Image Bite Politics

Series in Political Psychology

Series Editor
John T. Jost

Editorial Board
Mahzarin Banaji, Gian Vittorio Caprara, Chris Federico, Don Green, John
Hibbing, Jon Krosnick, Arie Kruglanski, Kathleen McGraw, David Sears,
Jim Sidanius, Phil Tetlock, Tom Tyler

Image Bite Politics: News and the Visual Framing of Elections
Maria Elizabeth Grabe and Erik Page Bucy

Social and Psychological Bases of Ideology and System Justification
John T. Jost, Aaron C. Kay, and Hulda Thorisdottir

Forthcoming Books in the Series:

The Political Psychology of Democratic Citizenship
Eugene Borgida, Christopher Federico, and John Sullivan

On Behalf of Others: The Psychology of Care in a Global World
Sarah Scuzzarello, Catarina Kinnvall, and Kristen Renwick Monroe

Image Bite Politics

NEWS AND THE VISUAL FRAMING OF ELECTIONS

Maria Elizabeth Grabe
and
Erik Page Bucy

OXFORD
UNIVERSITY PRESS

2009

OXFORD
UNIVERSITY PRESS

Oxford University Press, Inc., publishes works that further
Oxford University's objective of excellence
in research, scholarship, and education.

Oxford   New York
Auckland   Cape Town   Dar es Salaam   Hong Kong   Karachi
Kuala Lumpur   Madrid   Melbourne   Mexico City   Nairobi
New Delhi   Shanghai   Taipei   Toronto

With offices in
Argentina   Austria   Brazil   Chile   Czech Republic   France   Greece
Guatemala   Hungary   Italy   Japan   Poland   Portugal   Singapore
South Korea   Switzerland   Thailand   Turkey   Ukraine   Vietnam

Published by Oxford University Press, Inc.
198 Madison Avenue, New York, New York 10016
www.oup.com

Oxford is a registered trademark of Oxford University Press

Library of Congress Cataloging-in-Publication Data
Grabe, Maria Elizabeth.
Image bite politics : news and the visual framing of elections /
Maria Elizabeth Grabe and Erik Page Bucy.
p. cm.—(Series in political psychology)
Includes bibliographical references and index.
ISBN 978-0-19-537207-6
1. Elections—United States—Psychological aspects. 2. Presidential candidates—
United States—Public opinion. 3. Television broadcasting of news—United States.
4. Political psychology. 5. Public opinion—United States. I. Bucy, E. Page, 1963–
II. Title.
JK1967.G73 2009
324.973001'9—dc22

9 8 7 6 5 4 3 2 1

Printed in the United States of America
on acid-free paper

To Doris A. Graber and Roger D. Masters,
pioneers in the field of visual analysis.

Preface

Given the prevailing trajectories in media research, granting visuals their deserved status as reliable forms of political information requires somewhat of a paradigm shift in thinking about television news and democracy. Since the rise of broadcast media in politics, television has more often been vilified for committing civic sins and reviled as a vast cultural wasteland than commended as an equalizer of political knowledge. In defense of television news, we come at this project with uncommon conceptual and methodological tools for systematic visual analysis. Our aim is to present a new way of looking at the news and show how conceptions of media politics change when the focus is on the undervalued visual aspects of election coverage. In Kuhnian terms, we are less interested in "normal science" involving incremental extensions of existing approaches to news analysis than in helping to transform the very project of news analysis itself.

As with many original ideas that seemingly surface overnight, this book has been a long time in the making. The idea for *Image Bite Politics* germinated during the run-up to the 2000 election when we noticed that images were becoming a defining feature of election coverage and realized that a comprehensive visual analysis of the nightly news had never been performed. Such an analysis, we believed, held the potential to reveal important insights about network news coverage of presidential campaigns that had not come to light through conventional text-based investigations. Indeed, media researchers are in the habit of closely examining the transcript of television newscasts while ignoring the visuals.

At the outset, we wish to acknowledge the irony of needing an entire book's worth of words (close to 75,000!) to make a convincing case that visuals matter. Much of the inspiration for this endeavor also comes from the written word: academic tracts and research articles, political and journalistic memoirs, and printed news reports. Our professional histories as working journalists (Grabe as a television news producer for the South African Broadcasting Corporation, Bucy as a newspaper reporter in Los Angeles) molded our thinking about words and images, too. In a broader sense, *Image Bite Politics* has been in the making since our respective careers coalesced on opposite sides of the globe in the mid-1980s. The observations recounted here draw on the professional experiences that brought about our own epiphanies regarding the importance of moving images in the contemporary political landscape. In short, we lived it. Here, in the order of authorship, we chronicle key moments that made this book inevitable.

Images are far more than visual decorations for the audio track of television news stories. I came to this realization, and then made gainful use of it, during a five-year career as a documentary news producer for the South African Broadcasting Corporation (SABC). Fresh out of college and on a mission to be a barking watchdog over a misguided government, I joined the SABC's television news department in 1984. At that time, television was relatively new to the country, having been introduced only 8 years earlier by an apartheid government intent on retaining power and reluctant to allow disturbing images of violence in the townships to be broadcast within the country, let alone to the rest of the world. The government was also uneasy about broadcasting American-produced programming in which whites and blacks were portrayed as coexisting in apparent harmony. Such an implicit message of equality and diversity simply did not square with National Party policies.

Officially, the SABC was partially funded through government subsidies, but in practice the corporation was a state-controlled institution. The television news department was still in its infancy—run by former newspaper journalists with an incomplete understanding of the visual component of television news. At the same time, resistance to apartheid policies was escalating in violence throughout the country. In response, the government declared a state of emergency to suppress uprisings and gain control over the media. The result was a full-throttle chokehold on free speech. Under state-of-emergency regulations, newspapers were routinely punished for their criticisms of the government. Some presses were shut down for months and then struggled to regain readership after the state-imposed blackouts. Foreign journalists were thrown out of the country, and some were locked up without trial until being deported. Most tragically, South Africa's townships were literally burning, while citizens were denied access to information about the unfolding crisis.

At the SABC, widely viewed as the government's mouthpiece, watchful national intelligence officers were discreetly housed in news-rooms to monitor journalistic activities. Many of our home phone lines were tapped. Every completed news script and sound bite was subject to the approval of executive producers, who functioned as censors. But the most invasive censorship was reserved for the final drafts of our documentaries.

In a small, dark editing booth in the news department's Johannesburg headquarters, an executive producer would view the program, demand cuts, and sometimes review it again for approval. For two years, I ardu-ously resisted this process that turned my reports into incoherent, pro-government drivel. In return, I received poor marks on the company's "Sensitivity to the SABC's Broadcast Policies" evaluation scale and, con-sequently, received negligible raises. Prompted in part by one executive producer who ignored the visual track of my documentaries, I started part-time graduate work to learn more about visual communication. His habit was to take a seat in the editing booth, bow his head, shut his eyes, and listen attentively to the audio track, thumb and forefinger pinching his nose. The newspaperman in him was concerned about subversive words—but not televised images. It dawned on me that I could subvert the censors if I became a more astute visual communicator.

In evening graduate seminars at the Rand Afrikaans University, I learned about the persuasive power of visual information. Due to cultural sanctions against South Africa, libraries were short on cur-rent research publications, but I read everything I could get my hands on. At work, I applied this knowledge by driving the message home visually. This meant using unflattering camera angles to portray gov-ernment officials, selecting symbolically meaningful backgrounds for interviews, and relying on news visuals to contradict censor-imposed verbal phrases. Another key maneuver: I timed the submission of my documentaries to coincide with the availability of the executive pro-ducer who "watched" tape with his eyes closed. Still, other executive producers sometimes made cuts to my programs after I left the office, which I learned of as I watched my work on air. Livid at this trans-gression, I began staying in the studio control room on nights that my documentaries were slated for broadcast, handing the final version to the tape operator minutes before airtime. That strategy was generally effective, although some of my completed programs sat on the shelf rather than airing. To my surprise, one of my documentaries, critical (albeit heavily censored) of the government's clampdown on press freedom, aired. Ironically, the censorship process surrounding this documentary on press freedom sparked the high point of my SABC career.

With the final draft of this program I went through the familiar ritual of refusing the cuts recommended by executive producers. As usual they summoned their supervisor, Christo Kritzinger, a hot-tempered man who quickly became exasperated with my resistance to comply with censorship guidelines. I asked to see his boss, the chief director of news, Sakkie Burger. As we waited for Burger, Kritzinger ranted in Afrikaans: "I can't put my finger on it, but I know you're busy with subversive messages, god-dammit." The next morning, security police searched my cubicle for raw tape from the press freedom documentary, likely looking for recorded interviews with government critics.

In the instant of Kritzinger's comment, I understood my experiments in visual subversion had worked—an epiphany that was amplified by the visit from the security police. Within a month, I not only had resigned from the SABC but was also enrolled in graduate school in the United States, destined to study the visual component of television news.

As authors often say, books are not written in isolation. In this case there were star enablers. As living examples, my parents and brother inspire independence of thought. Annie, Jeanne, Lee, Martha, Mike, and Nancy, thank you for reading and/or listening to my rants about visuals. Mark, neglecting you made deadlines doable—but with serious ex post facto regret. Thank you for cooking comfort food, motivating me over morning coffee, and encouraging my voice. Tonya and Michael, "thank you" seems like a gross understatement, but please accept these two words for lack of a better way to acknowledge the layers of scaffolding you provided in the final stretch. Finally, I pay homage to a Scot named Martha, whose eyebrows were long enough to impair visual acuity. Her loyalty, guardianship, and passion for living are etched in memory.

—M.E.G.

As an undergraduate English major and former newspaper reporter, I came to appreciate the importance of news visuals and television's role in politics somewhat late in the game—only after experiencing the process for myself as a press aide and scheduler to former California governor Jerry Brown during his "quixotic" 1992 campaign for the Democratic presidential nomination. Gradually, I came to view newspapers as important for elite communication—and therefore to representative democracy—but less directly relevant for the mass public. As a general assignment reporter for the late, great *Los Angeles Herald Examiner*, I routinely quoted law enforcement authorities, politicians, and other public figures who I assumed were communicating with the *mass* public but were largely talking to themselves and other members of the *attentive* public and media establishment who paid close attention to the news. As reflected by circulation figures compared to viewership numbers, television easily wins out as the true medium of the masses (a fact that persists even in the Internet age).

This view was reinforced early in the 1992 presidential campaign season when, out on the hustings in New England, Brown would classify an event as either a success or failure based on how many television cameras showed up. Newspapers helped to set the tone, but when it came to reaching potential voters, the presence of cameras was all. In the preprimary season, Brown had enjoyed considerable name recognition—far more than Bill Clinton, Paul Tsongas, or other leading candidates initially—given his history as a somewhat flamboyant and iconoclastic two-term California governor. He had also run for the presidency twice before. But once the voting started, he found himself trailing the pack of major candidates and largely ignored by the media. Jerry lashed out at what he labeled the "black hole of media anonymity" that downplayed his presidential bid, but he pursued a shrewd strategy of accepting small donations through an 800 number and operating on a low budget to keep his candidacy alive.

Dogged to the end, Brown challenged Clinton in California and pursued the nominating contest to the floor of the Democratic National Convention, where, as a potential spoiler who refused to endorse the eventual nominee, he received renewed media attention of the magnitude that only national politics can provide. Walking into the Madison Square Garden convention hall as a deputy press secretary for the campaign in advance of Brown's arrival, I encountered a phalanx of television reporters—numbering close to 100—who began following *me* in the hopes that I would lead them to Jerry (he arrived a few minutes later through a side entrance). Brown probably had two motivations for taking his case all the way to the convention floor that year: his commitment to progressive causes, which he fought for during the platform writing process, and the need for one last round of national media attention. If you could attract the cameras and prestige press, even for a few days, you could go home satisfied with the realization that you still had it on some level.

After the campaign I became fascinated with the two intertwined worlds I had experienced—journalism and presidential politics—and decided to reconcile my interests in both by pursuing a PhD in mass communication. Actually, my path to an academic career was slightly more circuitous: after the campaign I had interviewed with Tom Hayden, then a California state senator, for a field rep position, but Willie Brown (the speaker of the house) ended up cutting his budget and, along with it, my opportunity to become a paid political staffer. Even after deciding on an academic career, I wasn't fully aware that television would become my eventual research focus. But it wasn't too long before a curious character at the University of Maryland would change all that.

When I first ran into John Newhagen during a visit to College Park, Maryland, in the spring of 1993, he was leading a group of graduate students to his research lab in the Journalism Building, where he was developing an approach-avoidance chair capable of measuring slight changes in viewer reactions either toward or away from a televised stimulus. Eventually, John published his approach-avoidance findings using data generated from a more reliable computer joystick that viewers used to move toward or away from the screen during exposure to images intended to induce anger, fear, or disgust. In graduate seminars John would press the case for visuals, arguing for their psychological and political significance. Over time, he convinced me that studying images was the most important thing you could do in media research. Suffice it to say, my appreciation for the psychological impact of emotion-laden images in the news is a direct reflection of his formative influence.

My acknowledgments for this project extend across three campuses over a period of several years. *Image Bite Politics* began to take shape while I was on sabbatical at Dartmouth College in the fall of 2005, when we outlined the book and identified the analyses that would be performed for each chapter. Roger Masters, a Renaissance scholar in the classic sense, generously shared his office and provided invaluable advice on research matters both large and small.

Also at Dartmouth, Deborah Brooks brought to my attention important new work on "thin-slice forecast" studies of election outcomes, which buttress our claims about the persuasive influence of news visuals. David Mindich of St. Michael's College offered similar encouragement from the perspective of journalism studies and provided access to his personal video library of memorable moments in televised politics. Markus Prior of Princeton University also merits thanks for generously forwarding copies of his working papers on visual knowledge, which are about to make a substantial contribution to political communication and psychology.

George Marcus of Williams College and Jamie Druckman of Northwestern University, stalwarts in the International Society of Political Psychology, provided helpful suggestions at different stages of this book's development. A tip of the hat to Frank Esser of the University of Zurich for recognizing the value of this work in its earliest incarnation and effectively applying the image bite concept in a cross-national context. I am also very fortunate to have trusted friends who double as research colleagues and intellectual sounding boards, among them Paul D'Angelo, Michael J. Filas, and Thomas Conte, who willingly lend advice when asked, regardless of the immediate demands on their time.

Hats off as well to friends and colleagues at the University of Michigan, who offered valuable feedback and much-welcomed camaraderie during my year as a visitor in the Department of Communication Studies. Special thanks to Russ Neuman for endorsing this project early on and making astute observations at just the right time. Conversations with Tony Collings, formerly of CNN and *Newsweek*, and Derek Valliant, formerly of National Public Radio and PBS, also informed my thinking about news practices and historical processes.

Parents are typically thanked in a pro forma fashion by book authors, but in this case my father, Thomas Bucy (a Michigan man himself), performed a hands-on role by reviewing multiple chapter drafts and offering a reader's perspective. The seniors in my Mass Media and Political Behavior course at Michigan will remember his guest lecture on the Kennedy assassination, particularly his visual analysis of the Zapruder film, for many years to come. Finally, throughout the vicissitudes of this project, the love and support of Amanda Berry provided a steady source of sustenance and was instrumental in bringing this project to completion. No one inspires me more.

—E.M.B.

Together we would like to thank our colleagues in the Department of Telecommunications and School of Journalism at Indiana University, especially David Weaver, Annie Lang, Walter Gantz, Andrew Bucksbarg, and Bob Affe for their professional and personal support throughout the project. Financial support from the Dean of Faculties Office, the Office of the Vice Provost for Research, and the School of Journalism at Indiana University, as well as the Joan Shorenstein Center on the Press, Politics, and Public Policy at Harvard University's John F. Kennedy School of Government, helped make this book possible by sustaining our data collection process.

The data for this book could not have been compiled without the dedicated assistance of Janis Cakars and Leigh Moscowitz, the primary coders for this project. We express our deepest thanks for their meticulousness and commitment over several years of coding. To Jacob Kytharampil, a tireless research assistant, and Adam Sheya at Indiana University's Center for Statistical and Mathematical Computing, who helped to shape the data analysis, we owe much gratitude. Finally, we would like to acknowledge the tremendous efforts of our editor at Oxford University Press, Lori Handelman, for her unwavering enthusiasm, encouragement, and confidence in the merits of this book.

Contents

Image Bite Politics

1

Why Visuals Matter

Newspapers make associations, and associations make newspapers. . . . We should underrate their importance if we thought they just guaranteed liberty; they maintain civilization.
—Alexis de Tocqueville
Democracy in America, 1840

Television thrives on unreason, and unreason thrives on television. It strikes at the emotions rather than the intellect.
—Sir Robin Day, BBC journalist
Financial Times, November 8, 1989

Before there was the vote, there was the word.

Democracy has always depended on communication for its philosophical foundations and practical realization. Indeed, the very concept of democracy (which derives from the ancient Greek *dēmokratia*, or "rule by the people") probably could not have been formulated without a developed language, medium of communication, deliberative tradition, and existence of a public sphere where citizens could gather to debate issues.[1-3] Technological advances and changing cultural practices have also played a role in the emergence of democracy. The development of the printing press and recognition of vernacular language in the late Middle Ages are widely regarded as liberating moments in Western civilization, allowing democratic discourse to overcome religious and monarchical strictures. Once control of knowledge was wrested from the monasteries and Latin was supplanted as the liturgical language by "common" dialects such as English and German, new ideas about liberty and human emancipation could flourish.

Curiously, the visual mode of communication is largely overlooked in the great narratives about politics, democracy, and the public sphere.[4-8] This is especially true in scholarly accounts of democracy's renaissance, in which special praise is reserved for the development of the printing press and its associated media—newspapers, journals, tracts, and pamphlets—for fostering a vibrant public sphere. Although primarily the province of educated elites, both then and now, the print culture has been hailed by historians and philosophers alike as promoting rational debate, particularly in times of social and political transformation.[9-11]

The impersonality and reproducibility of print, according to Schudson[10] (p. 40), "encouraged a faith in norms of rational discourse," thereby furthering Enlightenment ideals.[12,13] Newspapers in both Europe and the United States are lauded for promoting civic vitality, building a market for political controversy, and advancing public discourse.[10,14]

Television, although the most egalitarian news medium yet invented (for reasons explained in this chapter), receives no such approbation. Instead, the most relied upon source of news and information is accused of thriving on "unreason," contributing to an "idiot culture," and striking "at the emotions rather than the intellect."[15,16] As a news medium, television fails in the eyes of critics for two major reasons.[17] First, broadcast news is accused of distorting political reality. This criticism surfaces in analyses of information bias and the work routines of journalists,[18] in the charge that political coverage "charms" voters by making them feel informed while not delivering substantive information,[19] and in experimental findings holding that television news contributes "to the trivialization of public discourse and the erosion of electoral accountability" (p. 143[20]). Second, television news is accused of inappropriately intruding into democratic processes. Instead of purveying important information central to democratic decision making, broadcast journalists are described as "parasites of print" who have become "aggressively interventionist in controlling political storytelling," with special invective reserved for the shrinking sound bite[10] (p. 287) (a topic we investigate in Chapter 2).

Despite widespread condemnation of the medium, several converging trends have inexorably shifted politics onto a visual platform—the continued domination of television as the primary channel of political communication, campaign practices that have become increasingly geared toward image-making, and the need for presidents to actively shape the public-opinion environment while in office. These developments are not new, of course, but surprisingly little research attention has been given to the systematic analysis of political visuals. As political scientist Doris Graber observed two decades ago, "The television age demands a reconsideration of our print-age value structure, which routinely prizes abstractions conveyed through words more than the realities and feelings conveyed through pictures"[21] (p. 174).

This chapter surveys a vast terrain of theory, findings, and history to diagnose the origins and interrogate the legitimacy of neglecting the visual dimension of television news. Although television is an audiovisual medium, we are primarily focused on its visual component— precisely because it has been unappreciated (indeed much denigrated) as a source of information.

Moving away from contemporary media and politics, we look back in time to consider the natural history of the eye as a potent conduit of "meaning making." In the process we recount a watershed moment in evolution inspired by the development of sight and trace the late emergence of *Homo sapiens* and our quite recent adaptations for speech and writing. From neuroscientific research, we draw on findings that reveal how the human brain is wired for visual and, to a much lesser degree, verbal information processing. To further appreciate the cognitive and linguistic differences between words and images, we parse the analogical quality of visuals and their lack of explicit propositional syntax. Based on these arguments and evidence of visual primacy, the final section maps significant trends in cultural history in search of explanations for how written information has become revered (and visuals disparaged) by elites, and thereby serves to stratify society in a way that ultimately disserves democracy.

NEGLECTING THE VISUAL

Unlike other communication media, including print, radio, or even the Internet (which is multimedia in character but still largely text oriented), television is *quintessentially* an audiovisual medium and offers the most access to information to the largest potential audience. Indeed, there are more television sets per household in the United States than there are people.[22] Despite the rising popularity of online news, YouTube, and other file-sharing sites, television viewing still vastly outpaces Internet use, particularly for news about politics. Owing to its visual nature and simplicity as a technology, television also remains user-friendly and does not demand a high level of verbal literacy to understand and appreciate. Thus, for the mass public, television news provides easier access to information, particularly for less educated viewers, than other media channels, including newspapers and the Web.[23,24]

Ignoring the visuals of a televised news report means overlooking much of the meaning that viewers derive from the viewing experience.[25,26] Campaigns actively engage in visual framing strategies to promote desired candidate qualities and favored themes and to reinforce policy positions. Journalists routinely apply camera and editing techniques, including varying camera angles, lens movements, shot selections, and story packaging, that place candidates in a more or less favorable visual light.[27-29] The candidates' nonverbal behavior adds another dimension of visual information, evoking emotions, shaping impressions, and influencing audience attitudes.[30,31] Indeed, when citizens are evaluating leaders, televised portrayals are remarkably potent.[32,33] Yet with rare exception, news visuals are not emphasized in research, and are at best understated in public debate. Instead, verbally delivered and, especially, printed news has become the staple of research agendas.

The privileged position that words occupy in society is the product of a long tradition of rationalism that solidified during the Enlightenment in which logic and reason were elevated as the building blocks of scientific knowledge. Because verbal arguments are taken as the primary conduit of reason, theory building is skewed toward evidence gathering in support of this ontological position. Indeed, word bias reverberates in scholarly analyses of news texts and predictive models that assume voters are primarily influenced by issue positions and rational appeals. The rational-choice perspective carries this position to an extreme by treating human behavior as a cold-blooded exercise in interest calculation and excluding, for parsimony's sake, emotion-related variables from its models.[34,35] Because visuals are processed via emotional pathways in the brain, they are inherently affect laden. Thus, despite their statistical elegance, predictive models that overlook visuals fail to consider a major source of influence.

Given compelling evidence that visuals are instrumental in shaping public opinion,[36–40] one might expect the research community to pay close attention to the visual aspects of television news when studying political content. Yet prominent theories about news, including agenda setting and framing analysis, have virtually ignored the visual component of news broadcasts.[41,42] This oversight deserves renewed attention in light of findings that voters draw on a variety of information sources—visual images as well as verbal content—when forming impressions, acquiring knowledge, and arriving at political judgments (see Masters,[32] Benjamin and Shapiro,[36] Bucy,[43] and Drew and Weaver[44]).

Studying visual content does pose practical and methodological challenges that are mostly absent from studies relying on verbal transcripts of television news or print news sources. In particular, images (1) have an analogical quality that imbues them with direct resemblance to their physical referents, and (2) are less governed by explicit linguistic rules than are words. Investigating images therefore requires methodological resourcefulness and an investment of time and human resources that goes well beyond computerized content analyses of news databases to identify visual patterns and trends.

The dearth of visual analysis in an era of increasing media reliance[45,46] has prompted a small chorus of scholars to call for more research on the visual component of television, particularly of election news.[32,47–51] A few studies, most of which conflate the verbal narrative of news with the independent impact of images, have attempted to develop systematic procedures for coding news visuals (a literature surveyed in Chapter 3). Yet among the various coding schemes for evaluating news images that have been proposed over the years, including Graber's[50,51] "gestalt coding" procedure, Hans Kepplinger's[52] detailed categories for camera presentation techniques, and the different types of televised leader displays identified by Roger Masters and colleagues,[53,54] none have caught on in a significant way.

A common complaint among researchers is that news visuals are difficult to systematically isolate and quantify and too cumbersome and nuanced to code manually.[55] Thus, large-scale content analyses of television news tend to use verbal narratives (i.e., transcriptions of the audio track) or broad visual categories that can be coarsely coded to assess the general tenor of coverage (see, for example, Coleman and Banning,[56] and Media Tenor[57]). Despite their general usefulness, broad groupings or streamlined coding procedures do not provide the detail or subtlety necessary for isolating visual effects. An upshot of this content-analysis quandary is that public opinion researchers rarely include visual variables in their predictive models.

Together then, ontological, theoretical, methodological, and pragmatic barriers to studying visuals have contributed to an incomplete understanding of how media function in a democracy. By introducing an exacting coding system that reliably measures visual content and facilitates replication, this project aims to breathe new life into the analysis of political visuals. Rather than relying on coarse categories or impressionistic interpretations, our approach employs a detailed measurement system, including camera-shot distance and angles, facial expressions, candidate gestures, and contextual images, to connect news portrayals with shifts in public opinion at different stages in the campaign. Image handlers have aggressively pursued visual means to shape voter perceptions of candidates for decades (a colorful history that we review in Chapter 3), but scientific evidence regarding the centrality of visuals in shaping viewer impressions and attitudes is just now starting to catch up with political practice.

To understand why images are so central to the conduct and outcome of contemporary politics—and to lived experience more generally—we must appreciate the long human history of making sense of the world through vision, particularly since nonverbal communication preceded verbal language in modern humans by tens of thousands of years. In *The Nature of Politics*, Masters rightfully observes that "any complete understanding of the way individuals compete [for] and gain power must consider the symbolic gestures of emotion and dominance that originated in hominoid evolution but have been subtly influenced by human cultural practices" (p. 40[54]). Despite the critical role that nonverbal communication has played over the millennia, prevailing definitions of information, in vogue since the late age of print, continue to downplay the importance of visuals in political analysis. Our primary intention in writing this book is to establish the information value that news visuals have for viewers of political broadcasts. In the process we chronicle how news visuals shape viewer impressions of candidates and influence election outcomes. Countering the Gutenberg legacy requires cross-disciplinary reach and historical perspective, beginning with the natural history that produced humans.

A CONDENSED HISTORY OF *HOMO SAPIENS*

Appreciating the basic premise of this book—that television visuals are vastly underappreciated as a source of political information—begins with a nod to our distant past. At the risk of casting our argument in an outsized, epic context, we turn to a timeline of natural history that positions the emergence and subsequent ramifications of sight in an evolutionary perspective. By viewing the centrality of vision over time, the comparatively short history of language and the even shorter life span of the written word come to be seen as very recent adaptations. Compared to cultural occurrences, evolutionary events are enormously slow to materialize but can have tremendous consequences for species when they do. In this regard the emergence of the eye some 543 million years ago created havoc, dramatically hastening biodiversification and the development of species. From that period forward the eye was ever present, shaping specialized anatomical and cognitive functions that eventually brought *Homo sapiens* into existence.

Notwithstanding the importance of language in contemporary society, the human brain has had a remarkably short amount of time to adapt and specialize to oral and written forms of communication. Despite much controversy in dating particular evolutionary adaptations, the *sequence* of eyesight predating speech is uncontested and serves as a sobering reminder of why visuals, especially in relation to an audio-visual medium like television, are so consequential. With the assistance of an image-filled timeline, we now highlight a few key developments in this grand sequence of events.

From Life to Sight

Though debated, the formation of the Earth is widely dated to around 4.55 billion years ago (Fig. 1-1, panel 1).[58] Life emerged sometime thereafter, perhaps following a flurry of meteorite bombardments,[59] but the precise dating of the first life form is a contested topic.[60,61] Across debates and theories, there is some scientific consensus that abiogenesis (the origin of life from nonlife) occurred between 4.4 and 2.7 billion years ago (Fig. 1-1, panel 2).[62-64]

By all accounts life was slow to diversify. It took more than 2 billion years for three different animal phyla to evolve. Archaeologists, paleontologists, and evolutionary biologists trace a key moment in natural history to the Cambrian period approximately 543 million years ago (see Parker,[59] Morris[65]). At this point, an evolutionary "big bang" erupted. Spectacularly, over the next 5 million years life forms diversified from three to 38 animal phyla, with the exception of one or two extinctions, the same number we have today. Given that it took more than 2 billion years for animal life to initially evolve into three basic types, the degree of biodiversification that occurred in the early Cambrian period is nothing short of stunning—a blossoming referred to as the *Cambrian explosion*.

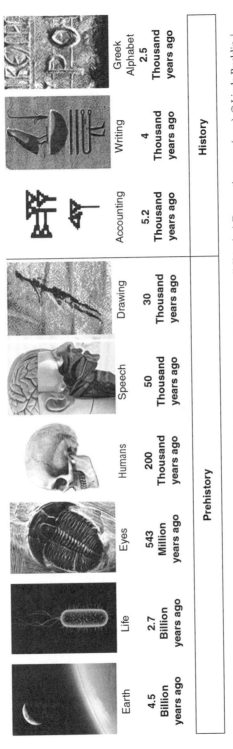

Earth	Life	Eyes	Humans	Speech	Drawing	Accounting	Writing	Greek Alphabet
4.5 Billion years ago	**2.7 Billion years ago**	**543 Million years ago**	**200 Thousand years ago**	**50 Thousand years ago**	**30 Thousand years ago**	**5.2 Thousand years ago**	**4 Thousand years ago**	**2.5 Thousand years ago**
			Prehistory				History	

Figure 1–1

Andrew Parker, a research fellow in Oxford University's Department of Zoology, describes this milestone in evolution as an event "that can be matched in significance only by the beginning of life itself" (p. 24[59]).

Through close analysis of the fossil record, Parker[59] has identified the development of vision in early animals as the accelerant that propelled biodiversity. Precambrian creatures were unable to see, but once the lights were "switched on," all animals had to either adapt or die; in a geological instant, the world was transformed. The first eye belonged to the trilobite, a small, hard-shelled marine arthropod that appeared about 543 million years ago during the early Cambrian period (see Fig. 1–1, panel 3). The birth of vision, according to Parker's[59] "light switch" theory of evolution, changed the rules of survival and accelerated evolutionary adaptations. Most notably, the development of eyesight gave rise to active predation and, over time, grouped different classes of species into predators and prey—a distinction that did not exist before vision.[59]

Indeed, the capacity to see—to fix one's prey in a line of sight or to espy a predator off in the distance—not only shaped animal behavior but also influenced physical appearances and development. "All animals needed to evolve to be adapted to vision before they were eaten, or before they were outwitted by their prey. The early Cambrian thus became a race for adaptation to vision"[59] (p. 279).[66] Animal body shapes, pigmentation, muscle development, physical movement, and behavioral tendencies, not to mention the positioning and type of eye, are all outcomes of sight. Indeed, the introduction of the eye effectively tore up the existing laws of life and gave rise to a frantic, chaotic period where new rules and shapes of existence prevailed. Following this momentous occasion in natural history, or evolutionary "chaos" as Parker[59] describes it, biodiversification settled back into a slower pace for more gradual adaptations.

Enter *Homo sapiens*

Modern humans did not emerge for another half-billion years. Estimates vary, but there is some level of consensus that *Homo sapiens* appeared approximately 200,000, and perhaps as long as 500,000, years ago, although with a thicker skull and brow ridge than we have today.[67] Anatomically modern humans are distinguished from earlier hominoids by the light build of their skeletons as well as by a high-vaulted cranium with a large, near-vertical forehead suitable for housing a large brain (see Fig. 1–1, panel 4). The oldest fossil evidence of modern humans, found in Africa, is about 130,000 years old, whereas evidence from the Near East dates back 90,000 years.[68,69]

Cultural evolution, evident from artifact remains, is often linked to an anatomical change, namely a mutation of the vocal tract that endowed *Homo sapiens* with finer control over sound production (see Fig. 1–1, panel 5). Specifically, physiological positioning of the larynx at the top of the trachea, which extended the vocal tract, permitted formation of a much greater variety of sounds, in both volume and pitch, than theretofore had been the case. Modifications to the tongue and associated muscles further enhanced vocal control. Thus, fully anatomically modern humans capable of speech, according to Diamond,[67] seem to have emerged between 40,000 and 60,000 years ago.

Other views of human evolution hold that *Homo sapiens* adapted for speech somewhere between 2.4 million and 50,000 years ago. The inexactness of this estimate reveals the scientific controversy surrounding the history of speech.[70] Deacon (quoted in Holden)[72] describes the development of speech as "a mystery with all the fingerprints wiped off" because there is no written record, and fossil evidence provides no concrete indication of the muscles and ligaments required for speech. Regarding the relatively vast time span in which speech might have surfaced, a number of potential clues have been identified. Stone tools, dating back some 2.4 million years, are viewed as an indication of linguistic capacity. Two million years ago, the hominid brain experienced rapid expansion—perhaps a sign of language adaptation. Recent identification of a "speech gene," thought to have originated between 100,000 and 200,000 years ago, offers another clue.[73,74] Cultural anthropologists conservatively estimate that humans were, 50,000 years ago, "creating art, burying their dead, [and performing other] symbolic behaviors that point unequivocally to language use" (p. 1316[72]).

Interestingly, speech may have developed as a gestural rather than an acoustic system that relied heavily on visual observation (see Hewes).[75] The so-called McGurk effect is still present in human communication: seeing the expression of the syllable "ga" while listening to a sound recording of the syllable "ba" typically results in hearing "da"—a sound that is anatomically between the other two. Speech reception may thus rely heavily on visual cues.[72,76,77]

The Emergence of Artifacts

Some time after speech evolved, the cultural inclinations of *Homo sapiens* inspired recordings of lived experience in visual form, manifested by what we now call painting and drawing. Artifacts scrawled on cave walls have survived to puzzle contemporary archaeologists in their attempts to date the origin of these drawings (see Fig. 1–1, panel 6). The main procedure for this process was stylistic dating, until radiocarbon dating was revolutionized through the development of accelerator mass spectrometric techniques. More controversy surrounds the precise age of prehistoric cave drawings (for instance, whether later generations of cave artists retouched the images using differently dated charcoal implements; see Pettitt and Bahn[78]), but if the new techniques and the dates they point to can be trusted, the oldest discovered cave paintings are around 30,000 years old.[79,80]

Evidence of writing systems, slightly easier to pinpoint but still an inexact science, is traditionally taken as the beginning of history—about 5,200 years ago—while the estimated 200,000-year existence of *Homo sapiens* preceding that point is referred to as *pre*history.[81] In demarcating human history, some archaeologists identify the emergence of pictographs and ideographs—visual depictions of ideas or concepts dating back some 7,000 to 12,000 years—as the first writing systems.[82] Others regard these artifacts as forms of proto-writing and therefore as evidence of prehistory. In these debates there is a general willingness to view accounting, inspired by economic necessity, as the beginning of the written word. The first known form of accounting, cuneiform script, surfaced about 5,200 years ago among the Sumerians, who used clay tablets to keep track of commodities and perhaps time units spent on labor (see Fig. 1–1, panel 7).[83,84] The use of hieroglyphs by the Egyptians some 4,000 years ago marks historical consensus as to the origin of the written word, as there is general agreement that hieroglyphs constitute a formal writing system (see Fig. 1–1, panel 8).[83,85]

When viewed over time, verbal language thus has a relatively short history, perhaps as short as 40,000 or 50,000 years, and the written word even less (just 5,200 years). Compare this to the highly developed neurological capacity for visual perception, which unquestionably evolved over millions of years as the hominoid brain increased in size and specialization. The visual acuity we take for granted today is the result of this lengthy evolutionary process. As important as the development of verbal language has been in steering the course of (recent) human history, it pales in comparison to the ramifications that the development of sight had on life forms that preceded *Homo sapiens*. In the long history of this vital sense lies an important reminder about the critical role of vision in processing information and guiding behavior.

To further the case for the primacy of images in the multimedia environment of the modern campaign, we next consider the biological basis of visual processing. At least five aspects of neurological response reveal the extent to which brain functioning privileges the image: (1) the speed with which visuals are processed, (2) the efficiency with which visual stimuli are classified and (3) stored in memory, (4) the way the visual system engages both emotional and "thinking" centers in the brain, and (5) interactions between different levels of processing during exposure to a visual stimulus. We elaborate on each of these points below.[86]

THE BIOLOGICAL BASIS OF VISUAL PROCESSING

Contrary to the preferences of political theorists for a rationally engaged public that relies on reason and deliberation to make informed decisions, visual experience remains the most dominant mode of learning[87]; indeed, visual processing is central to building synaptic connections and ultimately forms the basis of extended consciousness.[88] Because vision occurs in the visual cortex deep within the brain and not at the entry point of the cornea or when light hits the retina to produce eyesight, the eyes can be regarded as "a direct extension of the brain into the environment."[87] The most sophisticated of our senses to evolve, sight "send[s] more data more quickly and efficiently through the nervous system than any other sense."[87] Image processing is so efficient that basic recognition and emotional responding occur well before registering in conscious awareness.

Processing Speed

In his time scale of human action, Newell[89] describes different bands or levels of information processing and their corresponding units of time. At the lowest and fastest level is the biological band that accounts for operations among organelles, or structures *within* cells, as well as neuronal activity or synapse firings *between* cells. Whereas organelles perform their work on the order of microseconds (i.e., millionths of a second), neurons have a characteristic operation time of about a millisecond (i.e., one one-thousandth of a second). Up a level but still within the biological band are neural circuits, which provide the means through which the nervous system connects to and controls bodily systems. Neural circuits, including those that drive visual perception, operate on the order of tens of milliseconds (i.e., ten one-thousandths of a second), but still outside of conscious awareness.

Earlier debates over whether emotional reactions precede cognition have been superseded by findings in cognitive neuroscience that show sensory information reaches emotional brain centers before continuing on to cortical regions for further processing.[90,91] Libet and colleagues have estimated that it takes about half a second, or 500 milliseconds, for the brain to represent sensory data (i.e., sight, sound, smell, touch, taste) in consciousness.[92] However, affective responses and even visual recognition occur much faster. Once a facial image is presented for viewing, for example, perception of that image *as a face* occurs approximately 47 milliseconds after exposure,[83] the equivalent of about two frames of video or 1/20th of a second. By this time, sensory information from the optic nerve has already traveled through the thalamus to the limbic region of the brain, particularly the amygdala, "where the emotional import of the incoming sensory streams can be determined" (p. 37[34]). A second pathway, from the thalamus to the higher brain regions, including the visual, somatosensory, motor, and prefrontal cortices, supports conscious awareness or knowable feelings and appraisals (see LeDoux[91] and Mishkin and Appenzeller[94]).

The two pathways by which sensory data travel to different neurological regions process information at vastly different speeds. The thalamo-amygdala pathway to the limbic region yields appraisals in less than half the time it takes for sensory data to become consciously available via the cortical pathway (p. 37).[34] Thus, the body may begin to mobilize for fight or flight, or basic emotional assessments may place a person in a state of action readiness, before the mind realizes what is happening and makes a conscious decision to act. As is evident by this delay, the brain is built to anticipate likely occurrences, which it accomplishes by calling up memories and templates from past experience to continuously make predictions about the future (p. 57).[87] This principle applies to perceptual as well as motivational systems. "What we see is not what is on the retina at any given instant," Gazzaniga[95] (p. 75) explains, "but is a prediction of what will be there." The brain's anticipatory and emotional design is evolutionarily advantageous because in critical situations resources must be mobilized without the delay involved in making cognitive appraisals.

A fright reaction to a squirrel darting across a footpath illustrates this operation in action. Out of the corner of one's eye the quickly moving brown ball of fur may seem like a potential threat, perhaps a ravenous rodent or rabid dog. At the moment of movement detection (and threat perception), normal routines are abruptly halted and movement suspended. From a survival standpoint, the safest initial response is to rally resources and defensive reactions in anticipation of a threat until cognitively proven otherwise—an operation that could take seconds.[96,97] To ward off attack, our unsuspecting (and previously preoccupied but now focused) pedestrian lets out a panicked shriek before realizing the true nature of the rapidly approaching ball of fur. Of course, from the perspective of an onlooker, such a dramatic overreaction to an obvious nonthreat seems ludicrous, and a good laugh ensues. But by the time the squirrel was recognized, the brain had already instructed the body to mobilize for flight. Emotional responses are thus capable of guiding action and organizing behavior toward salient goals without much cognitive interference.[98]

The notion that visual stimuli are processed and that they form the basis of future action without first passing through consciousness is one of the most robust findings in cognitive neuroscience (see Barry[87]). In fact, very little of what the sensory system processes actually registers in awareness.[99] "Though we experience ourselves and the world through the apparent seamless immediacy of conscious awareness, the brain is active in ways not readily accessible to introspection"[100] (p. 52).[101] The mind, in other words, is always the last to know things.[95] In the case of vision, information gathered by the retina far exceeds what we consciously see. Marcus, Neuman, and MacKuen[34] refer to this as the "tip of the iceberg" phenomenon—neural processing facilitates a vast data collection of sensory information but supports only a small window of subjective awareness of that data.

Classifying Visual Stimuli

During the initial "pre-attentive" assessment of a visual stimulus, novelty overrides all other rules of image categorization, and processing is data-driven, determined by the unique features of the object in view.[102,103] At this point, as our example of the squirrel encounter suggests, a crude valence assessment about the stimulus—whether the object is inviting or uninviting, and therefore worthy of approach or avoidance—may be made, with little or no higher cognitive activity[104,105] (see also Kunst-Wilson, Raft, and Zajonc[106]). The interconnectedness of emotional centers with other brain regions ensures that sensory input deemed emotionally important receives further processing; hence, affective reactions frame conscious response. "Importantly," Marcus, Neuman, and MacKuen note, "affective processes determine *which* sensory information is represented in conscious awareness"[34] (p. 41 [italics added]).[107]

The biological primacy of vision is pertinent to our investigation of political news because the human perceptual system does not readily distinguish between visual stimuli originating from either the physical or the mediated world. In other words, the brain interprets media images *as if* they were real, preparing the body for an approach or avoidance response—even when higher-order cognitive processes are at work discounting them as symbolic in nature.[114] This holds for both entertainment and news; viewing scenes of vivid pornography on the one hand or a deadly war battle on the other is likely to result in appetitive or aversive activation (see Lang, Shin, and Lee[116]). Thus, there is no need for "the willing suspension of disbelief" when engaging with media fare. Reeves and Nass[113] call this tendency to respond to the mediated and physical worlds in a similar manner the *media equation*. From the standpoint of individual-level reactions, media in many ways do equal real life.

Given that the introduction of audiovisual media capable of conveying lifelike sound and images is a very recent occurrence in human history, initial psychological responses to mediated messages are consistent with evolutionary impulses. The brain has simply not had sufficient time and opportunity to adapt mechanisms to distinguish mediated messages from nonmediated ones. Consequently, humans respond to mediated images as if they represented a bona fide opportunity or threat—a situation of which media producers are all too aware—whereas the symbolic nature of the stimulus (e.g., moving specks of light on a television screen) is realized retrospectively, if at all.

Because visual processing has such a long evolutionary history compared to the acquisition of verbal language, the encoding of visual information is considered to be largely automatic—a neurologically hardwired process that occurs without conscious control. This is particularly true of intensely negative images that correspond to threats in the natural environment, which demand viewer attention and mobilize cognitive resources for processing.[26,117] "Even in a lifelong couch potato, the visual system never 'learns' that television is a pane of glowing phosphor dots" (p. 29[119]), or, nowadays, a liquid crystal or plasma display. Because the brain's affective circuitry interprets media images as reality and responds in real time according to literal visual circumstances, understanding perceptual processing has important implications for media-effects research (see Barry,[87] p. 59).

The ease with which visuals are processed owes in large part to the substantial neurological investment in vision, including specialized centers in the brain dedicated to visual processing, particularly of faces.[59,120] Neuroimaging studies have found that faces undergo specialized processing in the fusiform gyrus, in an area commonly called the fusiform face area. Other areas of the brain, notably the posterior superior temporal sulcus and lateral inferior occipital gyri, respond to faces as well "but are constrained by additional parameters of the stimulus such as expression or facial movement (p. 364[121])" (see also Haxby, Hoffman, and Gobbini[122]).[123] The substantial cranial real estate dedicated to vision is not unique to humans. A large portion of neurophysiology is devoted to vision in eyed animals generally, particularly in diurnal primates (who are active during the day), in which up to 50% of neocortex volume is constituted by the primary visual cortex.[59,124,125]

Forgetting "the News," Remembering the Visual

The results of numerous television learning studies indicate that viewers are hard-pressed to recall information they have just heard in a newscast (see Newhagen and Reeves,[26] Gunter,[126] and Robinson and Levy[127]), even though they may comprehend the story they just saw. One explanation for this finding is that structural features (pacing, editing, narrative structure, etc.) and content elements (story topic, emotion-laden images, etc.) of television messages direct attention to some message aspects more than others. Sequencing of verbal and visual content also plays a role. Intensely negative images of wars, disasters, or social mayhem can proactively enhance memory for audiovisual material that appears *after* the images are shown, while retroactively inhibiting memory for information that appears *before*.[26] Consequently, a typical news report containing both audio and video (and, perhaps, natural sound and text on screen) may be comprehended without the viewer fully processing the myriad details contained within it.[128]

As discussed, much of the work of visual perception is performed within the biological band before the mind has an opportunity to consciously assess and ascribe meaning to environmental events that impinge on moment-to-moment functioning. And yet once cognitive resources are mobilized to identify and make sense of visual stimuli, retention and recognition of visual information are highly efficient compared to verbal content, even when interest and motivation are not particularly pronounced. When shown brief (390-millisecond) images of news events and political leaders from network newscasts, for example, adult viewers are later able to correctly identify the images they have seen with 70% to 80% accuracy[129]; recognition performance only improves with longer exposures.[26] By contrast, when presented with multiple-choice questions about verbal information contained in the news narrative (audio track), with the opportunity to reread the questions as much and for as long as desired, viewers are able to correctly identify just 55% of statements contained in newscasts viewed just minutes earlier.[130] Tests of long-term memory six to seven weeks after exposure also show that television visuals are recalled much more easily than news story topics or narrative content, particularly when stories contain negative compelling images.[26]

Traditionally, information has been equated with factual knowledge present in verbal communication—the story narrative in the case of television. Until recently, much research involving television news focused on propositional memory or comprehension of the verbal stream and all but ignored the effects of the visual stream (see Newhagen and Reeves[26] and Graber[50]). Increasingly, however, a growing number of studies are showing that viewers process television using a combination of verbal content and nonverbal cues to make sense of messages that appear on the nightly news as well as in other program genres.[30,43,130,131] Among other dimensions of evaluation, viewers assess presidential reactions to compelling news events in terms of their emotional appropriateness (e.g., facial displays, gestures, voice tone), using a nonverbal heuristic to make sense of televised political behavior.[130,132]

In political news, negative viewer reactions can be triggered by violations of viewer expectations when a mismatch occurs between a familiar news setting and novel behavior on the part of a political actor or television personality (see Bucy and Newhagen[130] and Kaid, Downs, and Ragan[133]). Violations of viewer expectations also apply to the nonverbal emotional responses of political leaders to events in the news.[30] On television, editing plays a pivotal role. When there is a conflict or lack of correspondence between the visuals shown and words spoken during a broadcast, visual memory again wins out: viewers remember the images much better than the narration. Indeed, research on audiovisual redundancy has found that learning from television news can be enhanced when the visual and verbal streams of a broadcast are mutually reinforcing, or informationally redundant (for more on verbal correspondence with news visuals, see Chapter 2).[134,135]

Social Cognition

Importantly, the visual cortex resides in the thinking part of the brain, the neocortex, which is implicated in numerous higher-order functions, including association formation, planning, sensory integration, behavioral flexibility, problem solving, and memory.[125] Since much social behavior involves recognition of and responses to emotional cues, the visual system is centrally involved in the management of social complexity[124]—a capacity of particular relevance to contemporary politics. The careful observation of social developments has been integral to human advancement. Indeed, there is a positive relationship between social group size and neocortex size in primates and other animals (see Joffe and Dunbar[125] and Barton and Dunbar[136]). The "social brain" hypothesis, which has gained acceptance over the last three decades, holds that primates have evolved large brains and superior cognitive abilities to operate effectively in large, complex social groups.[137,138] The selective advantages of this ability to monitor individual and group behavior ensured that socially aware individuals succeeded in securing resources and attracting mates.[54,139]

Face processing is especially robust. The neural systems that underlie face perception allow humans to keep track of hundreds, if not thousands, of individual faces—a skill that "far exceeds our ability to memorize individual exemplars from any other class of objects" (p. 350[121,140]). In addition to being quickly recognized and identified, faces are also classified along a number of invariant dimensions referred to as "visually derived semantic categories," including race, sex, and age.[141] More broadly, other visually specified, albeit abstract, categories such as character traits and personality characteristics may also be assessed. "For example, most humans happily make a judgment about whether a face looks 'generous' or 'extroverted' " (p. 352[121]). Because they can reveal important cues about leadership (and, by extension, social and political stability), the faces of dominant individuals are subject to especially close scrutiny.

In politics, this tendency translates into considerable attention, and press coverage, focused on the nonverbal behavior of candidates, such as Howard Dean's "scream" in 2004 or Hillary Clinton's "emotional moment" in 2008 (see Fig. 1–2). These two episodes, almost exactly four years apart, are a study in contrasts. Both occurred in the early primary season, just after critical losses in the Iowa caucuses. In Dean's case, an aggressively shrill display seemed to reinforce impressions that he was a powder keg waiting to explode and therefore unsuitable for presidential consideration. Clinton managed to soften her stern image by welling up and showing her emotional side—but not to the point of actual tears. Both episodes represented nonverbal expectancy violations (see Burgoon and Walther),[142] but while in Clinton's case the evaluation was positive, in Dean's case the net effect was negative. Thus, images of leaders—one

Hillary Clinton's emotional moment  Howard Dean's scream

January 2008   January 2004

Figure 1–2 Clinton's and Dean's emotional displays

of the trademark visuals of the *close-up* medium of television—convey a substantial amount of social information beyond the content of the spoken words. This is particularly true when candidates are acting evasively, are showing signs of distress, or are behaving inappropriately in relation to the operative political setting or news context.[30,130]

When viewed from a behavioral perspective, nonverbal political communication, including gestures that serve as social signals and facial expressions that accurately convey emotion across cultures,[143] provides reliable insights into the affective state and behavioral intention of the communicator.[33,131] Televised leader displays also provide motivational cues on how viewers (i.e., citizens) should react, particularly in times of crisis or heightened anxiety.[43] As a result of evolutionary pressures, "humans have inherited a repertoire of social signals and emotions that continue to play an important role in interactions between leaders and followers" (p. 59[54]). The nonverbal display repertoires of presidential candidates are analyzed in detail in Chapter 4.

Levels of Processing

Although social life, including political groupings, gradually incorporated verbal elements, visual processing predated verbal communication and requires less conscious effort than reading.[95] "Brains were not built to read," Gazzaniga[95] (p. 56) has noted, which "is why many people have trouble with the process." Textual literacy and the use of a symbolic language facility operates at a much higher level of abstraction and takes place within what Newell refers to as the cognitive and rational bands of consciousness—self-aware activities that are orders of magnitude higher on the time scale of human action, which occur between 10^{-1} and 10^4 seconds, than events within the biological band, which occur between 10^{-4} and 10^{-2} seconds (p. 122[144]). The cognitive band addresses issues of comprehension and decision, followed by implementation and movement. Up a level from that, the rational band facilitates goal-oriented behavior and what is classically called reason. Interactions with the environment that evoke cognitive considerations take place on the order of seconds, whereas considerations within the rational band may play out over minutes or hours. Above both of these levels is the social band of human activity, in which political processes occur, unfolding over days, weeks, or months.[144]

With regard to dynamic symbol processing and the time scale of human action, Newhagen[145] (p. 398) asserts that meaning "will *always* be created at a level of analysis just below the particular level where it emerges and becomes apparent." That is, elaborate mental processes rest on more basic cognitive operations, whereas cognition emerges from neurological events at the biological level. Stimulus-driven or bottom-up processing is particularly salient when mismatches occur between internal states and environmental developments, or between expected and observed events, that prompt greater attentiveness and increased motivation for learning (p. 57[34]). In Marcus, Neuman, and MacKuen's affective intelligence model, disruptions to habitual routines, especially those perceived as threatening, elicit anxiety and feelings of uneasiness, activating the surveillance system of emotion that signals the need to look for solutions to novel circumstances (see also Gray[146]).

When the surveillance system is engaged, habitual routines are suspended and attention shifts to the novel or threatening occurrence so that learning can take place. Now, if a particular symbol in a narrative stream, such as an especially compelling image in a breaking news report, stands out from the expectations of its discursive context—the "mental horizon" in which it is embedded[147]—the symbol processor "must reach down a level to clarify its 'meaning'" (p. 398[145]). The terrorist attacks on the World Trade Center provide an apt example. The moment images of the airliners' impact appeared on television screens, "viewers abandoned the verbal stream, discursive processing ceased, and focus was redirected to the images themselves" (p. 398[145]). Information processing thus shifted down to a more basic level of emotional response. This disruption to habitual routines continued, in Newhagen's estimation, "for hours or days before message makers and receivers alike could sufficiently integrate the images into some meaningful context well enough to begin processing news about them 'normally' [that is,] at the level of shared cultural semiotic meaning" (p. 398[145]).

Because reading and the apprehension of spoken language require more deliberate cognitive effort than recognizing and deriving meaning from images, news *verbals* are poorly remembered compared to news *images*—particularly when they are compelling and dramatic. In contrast to images, verbal description is more experientially remote and less directly involving, especially for those with low levels of literacy. This is particularly true for political information, which requires an elaborated schema or existing base of knowledge for audiences to effectively integrate novel occurrences and new knowledge for later use (see Converse[148] and Lau and Sears[149]).

Yet despite the tendency to discard what was said and remember what was seen, verbal communication has been assigned a higher cultural value than visuals. Widely regarded as easy to understand and interpret, yet mysterious on account of their influence, images are discounted in research because they seem so intuitively obvious. Their ability to tap a nonrational aspect of experience, particularly in relation to propagandistic uses of symbols and so-called emotional triggers, has also caused many to regard them with suspicion. The mistake researchers make is to assume that visual processing, owing to its evolutionary priority, is associated *only* with basic actions related to survival, dominance, and procreation. As emphasized, visuals are equally processed in the thinking part of the brain and contain a great deal of nuanced social information important for political decision making, as elaborated upon below.

COGNITIVE AND LINGUISTIC CONSIDERATIONS

In *Descartes' Error*, Damasio[90] refuted the idea that reason is the final arbiter of perception and argued on the basis of neurological evidence that humans are not primarily thinking beings who also feel but feeling beings who also think. Both emotion and cognition come into play in the way that humans process visual and verbal forms of communication. Although images are capable of evoking basic emotional responses on a preattentive level and receive additional processing via the cortical pathway within a biological time scale, it would be a mistake to assume that they are therefore not subject to conscious appraisals and propositional evaluations. Within the cognitive and rational bands of processing, two issues warrant consideration once an audiovisual message becomes the focus of attention: the analogical quality of images and their lack of explicit syntactical rules.

Research on visual literacy and persuasion (see Messaris[150] and Messaris and Abraham[151]) points to inherent differences in how humans process visual and written forms of communication. Whereas images (whether still or full motion) are said to have an analogical quality in the way they represent physical objects and events in the nonmediated environment, words are abstract symbols with no physical resemblance to their referents.[152-155] This distinction is simply illustrated by considering the two mediated representations of an object in the physical world, a beloved gray tabby. Most readers would agree that the photograph in Figure 1–3, although a partial image, bears more resemblance to what a

Figure 1–3

common domestic short-haired cat looks like in the physical world than the three letters that form the word "cat."

Because images bear close resemblance to their physical referents on account of their analogical quality, a basic understanding of the content of visual messages requires less instruction than deriving meaning from the written word. The techniques involved in packaging visual content, including camera and editing operations, also resemble or at least simulate nonmediated perceptual experiences. For example, zoom-in camera lens movements mimic the physical experience of approaching an object, while zoom-outs resemble retreat or withdrawal movements. Moreover, camera actions such as pans (horizontal scanning) and tilts (vertical scanning) imitate head movements (for more on camera and editing techniques, see Chapter 5 and Messaris[150]).

From an entirely different perspective, film scholars argue that visual communication functions much like written language, complete with linguistic rules and conventions that are required for viewers to derive meaning from messages. Comprehension of visual media, they contend, requires substantial exposure and instruction on production conventions related to camera angle, shot distance, and time-compressing editing techniques.[156–160] Challenging this view, Messaris[150] refers to evidence that visually inexperienced media users have little trouble making sense of visual messages. This has been demonstrated by showing abstract and incomplete stick figure sketches to people in parts of the world where visual representation is not a common cultural phenomenon (see Cook,[161] Hudson,[162] and Kennedy and Ross[163]). Complicated point-of-view and time-compressed video sequences have also been comprehended without difficulty among first-time television viewers in an isolated Kenyan village.[164]

Thus, images are readily understood because their content directly corresponds to objects in the physical environment and because the production techniques used in packaging full-motion visuals simulate human perception. Yet the imitative qualities of visual messages may camouflage their constructed nature.[150,151] Through visual framing, varying shot distances, camera angles, and editing techniques, a *version* of the physical world is recorded and transformed, but without much transparency as to how a news report was assembled—a major criticism in the social construction of reality literature (see Gitlin[165] and Tuchman[166]). In this sense, television viewers are unlikely to be aware of a news report's constructedness or artificiality; journalists do not *fake* the news, so the argument goes, but they do *make* it (i.e., shoot, edit, narrate, and assemble raw footage into a cohesive package). At the most basic level, the very decision of what to include or exclude in a single camera shot is a transformative act (for more on visual framing and visual bias, see Chapters 3 and 5). Yet most viewers take these transformed versions of what occurred in the physical world on a given day at face value.

Visual images also differ from the written word in that they lack the explicit propositional syntax of formal language.[150] Propositions are the linguistic means of drawing conclusions, arguing causality, making generalizations, and forming associations between ideas. When a writer or speaker uses the propositional phrase "because of," listeners or readers understand explicitly that a causal claim is being made. News visuals are capable of make sweeping claims, yet the rules by which visuals function in making claims are far less formalized and rule based. For instance, the widely circulated photograph of Barack Obama in African dress with turban head cover, fed to media outlets from within the Hillary Clinton campaign during the 2008 Democratic primaries, made a potent visual claim that Obama was a Muslim. Despite the uproar about the dirty politics behind the picture's visual innuendo, the photograph was eagerly published and shown on television. Yet few (if any) mainstream news outlets would have been willing to publish the message had it been distributed as a verbal claim, that is, "Barack Obama is a Muslim"—a patently false statement.

Lack of explicit propositional syntax in visual communication makes claim-making difficult to detect or pinpoint—and preserves a measure of plausible deniability not afforded to news personnel (and political advertisers, for that matter) who use more semantically exacting verbal statements.[151] Combined with the analogical quality of visual communication, the absence of lexical rules leads to "reduced awareness of the process by which a particular visual impression is generated" (p. 219[151]), and therefore may render unsuspecting viewers more susceptible to persuasion. Lack of syntactical rules also makes the prospect of visual analysis somewhat daunting, which explains in part why researchers have shied from tangling with this analytical problem. Yet this persuasive quality, and the meaning that images impart, makes it imperative for the research community to develop the tools required for systematic analysis of news visuals. And perhaps there would be more inclination to take on the methodological challenges of studying visuals if the ontological biases against visuals were more widely and critically understood. With the purpose of tracking the origins of this bias against images, the final section of this chapter travels through 5,000 years of human cultural history, documenting the rise of print culture.

THE POMP AND CIRCUMSTANCE OF PRINT CULTURE

If the human brain and perceptual system have evolved for optimal information gain through visual processing, the question remains why visual-based media have not been embraced for their democratizing potential. Instead, television research is characterized by a disapproving normative tone, and the medium is ridiculed for thriving on unreason and promoting "culture death."[16,167] As we have noted, in scholarly analyses of media and democracy, research weight is signaled by studying the printed and, to some degree, spoken word when looking for evidence of media effects on political behavior. Even when the analytical focus is squarely on television news, the visual component of the medium is routinely ignored.[168]

Television emerged commercially in the late 1940s when academic derision of popular culture, especially of a visual nature, was in vogue. Then, as now, the visual form was treated as a threat to literary tradition, which had ascended during what Postman[16] referred to as the "Age of Typography" (see also Hartley,[169] Birkerts,[170] Briggs and Burke[171]). But the anxiety and concern about television was not limited to academic circles. Print journalists, politicians, clergy, and a host of self-appointed guardians of the public sphere eagerly verbalized their discontent with the medium, associating it with various "moral panics" over media sensationalism and civic decay.[172–174] The controversy surrounding television content highlights a contradiction between democratic thought and practice. While voluminous lip service has been paid to equality, informed citizenship, and political participation, elite fears about realizing social parity, supported by cultural practices intended to maintain hierarchy, permeate the democratic way of governance. Elite attitudes toward television, and the public spectacle associated with their expression, function to reaffirm social hierarchy.

Given its close fit with human information-processing capabilities, television is positioned to be an equalizing agent. Depending on how one defines information, the medium clearly has the capacity to shrink the gap between information haves and have-nots. Unlike some early research aimed at investigating television's purported inability to inform,[126,175–179] a growing body of literature[24,180–186] has demonstrated a positive association between public-affairs television viewing and political knowledge—a robust empirical finding that even television's staunchest critics begrudgingly concede (see Putnam[14]).

Despite the educated world's preference for printed information, audiovisual media have the capacity to transcend the inequities associated with learning from the written word. More than any other mass medium, television embodies the great promise of mass communication, which is to edify and uplift the masses. Because print requires textual literacy, it introduces cognitive barriers to learning and serves to stratify society rather than to equalize. As international demographic studies have found, one in five adults worldwide, two-thirds of them women, are illiterate.[187] In the United States, an estimated 20% to 25% of the adult population is functionally illiterate, preventing them from operating effectively in contemporary society,[188] and only about a third possess a four-year college degree. Needless to say, literacy for all remains an elusive target.[187] As much as the *New York Times* and *Washington Post* are venerated for providing the informational nutrients of democracy, the printing press has never been positioned to fulfill mass communication's great promise for a majority of citizens.

If the cultivation of an informed citizenry were a true priority, the diffusion of television into American households should have been embraced, studied, and taken seriously for its democratizing potential. As historians have noted, this was not the atmosphere, politically or academically, in which television was received. Even today, the rhetoric that frames the role of television in society has a jaundiced quality to it, whereas the written word is treated as the wellspring of any number of utopian outcomes, including self-governance, political accountability, social equality, individual advancement, and logical reasoning, among others (see, for example, Cipolla,[189] Eisenstein,[190] Goody and Watt,[191] Ong,[192] UNESCO[187]). Not only does the development of the written word serve as the starting point of recorded history but it also demarcates literacy, democracy, and civilization itself. "Looked at in the perspective of time, man's biological evolution shades into prehistory when he becomes a language-using animal; add writing, and history proper begins."[191]

Historians of writing and alphabetic literacy have begun to challenge assumptions about the socially corrective power of the written word. Literacy, or the skills required to employ the written word, has been increasingly questioned for its liberating potential and instead is seen as a mechanism that magnifies and exacerbates social cleavages.[193–198] As the noted sociologist Johan Galtung observed, "literacy is there to a large extent to create an illusion of equality" (quoted in Graff,[197] p. 49).

The optimism that surrounds the written word has recently been recategorized as a school of thought rather than a social fact and in some circles is referred to as the "literacy myth."[196,199] In these emerging counter-histories, both the oral tradition and visual modes of representation enjoy critical attention as conduits of socially relevant information. Yet both oral and visual modalities are given short shrift compared to the written word.[171,200,201] Also under scrutiny is the tendency among historians to rely on "texts from the summit of high culture," namely philosophical and theological writings—an approach to examining the past that Zaret equates with "looking the wrong way through a telescope" (Zaret,[11] p. 5; see also Burke[202]).

Upending utopian attitudes toward print, contrarian views regard the written word as an apparatus of religious propaganda, a tool that serves commerce, and a means for elites to exercise social control over the lower classes.[23] That was as true in ancient times as it is now.[196,204] In a dense, counter-account of the history of literacy, Graff[196] convincingly dispels the literacy myth. By tracing the origins of the idealism surrounding literacy, he exposes a darker legacy of the written word and shows that this mode of communication has more effectively served as a means of social stratification than social equality, distinguishing between those who have and have not mastered its use. Over the centuries, as print culture ascended, the visual and oral traditions were relegated to lesser cultural status and became synonymous with people of lower social standing.

To illuminate the intractability of this view, we next call on the work of historians to explain the social conditions that have exalted the print culture and prevented television from being taken more seriously as an information source. At the center of this analysis is the symbolic value that became associated with the written word. Television made a late entry onto the cultural stage, with front-row critics ardently invested in the print tradition and therefore not terribly receptive to the idea of broadcast media as valid information sources. This sentiment did not surface overnight but was in the making over the millennia as communication moved from an oral to a written and then printed footing. We briefly consider several key points in that transformation here.

Antiquity

The Western world's verbal tradition originates from Sumeria with the introduction of writing into a predominantly oral culture. From there writing spread to Mesopotamia, Egypt, and Greece. It took at least 2,500 years for the phonetic alphabet to develop and several more centuries for the first Greek and then Roman schools of instruction to emerge. Schooling in its earliest form was directed at male children of the upper classes, with instruction focused on diction and oral argumentation. Despite the dominant equation of early schooling with alphabetic literacy, there is no evidence that reading or writing was part of the early curriculum. Yet at a macro social level the link between the written word and social mobility was already in place. "Put writing in your heart that you may protect yourself from hard labour of any kind," an edict from Egyptian nobility of the New Kingdom advised, "the scribe is released from manual tasks; it is he who commands" (p. 314[191]).

By the fourth and fifth centuries BCE, male elites in Greece had acquired relatively high levels of literacy, although the business of state and commerce was mostly conducted within the oral tradition.[2,196,205] Nonetheless, historical records from this period have been held up as evidence of the connection between literacy and participatory democracy.[206] From evidence that handwritten notices and laws were posted publicly in the fourth and fifth centuries BCE in Athens, some historians extrapolate that high literacy rates enabled a public sphere.[191] But, as Graff[196] concludes, these postings offer flimsy confirmation that literacy was widespread. Laws and public notices could very well have been posted with the intent of having the literate read them out loud to a predominantly *illiterate* public.

The spread of the Christian and Jewish religious traditions after the first century, with their written gospels and Talmudic scrolls, is often attributed to the written word.[208] Yet evidence again points to the relatively small role that writing played in popularizing these "book" religions.[196] Scriptures were copied by hand and distributed to be read aloud so that followers could memorize and recite sections (see also Gandz[209]). Clergy were the gatekeepers (or "opinion leaders") in an early two-step flow model of communication from the written word to the people. Visual representations of religion were more direct means by which spiritual messages were conveyed during this period.[171] The Greek theologian Basil of Caesarea (330–379 CE) is quoted as saying that artists do as much for religion with images as orators do through their verbal eloquence. Similarly, Pope Gregory the Great (540–604 CE) described the role of images as "doing for those who could not read, the great majority, what writing did for those who could."[171,210]

Throughout antiquity the oral tradition, coupled with visual representation, dominated the transmission of religious and civic values—a historical interpretation at odds with the more common view that credits the written word for the rise of both religion and the public sphere.

The Middle Ages

During the Early Middle Ages (500–1000 CE), a period marked by devastating bouts of war and epidemic disease, literacy rates fell. The practice of writing and disseminating knowledge (mostly in Latin) was preserved in monasteries and by other religious institutions. Out of necessity, education tilted toward military preparedness rather than intellectual training, while the connection between religion and alphabetic literacy among the male elite solidified.[196]

In the early eighth century, church interiors underwent dramatic transformation, with decorative images displayed as a means of informing the illiterate. During the Middle Ages, religious art thus originated as instructional communication.[171] Through statues and stained glass windows, commoners learned from images "all that it was necessary that they should know—the history of the world from creation, the dogmas of religion, the examples of the saints, the hierarchy of virtues, the range of the sciences" (p. 7,[171] citing the French historian Emile Mâle). Throughout the medieval era, the oral tradition remained firmly in place as a primary form of information conveyance. In fact, the written word was shaped to be heard, not quietly read.[171,211]

Literacy patterns shifted during the tenth through thirteenth centuries, with rising prosperity, population increases, economic diversification, and governmental secularization. Royalty and nobility were increasingly trained in the use of the written word, as were administrators and merchants, and their assistants and clerks. Instruction, spearheaded by religious institutions, was still given in Latin; although spreading, literacy was not yet a common phenomenon.[171,196]

The early part of the fourteenth century was defined by economic hardship, war, and population declines due to pestilence and disease (mostly, the Black Plague). As recovery commenced, a humanist tradition, fueled by renewed interest in classic Greek and Roman thinking about the state and society, spread from Italy throughout Europe. Initiated by the educated elite, the humanist movement provided the impetus for social, political, and cultural reform. Informed citizenship certainly counted among humanist ideals, but ultimately humanism was a movement among the elite, for the elite. Nevertheless, it sparked an awakening that helped inspire the Renaissance.[171,196]

The fifteenth and sixteenth centuries witnessed the flowering of the Renaissance, emergence of the printing press, and succession of the Reformation—dramatic events in social, political, and economic life. In the mid-fifteenth century, Johan Gutenberg's printing office in Mainz, Germany, commenced mechanical book production.[212] Largely absent from historical accounts of this period are mentions of how religious images were printed from woodcut blocks in Europe a hundred years *before* Gutenberg introduced movable type.[171] Playing cards, satirical posters, and calendars also preceded the printing of books. Moreover, much of what was printed after the invention of the printing press was image based. The more pressing demand for printed *images* in a society where the underclasses were not taught to read trumped the need for printed *texts*.[196]

Unlike most historians who attribute legendary qualities to Gutenberg's invention, Graff underplays the role of the printing press in

Image printing	Text printing	Newspaper	Photography	Telegraph	Movies	Radio	Television	WWW
6 Hundred years ago	5.6 Hundred years ago	4 Hundred years ago	1.8 Hundred years ago	1.6 Hundred years ago	1.1 Hundred years ago	1 Hundred years ago	80 Years ago	20 Years ago

Figure 1–4

advancing widespread literacy. "Print did not produce deterministically
or mystically readers and literates without intermediate steps, such
as schooling. The level of literacy was not raised rapidly by printing"
(p. 117[196]; see also Zaret[11]). Visual depictions and the spoken word continued to serve the cause of mass education, most notably among the
lower classes. Bookshops, coffee houses, and reading rooms also provided gathering places where the printed word could be read aloud
and publicly considered (see Habermas[9]).

Many historians regard literacy and the advent of printing as the
kindling that ignited the Renaissance. While these developments
played an important role in the cultural rebirth that took place during
this time, Graff argues that the contribution of the printing press in particular has been greatly exaggerated: "The activities of the Renaissance
were well developed *before* the invention of moveable typography.
The contribution of printing to the Renaissance, while important, was
relatively late (about 150 years into the movement) and specific. More
important was a transition from a primarily oral culture to one more
literary and visual" (p. 83[196]).

This period also witnessed the emergence of tangible distinctions
between the social value of textual and visual modes of representation. Pursuing a career in the visual arts, whether as a painter, sculp-
tor, or architect, was not encouraged among the nobility or successful
merchant class. These labor-intensive pursuits, though creative, were
considered befitting the children of shopkeepers and clerks, while the
scions of elites were encouraged to become writers in the humanist
tradition. Schooling for writers and visual artists differed markedly.
The former received training in classical literacy, learning to read and
write in Latin, while the latter were trained as craftsmen, by appren-
ticeship.[196] In this way two parallel literacies developed: one visual,
practical, and common; the other, centered around the written word,
associated with intellect and reserved for those at the very top of the
social hierarchy.

Decades after the printing press was developed, religious and political leaders saw in this media technology the potential for building
a godly and civil society. With the press's capabilities for mass reproduction mass literacy could be pursued in a manner never before
attempted. At the vanguard of the movement were humanists and reformers of religion and society. "The press was a tool, but the ideas
came not from its agency" (p. 119[196]). Along these ideological lines
church and state assumed more responsibility for the underclasses in
the late fifteenth century and beyond, and literacy became more tightly
associated with a Christian type of knowledge. The Dutch theologian
Desiderius Erasmus, also known as the "Prince of Christian Humanism," played a prominent role in imposing a high-minded approach
to education. Modern languages were considered inferior to classical

languages, and popular folk tales were held in contempt. Despite enthusiastic pronouncements in favor of mass literacy, the humanist movement showed great hesitation in making literacy a universal phenomenon.[196,202]

As the Reformation gathered force in the early sixteenth century, the printing press provided the opportunity for the first test of a propaganda campaign through printing: the medium would help launch a religious reform movement of unprecedented proportions. Of course, printing technology alone did not inspire the Reformation but merely provided a "tried and tested vehicle for both reformers and their opposition to spread their ideas" (p. 133[196]). Similarly, the increased availability of printed materials did not increase literacy of its own accord but did make the flow of communication more efficient. In this way the writings of Protestant reformer Martin Luther were distributed quickly and widely. At the same time, orations, performative rituals, and visual materials were instrumental in supplementing the printed word and popularizing Luther's ideas.

Briggs and Burke,[171] much like Graff,[196] are skeptical of those who argue that the Reformation would not have occurred without the printing press. The assertion that at the heart of the Reformation was a battle between the visual form and written word also appears questionable. Catholics adhered to a strong visual culture to inform the uneducated about biblical lessons, while some Protestants—in particular John Calvin—viewed visual depictions of religion as blasphemous.[202] Martin Luther did not oppose visual depictions of religion and commissioned printing of religious imagery as a means of spreading reformist ideas to what he called *simple folk* (p. 65[171]). Although the Calvinist wing of Protestantism fought a symbolic battle against Catholicism by destroying visual representations in cathedrals, the Reformation overall was focused on much larger issues.[202]

Absent from most celebratory accounts of the printing press as a democratizing force following the Reformation are the ways in which the printed word was controlled and intentionally deployed to *hinder* democratic principles. Religious leaders initially attempted to restrict distribution of printed Bibles, particularly those printed in common languages, because they enabled churchgoers to read the gospel for themselves, thus eroding attendance and encouraging challenges to their spiritual authority.[171] In response to the new technology, government officials were preoccupied with the establishment of censorship and issuance of printing licenses; moreover, they feared that reading would invite public criticism of their reign. Among the male elite, fears about the potential of the written word to stir emotion among women surfaced. *Progressive* thought on the topic held that women should be permitted to read, provided their reading was limited to the Bible. Only "a few brave people argued that upper class women should be allowed to read the classics" (p. 51[171]). It was not until the mid-1700s, when women were considered literate enough, that books specifically targeted at their interests started to appear in Western literature.

Modernity

With a few exceptions, early modern (1600–1800) Europe was characterized by restricted literacy. A minority of the population, mainly urbanites, men, and Protestants, were able to read, and even fewer were able to write.[196,202] Political uprisings, including the French and American revolutions, as well as the English Civil War, were emboldened and to some extent organized through popular media (see Zaret[11]). Propaganda campaigns, familiar as a means of promoting religion over the centuries, were now orchestrated in the service of politics.[11,202]

Many of these printed materials, which were distributed illicitly in the form of placards, handbills, and other media due to censorship, featured cartoonlike images ridiculing leaders and calling on the people to rise up against oppressive rule. Along with printed media and visual representations, the spoken word fomented much of the fervor that brought about social and political change. Coffeehouses and taverns continued to serve as meeting places where citizens debated issues, coordinated efforts, and exchanged information.[9,11,171,196,202] Over time, non-elites became more invested in political matters as opportunities for civic involvement increased and information relevant to self-governance became more accessible.

During the eighteenth century, literacy increased throughout Europe and North America. But with this growth in learning came renewed concerns about the content of educational curricula for the underclasses. In some circles a servant's ability to read his master's letters was considered too much education.[196] Schools were therefore tailored to match the social hierarchy, with different programs of study developed for students from different social classes. Children from lower-class families were trained for four years in reading, writing, and arithmetic (the so-called three R's) with heavy-handed moral instruction and additional focus on "performing one's role in society" (p. 179[196]). Overwhelmingly, the destined societal duty of lower-class children was labor. Thus, agriculture became a staple of their four-year curriculum. Upper-class children were also schooled in the three R's—needless to say, with no emphasis on agriculture—and they also received an additional four years of training in hard science, commerce, languages, and social science.

Despite documented resistance to universal education by important thinkers of the day, including Voltaire and Rousseau, the Enlightenment is widely viewed as an educational movement. Classist views were prevalent among leading philosophers and architects of social policy, who remained darkly skeptical about the social desirability of commoners' becoming literate, as well as their ability to do so. Most pressing were concerns that literacy would divorce "the people" from hard labor.[196,202] Religious authorities were less opposed to the idea of mass literacy, recognizing the potential of a managed education system to spread the gospel as part of the curriculum.

As the ideals of the Enlightenment evolved and proliferated, something approximating universal literacy was achieved. As a measure of estimating literacy rates, historians rely on the ability to sign a marriage license or last will and testament. By 1795, approximately 90% of men in New England were able to sign their names to a will, whereas about 42% of women were able to do so. Such gains reinforced popular (and simplistic) assumptions about the written word enabling democratic self-governance. The rise of literacy and its dissemination to the popular classes, Graff noted, was "associated with the triumph of light over darkness, of liberalism, democracy, and universal unbridled progress" (p. xxxvii[197]). This sentiment has gained strength over the ensuing centuries. A stamp issued by the U.S. Postal Service in 1978, featuring an illustration of a quill pen and ink well, exemplified this view by proclaiming: "The ability to write. The root of democracy" (p. xxxv[197]).

By the 1830s, opposition to universal schooling had waned in North America and most of Europe.[197] Elite fears about an educated working class were redirected.[213] The new thinking held that education, following the religious model, could deliver an underclass well trained in the social order—complete with political and moral restraint. Literacy alone, "isolated from its moral basis—was feared as potentially subversive" (p. 23[197]). However, as morality and literacy became entwined, literacy was seen as "speeding and easing moral instruction, [with] morality guiding and restraining the potentially dangerous uses of literacy" (p. 26[197]). Instruction in mastering the use of the written word was also believed to generate a productive and disciplined labor force, which was thought to be more orderly, punctual, and well mannered than an uneducated working class.

Perhaps most significantly, through formal education manual laborers were taught to abandon ambitions of social mobility. "Schooling had the additional important task of assuring that manual workers did not aspire to rise above their station in life. Farmers or agricultural workers, for example, must be educated *not* to view their activities as narrow or regard them with contempt and disgust; they were not to be schooled so that they would want to leave their work, in order to attain to a position of importance and influence" (p. 31[197]). Historic documents (see Graff)[197] show that ideas about individual progress, liberation, equality, and democracy were far removed from the discourse surrounding the establishment of public education. Novels, for example, were considered a threat to profound and disciplined thought among young men but were *prescribed* for young, unmarried women.[197] Referring to socially stratified educational programs, a report issued by the National Society of Canada in 1841 observed that the people should not be hindered "from obtaining Knowledge, but [the state] can do something towards making that knowledge the safest and the best" (p. 45[197]). Class distinctions also manifested in the ways that students were trained to speak, primarily in the form of word choice and tone, as well as the printed media they consumed.[202,214]

By the early twentieth century, elite concerns about the revolutionary threat of the lower classes, reawakened by the harsh reality of the Industrial Revolution, were evident in the writings of Charles Babbage, Emile Durkheim, Gustave Le Bon, and Antonio Gramsci, among other social thinkers.[171] This was also the point at which the term *mass culture*, distributed through mass media (newspaper, film, photography), was coined. Popular media outlets provided a break from the grinding monotony of factory work and became associated with the mass introduction of leisure time.[215] With the proliferation of low cost entertainment, a distinction between highbrow and lowbrow media culture was emerging.[216]

As early as the seventeenth century a line was drawn between news consumed by the upper and lower classes. Lowbrow news, initially consisting of ballads, chapbooks, and *corantos* (small booklets issued at semiregular intervals), was dismissed as sensational and crude. These popular media forms were distinguished by their visual depictions of murders and scandals and use of large type—a style not much different from today's tabloids.[11,46,202,217-220] By contrast, proper newspapers were described as instruments of didactic virtue, capable of fulfilling the great promise of mass communication.[221] Joseph Pulitzer, the reform-minded editor and publisher who endowed the first school of journalism at Columbia University (even while his papers engaged in sensationalism and practiced yellow journalism), saw newspapers as an "organ of truth."[222] The noted editor Samuel Bowles, articulating the great promise, asserted that the "brilliant mission of the newspaper . . . is to be the high priest of history, the vitalizer of society, the world's great informer, the earth's high censor, the medium of public opinion and the circulating life blood of the whole human mind" (quoted in Harris,[223] p. 3). These distinctions between tabloid and highbrow news sharpened over time and are reflected in virtually all forms of media today.

When radio burst onto the scene in the United States, members of the elite print press responded with outrage in what is referred to as the Press–Radio War of the 1930s.[224-226] Newspaper reporters dismissed radio reporting as a working-class occupation, akin to working at a grocery store, and called radio news a threat to an informed citizenry. Broadcast journalism was derided as a variant of show business rather than credited as an equal player in the news business. Radio broadcasts were accused of stirring emotion in a dangerous way, and the rantings of early radio demagogues such as Father Coughlin were held up as portentous examples. Observed one print reporter, "The radio, through the magic inherent in the human voice, has a means of appealing to the lower nerve centers and of creating emotions, which the hearer mistakes for thoughts" (Irwing, quoted in Jackaway, p. 65).[225]

Beyond such pontifications, specific steps were taken to dissuade radio journalists' nascent pursuit of news. The Associated Press wire service banned radio stations from receiving its news bulletins, and print journalists sought legislation (which never passed) that would have prevented CBS News reporters from gaining admission to congressional press galleries. When it became clear that radio news was not going away, newspaper companies set out to control the new industry by buying up stations and putting print journalists in charge of writing and editing radio news copy.[225,227]

When television news emerged in the late 1940s (see Conway[224]), the small-screen medium drew the same criticisms that were leveled against radio—this time from both print and radio journalists.[171,224,225] Upon his return from World War II, the celebrated radio reporter Edward R. Murrow described television news as "mindless," while his colleague Howard K. Smith made it known that television news was not a "manly" career pursuit—unworthy of serious consideration as a professional career for young educated men.[227,228] Both stayed clear of television for as long as they could but of course are now well known for their illustrious careers in broadcast news.

The Democratic and Republican national conventions of 1948 and 1952 were instrumental in popularizing the new medium and drove television's meteoric diffusion into American homes.[224,228] By mid-1947, roughly 7,000 television sets had been sold in the United States; a year later that number had risen to 400,000. By the 1952 Republican National Convention, some 18 million receivers had entered American households.[228] Television was now mainstream and Murrow its rising star. By the time of his speech to the Radio-Television News Directors Association in 1958, Murrow had become a reluctant advocate of the medium's civic promise. Now, speaking with some candor about what was happening to broadcasting, he observed that television could teach, illuminate, and even inspire—providing that the will existed to realize its democratizing potential.[229] "There is a great and perhaps decisive battle to be fought against ignorance, intolerance, and indifference," he said. "This weapon of television could be useful."[226] By November 1963 a Roper poll commissioned by the Television Information Office[230] found that television was the main source of news for most Americans—a statistic that holds true today.[231]

Breaking with the Gutenberg Legacy

This brief history of human communication has highlighted the central role that oral and visual forms have played in Western culture even after the invention of writing and printing. Although the print-ing press liberated the written word from monastic control, literacy barriers have prevented textual media from becoming "the world's great informer," as Samuel Bowles hoped for newspapers. Instead of being read by the masses, elite print media often set the agenda for *other* media outlets, including broadcast news organizations, extend-ing their reach and influence indirectly. Even as the newspaper indus-try contracts, the traditional press continues to serve the interests of the upper echelons of society, who have always enjoyed access to the printed word as a forum for exchange (see McChesney[236]).

Over time, both oral and visual forms of communication, though more accessible than textual representations, became devalued as their association with cultural practices at the lower end of the social hier-archy grew. By the time of the Enlightenment, this division between the cultural status of the printed word and other forms of communi-cation had become evident. During this period, social mobility based on individual achievement rather than fixed class position at birth also became possible. Hierarchy maintenance under such fluid conditions required new symbolic mechanisms for drawing—and maintaining—separations between social classes.

Comfortably at hand was the printed word, which could be con-toured to fit class variations in the skill level required to command it. Text-based media already evidenced distinctions between lowbrow and highbrow content, especially in the widely consumed newspaper genre. Equally important, the biological primacy of visual processing among *Homo sapiens*, which gives images their universality, disquali-fied visually based media as a means of drawing class distinctions. Perhaps because of the inherently egalitarian quality of visuals, cul-tural practices that function to maintain social hierarchies disparaged image-based media as inferior to words. Humans, after all, are the only word-using animal, which regrettably has invited a disturbing construction of images as "the medium of the subhuman, the savage, the 'dumb' animal, the child, the woman, [and] the masses"[237] (p. 24). The upshots of such constructions are attitudes that survive both po-litical and technological revolutions.

Indeed, the introduction of radio and television had the potential to reanimate oral and visual traditions (see McLuhan[13]), but the sym-bolic investment in printed media as both socially distinguishing and democracy-enhancing was already complete. Thus, granting radio the status of the old oral tradition was not about to happen, and efforts were undertaken to bar broadcasters from news gathering altogether. The most vehement criticism, bordering on moral disparagement, has been leveled at television—despite the medium's audiovisual richness, cognitive accessibility, and nondiscriminatory nature. Even today, television news is referred to as *infotainment*, as if it conveyed no serious information at all. The characterization of broadcast news by Pulitzer Prize–winning journalist Carl Bernstein as servant to an "idiot culture" continues to represent elite sentiment about television, and about audiovisual media more generally (see Bernstein,[15] Postman,[16] Mitchell[237]).[238]

Examining the reasons why the most accessible technology in the history of human communication has not been embraced in academic and other circles is an important pursuit, with implications for the practice and understanding of democratic politics. The principles that underlie this resistance may be undemocratic themselves, lending urgency to the careful and unprejudiced analysis of television's content and form. Consequently, throughout this book we break with the time-honored Gutenberg legacy and instead take the visual dimension of television news seriously.

NOTES

1. Innis[2] observed that a harmonious balance between oral and written forms of communication contributed to the flourishing of Greek civilization in the time of Plato around the fifth century BCE. Plato's dialogues, Innis felt, brilliantly combined the vitality of the spoken word with the power of writing. By contrast, he warned that Western culture in the mid-twentieth century was imperiled by an advertising-obsessed media system consumed by "present-mindedness" and the "continuous, systematic, ruthless destruction of elements of permanence essential to cultural activity" (p. 15[3]).
2. Innis, Harold. 1950. *Empire and communications*. Oxford: Clarendon Press.
3. Innis, Harold. 1952. *Changing concepts of time*. Toronto: University of Toronto Press.
4. For notable exceptions examining the role of art in politics, see Edelman,[5] Frascina,[6] Mosse,[7] and Petropoulos.[8]
5. Edelman, Murray. 1995. *From art to politics: How artistic creations shape political conceptions*. Chicago: University of Chicago Press.
6. Frascina, Francis. 2000. *Arts, politics, and dissent: Aspects of the art Left in sixties America*. Manchester, UK: Manchester University Press.
7. Mosse, George M. 1973. *The nationalization of the masses*. New York: Howard Fertig.
8. Petropoulos, Jonathan. 1999. *Art as politics in the Third Reich*. Chapel Hill: University of North Carolina Press.
9. Habermas, Jurgen. 1962/1989. *The structural transformation of the public sphere: An inquiry into a category of bourgeois society*. Translated by Thomas Burger, with the assistance of Frederick Lawrence. Cambridge, MA: MIT Press.
10. Schudson, Michael. 1998. *The good citizen: A history of American civic life*. New York: Free Press.
11. Zaret, David. 2000. *Origins of democratic culture*. Princeton, NJ: Princeton University Press.

12. McLuhan[13] (p. 173) similarly argued that the precision and linear sequencing of typographical communication promoted specialization, hyperrationalization, and detachment, with the effect of encouraging the separation of thought and action from feeling and emotion. Television, he argued, implodes these divisions.

13. McLuhan, Marshall. 1964/1994. *Understanding media: The extensions of man.* Cambridge, MA: MIT Press.

14. Putnam, Robert D. 2000. *Bowling alone: The collapse and revival of American community.* New York: Simon and Schuster.

15. Bernstein, Carl. 1992, June 8. The idiot culture: Reflections of post-Watergate journalism. *The New Republic* 22–26.

16. Postman, Neil. 1986. *Amusing ourselves to death: Public discourse in the age of show business.* New York: Penguin Books.

17. Bucy, Erik P., and Paul D'Angelo. 1999. The crisis of political communication: Normative critiques of news and democratic processes. *Communication Yearbook* 22:301–339.

18. Bennett, W. Lance. 2007. *News: The politics of illusion.* 7th ed. New York: Pearson Longman.

19. Hart, Roderick P. 1999. *Seducing America: How television charms the modern voter.* 2nd ed. Thousand Oaks, CA: Sage.

20. Iyengar, Shanto. 1991. *Is anyone responsible? How television frames political issues.* Chicago: University of Chicago Press.

21. Graber, Doris A. 1988. *Processing the news: How people tame the information tide.* 2nd ed. New York: Longman.

22. Potter, W. James. 2008. *Media literacy.* Los Angeles, CA: Sage.

23. Grabe, Maria Elizabeth, and Rasha Kamhawi. 2004. Cognitive access to new and traditional media: Evidence from different strata of the social order. In *Media access: Social and psychological dimensions of new technology use,* ed. P. Bucy and J. Newhagen, pp. 27–46. Mahwah, NJ: Lawrence Erlbaum Associates.

24. Grabe, Maria Elizabeth, Rasha Kamhawi, and Narine Yegiyan. Informing citizens: How people with different levels of education process television, newspapers, and Web news. *Journal of Broadcasting and Electronic Media* (in press).

25. Newhagen, John E. 2002. The role of meaning construction in the process of persuasion for viewers of television images. In *The persuasion handbook: Developments in theory and practice,* ed. James P. Dillard and Michael W. Pfau, pp. 729–748. Thousand Oaks, CA: Sage.

26. Newhagen, John E., and Byron Reeves. 1992. The evening's bad news: Effects of compelling negative television news images on memory. *Journal of Communication* 42(2):25–41.

27. Grabe, Maria Elizabeth. 1996. The South African Broadcasting Corporation's coverage of the 1987 and 1989 elections: The matter of visual bias. *Journal of Broadcasting and Electronic Media* 40(1):1–27.

28. Kepplinger, Hans Mathias. 1982. Visual biases in television campaign coverage. *Communication Research* 9(3):432–446.

29. Messaris, Paul, and Linus Abraham. 2001. The role of images in framing news stories. In *Framing public life: Perspectives on media and our understanding of the social world,* ed. Stephen D. Reese, Jr., Oscar H. Gandy, and August E. Grant, pp. 215–226. Hillsdale, NJ: Lawrence Erlbaum.

30. Bucy, Erik P. 2000. Emotional and evaluative consequences of inappropri-ate leader displays. *Communication Research* 27(2):194–226.

31. Sullivan, Dennis G., and Roger D. Masters. 1988. "Happy warriors": Lead-ers' facial displays, viewers' emotions, and political support. *American Journal of Political Science* 32(2):345–368.

32. Masters, Roger D. 2001. Cognitive neuroscience, emotion, and leadership. In *Citizens and politics: Perspectives from political psychology*, ed. James H. Kuk-linski, pp. 68–102. New York: Cambridge University Press.

33. Masters, Roger D., and Denis G. Sullivan. 1993. Nonverbal behavior and leadership: Emotion and cognition in political information processing. In *Explorations in political psychology*, ed. Shanto Iyengar and William J. McGuire, pp. 150–182. Durham: Duke University Press.

34. Marcus, George E., W. Russell Neuman, and Michael MacKuen. 2000. *Affective intelligence and political judgment*. Chicago: University of Chicago Press.

35. Somit, Albert, and Steven A. Peterson. 1998. Biopolitics after three dec-ades: A balance sheet. *British Journal of Political Science* 28:559–571.

36. Benjamin, Daniel J., and Jesse M. Shapiro. 2008. Thin-slice forecasts of gu-bernatorial elections. *Review of Economics and Statistics* 90.

37. Lanzetta, John T., Denis G. Sullivan, Roger D. Masters, and Gregory J. McHugo. 1985. Emotional and cognitive responses to televised images of political leaders. In *Mass media and political thought: An information-processing approach*, ed. Sidney Kraus and Richard M. Perloff, pp. 85–116. Beverly Hills, CA: Sage.

38. Rosenberg, Shawn W., Lisa Bohan, Patrick McCafferty, and Kevin Harris. 1986. *American Journal of Political Science* 30(1):108–127.

39. Rosenberg, Shawn W., and Patrick McCafferty. 1987. The image and the vote: Manipulating voters' preferences. *Public Opinion Quarterly* 51(1):31–47.

40. Todorov, Alexander, Anesu N. Mandisodza, Amir Goren, and Crystal C. Hall. 2005. Inferences of competence from faces predict election outcomes. *Science* 308(10):1623–1626.

41. Agenda setting holds that mass media set the topics of issue discussion among the public, influencing judgments about the relative importance of political issues. Framing is the process whereby certain aspects of a per-ceived reality (e.g., depictions of a political candidate in a television news report) are highlighted at the expense of other information. In this way a problem is constructed, causal interpretation and moral evaluation of-fered, and remedies to a problem recommended.[42] For an explication of visual framing, see Chapter 3 in this book.

42. Iyengar, Shanto, and Jennifer A. McGrady. 2007. *Media politics: A citizen's guide*. New York: W. W. Norton.

43. Bucy, Erik P. 2003. Emotion, presidential communication, and traumatic news: Processing the World Trade Center attacks. *Harvard International Journal of Press/Politics* 8(4):76–96.

44. Drew, Dan, and David H. Weaver. 2006. Voter learning in the 2004 presi-dential election: Did the media matter? *Journalism and Mass Communication Quarterly* 83(1):25–42.

45. Gitlin, Todd. 2002. *Media unlimited: How the torrent of images and sounds overwhelms our lives*. New York: Metropolitan Books.

46. Stephens, Mitchell. 1998. *The rise of the image, the fall of the word*. New York: Oxford University Press.

47. Adams, William, and Fay Schreibman. 1986. *Television network news: Issues in content research*. Washington, DC: George Washington University.

48. Fyfe, Gordon, and John Law. 1988. On the invisibility of the visual. *Sociological Review Monograph* 35:1–14.

49. Graber, Doris A. 1986. Mass media and political images in elections. *Research in Micropolitics* 1:127–160.

50. Graber, Doris A. 2001. *Processing politics: Learning from television in the Internet age*. Chicago: University of Chicago Press.

51. Graber, Doris A. 2004. Methodological developments in political communication research. In *Handbook of political communication research*, ed. Lynda Lee Kaid, pp. 45–67. Mahwah, NJ: Lawrence Erlbaum.

52. Kepplinger, Hans Mathias. 1991. The impact of presentation techniques: Theoretical aspects and empirical findings. In *Television and political advertising, vol. 1: Psychological processes*, ed. Frank Biocca, pp. 173–194. Hillsdale, NJ: Lawrence Erlbaum.

53. Masters, Roger D., Dennis G. Sullivan, John T. Lanzetta, Gregory J. McHugo, and Basil G. Englis. 1986. Facial displays and political leadership. *Journal of Biological and Social Structures* 9:319–343.

54. Masters, Roger D. 1989. *The nature of politics*. New Haven: Yale University Press.

55. McLuhan was perhaps the first to comment on the difficulty or, in his view, pointlessness of analyzing television content. "Since [television] has affected the totality of our lives, personal and social and political, it would be quite unrealistic to attempt a 'systematic' or visual presentation of such influence. Instead, it is more feasible to 'present' TV as a complex *gestalt* of data gathered almost at random."[12] While we agree that studying the broader effects of media technology is important, we disagree that systematically analyzing television content is a nonproductive enterprise.

56. Coleman, Renita, and Stephen A. Banning. 2006. Network TV news' affective framing of the presidential candidates: Evidence for a second-level agenda-setting effect through visual framing. *Journalism and Mass Communication Quarterly* 83(2):313–328.

57. Media Tenor. 2007. *Research Report* Nr. 157. Berlin: InnoVatio Verlags AG. http://www.mediatenor.com. Accessed May 11, 2008.

58. Dalrymple, G. Brent. 1991. *The age of the Earth*. Palo Alto, CA: Stanford University Press.

59. Parker, Andrew. 2003. *In the blink of an eye: How vision sparked the big bang of evolution*. New York: Perseus.

60. A key point in this process occurred in 1924, when Alexander Oparin experimentally identified the necessary components for the evolution of life. In *The Origin of Life on Earth*, Oparin[61] described a primeval soup of non-living organic materials capable of a primitive metabolism sufficient to sustain cell integrity. This experimental work is still at the core of contemporary theories about the origin of life.

61. Oparin, Alexander I. 1938. *The origin of life on earth*. New York: Dover.

62. Brasier, Martin D., Owen R. Green, Andrew P. Jephcoat, Anette K. Kleppe, Martin J. Van Kranendonk, John F. Lindsay, Andrew Steele, and Natalie V. Grassineau. 2002. Questioning the evidence for Earth's oldest fossils. *Nature* 416:76–81.

63. Schopf, J. William, Anatoliy B. Kudryavtsev, David G. Agresti, Thomas J. Wdowiak, and Andrew D. Czaja. 2002. Laser–Raman imagery of Earth's earliest fossils. *Nature* 416:73–76.

64. Wilde, Simon A., John W. Valley, William H. Peck, and Colin M. Graham. 2001. Evidence from detrital zircons for the existence of continental crust and oceans on the Earth 4.4 Gyr ago. *Nature* 409:175–178.

65. Morris, Simon Conway. 1997. *The crucible of creation: The Burgess Shale and the rise of animals.* New York: Oxford University Press.

66. In the case of the trilobite, ancestral forms may have been somewhat soft-bodied but over time developed a hard exoskeleton as a defensive measure—an adaptation that served this class of three-lobed animals well for almost 300 million years.[59]

67. Diamond, Jared. 1992/2006. *The third chimpanzee: The evolution and future of the human animal.* New York: Harper Perennial.

68. Goodman, Morris, Danilo A. Tagle, David H. A. Fitch, Wendy Bailey, John Czelusniak, Ben F. Koop, Philip Benson, and Jerry L. Slightom. 1990. Primate evolution at the DNA level and a classification of hominoids. *Journal of Molecular Evolution* 30(3):260–266.

69. Smithsonian Human Origins Program. 2008. *Homo sapiens.* http://anthropology.si.edu/humanorigins/ha/sap.htm. Accessed March 28, 2008.

70. The history of speech became so hotly debated in the nineteenth century that the British Academy in London and Société de Linguistique in Paris discouraged members in the 1860s from discussing and studying the origin of language and speech, as it was then seen as a speculative and futile theoretical pursuit.[71,72] Even today, there is little agreement.

71. Hoccett, Charles F. 1960. The origin of speech. *Scientific American* 203:88–96.

72. Holden, Constance. 2004. The origin of speech. *Science* 303(5662):1316–1319.

73. Balter, Michael. 2002. Language evolution: "Speech gene" tied to modern humans. *Science* 297(5584):1105.

74. This estimate is consistent with the assessment of Jared Diamond[67] (pp. 55–56), who doesn't "suggest that the Great Leap Forward began as soon as the mutations for altered tongue and larynx anatomy arose. Given the right anatomy, it must have taken humans thousands of years to perfect the structure of language as we know it—to arrive at the concepts of word order and case endings and tenses, and to develop vocabulary."

75. Hewes, Gordon W. 1984. The invention of phonemically-based language. In *Language development: A reader*, ed. Andrew Lock and Eunice Fisher, pp. 49–58. London: Open University Press.

76. McGurk, Harry, and John MacDonald. 1976. Hearing lips and seeing voices. *Nature* 264(5588):746–748.

77. Wright, Daniel, and Gary Wareham. 2005. Mixing sound and vision: The interaction of auditory and visual information for ear-witnesses of a crime scene. *Legal and Criminological Psychology* 10(1):103–108.

78. Pettitt, Paul, and Paul Bahn. 2003. Current problems in dating paleolithic cave art: Candamo and Chauvet. *Antiquity* 77(295):134–141.
79. Valladas, Hélène. 2003. Direct radiocarbon dating of prehistoric cave paintings by accelerator mass spectrometry. *Measurement Science and Technology* 14:1487–1492.
80. Valladas, Hélène, Jean Clottes, Jean-Michel Geneste, M. A. Garcia, Maurice Arnold, Hélène Cachier, and Nadine Tisnerat-Laborde. 2001. Evolution of prehistoric cave art. *Nature* 413:479.
81. Clarke, Grahame. 1977. *World prehistory: A new perspective.* Cambridge: Cambridge University Press.
82. Hooker, James T. 1990. *Reading the past: Ancient writing from cuneiform to the alphabet.* Berkeley: University of California Press.
83. Mitchell, Larkin. 1999. Earliest Egyptian glyphs. *Archaeology* 52(2):28–29.
84. Schmandt-Besserat, Denise. 1996. *How writing came about.* Austin: University of Texas Press.
85. Houston, Stephen D. 2004. *The first writing script invention as history and process.* New York: Cambridge University Press.
86. We acknowledge that our arguments apply to those with vision, putting aside questions about how information processing for blind people might differ.
87. Barry, Ann Marie. 2005. Perception theory. In *Handbook of visual communication,* ed. Ken Smith, Sandra Moriarty, Gretchen Barbatsis, and Keith Kenney, pp. 45–62. Mahwah, NJ: Lawrence Erlbaum.
88. Damasio, Antonio R. 1999. *The feeling of what happens.* New York: Harcourt Brace.
89. Newell, Allen. 1990. *Unified theories of cognition.* Cambridge, MA: Harvard University Press.
90. Damasio, Antonio R. 1994. *Descartes' error: Emotion, reason and the human brain.* New York: G. P. Putnam's Sons.
91. LeDoux, Joseph. 1996. *The emotional brain: The mysterious underpinnings of emotional life.* New York: Simon and Schuster.
92. Libet, Benjamin, Dennis K. Pearl, David Morledge, Curtis A. Gleason, Yoshio Morledge, and Nicholas Barbaro. 1991. Control of the transition from sensory detection to sensory awareness in man by the duration of a thalamic stimulus. *Brain* 114:1731–1757.
93. Watanabe, Shoko, Ryusuke Kakigi, Sachiko Koyama, and Eiji Kirino. 1999. Human face perception traced by magneto- and electro-encephalography. *Cognitive Brain Research* 8(2):125–142.
94. Mishkin, Mortimer, and Tim Appenzeller. 1987. The anatomy of memory. *Scientific American* 256:80–89.
95. Gazzaniga, Michael Saunders. 1998. *The mind's past.* Berkeley: University of California Press.
96. Gilbert, Daniel T. 1991. How mental systems believe. *American Psychologist* 46:107–119.
97. Gilbert, Daniel T., Douglas S. Krull, and Patrick S. Malone. 1990. Unbelieving the unbelievable: Some problems with the rejection of false information. *Journal of Personality and Social Psychology* 59:601–613.
98. Davidson, Richard J., and William Irwin. 1999. The functional neuroanatomy of emotion and affective style. *Trends in Cognitive Sciences* 3(1):11–21.

99. Zimmermann, Manfred. 1989. The nervous system in the context of information theory. In *Human physiology,* ed. Robert F. Schmidt and Gerhard Thews, 2nd ed., pp. 166–173. Berlin, Germany: Springer-Verlag.

100. Marcus, George E. 2002. *The sentimental citizen: Emotion in democratic politics.* University Park: Pennsylvania State University Press.

101. In other words, we experience far more than we understand. "Yet it is experience, rather than understanding," McLuhan[13] argued, "that influences behavior."

102. Broadbent, Donald E. 1977. The hidden preattentive process. *American Psychologist* 32(2):109–118.

103. Paivio, Allan. 1971. *Imagery and verbal processes.* New York: Holt, Rinehart and Winston.

104. Bargh, John. 1988. Automatic information processing: Implications for communication and affect. In *Communication, social cognition, and affect,* ed. Lewis Donohew, Howard E. Sypher, and E. Tory Higgins, pp. 9–32. Hillsdale, NJ: Lawrence Erlbaum.

105. Fazio, Russell H., David M. Sanbonmatsu, Martha C. Powell, and Frank R. Kardes. 1986. On the automatic activation of attitudes. *Journal of Personality and Social Psychology* 50:229–238.

106. Kunst-Wilson, William Raft, and Robert B. Zajonc. 1980. Affective discrimination of stimuli that cannot be recognized. *Science* 207:557–558.

107. Consistent with this realization, emotion has emerged as an increasingly important variable in studies examining the processing of television news and, for that matter, political advertising (see, for example, Biocca,[108] Brader,[109] Bucy,[30,43] Grabe and Kamhawi,[110] Grabe, Lang, and Zhao,[111] Grabe, Kamhawi, and Yegiyan,[24] Newhagen,[112] Reeves and Nass[113]).

108. Biocca, Frank, ed. 1991. *Television and political advertising,* vol. 1, *Psychological processes.* Hillsdale, NJ: Lawrence Erlbaum.

109. Brader, Ted. 2005. *Campaigning for hearts and minds: How emotional appeals in political ads work.* Chicago: University of Chicago Press.

110. Grabe, Maria Elizabeth, and Rasha Kamhawi. 2006. Hard wired for negative news? Gender differences in processing broadcast news. *Communication Research* 33(5):346–369.

111. Grabe, Maria Elizabeth, Annie Lang, and Xiaoquan Zhao. 2003. News content and form: Implications for memory and audience evaluations. *Communication Research* 30(4):387–413.

112. Newhagen, John E. 1998. TV news images that induce anger, fear, and disgust: Effects on approach-avoidance and memory. *Journal of Broadcasting and Electronic Media* 42(2):265–276.

113. Reeves, Byron, and Clifford Nass. 1996. *The media equation: How people treat computers, television, and new media like real people and places.* New York: Cambridge University Press.

114. Physiological manifestations of a stress response include the release of hormones (particularly adrenaline), heart-rate acceleration, pupil dilation, enhanced respiration, nostril flaring, liberation of nutrients and dilation of blood vessels for muscular action, and the inhibition of unnecessary functions, among other bodily preparations (see Gleitman, Reisberg, and Gross[115]).

115. Gleitman, Henry, Daniel Reisberg, and James Gross. 2007. *Psychology*. 7th ed. New York: W. W. Norton.

116. Lang, Annie, Mija Shin, and Seungwhan Lee. 2005. Sensation seeking, motivation, and substance use: A dual system approach. *Media Psychology* 7(1):1–29.

117. Messages containing strong positive emotion, on the other hand, are likely to be more complex and require increased cognitive effort, propositional evaluation, and additional time to process.[118]

118. Leventhal, Howard, and Klaus Scherer. 1987. The relationship of emotion to cognition: A functional approach to a semantic controversy. *Cognition and Emotion* 1(1):3–28.

119. Pinker, Steven. 1997. Words and rules in the brain. *Nature* 387:547–548.

120. Kanwisher, Nancy, Josh McDermott, and Marvin M. Chun. 1997. The fusiform face area: A module in human extrastriate cortext specialized for face perception. *Journal of Neuroscience* 17(11):4302–4311.

121. O'Toole, Alice J. 2005. Psychological and neural perspectives on human face recognition. In *Handbook of face recognition*, ed. Stan Z. Li and Anil K. Jain, pp. 349–369. New York: Springer.

122. Haxby, James V., Elizabeth A. Hoffman, and M. Ida Gobbini. 2000. The distributed human neural system for face perception. *Trends in Cognitive Sciences* 4(6):223–233.

123. More specifically, Haxby and colleagues[122] have proposed a *distributed neural system* for human face perception, which posits that the invariant aspects of faces contribute to face recognition, whereas the changeable aspects of faces, including eye gaze direction, facial expressions, and lip movements, serve social communication functions (p. 364[121]). The distributed neural model identifies three core brain areas and proposes four associated areas as part of an extended system for face processing keyed to specific tasks.

   In the core system, the fusiform gyrus is thought to represent information about facial identity and other categorical or unchanging properties of faces. The posterior superior temporal sulcus is identified as the site for encoding the changeable aspects of faces, including gaze direction, eye and mouth movement, head orientation, and variable expressions. The lateral inferior occipital gyri form the third core component and are thought to be involved in the early perception of facial features as well as distributing information to the two other core areas.

   The four brain regions proposed as the extended system for face processing include the intraparietal sulcus (involved in spatially directed attention); auditory cortex (involved in prelexical speech perception from lip movements); anterior temporal area (involved in the retrieval of personal identity, name, and biographical information); and a set of limbic structures, including the amygdala and insula (involved in the perception of emotion from expressions).[121,122]

124. Barton, Robert A. 1996. Neocortex size and behavioural ecology in primates. *Proceedings of the Royal Society of London: Biological Sciences* 263:173–177.

125. Joffe, Tracey H., and Robin I. M. Dunbar. 1997. Visual and socio-cognitive information processing in primate brain evolution. *Proceedings of the Royal Society of London: Biological Sciences* 264(1386):1303–1307.

126. Gunter, Barry. 1987. *Poor reception: Misunderstanding and forgetting broadcast news*. Hillsdale, NJ: Lawrence Erlbaum.

127. Robinson, John P., and Mark R. Levy. 1986. *The main source: Learning from television news*. Beverly Hills, CA: Sage.

128. Lang, Annie. 1995. Defining audio/video redundancy from a limited-capacity information processing perspective. *Communication Research* 22(1):86–115.

129. Bucy, Erik P. 1998. The emotional appropriateness heuristic: Viewer assessments of televised presidential reactions to compelling news events. PhD diss., University of Maryland.

130. Bucy, Erik P., and John E. Newhagen. 1999. The emotional appropriateness heuristic: Processing televised presidential reactions to the news. *Journal of Communication* 49(4):59–79.

131. Bucy, Erik P., and Samuel D. Bradley. 2004. Presidential expressions and viewer emotion: Counterempathic responses to televised leader displays. *Social Science Information/Information sur les Sciences Sociales* 43(1):59–94.

132. For leader reactions to be deemed appropriate, they must be meaningfully related to the message that preceded them and emotionally compatible with the tone of the setting in which they occur.[30]

133. Kaid, Lynda Lee, Valerie Cryer Downs, and Sandra Ragan. 1990. Political argumentation and violations of audience expectations: An analysis of the Bush-Rather encounter. *Journal of Broadcasting and Electronic Media* 34(1):1–15.

134. Drew, Dan, and Thomas Grimes. 1987. Audio-visual redundancy and TV news recall. *Communication Research* 14(4):452–461.

135. Grimes, Tom. 1991. Mild auditory-visual dissonance in television news may exceed viewer attentional capacity. *Human Communication Research* 18(2):268–298.

136. Barton, Robert A., and Robin I. M. Dunbar. 1997. The evolution of the social brain. In *Machiavellian intelligence II: Extensions and evaluations*, ed. Andrew Whiten and Richard W. Byrne, pp. 240–263. New York: Cambridge University Press.

137. Brothers, Leslie. 1990. The social brain: A project for integrating primate behavior and neurophysiology in a new domain. *Concepts in Neuroscience* 1:27–51.

138. Byrne, Richard W., and Andrew Whiten, eds. 1988. *Machiavellian intelligence: Social expertise and the evolution of intellect in monkeys, apes, and humans*. New York: Oxford University Press.

139. Masters, Roger D. 1981. Linking ethology and political science: Photographs, political attention, and presidential elections. *New Directions for Methodology of Social and Behavioral Science* 7:61–80.

140. Equally impressive, O'Toole[121] (p. 350) notes, is our ability "to state with confidence that a face is one we have never seen before."

141. Bruce, Vicki, and Andy Young. 1986. Understanding face recognition. *British Journal of Psychology* 77(3):305–327.

142. Burgoon, Judee K., and Joseph B. Walther. 1990. Nonverbal expectancies and the evaluative consequences of violations. *Human Communication Research* 17(2):232–265.

143. Ekman, Paul. 1982. *Emotion in the human face*. New York: Cambridge University Press.
144. Newell, Allen. 1990. *Unified theories of cognition*. Cambridge, MA: Harvard University Press.
145. Newhagen, John E. 2004. Interactivity, dynamic symbol processing, and the emergence of content in human communication. *The Information Society* 20:395–400.
146. Gray, Jeffrey A. 1987. *The psychology of fear and stress*. 2nd ed. Cambridge: Cambridge University Press.
147. Hall, Stuart. 1980. Encoding/decoding. In *Culture, media, language: Working papers in cultural studies, 1972–79*, ed. Stuart Hall, Dorothy Hobson, Andrew Lowe, and Paul Willis, pp. 128–138. London: Hutchinson.
148. Converse, Philip E. 1964. The nature of belief systems in mass publics. In *Ideology and discontent*, ed. David E. Apter, pp. 206–261. New York: Free Press.
149. Lau, Richard R., and David O. Sears, eds. 1986. *Political cognition: The 19th annual Carnegie symposium on cognition*. Hillsdale, NJ: Lawrence Erlbaum.
150. Messaris, Paul. 1994. *Visual literacy: Image, mind, and reality*. Boulder, CO: Westview Press.
151. Messaris, Paul, and Linus Abraham. 2001. The role of images in framing news stories. In *Framing public life: Perspectives on media and our understanding of the social world*, ed. Stephen D. Reese, Jr., Oscar H. Gandy, and August E. Grant, pp. 215–226. Hillsdale, NJ: Lawrence Erlbaum.
152. Barthes, Roland. 1967. *Elements of semiology*. Translated by Annette Lavers and Colin Smith. London: Jonathan Cape.
153. Chandler, Daniel. 2007. *Semiotics: The basics*. London: Routledge.
154. De Saussure, Ferdinand. 2006. *Writings in general linguistics*. Oxford: Oxford University Press.
155. Peirce, Charles S. 1934. *Collected papers, vol. V: Pragmatism and pragmaticism*. Cambridge, MA: Harvard University Press.
156. Mangan, James. 1978. Cultural conventions of pictorial representation: Iconic literacy and education. *Educational Communication and Technology* 26(3):245–267.
157. Metz, Christian. 1991. *Film language: A semiotics of the cinema*. Translated by Michael Taylor. Chicago: University of Chicago Press.
158. Monaco, James. 1981. *How to read a film: The art, technology, language, history and theory of film and media*. New York: Oxford University Press.
159. Saint-Martin, Fernande. 1990. *Semiotics of visual language*. Bloomington: Indiana University Press.
160. Sebeok, Thomas A., and Jean Umiker-Sebeok. 1995. *Advances in visual semiotics*. New York: Mouton de Gruyter.
161. Cook, Bruce L. 1981. *Understanding pictures in Papua New Guinea*. Elgin, IL: David C. Cook Foundation.
162. Hudson, William. 1960. Pictorial depth perception in subcultural groups in Africa. *Journal of Social Psychology* 52:183–208.
163. Kennedy, John M., and Abraham S. Ross. 1975. Outline picture perception by the Songe of Papua. *Perception* 4:391–406.

164. Hobbs, Renee, Richard Frost, Arthur Davis, and John Stauffer. 1988. How first-time viewers comprehend editing conventions. *Journal of Communication* 38(4):50–60.

165. Gitlin, Todd. 1980. *The whole world is watching: Mass media in the making and unmaking of the New Left.* Berkeley: University of California Press.

166. Tuchman, Gaye. 1978. *Making news: A study in the construction of reality.* New York: Free Press.

167. Morris, Simon Conway. 2006. Darwin's dilemma: The realities of the Cambrian "explosion." *Philosophical Transactions of the Royal Society B: Biological Sciences* 361(1470):1069–1083.

168. The more general area of critical television studies (including fictional content) has also been dominated since its inception by an abiding concern about the corrupting influence of the medium. Academic analyses of television constitute one of the few areas of research where the successful student, according to Hartley[169] (p. 66), is the one "who could catalogue most extensively the supposed evils associated with [the medium], although of course these evils only affected *other* people, possibly because students were not encouraged to watch TV themselves, only to opine haughtily about it."

169. Hartley, John. 1999. *Uses of television.* New York: Routledge.

170. Bikerts, Sven. 2006. *The Gutenberg elegies: The fate of reading in an electronic age.* New York: Faber and Faber.

171. Briggs, Asa, and Peter Burke. 2005. *A social history of the media: From Gutenberg to the Internet.* Malden, MA: Polity Press.

172. Grabe, Maria Elizabeth, Shuhua Zhou, and Brooke Barnett. 2001. Explicating sensationalism in television news: Content and the bells and whistles of form. *Journal of Broadcasting & Electronic Media* 45(4):635–655.

173. Ryu, Jung S. (1982). Public affairs and sensationalism in local TV news programs. *Journalism Quarterly* 59(1):74–78, 137.

174. Slattery, Karen L., and Hakanen, Ernest A. 1994. Sensationalism versus public affairs content of local TV news: Pennsylvania revisited. *Journal of Broadcasting & Electronic Media* 38(2):205–216.

175. Becker, Lee B., and Charles D. Whitney. 1981. The effects of media dependencies on audience assessment assessments of government. *Communication Research* 2:167–188.

176. McClure, Robert D., and Thomas Patterson. 1976. Print vs. network news. *Journal of Communication* 26(2):23–28.

177. Neuman, W. Russell. 1976. Patterns in recall among television news viewers. *Public Opinion Quarterly* 40:115–123.

178. Nordenstreng, Karl. 1972. A policy for news transmission. In *Sociology of mass communications*, ed. Denis McQuail, pp. 386–405. Harmonsworth: Penguin.

179. Robinson, Michael J. 1974. The impact of the televised Watergate hearings. *Journal of Communication* 24:17–30.

180. Chaffee, Steven H., Xinshu Zhao, and Glenn Leshner. 1994. Political knowledge and the campaign media of 1992. *Communication Research* 21(3):305–324.

181. Holbert, R. Lance, William L. Benoit, Glenn J. Hansen, and Wei-Chun Wen. 2003. The role of communication in the formation of an issue-based citizenry. *Communication Monographs* 69(4):296–310.

182. Neuman, W. Russell, Marion Just, and Ann N. Crigler. 1992. *Common knowledge: News and the construction of political meaning*. Chicago: University of Chicago Press.

183. Van der Molen, Juliette H. W. and Thom H. A. Van der Voort. 2000. Children's and adults' recall of television and print news in children's and adult news formats. *Communication Research* 27(2):132–160.

184. Weaver, David H., and Dan Drew. 2001. Voter learning and interest in the 2000 presidential election: Did the media matter? *Journalism and Mass Communication Quarterly* 78(4):787–798.

185. Weaver, David H., and Dan Drew. 2006. Voter learning in the 2004 presidential election: Did the media matter? *Journalism and Mass Communication Quarterly* 83(1):25–42.

186. Wicks, Robert H. 1995. Remembering the news: Effects of medium and message discrepancy on news recall over time. *Journalism and Mass Communication Quarterly* 72(3):666–681.

187. UNESCO. 2008. *Education: Literacy portal*. http://portal.unesco.org/education/en/ev.php- URL_ID=54369andURL_DO=DO_TOPICandURL_SECTION=201.html. Accessed March 12, 2008.

188. Gee, James P. 1989a. The legacies of literacy: From Plato to Freire through Harvey Graff. *Journal of Education* 171(1):147–166.

189. Cipolla, Carlo M. 1969. *Literacy and development in the West*. Harmondsworth, UK: Penguin Books.

190. Eisenstein, Elizabeth L. 2005. *The printing revolution in Early Modern Europe*. Cambridge: Cambridge University Press.

191. Goody, Jack, and Ian Watt. 1963. The consequences of literacy. *Comparative Studies in Society and History* 5(3):304–345.

192. Ong, Walter, J. 1982. *Orality and literacy*. London: Methuen.

193. Berg, Ivar. 1971. *Education and jobs: The great training robbery*. Boston, MA: Beacon Press.

194. Cook-Gumperz, Jenny, ed. 1986. *The social construction of literacy*. Cambridge: Cambridge University Press.

195. Disch, Robert, ed. 1973. *The future of literacy*. Englewood Cliffs, NJ: Prentice-Hall.

196. Graff, Harvey J. 1987. *The legacies of literacy: Continuities and contradictions in western culture and society*. Bloomington: Indiana University Press.

197. Graff, Harvey J. 1991. *The literacy myth: Cultural integration and social structure in the nineteenth century*. New Brunswick, NJ: Transaction.

198. Marcus, Joyce. 1992. *Mesoamerican writing systems: Propaganda, myth, and history in four ancient civilizations*. Princeton, NJ: Princeton University Press.

199. Halverson, John. 1992. Goody and the implosion of the literacy thesis. *Man* 27(2):301–317.

200. Lesy, Michael. 2007. Visual literacy. *Journal of American History* 94(1):143–153.

201. One reason the history of literacy, or human history generally, might have bestowed utopian qualities on the written word is practical: the written word leaves a physical artifact behind that can be retrieved to serve as an

account of history. The oral tradition, in contrast, leaves relatively imper-
manent traces of how it shaped human behavior over centuries. And, as
oral content became recorded in written form, it was counted as evidence
of *written* culture. What remains puzzling is that visual representation,
which leaves behind full-blown retrievable artifacts, has not been treated
more seriously as historical evidence. Burke[202] articulates the conventional
historical view of visual representation by calling it oblique and in need
of interpretation—something the written or printed word apparently does
not call for.

202. Burke, Peter. 1994. *Popular culture in Early Modern Europe*. Burlington, VT:
     Ashgate.
203. The same charge could be made about the oral and visual traditions.
204. See Marcus[198] for a forceful account of how ancient Mesoamerican (Aztec,
     Zapotec, and Mayan) writing systems served to exercise control over illit-
     erate classes and were used by elites as a tool to gain prestige, leadership,
     advantageous marriages, and territory.
205. Havelock, Eric A. 1963. *Preface to Plato*. Cambridge, MA: Harvard Univer-
     sity Press.
206. Plato was a staunch critic of the written word, commenting on its
     superficiality, static quality, and inefficiency in facilitating queries and
     exchanges. He also expressed concern that the written word would dis-
     courage reliance on memory and ultimately erode intellectual faculties
     (Gee,[188,207] Goody and Watt[191])—a charge equally applicable to the Internet
     and other digital media today.
207. Gee, James P. 1989b. Orality and literacy: From the savage mind to ways
     with words. *Journal of Education* 171(1):39–60.
208. During the century after the birth of Christ, schooling became the work
     of religion. This marks the early origins of the historically persistent prac-
     tice of fusing moral instruction and alphabetic literacy—a trend that car-
     ried through the Middle Ages and Enlightenment and into contemporary
     times.
209. Gandz, Solomon. 1935. Oral tradition and the Bible. In *Jewish studies in
     memory of George A. Kohut, 1874–1933*, ed. Salo W. Baron and Alexander
     Marx, pp. 248–269. New York: Alexander Kohut Memorial Foundation.
210. The Byzantine tradition departed dramatically on the use of images for
     religious instruction: both Islam and Judaism banned the human form in
     visual depictions of religion.[171]
211. Chaytor, Henry J. 1945. *From script to print*. Cambridge: Cambridge Uni-
     versity Press.
212. Wood block printing was practiced in China and Japan from around the
     eighth century onward.[171]
213. During this period some elites became interested in the culture and tradi-
     tions of ordinary people as an object of study, a precursor to the academic
     study of popular culture.[202]
214. Elites were to speak correctly and properly, according to formal rules, and
     avoid regional dialects, informal language, and technical (labor-oriented)
     terms used by the peasantry. Dignity, reserved tonality, and nonchalance
     were prescribed. Schools offered formal instruction on these matters
     while courtesy books (most famously a rediscovered title from 1561 called

Courtier by the humanist Renaissance writer Baldasare Castiglione) disseminated information about the acme of patrician behavior.

215. Jarvie, Ian. 1982. The social experience of movies. In *Film/culture: Explorations of cinema in its social context*, ed. Sari Thomas, pp. 247–268. Metuchen, NJ: Scarecrow.

216. Gans, Herbert J. 1999. *Popular culture and high culture: An analysis and evaluation of taste* (rev. ed.). New York: Basic Books.

217. Bird, S. Elizabeth. 1992. *For inquiring minds: A cultural study of supermarket tabloids*. Knoxville, TN: University of Tennessee Press.

218. Shaw, Donald L., and John W. Slater. 1985. In the eye of the beholder? Sensationalism in American press news, 1820–1860. *Journalism History* 12(3–4):86–91.

219. Stephens, Mitchell. 1985. Sensationalism and moralizing in 16th and 17th-century newsbooks and news ballads. *Journalism History* 12(3–4):92–95.

220. Stevens, John D. 1985. Sensationalism in perspective. *Journalism History* 12(3–4):78–79.

221. Stoddard, Henry L. 1946. *Horace Greeley: Printer, editor, crusader*. New York: Putnam.

222. Juergens, George. 1966. *Joseph Pulitzer and the New York World*. Princeton, NJ: Princeton University Press.

223. Harris, Brayton. 1999. *Blue and gray in black and white: Newspapers in the Civil War*. London: Brassey's.

224. Conway, Mike. 2007. A guest in our living room: The television newscaster before the rise of the dominant anchor. *Journal of Broadcasting and Electronic Media* 51(3):457–478.

225. Briggs and Burke[171] report the same hostility from newspaper journalists toward broadcasters in Germany.

226. Murrow, Edward R. 1958. Industry leaders speech. http://www.rtnda.org/pages/media_items/edward-r.-murrow-speech998.php. Accessed June 5, 2008.

227. Conway, Mike. 2007. Before the bloggers: The upstart news technology of television at the 1948 political conventions. *American Journalism* 24(1): 33–58.

228. Mickelson, Sig. 1998. *The decade that shaped television news: CBS in the 1950s*. Westport, CT: Praeger.

229. Otherwise, he said, "it's nothing but lights and wires in a box."[226]

230. Roper Organization Inc. 1979. *Public perspectives of television and other mass media: A twenty-year review 1959–1978*. New York: Television Information Office.

231. The precise wording of the Roper question was, "First, I'd like to ask you where you usually get most of your news about what is going on in the world today—from the newspapers or radio or television or magazines or talking to people or where?" The multibarrelled wording of this question has fueled criticism, analysis, and counter-studies in mass media research circles for decades—even while television was strengthening its position as the most widely used source of information (see, for example, Lemert,[232] Reagan and Ducey,[233] Stempel,[234,235]).

232. Lemert, James B. 1980. News media competition under conditions favorable to newspapers. *Journalism Quarterly* 47:272–280.

233. Reagan, Joey, and Richard V. Ducey. 1983. Effects of news measure on selection of state government news sources. *Journalism Quarterly* 60(2):211–217.
234. Stempel, Guido H. III. 1973. Effects on performance of a cross-media monopoly. *Journalism Monographs* 29:1–30.
235. Stempel, Guido H. III. 1991. Where people *really* get most of their news. *Newspaper Research Journal* 12:2–9.
236. McChesney, Robert W. 2004. *The problem of the media: U.S. communication politics in the twenty-first century.* New York: Monthly Review Press.
237. Mitchell, W. J. Thomas. 1994. *Picture theory: Essays on verbal and visual representation.* Chicago: University of Chicago Press.
238. See, for example, http://www.msnbc.msn.com/id/21595196/.

2

Image Bite News

Concern about the dwindling amount of airtime allotted to presidential candidates in network news coverage of elections constitutes one of the major criticisms of media and politics today. The distillation of an entire day's worth of campaigning into a single pithy quotation, phrase, or sound bite, although an established industry convention, has become a source of great consternation among scholars and pundits alike. The problem is seen as twofold: a reduction in the overall volume of election coverage given to campaigns and a decrease in the amount of speaking time allotted to candidates in individual news reports. Television news, in particular, stands accused of not granting politicians enough verbal access to the public sphere. Broadcast news organizations have been disparaged for the growing tendency of reporters to voice-over candidate statements with narrative commentary and for compelling candidates and officeholders to speak and act on television's terms—namely, in sound bite form.[1-3] Candidates, when they are allowed to speak, are simply being heard less. With documentation of the shrinking sound bite, an assumption has emerged, "that as sound bite length decreases, viewers of television newscasts are provided a more distorted, filtered picture of the candidates, their positions on key issues, and the race itself" (p. 408[4]; see also Hallin[5]).

Though damning from a rhetorical perspective that situates mediated discourse as an important channel of policy debate, these criticisms ignore what viewers of the evening news *do* receive in ample supply during presidential elections: images of candidates that convey important cues about status, viability, and temperament as well as physical and mental fitness for office. Indeed, news images of political leaders form indelible impressions, stirring emotion and conveying "important information that is attended to, processed, and remembered long after the words are forgotten" (p. 372[6]). In this chapter we compare the prevalence of sound and image bites in network news coverage over the past four general election cycles to argue that image bites—audiovisual segments in which candidates are shown but not necessarily heard—are vastly underappreciated as a source of political information.

Our motivation for this analysis stems from two separate streams of research. The first is the television news literature, which has documented a steady decrease in sound bite length while repeatedly calling for increased analysis of other elements of news broadcasts, particularly visuals (see Graber,[7,8] Griffin,[9] Lowry and Shidler[10,11]). With rare exception, however,[12–15] scholars have not taken up this call. The second stream involves research on the nonverbal display behavior of political leaders, which has examined images aired on the nightly news from the perspective of behavioral biology and cognitive neuroscience, as discussed in the first chapter. Research conducted in the biopolitics tradition (see Somit and Peterson[16]) has found that visual displays of political leaders are efficiently processed and readily remembered by viewers, are judged for their appropriateness in relation to the immediate news context,[17,18] and influence viewer emotions and evaluative appraisals—including, potentially, voting decisions. With enhanced understanding of visual information processing, it is possible to look more scientifically at the likely effects of news coverage of campaigns rather than simply bemoan the faster-paced, more visually gripping character of contemporary news[9] and its purportedly harmful impact on informed citizenship.[1]

Despite the visual nature of television, research analyzing the content of presidential-candidate appearances on the news has focused almost exclusively on the verbal side of the message, documenting the amount of time candidates are simultaneously seen *and* heard,[19,20] the length and tone of their statements,[10,11,21] and the interpretive frames journalists use to package sound bites in televised reports.[22,23] Yet such preoccupation with the shrinking sound bite, which treats the accompanying visuals as accidental elements of televised political speech, not only overlooks television's single most distinguishing feature— its ability to generate a real-time stream of images rich in referential meaning—but also fails to consider the influence that images have on viewers.[24,25] As the information-processing literature has shown, these effects are considerable when compared to the verbal component of the news. Moreover, fixation on sound bite length assumes that the longer the sound bite, the better the quality of news coverage.[4,26]

Our investigation calls these assumptions into question and makes a decisive turn toward the visual dimension of media politics. Despite the academic emphasis on policy debate and issue discussion in election campaigns, expressive displays emitted by candidates do not lose their relevance to audiences—or to journalists and other critics—when broadcast on the nightly news. Indeed, owing to the close-up nature of television, they arguably take on added importance, as Hillary Clinton's emotional moment during the 2008 New Hampshire primary aptly illustrated (see Givhan,[27] Kantor[28]). Given the rise of a more interpretive style of broadcast journalism since the 1980s, with reporters and correspondents inserting more of their own opinion and commentary into political coverage and candidates being verbally confined to an ever dwindling amount of air time,[12,19] news visuals have assumed an increasingly central yet largely unrecognized role in informing viewers.[29]

With regard to the volume of coverage, the question that has to be asked is whether image bites now occupy more candidate airtime than sound bites—and what the implications of this development might be for democratic politics. Anecdotally, Griffin[9] (p. 133) has argued that image bites of politicians and other newsmakers "are far more common than the interview 'sound bites' that have been given greater attention in news research." But this statement has not received rigorous empirical scrutiny.[31] To document the extent to which presidential candidates visually appear on the nightly news, this investigation draws on our longitudinal analysis of presidential news coverage from the 1992, 1996, 2000, and 2004 general elections. For each year, the political reporting of the main broadcast networks (ABC, CBS, and NBC) was coded for visual information (see Appendix 1 for details). In this analysis, we summarize the frequency and duration of candidate image bites that were broadcast, in which candidates were shown but not heard speaking, and compare them to sound bites in which candidates were simultaneously seen and heard. We also assess sound bite content—what the candidates are actually saying in these televised actualities—and introduce a typology for classifying the different types of sound and image bites that appear on the news (see Appendix 2 for details).

DARMAN'S HUNCH, OR WHY SEEING IS REMEMBERING

Beyond the pacing of newscasts and apportionment of candidate speaking time, an important information consideration concerns the degree of correspondence between the audio and visual components of a news report. When there is a conflict or lack of correspondence between the pictures shown and words spoken during a broadcast, viewers remember the images more readily than the verbal narration. This explains why memory tends to be poor for news stories and content details but generally good for news images,[34] particularly negative compelling images that elicit anger, fear, or disgust.[35] As confirmed by the audiovisual redundancy literature,[36–38] a mismatch between the verbal message of a news report and the visuals shown on screen impairs memory for verbal information. A similar phenomenon has been demonstrated in studies investigating visual primacy or dominance—the tendency for visuals to dominate awareness of stimuli of similar or greater intensity presented simultaneously in other modalities (see Noller[39]; Posner, Nissen, and Klein[40]). In both cases, dissonance is caused by conflicting streams of information, which is thought to increase complexity to the point of overloading attentional capacity.[37] An analysis by Graber[8] (pp. 92–93) of 189 news stories from the three major networks plus PBS found that nearly 40% of all visual scenes reinforced or clarified the verbal narration; that is, about two-fifths of the news images analyzed were in some way redundant with the accompanying verbal information.

In televised politics, mismatches between the audio and video tracks of a broadcast news report may work to a candidate's benefit or detriment, depending on the nature of the visuals. This came to light perhaps most famously during the 1984 general election when Lesley Stahl of CBS News aired what she thought was a critical report, 5 minutes and 10 seconds in length, of the Reagan campaign's duplicitous stagecraft—the public relations technique of using feel-good imagery to deflect attention away from the president's more controversial policies. While the report's narration was sharply critical, the video track was highly flattering of Reagan.

The images featured Reagan juxtaposed with an oversized American flag, smiling in a series of close-up shots, ably lifting weights and tossing out one-liners, handing off the Olympic torch, cutting a ribbon on a new nursing home, awarding medals to athletes with disabilities, and being cheered by supporters waving hand-held flags. Shortly after the report aired, a *Washington Post* reporter showed the newscast to a group of 100 people visiting the Smithsonian Institution—first without Stahl's critical voiceover and then with. Even with the voiceover, Stahl said, "most of the audience thought it was either an ad for the Reagan campaign or a very positive news story. Only a handful heard what I said" (p. 211[41]).

Expecting a barrage of criticism from the White House after the report aired, she instead received a congratulatory call from Deputy Chief of Staff Dick Darman. As Darman explained, "You guys in Televisionland haven't figured it out, have you? When the pictures are powerful and emotional, they override if not completely drown out the sound. Lesley, I mean it, nobody heard you" (quoted in Stahl,[41] p. 211). Darman had it mostly right. The visuals probably did prevail, but not just because the images were emotionally evocative; Stahl's verbal narration also conflicted with the video material shown.

Though surprising to Stahl, who thought she would surely anger the president's staff, Darman's reaction was consistent with an understanding of visual primacy. Stahl's biting verbal commentary may have been apprehended by sophisticated viewers with an appreciation for irony or by liberal partisans with distaste for the White House's tactics. However, for politically inattentive or uninformed viewers—that is, the vast majority of the viewing audience[42]—the favorable images in all likelihood did drown out the audio narration. Darman's hunch has been borne out by a series of political information–processing studies conducted since the 1980s that have examined the effects of televised leader displays on audiences across a variety of election and governing conditions (see Bucy,[17,43] Bucy and Newhagen,[18] Lanzetta et al.,[44] Masters and Sullivan[45]). When forming impressions of others, in social settings or more formal contexts such as election contests, individuals tend to rely heavily on information gathered through the visual channel.[46–47]

Considered from this point of view, television news is an ideally situated medium of political evaluation that has the capacity to visually inform viewers about aspects of the candidates that might otherwise remain unspoken (see Meyrowitz[24]). Despite their brevity, sound and image bites afford audiences the opportunity to closely examine the faces and body language of newsmakers as they speak and witness the social interactions of candidates during important campaign exchanges. As discussed in Chapter 4, the visual processing system is particularly attuned to recognizing and decoding facial expressions, which have tremendous heuristic value in social evaluation and impression formation.

Although the news audience is fragmenting with the growth of cable news channels, news magazine shows, and other soft news formats,[48] news-related programming now occupies a greater share of airtime than ever before.[2] Even in the era of online news and cell phone news feeds, network newscasts still draw the largest audiences for news.[20,49] The continued prominence of network news and dependence of political campaigns on audiovisual media promotes unprecedented viewer scrutiny of candidates. Widescreen and high-definition television monitors also bring candidates into closer view than ever. Indeed, "never before have leaders been in such frequent, widespread, and close-up visual contact with followers" (p. 61[50]). Despite this, however, scholarly analyses of sound bites generally ignore the experimental research relating to television visuals and focus instead on the length of candidate statements aired on the evening news.

SOUND BITE NEWS

Dramatic technological advances in editing and the rise of journalistic mediation led to a more interpretive style of reporting between the late 1960s and 1980s.[19] The fundamental shift, Hallin noted, was a change in focus from what candidates were saying *in* the campaign to what journalists were saying *about* the campaign. Rather than setting the scene and letting candidate actualities dominate the report, correspondents began to treat candidate statements as "raw material to be taken apart, combined with other sounds and images, and reintegrated into a new narrative" (pp. 9–10[19]). This more aggressive posture toward the news narrative became particularly evident in the 1980s as journalists struggled to assert editorial autonomy and get out from under the manipulative grasp of image handlers and professional operatives, particularly those of the Reagan–Bush campaigns.[51] At the same time, economic pressures from cable and increased profit expectations prompted by deregulation forced news executives to look for more effective ways of maintaining audience attention. Campaign visuals, including both full-motion images and graphics, were used much more extensively, and news reports became faster paced, more tightly structured, and shorter in length, reflecting the sensibility of advertising.[19]

Safire[52] defines the term *sound bite* as a "snappy snippet of taped comment or news" (p. 733)—in other words, an audiovisual segment in which a candidate or other quoted source is simultaneously shown and heard. Though associated with television, the term sound bite merges the idea of an audio or radio actuality (a recorded quote or statement from a news source) with the data-packet formatting of digital computing (into binary bits, or bytes). Daniel Schorr, a veteran Washington correspondent and senior news analyst for National Public Radio, dates its use to the early 1960s, when he worked at CBS News. "It came out of the editing room, in the days before videotape. When the producer saw the excerpt he wanted, he'd tell the film editor, 'Take that bite'; out of longer interviews, the bite would be 30 to 45 seconds" (quoted in Safire,[52] p. 733). As discussed below, the average length of a sound bite has shrunk dramatically since then, to just under 8 seconds. But the idea of encapsulating key political sentiments in a campaign context with a short memorable phrase predates the electronic media era entirely, originating in American politics in the early nineteenth century in the form of campaign slogans that were introduced by a candidate's partisans.[52,53]

In the pretelevision era, slogans acted as a way of popularizing a candidacy or presidential ticket but were generally not the dominant mode of campaign communication. Speeches by candidates and their surrogates, newspaper coverage of elections, and organized party events were largely responsible for disseminating a candidate's views to the public. With the rise of television in politics, however, campaigns began to rely on advertising and televised appearances to reach voters, and candidates were compelled to modify their communication style to accommodate the new medium. Scholars of mediated politics have long argued that the truncated message environment of both spot advertising and network newscasts (which doubled in length to 30 minutes in the early 1960s) encourages discussion and presentation of issues and ideas in bite-size form (see Jamieson[56]). This trend is generally seen as a cause for alarm, and broadcast news has been persistently chided for trivializing political discourse and constricting public debate (see Bucy and D'Angelo[51]). The picture at first glance does appear troubling: research has documented a dramatic shrinkage of candidate sound bites from over 40 seconds in the late 1960s to under 10 seconds by the 1988 election (see Adatto,[57] Hallin[5]).

Although efforts have been made to offer presidential candidates more time on the network evening news, as when CBS unilaterally decided in 1992 to maintain a 30-second sound bite minimum (which the network quickly revised downward to 20 seconds and subsequently abandoned),[58] the average length of sound bites continues to decline. In 1988, the mean sound bite length was 9.8 seconds; by the 2000 election the mean length had contracted another 20%, down to 7.8 seconds.[20] During this time period, with the exception of the unusual 1992 general election campaign, which featured three ostensibly major candidates— the two major party nominees plus Independent Ross Perot—the total number of campaign stories and minutes of news time devoted to general election news decreased while the frequency and proportion of journalists' speaking time increased.[20,23,59]

Over our sample period we would expect the amount of news time devoted to candidates and campaign stories in general election coverage to continue to decrease. Research findings that anchors and correspondents now appear more frequently and dramatically on screen while candidates are confined to a dwindling amount of airtime leads to the additional expectation that journalists will be seen speaking for a longer average duration than candidates.

Findings for Volume of Coverage

To determine whether the amount of network news time devoted to campaign coverage continued to gradually decrease over time, we examined all 178 newscasts in our sample of four consecutive election campaigns, totaling approximately 62 hours of program material. Overall, there were 2,173 individual news stories, of which 20% ($n = 437$) were defined as campaign stories. On average, there were 2.59 campaign stories per newscast. Nine newscasts did not feature campaign stories. The total duration of all campaign coverage was 906 minutes, with an average story length of just over 2 minutes per story. Table 2–1 summarizes the volume of coverage by election year, the amount of speaking time devoted to journalists and candidates in sound bite segments, and the amount of airtime journalists and candidates were allotted in televised sound and image bite segments.

As shown in Table 2–1, the number of campaign stories varied significantly across elections.[60] Post hoc Tukey tests showed that there were significantly more campaign stories in 1992 than in any other year.[61] There were no other significant paired comparison differences for election years

Table 2–1 Comparisons for Volume of Coverage and Sound and Image Bite Means over Time

Variable	Overall	Election Year			
		1992	1996	2000	2004
Volume of Coverage per Newscast					
Number of campaign stories	2.59	3.62	2.24	2.23	2.69*
SD	1.40	1.32	1.51	1.24	1.00
Duration of campaign stories (in secs.)	321.70	475.76	214.48	298.23	298.93*
SD	189.08	199.88	141.27	173.11	135.64
Audiovisual Bites					
Sound Bites					
Duration of individual candidate sound bites	8.52	9.19	9.23	8.03	7.73†
SD	5.24	6.03	5.17	5.15	4.34
Number of candidate sound bites per story	2.31	2.20	2.35	2.40	2.33
SD	1.60	1.54	1.78	1.60	1.54
Total duration of candidate sound bites per story	18.99	17.91	18.78	21.97	17.76
SD	19.68	12.35	12.70	31.51	16.71
Duration candidate is seen and heard per story	18.59	17.73	18.27	21.53	17.27
SD	18.82	12.16	12.15	30.67	14.83
Duration journalist is seen and heard per story	34.22	34.79	27.84	34.20	38.29*
SD	22.12	23.14	16.16	18.99	26.33
Image Bites					
Duration of candidate image bites per story	22.99	21.76	22.57	23.20	25.83
SD	18.23	17.57	17.97	18.04	20.19
Duration of journalist image bites per story	9.13	13.46	5.00	6.49	9.43*
SD	14.50	21.81	3.07	5.35	14.20

Sound bites include footage where the candidate is *shown speaking* (seen and heard) plus footage where the candidate is *heard but not shown*. Image bites include footage where the candidate is *shown but not heard*. All durations are presented in seconds. SD stands for standard deviation. *Statistically significant difference across years. †Difference across years approached significance.

on the number of campaign stories. The duration of campaign stories also varied significantly over time, showing a sharp decrease at first, which then stabilized across the 2000 and 2004 campaigns.[62] In 1992, the networks dedicated close to 8 minutes per newscast to presidential campaign news. This figure dropped to about 3.5 minutes in 1996, and picked up to around 5 minutes in the 2000 and 2004 election years. Post hoc tests for the campaign story durations show significantly longer coverage in 1992 than in any other election year.[63] Moreover, in 1996, campaign story durations hit a low point and were shorter than in other election years, and significantly more so in 2004.[64] Thus, the volume of coverage shrank sharply from 1992 to 1996, but this trend did not continue toward the 2004 election. In fact, after the sharp decline in 1996, it picked up in 2000 and 2004 but remained significantly lower than in 1992.

Sound Bite Findings

Looking at the length of time candidates were allowed to speak on air, we find that the average duration of candidate sound bites did continue to decline, although not dramatically. In 1992 and 1996 the average duration of sound bites was 9.19 and 9.23 seconds, respectively. In 2000 it shrank to 8.03 seconds and waned further to 7.73 seconds in 2004. These differences only approached statistical significance, but there is a notable pattern of decline over time.[65] Post hoc tests revealed no significant differences between pairs.[66] Further analysis showed that the number of bites per candidate and the total duration of sound bite time per story did not fluctuate significantly.

Examining the data for potential differences between political parties revealed some variation but no dramatic differences (see Table 2–2). For all four election years combined, the average duration of sound bites did not vary significantly between Democrats ($M = 8.74$ seconds) and Republicans ($M = 8.45$ seconds). Separate year-by-year examinations, again, did not produce significant differences between parties, except for 2004, when individual sound bites featuring Democrats were significantly longer than those featuring Republicans. Democrats and Republicans appeared in roughly the same number of bites in each election year, yet the total duration of candidate sound bites per news story differed by party, approaching significance.[67] As Table 2–2 shows, Democrats ($M = 20.78$ seconds) received more sound bite time across election years than Republicans ($M = 17.25$ seconds). A closer look at individual years shows fluctuation between the two parties in terms of who was allotted more sound bite time. During the 1996 election, Republicans received significantly more sound bite time than Democrats.[68] Yet in 2004, Democrats received more bite time than Republicans, approaching statistical significance.[69]

Finally, it is worth mentioning that there were no significant fluctuations over time for Democrats or Republicans for either the number of

Table 2–2 Sound and Image Bite Comparisons between Political Parties over Time

| | Party Affiliation | | | | | | | | | |
| | Republicans | | | | | Democrats | | | | |
Variables	'92	'96	'00	'04	Overall	'92	'96	'00	'04	Overall
Individual sound bite size duration	9.98	9.84	7.41	6.67	8.45	8.78	8.14	8.90	8.85*	8.74
SD	6.87	5.81	4.32	3.58	5.47	5.21	3.81	5.93	4.79	5.07
Number sound bites per story	1.94	2.47	2.18	2.23	2.20	2.31	1.85	2.53	2.43	2.34
SD	1.50	1.84	1.33	1.22	1.48	1.48	1.00	1.74	1.81	1.62
Sound-bite duration volume per story	17.04	20.13	17.53	14.81	17.25	18.00	14.77[†]	26.68	20.86[†]	20.78[†]
SD	12.27	12.63	13.17	11.78	15.23	11.77	10.59	18.54	10.33	14.39
Image-bite duration volume per story	21.62	23.83	23.09	27.68	23.64	21.51	20.88	22.99	24.13	22.29
SD	15.89	18.62	15.54	23.77	18.13	18.86	15.08	19.79	15.52	7.93

Durations are represented in seconds. *Statistically significant difference between Democrats and Republicans for a given year. [†]Differences between Democrats and Republicans for a given year approached statistical significance.

61

bites or total duration of bites. However, for average bite size there was a dramatic and significant decline over time for Republicans.[70] In fact, post hoc comparisons between years show that there was a significant difference between 1992 and 2004 in terms of individual Republican sound bite lengths.[71] On the other hand, the bite sizes for Democrats remained stable over time. The overall decline in bite sizes, reported earlier in this chapter, appears to be driven by Republican sound bite lengths. Figure 2–1 graphically represents these trends.

Findings for Candidates versus Journalists

To assess whether journalists were seen speaking for longer average durations than candidates, a *seen and heard* measure was devised (see Appendix 2). The reasoning here is that candidates and journalists play substantially different roles in election stories and there are structural conventions in broadcast news associated with their presentation. Journalists narrate relatively long portions of election stories, making average or total sound bite durations per story artificially longer for reporters than candidates.

As reported in Table 2–1, journalists dominated as visible talking heads at a statistically close to significant level.[72] Overall, reporters and

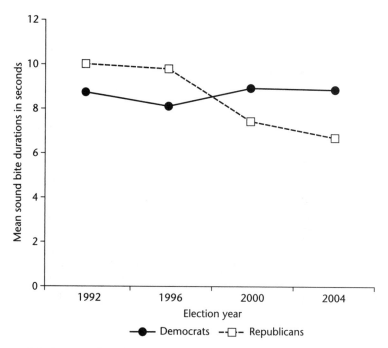

Figure 2–1 Average duration of sound bites for Republicans and Democrats over time.

anchors were seen speaking at an average of 34.22 seconds per election story. By contrast, candidates were seen speaking for an average of 18.59 seconds per story—a little more than half the time allocated to journalists. One-way ANOVA tests revealed a significant increase on the seen and heard measure for journalists over time[73] while there were no significant over-time fluctuations for candidates. Figure 2–2 visually depicts these trends.

Sound Bite Content

Only analyzing sound bite and campaign story *length*, however, ignores the *content* of candidate statements and overlooks the possibility that even the briefest of comments or utterances may have sizable political impact.[4,26,74,75] Take, for example, George H. W. Bush's 1988 convention pledge: "Read my lips: no new taxes," reprised by the Democrats to detrimental effect during the 1992 campaign.[76] The Clinton campaign exploited Bush's fateful guarantee, which consultant James Carville described as "the most famous broken promise in the history of American politics" (quoted in Hegedus and Pennebaker[77]), in both advertising and televised debates. In the third and final debate, Clinton cast the pledge as a cynical ploy that reflected on Bush's

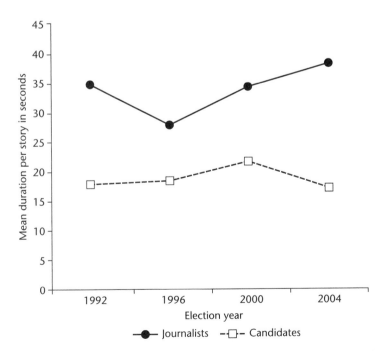

Figure 2–2 Average duration of candidate versus journalist *seen and heard* appearances over time

character. "The mistake that was made was making the 'read my lips' promise in the first place just to get elected, knowing what the size of the deficit was. You just can't promise something like that just to get elected if you know that circumstances may overtake you" (quoted in Hegedus and Pennebaker[77]). Similarly, the Republicans in 2004 used a short but contradictory statement by John Kerry to critique his lack of resolve. When pressed by a heckler about why he had voted against an appropriations bill to support the war in Iraq, Kerry said, "I actually did vote for the $87 billion before I voted against it" (quoted in Thomas,[78] p. 70). Technically, he was referring to different *versions* of the bill, but this critical point was lost in translation. Kerry was subsequently branded as a "flip-flopper," an image powerfully reinforced in George W. Bush's campaign advertising, and one that he never managed to shake.

Under certain circumstances, then, even short sound bites can have political consequences, particularly when recycled in advertising and other campaign attacks. Yet blanket criticism of the *shrinking* sound bite reflects the untested assumption that brief candidate statements invariably misinform voters, contribute to a distorted view of the campaign, and negatively impact the speaker's candidacy while longer actualities enhance news quality, increase voter learning, and improve a candidate's prospects for election. The sheer *length* of a sound bite does not necessarily correlate with increased substance: politicians are famous for filling rooms (and broadcasts) with hot air. As Stephens[76] argues in *The Rise of the Image, the Fall of the Word*, 30 seconds of well-selected news visuals are far more informative than a string of spoken platitudes. "In assuming politicians will dispense disproportionately more truth and meaning in 30 seconds than in seven, the argument gives too much credit to mere length" (p. 144). Carville puts the issue in terms of the old "less is more" adage: "The communications business is the only one in the world where you multiply by subtracting. The less you say, the more you're heard" (quoted in Auletta,[79] p. 64).

To move beyond concerns about length, sound bite *content* should also be considered. Previous research has analyzed candidate statements for their informational context or origin[10,11] but sound bite substance has not been explicitly examined in news analysis. Therefore, we investigate the substantive content or meaning of these "snappy snippets of taped comment or news." As detailed in Appendix 2, we identified seven options of sound bite content, including: speaking time devoted to policy positions, reactions to the news, attacks on opponents, defending one's role in a controversy, predicting victory, calls to rally the troops, and an "other" category for cases that did not fit. The duration of sound bite substance was recorded in seconds, with each sound bite assigned to a single content option.

Findings for Sound Bite Content

The largest portion of sound bite time, 40.79%, was spent on attacks against opponents, whereas only 3.52% of bite time was allocated to defenses against attacks (see Table 2–3). Thus, the biggest chunk of bite content was taken up by attack and defense rhetoric. Another sizable portion of bite time, 29.88%, contained candidate statements on issues, either explaining policy positions or responding to news events of national and international interest. Declarations of victory and appeals for voter support—calls to "rally the troops"—took up 11.09% of bite time. Another 14.72% of bite time was taken up by topics that did not fit into the above options.

Table 2–3 Content of Sound Bites

Sound Bite Content	Percentage of Total Bite Time (1992–2004 combined)
Attacks on opponents	40.79
Defensive rhetoric	3.52
Issue discussion of policies or news events	29.88
Calls to rally supporters	11.09
Other	14.72

Table 2–4 Comparisons of Means for Sound Bite Content over Time

Sound Bite Content	Mean Durations per Election Year				
	Overall	1992	1996	2000	2004
Issue discussion of policies or news events	14.30	14.12	14.47	16.12	12.78
SD	5.74	9.79	12.02	13.65	12.36
Attacks on opponents	14.85	15.96	15.97	12.60	15.07
SD	11.54	10.72	10.42	9.27	13.85
Defensive rhetoric	10.20	8.89	11.67	15.17	7.00*
SD	5.65	2.57	6.50	8.51	2.08
Calls to rally supporters	11.11	10.63	10.05	12.77	10.46
SD	2.50	10.91	6.32	8.78	8.34
Other	9.81	10.00	11.38	10.54	7.00
SD	9.87	6.79	9.50	3.33	4.78

All durations are presented in seconds. *Statistically significant difference across years.

Table 2-5 Attack and Defensive Sound Bites for Republicans and Democrats over Time

	Party Affiliation									
	Republicans					Democrats				
Variables	'92	'96	'00	'04	Overall	'92	'96	'00	'04	Overall
Attacks on opponents	16.20	17.28	12.23	10.62	14.05	15.70	9.67†	13.05	18.30*	15.80
SD	10.54	1.55	8.32	7.22	9.53	11.16	7.53	10.47	16.48	13.57
Defensive rhetoric	10.50	11.50	9.50	7.00	8.87	7.60†	12.00	18.00	0.00	7.59
SD	2.65	9.19	0.71	2.08	3.60	1.82	--	9.42	--	3.60

Duration is represented in seconds. *Statistically significant difference between Democrats and Republicans for a given year. †Differences between Democrats and Republicans for a given year approached statistical significance.

The mean durations for these content categories remained reasonably stable over time. Only one category, defenses against attacks, fluctuated significantly across elections.[80] As shown in Table 2–4, attacks on opponents and issue-related bites were the two categories with the highest volume, followed by calls to rally supporters, and defensive rhetoric. The 2000 election was the only campaign in which the mean for sound bites about issues surpassed the mean for attack-oriented bites. In stories that featured these bites, the overall mean duration for issue discussion was 16.12 seconds per story, compared to 12.60 seconds per story of attack discourse. The 2000 election also featured the most defensive rhetoric.

Although there were no significant differences overall between Republicans and Democrats in terms of the sound bite content categories, a few notable differences in specific election years emerged. Interestingly, these are specific to attack and defense rhetoric, as summarized in Table 2–5. In the 1992 election, a near-significant[81] difference emerged between the two parties on defensive bites: Republicans were shown for a longer amount of time in defensive mode. In 1996, Republican candidates were also portrayed on the attack more than Democratic candidates,[82] but in 2004 the Democrats were shown significantly more in attack mode.[83] Another trend worth noting might signal emerging political strategies within the parties: over time there was a significant *decline* in Republican attacks aired on network news,[84] while attack bites from Democrats increased (although not at a statistically significant level). Figure 2–3 illustrates these trends visually.

IMAGE BITE NEWS

Sound bites play an important, if not controversial, role in election coverage, but the biggest untold story of televised coverage of presidential campaigns is the prevalence of candidate *image bites*. Although scholars have called for greater attention to "video bites"[10,11] and systematic investigation of news visuals generally,[7,8] the visual aspect of news remains understudied. Research on ambient or background sound in television news (e.g., cheering, jeering, music, natural sound) is perhaps even more overlooked than visuals, despite its potentially powerful communicative outcomes. This is due in part to a normative, social-scientific bias against audiovisual media and a tendency to dismiss television as a superficial or entertainment medium that lacks the seriousness of print. As Graber[8] (p. 93) has observed, "The belief that audiovisuals are poor carriers of important political information has become so ingrained in conventional wisdom that it has throttled research."

Yet the myth that television is an intellectual lightweight is convincingly countered by empirical findings that show television news to be positively associated with political knowledge[85,86] and experimental

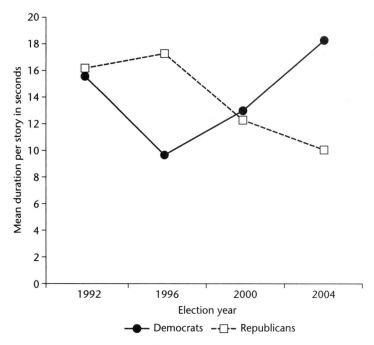

Figure 2–3 Average duration of Democratic and Republican attack bites over time

literature that has demonstrated how emotional displays of political leaders are capable of influencing viewer attitudes even when embedded in the background of a TV newscast during which the leader's voice is not heard[17,45] (see Chapter 4). Investigation of image bites seems duly warranted on several accounts. First, nonverbal emotional displays can serve as a potent vehicle for expression by candidates, whether intended or not. Second, viewers readily distinguish between different types of televised displays, which are frequently shown at close-up range—and increasingly in high definition. And third, the emotional and evaluative reactions that viewers experience upon exposure to visual portrayals of candidates can translate into lasting feelings, attitudes, and political behaviors.[43,44]

Lacking the pithy verbal content of sound bites, image bites are nevertheless informationally and politically potent. Indeed, in the course of a few ill-advised seconds during a speech to supporters on the night of the 2004 Iowa caucuses, Howard Dean issued a shrill call to rally the troops and demonstrated the power of an image bite to undermine a candidate's electoral viability. In news commentaries after the episode, Dean was characterized as having "blown up his presidential

Table 2–6 A Basic Typology of Sound and Image Bites

Bite Type	Presentation Modality	
	Sound	Image
Gaffe	Verbal Blunder	Inappropriate Nonverbal Display
Iconic Moment	Memorable Quotation	Signature Expression

aspirations . . . with what appeared to be a painful, primal scream" (p. A25[87]). Maureen Dowd[88] (p. A27) of the *New York Times* observed that "Dr. Dean's snarly, teeth-baring Iowa finale was so Ross Perot-scare-off-the-women-and-horses crazy that some Democrats on Capitol Hill, already anxious about the tightly wound doctor, confessed they could not imagine that jabbing finger anywhere near The Button."[89] Both sound and image bites derive their notoriety and persuasive force at the extremes, particularly from gaffes and iconic moments. At their most memorable, they are characterized on the one hand by the signature expressions of perceived greatness and, on the other, by the irreparable slips and embarrassing acts that destroy candidacies.

Crossing the presentation modality (sound, image) with the extreme forms that bites can take (gaffe, iconic moment) produces the following 2 × 2 table (see Table 2–6). This simple typology offers a basic category system for classifying the remarkable campaign moments that become etched into collective memory. Each combination of sound/image type has an unforgettable or poignant quality and could generally qualify as a memorable or defining campaign moment. In an analysis of the 1988 vice-presidential debate between Senators Lloyd Bentsen and Dan Quayle, Clayman[74] (p. 119) described a *defining campaign moment* as a compelling remark or interactional exchange that becomes the primary focus of attention immediately after the event and which is extensively scrutinized, replayed, excerpted, paraphrased, and referenced in the news—and then recycled in subsequent political encounters. Though brief, a defining moment is "taken to symbolize the original event in its entirety" and may resonate for years afterward (p. 119[74]). Bentsen's chiding of Quayle for daring to compare his political experience to John F. Kennedy's was instantly recognized as the single most noteworthy moment of the vice-presidential debate, airing on each of the network newscasts the next evening.[74] Bentsen dressed down the considerably younger Quayle with a multipart assertion:

Senator, I served with Jack Kennedy.
I knew Jack Kennedy.
Jack Kennedy was a friend of mine.
Senator, you're no Jack Kennedy. (quoted in Clayman,[74] p. 132)

In our category system, Bentsen's deftly spoken retort represents an iconic sound bite, or what could be classified as a memorable or famous quotation (see Bartlett[91]). Iconic sound bites consist of planned one-liners and eloquent, moving, or pointed extemporaneous comments that break through the barrage of televised verbal statements made during the course of a presidential campaign. Such dramatic utterances, in the view of one TV critic, stand out "like a tornado on a flat plain" (p. C1[92]), making other statements seem mundane, overly scripted, or forgettable. Oftentimes they surface during a debate, perhaps as part of a rehearsed strategy. Regardless of how much advance planning goes into phrasing sound bites, their appeal seems to stem more from a convincing and well-timed delivery than the bites' content per se. One of the biggest applause lines from the 1984 debates between Ronald Reagan and Walter Mondale occurred when Reagan addressed the question of his age with a lively, and unexpected, riposte aimed at the younger Mondale: "I want you to know that also I will not make age an issue of this campaign. I am not going to exploit, for political purposes, my opponent's youth and inexperience."[93] The line caused the entire auditorium to erupt and drew a hearty, almost uncontrollable laugh from Mondale.

Verbal gaffes, by contrast, are the stuff of which campaign blunders are made. Perhaps the most damaging statement made by a major party nominee in any televised debate was Gerald Ford's assertion in a 1976 encounter with Jimmy Carter, "There is no Soviet domination of Eastern Europe, and there never will be under a Ford administration."[94] At the time, a half-dozen countries in Central and Eastern Europe belonged to the Moscow-controlled Warsaw Pact. During the 1988 presidential campaign, Democratic candidate Michael Dukakis gave what many observers regarded as an unimpassioned, emotionally flat response to a question during a nationally televised debate about the hypothetical rape and murder of his wife. At the start of the debate, CNN's Bernard Shaw posed the question, "Governor, if Kitty Dukakis were raped and murdered, would you favor an irrevocable death penalty for the killer?" After a brief pause, the candidate, who was known for his anti–capital punishment view, coolly replied, "No, I don't, Bernard. And I think you know that I've opposed the death penalty during all of my life. I don't see any evidence that it's a deterrent, and I think there are better and more effective ways to deal with violent crime."[95] Both in substance and delivery, Dukakis left the impression that he lacked compassion and the ability to express outrage. As rhetorical critics Craig Smith and Michael Hyde[96] noted, Dukakis's calm demeanor "was deemed inappropriate by many watching the debate, and reinforced Bush's charge that Dukakis was 'the iceman'" (p. 462).

On the visual side of the ledger, image gaffes consist of inappropriate nonverbal displays that stand out as incongruent with the immediate communication setting or larger news context.[17,18] When George H. W. Bush glanced at his watch during a town hall debate with Bill Clinton and Ross Perot in 1992, he was widely viewed as having violated the accepted norms of televised political behavior. *Newsweek* reported in its coverage of the debate that "[i]t was a gesture familiar to Bush watchers. A sudden flick of the lanky wrist, a quick glance down at the watch. . . . But last Thursday, when Bush obviously and impatiently checked the time halfway through the second presidential debate, some 80 million viewers could not help but read a larger meaning into a familiar habit" (McDaniel,[97] p. 33). Bush's impatience became a metaphor for his attitude toward the campaign and his term in office. During the presidential debates of 2000, Al Gore "lost personality points even as he scored debating points" in the words of *Newsweek's*[98] editors, appearing strident and audibly sighing during the first debate with George W. Bush and even invading Bush's personal space at one point in the third and final debate. Nonverbally, Gore conveyed a clear message of impudence—in stark contrast to Bush's folksy likeability[90]—and was immediately mocked as pompous and condescending in a series of uproarious *Saturday Night Live* skits featuring Darrell Hammond and Will Ferrell.

In American politics, televised nonverbal displays "have proved both disastrous and beneficial for those seeking or holding public office" (p. 78[99]). As for their salutary consequences, iconic image bites are the stuff of which lasting impressions are made. These are the signature expressions and desirable candidate behaviors that inspire and reassure while capturing the larger meaning of a political performance. In recent elections two episodes stand out, both from acceptance speeches at Democratic National Conventions. In 2004, John Kerry invoked his war-hero past (but not his anti-Vietnam activism) by bounding to the podium, saluting convention-goers, and proclaiming, "I'm John Kerry and I'm reporting for duty." The line—borrowed from an old Wesley Clark speech—"brought down the house" (p. 81[100]). The image of Kerry saluting delegates reinforced the convention message of "a strong America," and his performance, in the words of one convention delegate, offered "a true reflection of his patriotism and his life" (quoted in Nagourney,[101] p. A1). Four years earlier, Al Gore's extended embrace of his wife as he made his way to the podium for his 2000 acceptance speech made headlines and seemed to give Gore a better than expected postconvention bounce. The "20-point kiss," as it came to be known,[90] also put candidate Gore in an improved political position. As Klein[90] (p. 154) describes the moment:

> As he arrived at the podium, Gore planted a big wet smooch on his wife, Tipper. . . . It was not a perfunctory kiss; it went on for a while, mouth to mouth. Tongues seemed to be involved. The

crowd applauded and then, as the kiss continued, began to cheer. Everyone on Gore's staff was surprised. It was a spontaneous moment, and it was filled with "low information signals." . . . It said to the world that maybe Al Gore wasn't such a stiff after all. In fact, he seemed a pretty passionate guy.

Depending on the tracking poll, Gore received anywhere from a 12- to 17-point spike in public opinion following his convention speech. "He walked around for days after that with a smile on his face," an aide later recalled. "I think it was because he knew—it wasn't the speech, it was the kiss" (quoted in Klein,[90] p. 154). Unfortunately for Gore, he could not easily replicate the surprising enthusiasm this visual generated when he set out on the campaign trail (unlike Bill Clinton, whose signature expressions wore easily and could be used repeatedly). The 20-point kiss did not translate into an enduring lead.

Because of the visual proximity that the camera lens affords, electronic media demand that politicians remain extraordinarily mindful of their nonverbal communication.[24] "The lens magnifies everything," the acclaimed playwright Arthur Miller[102] (p. 37) once observed, "one slight lift of an eyelid and you look like you're glaring." During a political debate, major speech, or other high-profile televised event, a few seconds of the wrong nonverbal cues could lead to a fall in the polls, accompanied by eroded faith in leadership ability.[24,54] As a consequence, the communicative behavior and visual presentation of public figures has become increasingly central to evaluations of political effectiveness.

Anecdotal observation and qualitative analysis of television news formats[2] suggest that candidate image bites are much more common than sound bites. On the newscaster side of the equation, on-air shots of journalists have been increasing in frequency and shortening in duration, contributing to the quickening pace and increasing journalistic mediation of political news.[12] However, television news researchers have not yet directly compared journalist and candidate sound and image bites, offering no benchmarks for assessing the relative frequency of these two distinct forms of presentation. The following analysis addresses the issues raised by the foregoing discussion.

Sound and Image Bite Comparisons

Importantly, sound and image bites are conceptually distinct. A sound bite may consist of several separate pieces of video and audio spliced together to form a coherent statement from the candidate. By contrast, an image bite constitutes a single uninterrupted piece of video material in which the candidate is shown but not heard (i.e., an individual camera shot, which could be quite short—see Appendix 2). Thus, individual sound bite averages, because of inherent structural characteristics, are longer than average image bite occurrences. Here, the logical solution to make valid and fair comparisons between image and sounds bites pointed to calculating total bite durations for each candidate across entire stories.

Over each of the four elections analyzed, image bites made up a substantially larger percentage of total campaign coverage than sound bites. In fact, sound bites constituted 14.28% of all election coverage, whereas image bites accounted for 25.07%. For the 1992 election, sound bites accounted for 10.48% and image bites 22.88% of campaign coverage. In 1996, the gap between sound (16.88%) and image (30.32%) bite portions of election coverage opened slightly. The 2000 election data reveal similar proportions, with sound bites taking up 16.07% and image bites 29.52% of campaign story time. In 2004, sound bites (16.66%) and image bites (20.02%) were proportionally the closest in size, with image bites still constituting a greater percentage of coverage.

Overall, there was a significant difference between the amount of time that candidates appeared in sound and image bites per story (see Table 2–1).[103] Candidates were featured more prominently in image bites than sound bites. Although the average duration of all sound and image bites within stories did not vary significantly over time, a

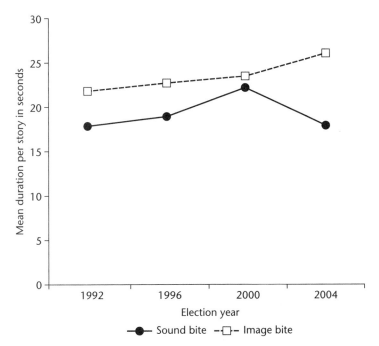

Figure 2–4 Average total duration of candidate sound and image bites over time

consistent increase in image bite lengths could be observed (see Fig. 2–4). Sound bite durations per story show a less consistent pattern, increasing from 1992 to 2000, then decreasing notably in 2004. Post hoc Tukey tests for the sound bite variable and Dunnett C tests for image bites did not produce any significant paired comparisons.

Comparisons across parties also failed to produce significant differences. Both overall and for each election year, Democrats and Republicans were seen in image bites at similar rates (see Table 2–2).

Image Bite Comparisons: Candidates versus Journalists

The image bite findings were almost the exact opposite of the findings for sound bites: candidates were seen (but not heard speaking) significantly more often than journalists.[104] On the other hand, journalists were seen speaking more than candidates, as we reported earlier. Indeed, while candidates were presented in image bites an average of 22.99 seconds per story, journalists were featured an average of just 9.13 seconds per story. Within individual stories, journalists thus dominated candidates in talking head mode whereas candidates were presented in *shown but not heard* segments for longer periods of time. As reported above, there were no significant differences for the duration of candidate image bite means over time. But for journalists, there were significant differences over the course of the four election years.[105] Dunnett C tests revealed significant variation between the 1992 and 1996 elections, when there was a sizable drop in journalist image bites.[106] As with the sound bite comparisons between journalists and candidates, the 1996 election surfaces as the one in which journalists were the least visible (see Table 2–1).

DISCUSSION

Images are the *lingua franca* of politics, yet they remain among the least scrutinized and least understood aspects of political news. Image bites do not reveal the logic of candidate arguments or the details of policy positions. However, for a critical component of the electorate, which is only semi attentive to civic affairs,[42] political decisions may be based more on affective attachments and nonverbal signals expressed by leading politicians on television than careful consideration of issue positions.[17] Indeed, in a political environment increasingly dependent upon electronic media, an awkward, unappealing, or inappropriate communication style is becoming difficult to counteract with policy proposals—and may become the focus of public discussion, as losing candidates learned in each of the four elections we analyze (for an analysis of visual framing, see Chapter 3). This sort of nonverbal information is precisely what television excels at presenting. Appreciating the information value of candidate displays, and therefore of the potential influence of image bites, opens a window on understanding television news that did not appear to exist when the audio track alone was treated as important.

Consistent with other research, this analysis documented a continued decline in candidate sound bite length over time, from 9.19 seconds in 1992 to 7.73 seconds by 2004. At the same time, there was no significant variation in the *number* of sound bites per news story (2.31 on average), so presidential candidates were shown speaking with the same frequency over our 12-year sample period but were heard for shorter periods of time. It is important to note that the decline in sound bite sizes can be attributed specifically to Republicans in 2000 and 2004. In fact, sound bites from George W. Bush in both elections reflect a sharp decrease in length while bites for Kerry and Gore increased in length during the same two elections. Perhaps the Bush campaign favored message discipline through economic word use and strategically tutored their candidate to speak plainly, in sound bite sizes; alternatively, the networks might have been more willing to verbally cut Bush off. Kerry and Gore, on the other hand, might have been more inclined to display their intellectual prowess through more nuanced, lengthy statements that were difficult to condense.

As documented by previous studies and confirmed by our analysis, journalists do indeed claim a larger percentage of news story time, particularly if sound bites are taken into consideration. Although the total volume of campaign coverage decreased, a trend surely destined to displease television's critics, the average amount of airtime dedicated to presidential campaign news per newscast remained responsive to changing election conditions. Campaign coverage decreased precipitously during the noncompetitive and lackluster 1996 race, to 3.5 minutes per newscast, but rebounded somewhat during the close 2000 and 2004 elections to almost 5 minutes, or over 20% of the 22-minute nightly newscast.

In terms of content, the substance of candidate sound bites revealed some interesting patterns. The largest portion of sound bite time (40.79%) was devoted to attack-and-defense rhetoric, but almost a third (29.88%) of bite time featured candidate statements that were either issue oriented or responses to news developments. As the political advertising literature has shown, political attacks are far more likely to focus on salient issues—candidate views, legislative votes, policy positions, and qualifications for office—than personal characteristics.[107] Assuming that political attacks aired on the nightly news are similarly issue focused, attack rhetoric logically could be grouped with issue content. Combining the categories in this manner means that over 70% of sound bite content was essentially issue focused. Indeed, sound bites may be short, but they are not devoid of verbal substance.

Clayman[74] describes the reproduction of candidate quotations and sound bites as a "profoundly consequential matter" for democracy. "As the news media have become increasingly central to the conduct of public affairs, political battles are now waged largely through the brief verbal excerpts that make their way into the daily news" (p. 119). If sound bites are largely issue oriented, as our analysis has found, then their contribution to policy debates—and to highlighting differences between candidates during elections—may be more substantial than commonly assumed. This is particularly relevant to partisan politics. The very nature of broadcast media, with their fast-paced editing and increasing audiovisual speed, resists long, complex messages. Broadcast news, as with television generally, acts as a "simplifying lens," in the words of Scheuer,[108] favoring clear-cut issues over diffuse or complicated policy discussions (see also Patterson[109]).

On account of this structural or nonideological bias, Scheuer maintains, television's sound bite sensibility ultimately favors political ideas and positions on the Right, which tend to be clear-cut, self-regarding, and easier to articulate than positions on the Left, which tend to involve contextual explanations of remote causes or effects and advocate the welfare of others. Television, he asserts, filters out "complex ideas in favor of blunt emotional messages that appeal to the self and to narrower moral-political impulses" (p. 10[108]).[110] Conservative promises to cut taxes and safeguard individual rights, for instance, are an easier sell than liberal ideas about the need to increase social welfare spending and use taxpayer money to develop alternative energy sources. As a result, news coverage and other television fare function as a brake on liberal ideas while acting as an accelerator of conservative messages and values. To Scheuer[108] (p. 10), the medium's "increasing dominance of our political culture has been a central factor in the resurgence of American conservatism" and eclipse of liberalism in recent decades. We return to questions of bias and partisanship in Chapter 5, with surprising results, in our visual examination of the "liberal media bias" accusation against mainstream news.

Perhaps most striking in this analysis were the findings for candidate image bites, which constituted a greater percentage of total campaign coverage than sound bites. This result was expected, given television's status as a visual medium. Consistent with this pattern, candidates were featured more often in image bites ($M = 22.99$ seconds per news story) than they were in sound bites ($M = 18.59$ seconds). Even as sound bites continue to shrink, the amount of time candidates are appearing visually in newscasts is actually *increasing* in duration, rising gradually each election year. This suggests that viewers of the evening news are receiving more direct visual cues about candidates than verbal information. Because pictures are perceived as firsthand knowledge about political actors and events, including presidential candidates and campaign-related developments, news visuals are undoubtedly delivering more information to viewers than previously acknowledged. With greater appreciation for visual processing, nonverbal communication, and voter learning from television news, research can begin to redress this oversight by investigating the effects of image bites on political evaluations and outcomes (see, for example, Benjamin and Shapiro[111]).

Given that presidential candidates were seen in image bites more than twice as much as journalists over all election years ($M = 22.99$ seconds per story compared to $M = 9.13$ seconds), the journalistic domination of broadcast news is not as one-sided or complete as commonly argued. If using a verbal yardstick to measure candidate appearances on the evening news, the airtime available to candidates has indeed declined. However, if using the *shown but not heard* visual standard, the amount of time allocated to candidates relative to journalists is quite favorable. Granted, candidates are speaking less, but this does not mean that viewers are receiving no useful political knowledge. Visuals carry a plenitude of social information, and the nonverbal communication they convey forms the basis of political impressions and assessments.

CONCLUSION

Before a new era of more scientifically and less normatively based research on visual communication can truly commence, two unfounded assumptions need to be rethought. The first concerns the expedient commonplace that visuals merely serve as window dressing for or decorative distraction from the verbal component of television news, which is studied as the "real" content. Overlooking television's visuals treats the medium as if it were something else entirely, namely, radio, discounting the unique contributions and persuasive influence that images have on political understanding[25] and misrepresenting the value that television has to viewers—and to democratic processes generally. Despite the ease with which news transcripts can now be retrieved through electronic databases, studying only the text of an audiovisual message while ignoring both the visuals and other nonverbal elements of newscasts, such as vocal tone and ambient sounds, is insufficient. Thus, it seems premature to characterize network television's coverage of recent U.S. presidential elections as "nightmarish," lacking both substance and quality content,[1] without systematically taking images into account.

The second assumption, embraced by rational choice theorists and scholars who view campaigning as a primarily rhetorical exercise, holds that political visuals are, by their very nature, strictly emotional and tap a nonrational aspect of experience void of information gain. Drawing on neuroscientific research, recent advances in understanding the effects of nonverbal communication on audiences demonstrate that visuals, even when shown without accompanying sound, are a rich source of information (see Chapters 4 and 7). In the heat of an election, mediated images are politically consequential and offer voters a vivid display of a candidate's electoral suitability. Like Doppler radar images of clear weather patterns or incoming storms, candidate depictions are indeed reliable forms of information.

Taking television seriously requires that we reconsider whether, in an increasingly visual and journalist-centered news environment, it makes sense to ask if television impedes careful thought, discourages contemplation, or distorts viewers' sense of political consequences, as many scholars have argued. A confluence of political, organizational, technological, and economic factors has produced the commercial media system that we have.[112] Rather than awkwardly fitting research questions and assumptions that are more appropriate for a noncommercial, government-controlled, or print-based media system onto network television, perhaps the medium should finally be considered at face value for what it *does* deliver—a real-time stream of images rich with social significance whose persuasive influence can be subject to empirical examination. With regard to political news, this suggests a research program focused on the visual framing of election campaigns, the character of candidate displays, and the potential for visual forms of bias—topics addressed in subsequent chapters.

NOTES

1. Farnsworth, Stephen J., and S. Robert Lichter. 2003. *The nightly news nightmare: Network news coverage of U.S. presidential elections, 1988–2000*. Lanham, MD: Rowman and Littlefield.
2. Griffin, Michael. 1992. Looking at TV news: Strategies for research. *Communication* 13:121–141.
3. Patterson, Thomas E. 1993. *Out of order*. New York: Knopf.
4. Russomanno, Joseph A., and Stephen E. Everett. 1995. Candidate sound bites: Too much concern over length? *Journal of Broadcasting and Electronic Media* 39(3):408–415.
5. Hallin, Daniel C. 1992. Sound bite news: Television coverage of elections, 1968–1988. *Journal of Communication* 42(2):5–24.
6. Moriarty, Sandra E., and Mark N. Popovich. 1991. Newsmagazine visuals and the 1988 presidential election. *Journalism Quarterly* 68(3):371–380.
7. Graber, Doris A. 1996. Say it with pictures. *Annals of the American Academy of Political and Social Science* 546:85–96.
8. Graber, Doris A. 2001. *Processing politics: Learning from television in the Internet age*. Chicago: University of Chicago Press.
9. Griffin, Michael. 1992. Looking at TV news: Strategies for research. *Communication* 13:121–141.
10. Lowry, Dennis T., and Jon A. Shidler. 1995. The biters and the bitten: An analysis of network TV news bias in campaign '92. *Journalism and Mass Communication Quarterly* 69(2):341–361.

11. Lowry, Dennis T., and Jon A. Shidler. 1998. The sound bites, the biters, and the bitten: A two-campaign test of the anti-incumbent bias hypothesis in network TV news. *Journalism and Mass Communication Quarterly* 75(4):719–729.

12. Barnhurst, Kevin G., and Catherine A. Steele. 1997. Image-bite news: The visual coverage of elections on U.S. television, 1968–1992. *Press/Politics* 2(1):40–58.

13. Grabe, Maria Elizabeth. 1996. The SABC's coverage of the 1987 and 1989 elections: The matter of visual bias. *Journal of Broadcasting and Electronic Media* 40(1):1–27.

14. Kepplinger, Hans Mathias. 1982. Visual biases in television campaign coverage. *Communication Research* 9(3):432–446.

15. Messaris, Paul, and Linus Abraham. 2001. The role of images in framing news stories. In *Framing public life*, ed. Stephen D. Reese, Oscar H. Gandy Jr., and August E. Grant, pp. 215–226. Mahwah, NJ: Lawrence Erlbaum.

16. Somit, Albert, and Steven A. Peterson. 1998. Biopolitics after three decades: A balance sheet. *British Journal of Political Science* 28:559–571.

17. Bucy, Erik P. 2000. Emotional and evaluative consequences of inappropriate leader displays. *Communication Research* 27(2):194–226.

18. Bucy, Erik P., and John E. Newhagen. 1999. The emotional appropriateness heuristic: Processing televised presidential reactions to the news. *Journal of Communication* 49(4):59–79.

19. Hallin, Daniel C. 1992. Sound bite news: Television coverage of elections, 1968–1988. *Journal of Communication* 42(2):5–24.

20. Lichter, S. Robert. 2001. A plague on both parties: Substance and fairness in TV election news. *Harvard International Journal of Press/Politics* 6(3):8–30.

21. Robinson, Michael J., and Margaret A. Sheehan. 1983. *Over the wire and on TV: CBS and UPI in campaign '80*. New York: Russell Sage Foundation.

22. Levy, Mark R. 1981. Disdaining the news. *Journal of Communication* 31(3):24–31.

23. Steele, Catherine A., and Kevin G. Barnhurst. 1996. The journalism of opinion: Network news coverage of U.S. presidential campaigns, 1968–1988. *Critical Studies in Mass Communication* 13(3):187–209.

24. Meyrowitz, Joshua. 1985. *No sense of place: The impact of electronic media on social behavior*. New York: Oxford University Press.

25. Newhagen, John E. 2002. The role of meaning construction in the process of persuasion for viewers of television images. In *The persuasion handbook: Developments in theory and practice*, ed. James. P. Dillard and Michael W. Pau, pp. 729–748. Thousand Oaks, CA: Sage.

26. Stephens, Mitchell. 1998. *The rise of the image, the fall of the word*. New York: Oxford University Press.

27. Givhan, Robin. 2008, January 8. A chink in the steely façade of Hillary Clinton. *Washington Post*, p. C1.

28. Kantor, Jodi. 2008, January 9. A show of emotion that reverberated beyond the campaign. *New York Times*, p. A14.

29. Lehtonen[30] argues that growing information complexity and a widening imbalance between information supply and individual processing ability (or "information discrepancy") places renewed emphasis on images to the point that "visual impressions will have a greater impact as stimuli than verbal language" (p. 104; see also Stephens[26]).

30. Lehtonen, Jaako. 1988. The information society and the new competence. *American Behavioral Scientist* 32(2):104–111.

31. Our analysis is, as far as we can tell, the first to do so (see also Bucy and Grabe[32]). Previously, in a study titled "Image Bite News," Barnhurst and Steele[12] examined the growing visual presence of broadcast journalists and anchors in presidential election coverage from 1968 to 1992. Ironically, they did not examine the frequency and duration of candidate image bites. Earlier, Masters, Frey, and Bente[33] documented the prevalence of what they called "visual quotes"—distinct shots in which "an identifiable political actor is on the screen" (p. 380)—in a sample of newscasts from France, Germany, and the United States from March 1987, but they did not report the occurrence of sound bites for comparison.

32. Bucy, Erik P., and Maria Elizabeth Grabe. 2007. Taking television seriously: A sound and image bite analysis of presidential campaign coverage, 1992–2004. *Journal of Communication* 57:652–675.

33. Masters, Roger D., Seigfried Frey, and Gary Bente. 1991. Dominance and attention: Images of leaders in German, French, and American TV news. *Polity* 25:373–394.

34. Newhagen, John E., and Byron Reeves. 1992. This evening's bad news: Effects of compelling negative television news images on memory. *Journal of Communication* 42(2):25–41.

35. Newhagen, John E. 1998. TV news images that induce anger, fear, and disgust: Effects on approach-avoidance and memory. *Journal of Broadcasting and Electronic Media* 42(2):265–76.

36. Drew, Dan G., and Thomas Grimes. 1987. Audio-visual redundancy and TV news recall. *Communication Research* 14(4):452–461.

37. Grimes, Tom. 1991. Mild auditory-visual dissonance in television news may exceed viewer attentional capacity. *Human Communication Research* 18:268–298.

38. Lang, Annie. 1995. Defining audio/video redundancy from a limited capacity information processing perspective. *Communication Research* 22:86–115.

39. Noller, Patricia. 1985. Video primacy—a further look. *Journal of Nonverbal Behavior* 9(1):28–47.

40. Posner, Michael I., Mary Jo Nissen, and Raymond M. Klein. 1976. Visual dominance: An information-processing account of its origins and significance. *Psychological Review* 83(2):157–171.

41. Stahl, Lesley. 1999. *Reporting live.* New York: Simon and Schuster.

42. Neuman, W. Russel. 1986. *The paradox of mass politics: Knowledge and opinion in the American electorate.* Cambridge, MA: Harvard University Press.

43. Bucy, Erik P. 2003. Emotion, presidential communication, and traumatic news: Processing the World Trade Center attacks. *Harvard International Journal of Press/Politics* 8(4):76–96.

44. Lanzetta, John T., Dennis G. Sullivan, Roger D. Masters, and Gregory J. McHugo. 1985. Emotional and cognitive responses to televised images of political leaders. In *Mass media and political thought: An information-processing approach,* ed. Sidney Kraus and Richard M. Perloff, pp. 85–116. Beverly Hills, CA: Sage.

45. Masters, Roger D., and Denis G. Sullivan. 1993. Nonverbal behavior and leadership: Emotion and cognition in political information processing. In *Explorations in political psychology*, ed. Shanto Iyengar and William J. McGuire, pp. 150–182. Durham, NC: Duke University Press.

46. Ekman, Paul, Wallace V. Friesen, Maurice O'Sullivan, and Klaus Scherer. 1980. Relative importance of face, body, and speech in judgments of personality and affect. *Journal of Personality and Social Psychology* 38(2):270–77.

47. Englis, Basil G. 1994. The role of affect in political advertising: Voter emotional responses to the nonverbal behavior of politicians. In *Attention, attitude, and affect in response to advertising*, ed. Eddie M. Clark, Timothy C. Brock, and David W. Stewart, pp. 223–247. Hillsdale, NJ: Lawrence Erlbaum.

48. Patterson, Thomas E. 2000. *Doing well and doing good: How soft news and critical journalism are shrinking the news audience and weakening democracy—and what news outlets can do about it.* Faculty Research Working Paper Series (RWP01–001). Cambridge, MA: John F. Kennedy School of Government, Harvard University.

49. Project for Excellence in Journalism. 2004. *The state of the news media 2004.* http://www.stateofthenewsmedia.org/. Accessed January 15, 2006.

50. Bucy, Erik P., and Samuel D. Bradley. 2004. Presidential expressions and viewer emotion: Counterempathic responses to televised leader displays. *Social Science Information/Information sur les Sciences Sociales* 43(1):59–94.

51. Bucy, Erik P., and Paul D'Angelo. 1999. The crisis of political communication: Normative critiques of news and democratic processes. *Communication Yearbook* 22:301–339.

52. Safire, William. 1993. *Safire's new political dictionary: The definitive guide to the new language of politics.* New York: Random House.

53. Slogans, which are even more compact than sound bites, are brief messages or catch phrases that crystallize an idea, define an issue, or serve as a rallying cry.[52] Some of the more memorable presidential campaign slogans include "Tippecanoe and Tyler Too" (1840), "Rum, Romanism, and Rebellion" (1844), "In Hoover We Trusted, Now We Are Busted" (1928), "I Like Ike" (1952), "Let's Get America Moving Again" (1960), "In Your Heart You Know He's Right" (1964), "Nixon's the One" (1968), and "Putting People First" (1992). Edelman[54] has referred to evocative expressions, slogans, or sayings as condensation symbols. The use of such symbols, which stir "vivid impressions involving the listener's most basic values," has a long and interesting history (see Graber,[55] p. 289).

54. Edelman, Murray. 1964. *The symbolic uses of politics.* Urbana: University of Illinois Press.

55. Graber, Doris A. 1976. *Verbal behavior and politics.* Urbana: University of Illinois Press.

56. Jamieson, Kathleen H. 1988. *Eloquence in an electronic age: The transformation of political speechmaking.* New York: Oxford University Press.

57. Adatto, Kiku. 1990. *Sound bite democracy: Network evening news presidential campaign coverage, 1968 and 1988* (Research Paper R-2). Cambridge, MA: Harvard University, Joan Shorenstein Barone Center.

58. Ross, E. 1992, September 25. Networks adjust election coverage. *Christian Science Monitor*, p. 12.

59. Grabe, Maria Elizabeth, Shuhua Zhou, and Brooke Barnett. 1999. Sourcing and reporting in news magazine programs: *60 Minutes* versus *Hard Copy*. *Journalism and Mass Communication Quarterly* 76(2):293–311.

60. $F(3, 169) = 12.10, p < 0.001, \eta^2 = 0.18$.

61. $p < 0.001$.

62. $F(3, 169) = 15.73, p < 0.001, \eta^2 = 0.25$.

63. Dunnett C: $p < 0.05$.

64. Dunnett C: $p < 0.05$.

65. $F(3, 408) = 2.42, p < 0.067, \eta^2 = 0.02$.

66. This analysis was performed for comparison with existing research on the average duration of individual sound bites. Yet the average duration of a candidate's individual talking head appearances does not give a comprehensive account of the person's presence in election stories—for that, both image bite and sound bite appearances must be tabulated.

67. $t(378) = 1.72, p < 0.086$.

68. $t(113) = 2.77, p < 0.007$.

69. $t(113) = 1.96, p < 0.052$.

70. $F(3, 202) = 5.42, p < 0.001$.

71. Tukey: $p < 0.006$.

72. $t(72) = -1.87, p < 0.065$.

73. $F(3, 411) = 5.51, p < 0.001, \eta^2 = 0.02$. Post hoc Tukey tests showed significant differences between 1992 and 1996 ($p < 0.026$), and 1996 and 2004 ($p < 0.001$). Of the four election years examined, journalists were seen and heard the least in 1996.

74. Clayman, Steven E. 1995. Defining moments, presidential debates, and the dynamics of quotability. *Journal of Communication* 45(3):118–146.

75. Scheuer, Jeffrey. 1999. *The sound bite society: Television and the American mind*. New York: Four Walls Eight Windows.

76. In his convention address, Bush prefaced his "read my lips" pledge by asserting, "My opponent won't rule out raising taxes. But I will. And the Congress will push me to raise taxes, and I'll say no, and they'll push, and I'll say no, and they'll push again, and I'll say, to them, 'Read my lips: no new taxes'" (see the Commission on Presidential Debates Web site, http://www.debates.org/pages/debtrans.html).

77. Hegedus, Chris, and D. Alan Pennebaker. 1993. *The war room*. Santa Monica, CA: Trimark Home Video.

78. Thomas, Evan. 2004a, November 15. Trench warfare. *Newsweek*, pp. 62–71.

79. Auletta, Ken (2004, September 20). Kerry's brain. *The New Yorker*, 80(27), 64–79.

80. $F(3, 21) = 3.21, p < 0.044$. Post hoc Tukey tests show a significant ($p < 0.037$) difference between 2000 and 2004.

81. $t(7) = -1.96, p < 0.091$.

82. $t(33) = -2.09, p < 0.065$.

83. $t(67) = 2.35, p < 0.022$.

84. $F(3, 105) = 3.29, p < 0.024$. Post hoc Tukey tests show a significant ($p < 0.036$) difference between 1996 and 2004.

85. Drew, Dan D., and David H. Weaver. 2006. Voter learning in the 2004 presidential election: Did the media matter? *Journalism and Mass Communication Quarterly* 83(1):25–42.

86. Putnam, Robert D. 2000. *Bowling alone: The collapse and revival of American community*. New York: Simon and Schuster.

87. Kamen, Al. 2004, January 21. A meltdown in history. *Washington Post*, p. A25.

88. Dowd, Maureen. 2004, January 22. Riding the crazy train. *New York Times*, p. A27.

89. Of course, Dean's political prospects in the Democratic primaries had already begun to wane before the scream episode; the candidate's shrill outburst, "too precipitous and undignified [for Dean] to be a plausible president in a serious time" (p. 182[26]), simply finished him off.

90. Klein, Joe. 2006. *Politics lost: How American democracy was trivialized by people who think you're stupid*. New York: Doubleday.

91. Bartlett, John. 2002. *Bartlett's familiar quotations: A collection of passages, phrases, and proverbs traced to their sources in ancient and modern literature*. 17th ed. Boston: Little, Brown.

92. Shales, Tom. 1988, October 6. Bentsen and Quayle: A single point of light. *Washington Post*, p. C1.

93. Commission on Presidential Debates. 1984. *Debate transcript, October 21, 1984: The second Reagan-Mondale presidential debate*.

94. Commission on Presidential Debates. 1976. *Debate transcript, October 6, 1976: The second Carter-Ford presidential debate*. http://www.debates.org/pages/debtrans.html. Accessed February 5, 2008.

95. Commission on Presidential Debates. 1988. *Debate transcript, October 13, 1988: The second Bush-Dukakis presidential debate*. http://www.debates.org/pages/debtrans.html. Accessed February 5, 2008.

96. Smith, Craig R., and Michael J. Hyde. 1991. Rethinking "the public": The role of emotion in being-with-others. *Quarterly Journal of Speech* 77:446–466.

97. McDaniel, Ann. 1992, October 26. Mourning in America. *Newseek*, p. 33.

98. *Newsweek*. 2000, November 20. Face to face combat. p. 92.

99. Shields, Stephanie A., and Kathleen A. MacDowell. 1987. "Appropriate" emotion in politics: Judgments of a televised debate. *Journal of Communication* 37(4):78–89.

100. Thomas, Evan. 2004b, November 15. Teaming up. *Newsweek*, pp. 72–81.

101. Nagourney, Adam. 2004, July 30. Kerry accepts nomination, telling party that he'll restore "trust and credibility." *New York Times*, p. A1.

102. Miller, Arthur. 2001, June. American playhouse: On politics and the art of acting. *Harper's Magazine*, pp. 33–43.

103. $t (343) = 6.82, p < 0.001$.

104. $t (592) = 18.51, p < 0.001$.

105. $F (3, 170) = 3.71, p < 0.019, \eta^2 = 0.05$.

106. Tukey: $p < 0.05$.

107. Geer, John G. 2006. *In defense of negativity: Attack ads in presidential campaigns*. Chicago: University of Chicago Press.

108. Scheuer, Jeffrey. 1999. *The sound bite society: Television and the American mind*. New York: Four Walls Eight Windows.

109. Patterson, Thomas E. 1980. *The mass media election: How Americans choose their election*. New York: Praeger.

110. " 'Simpler' here emphatically does not mean simplistic or simpleminded. A simpler theory of government and the social contract is one that de-

mands less of individuals and offers less in return; that argues for smaller government, lower taxes, fewer services, and less regulation, preferring to leave the market alone rather than to curb or offset it; that seeks to maximize personal autonomy over other freedoms, and implies that government—not other institutions or individuals—is the primary threat to individual freedom" (pp. 10–11[108]).

111. Benjamin, Daniel J. and Jesse M. Shapiro (2008). Thin-slice forecasts of gubernatorial elections. *Review of Economics and Statistics, 90.*

112. Among other developments, these include advances in digital editing and satellite transmission technology; growing pressures for profits; and the professionalization of political advocacy, which has produced an increasing amount of media management—and journalistic reclaiming of airtime for news interpretation and analysis (see Bucy and D'Angelo,[51] Hallin[5]).

3

Visual Framing

Contemporary elections are built on a visual foundation. Candidates must appear telegenic enough to invite—and sustain—close viewer scrutiny, and the events that campaigns stage, if they are to be effective, must strengthen and reinforce the candidate's personal appeal and policy initiatives. Since the rise of television as a political force, candidate images have largely been constructed visually through deliberate campaign strategies designed to promote desired qualities and favored themes. Visual portrayals facilitate different levels of intimacy between candidates and viewers, highlight appealing or unappealing personal attributes of candidates, and have the potential to craft enduring images that affect electoral support. In recent elections, political strategists for both parties have attempted to dress their candidates in a populist suit, with folksy appeals that prove awkwardly fitting for elitist candidates and come across as inauthentic. As we show in this chapter, media framing of the election process readily reflects the themes that campaigns promote, but at the same time it reveals problems candidates have in donning their designated visual frame.

The previous chapter analyzing image and sound bites documented the extent to which *television news producers* control the amount of visual and verbal airtime that candidates receive. Here, we investigate the influence of *image handlers* on the manner in which candidates are visually framed in televised appearances, tracking variables most likely to reveal decisions made by campaign consultants as opposed to those made by news producers or even the candidates themselves.[1] Although not given much attention in academic research or the popular press, political consultants are nevertheless a potent force shaping American democracy (see Nimmo,[9] Sabato[10]). Relatively hidden behind other actors on the political stage, image handlers function as the executive producers of the election spectacle, developing, testing, and micromanaging a candidate's public persona. Our analysis of network news coverage takes a magnifying glass to the visual frames or thematic portrayals of candidates that all this political advice produces.

To explicate the visual framing process, this chapter examines the salient candidate image frames evident in television coverage of the presidential elections, the constituent elements of these frames, and the campaign conditions associated with the use of specific frames. In our analysis, we identify three visual frames that materialize in general election news—the ideal candidate, the populist campaigner, and the sure loser—and report on how these frames manifest themselves visually across election years and candidates. The analysis focuses on how the image management strategies of campaigns, which deliberately promote particular themes, symbolic meanings, and character qualities, are revealed in news coverage of individual candidates. We conclude by commenting on how comfortably candidates appear to "wear" their visually constructed frames; the better the fit, the more likely voters are to accept this construction (artificial though it may be) as natural and veracious. Yet, as with a poorly tailored suit, no amount of handling can compensate for an ill-fitting image. To the degree that candidates have difficulty sounding certain themes and embodying their consultant-constructed image, they risk coming across as contrived, inauthentic, and untrustworthy—qualities detrimental to cultivating widespread voter support.

IMAGE AND LEADERSHIP

The expectations of major party nominees running for president are considerable. Not only must leading candidates present credible plans about running the government, managing the economy, conducting international diplomacy, and commanding national defense but they must also project a likable, plain-folks image that appeals to a majority of the electorate. And, as the 2008 election has shown, the extended job interview that constitutes running for president now lasts the better part of two years. Driven by ever increasing public expectations to be able to do "something about everything" (p. 7[11]), presidents and those vying for office have come to rely on image handlers—the "vast army of pollsters, public relations specialists, and press assistants" (p. 753[12]) that surround the modern presidency—for advice on getting the appearance of things right. The expectations that the public has of presidential performance are such that scholars have identified the persistence of an expectations gap that "exists between what the public expects and what presidents can actually accomplish" (p. 8[13]). Public opinion research has attributed the inevitable decline in approval ratings that presidents experience—the so-called decay curve that sets in after an initial honeymoon period and early legislative efforts—to the existence of this gap.[14-17]

To make up for the inherent inability to actually do something about everything, presidents and their advisors pursue policy agendas as much to address substantive issues as to advance a desired image. Careful crafting of image is important because images tap into shared values and culturally resonant themes that form the basis of affective attachments on which evaluations of public figures often rest.[18] Affective orientations are politically consequential, even for highly informed citizens, because they contribute to enduring support by encouraging commitments based on general attachments rather than specific assessments of individual policies or decisions, which are subject to parsing and disagreement (see Almond and Verba,[19] Lipset[20]). Purely instrumental decision making, where the pros and cons of each policy proposal are carefully weighed and considered, can divide even favorable partisans, as occurs among attentive voters during hotly contested primary races.

Moreover, as the smearing of John Kerry's distinguished Vietnam service record showed in 2004, accomplishments alone do not mark a successful candidate or officeholder.[21] Nor do rational arguments or an encyclopedic command of the issues. "What is important is how a president's [or candidate's] message is communicated and how it appears to the public" (p. 65[13]). The assumption underlying this image-based approach to campaigning is that defining a candidate's character conditions public reaction, shaping how political developments are evaluated. Early in the 2008 primaries, Barack Obama was endorsed by Senator Edward Kennedy, Caroline Kennedy, and other members of the Kennedy family and was presented in the press as the adopted heir to Camelot both for his association with the dynastic political family and his ability to inspire, similar to John and Robert Kennedy.[24] On the day of the Kennedy endorsement at American University in Washington, D.C., throngs of supporters were shown ecstatically reaching out to the first major African American presidential candidate, giving him a star-like quality.

Theoretically, the process by which media coverage influences the criteria that viewers use to evaluate political candidates and institutions can be explained by priming. The more prominent an issue, event, or theme becomes in the public consciousness—that is, the more media coverage it receives—the more it tends to shape how leaders are judged.[25] Priming applies to evaluations of candidate character as well as issue positions. Interestingly, priming effects are most likely to occur among people who are both highly knowledgeable about political affairs and trusting of the media.[26] Thus, media coverage consistently infused with character frames can lead citizens to give greater weight to trait information when evaluating candidates (see Druckman and Holmes,[27] Mendelsohn[28]).

Evidence of image priming could also be seen in the days leading up to the 2008 New Hampshire primary, when Hillary Clinton took steps to appear more accessible after placing second in the Iowa caucuses by forgoing her standard stump speech and interacting more personally with voters. She almost teared up in front of a small group of undecided voters in response to a sympathetic question about how she was holding up on the campaign trail.[29,30] This emotional display, subdued and momentary, led all three network newscasts as the main political story the night before the primary, focusing attention on her image. Although initially portrayed in press accounts as a chink in Clinton's otherwise steely façade, this character-softening moment helped to humanize her in the eyes of some voters, winning over wavering supporters and contributing to her victory over Obama in the Granite State.[32,33] "As displays of emotion go," the *Washington Post* reported (p. C1[32]), "this one was tasteful and reserved—and ever so brief. It was like one of those perfect flickers of sadness that won Helen Mirren an Oscar for *The Queen*. It was dignified, yet human." Reporters covering the campaign scrambled to determine whether Clinton's choking up represented true, heartfelt sentiment or careful calculation designed to emotionally connect with voters.[29]

Contemporary candidates are not unique in their fixation with projecting a desirable image. The necessity of reaching a geographically dispersed electorate with a unifying appeal led candidates as early as Andrew Jackson in the 1820s to accept political advice and consciously adopt policies as well as a communication style that encouraged the public to see the candidate as a man of the people. Waterman, Wright, and St. Clair[13] identify three historical images that presidents have embraced over the past two centuries: the common man, the master politician, and the Washington outsider. These images, which say as much about the public's prevailing attitudes and expectations during different periods in American history as they do about the people who run for office, are instrumental in focusing mass attention on a single, grand narrative—of rustic self-reliance, legislative acumen, or anti-Washington populism. While each of these historical images has resonated at different times (the common man throughout much of the nineteenth century and master politician for most of the twentieth century), the outsider image has prevailed since the plainspoken Jimmy Carter, a one-term governor from Georgia, was elected to office on a wave of post-Watergate, anti-Washington sentiment in 1976.[13] We find elements of each of these historical images in the visual framing of election coverage. The master politician is represented in the depiction of the ideal candidate, while the common man and Washington outsider are clearly evident in our populist campaigner frame.

HISTORICAL MARKERS OF IMAGE HANDLING

Although perfected by image-conscious presidents in the television era, impression management is as old as American democracy itself. The history of campaign consulting is told with reference to many different starting points, defining moments, and record-setting events. Most sources point to five structural developments that paved the way for modern political consulting: the establishment of public relations as a profession; the rise of broadcast media and political advertising as a primary vehicle of campaign communication; the decline of political parties as central decision-making bodies; American trust in—and infatuation with—experts; and the growing amount of money spent on campaigns (see De Vries;[34] Farrell, Kolodny, and Medvic;[35] Nimmo;[9] Sabato;[10] Schultz;[36] Thurber, Nelson, and Dulio).[37,38]

Political advisors, both formal and informal, have played a key role in candidate packaging and promotion since colonial times. Friedenberg,[44] in reviewing the prehistory of media consultation, describes how George Washington was advised to publicly celebrate his 1758 candidacy for the Virginia House of Burgesses. He did so by distributing 160 gallons of rum, beer, wine, and hard cider among his constituents. With only 391 eligible voters in his district, Washington is said to have distributed more than a quart and a half per person, which opened him to accusations of buying votes. John Beckley, the first clerk of the U.S. House of Representatives, is recognized as the first political campaign manager. In handling Thomas Jefferson's campaign of 1796, Beckley launched what may have been the first "media blitz" in American politics, "flooding what he perceived to be the critical swing state of Pennsylvania with thirty thousand sample ballots and thousands of political handbills extolling Jefferson's virtues" (p. 13[44]).

In the nineteenth century, presidential candidates were frequently advised by other politicians—and occasionally by future presidents. Andrew Jackson's presidential campaigns of 1828 and 1832, advised by Martin Van Buren, are regarded as prototypes of today's media-driven campaigns. After the election of 1824, in which Jackson won a plurality of the popular vote but lost in the Electoral College to John Quincy Adams (similar to Al Gore's loss to George W. Bush in 2000), Van Buren labored from his Tammany Hall base in New York to create a national party organization to mobilize voters.[45] Notably, Van Buren worked at the grassroots level with local volunteers and sympathetic newspapers to secure favorable coverage of General Jackson as a statesmanlike war hero and to transform presidential campaigning into a more public experience. During the election of 1828, the Jackson campaign made extensive use of printed literature and color lithographs. Rallies were held; parades were staged; and hickory brooms, canes, and sticks were given away to remind voters of "Old Hickory."[44] In 1832, Van Buren helped Jackson organize the new, nationally based Democratic Party following the model of a political machine, with the pragmatic goal of winning elections, controlling government, and doling out patronage to maintain support.[45,46] At the end of Van Buren's first term as president in 1840, a young Abraham Lincoln, then a member of the Illinois House of Representatives, wrote strategy memos to organize fellow Whig Party members in his state in support of William Henry Harrison's successful bid to unseat Van Buren.[45]

Over time, political consulting became more formalized and began to embrace the tools and techniques of mass persuasion. The election of 1896 between William McKinley and William Jennings Bryan, a watershed in presidential politics, was particularly noteworthy for the McKinley campaign's adroit use of (pro-Republican and anti-Democratic) persuasive appeals, strategic championing of issues, and targeting of likely voters.[47] McKinley employed the services of Republican political boss Mark Hanna, who, as chairman of the Republican National Committee, raised an unprecedented $3.5 million for the McKinley effort and enlisted the services of some 1,400 surrogate speakers.[48] In addition, almost 300 different campaign circulars were tailored for targeted groups at different stages in the campaign.[47] Hanna's fund-raising efforts, particularly from corporate sources, were so successful they sparked the first major effort geared toward campaign finance reform.[40,45] Market research developed rapidly after 1900, incorporating such audience feedback techniques as ad testing, questionnaire-based surveys, house-to-house interviewing, and random sampling theory in the early decades of the twentieth century.[50] Public relations emerged as a profession soon thereafter.

By 1928, Edward Bernays—the father of "spin,"[51] or modern public relations—was urging political leaders to embrace from big business "the methods of appealing to the broad public" (p. 110[52]). Along with newsman Walter Lippmann, Bernays had worked during the First World War for the U.S. government's Committee on Public Information, to "package, advertise, and sell the war as one that would 'Make the World Safe for Democracy'" (p. 3[53]). A nephew of Sigmund Freud, Bernays attempted to bring scientific principles to public relations practices.[44] To win public support, Bernays encouraged politicians to systematically assess citizens' "desires and demands" and combine this knowledge with the artful dramatizing of issues to attract media coverage. The pairing of citizen concerns with staged events covered as news almost guaranteed widespread attention and interest, Bernays[52] felt. "Events and activities must be created in order to put ideas into circulation," he asserted (p. 118). A candidate campaigning to lower taxes, for example, should "not merely tell people that the high tariff increases the cost of the things they buy" but should "create circumstances which would make his contention dramatic and self-evident" (p. 121).

> He would perhaps stage a low-tariff exhibition simultaneously in twenty cities, with exhibits illustrating the additional cost due to the tariff in force. . . . He would have groups, whose interests were especially affected by the high cost of living, institute an agitation for lower schedules. He would dramatize the issue, perhaps by having prominent men boycott woolen clothes, and go to important functions in cotton suits, until the wool schedule was reduced. He might get the opinion of social workers as to whether the high cost of wool endangers the health of the poor in winter. (p. 121)

The route to public acceptance involved successfully harnessing "as many of the basic emotions as possible" to reinforce the candidate's own values and policy positions. Far from an empty vessel beholden to voter prejudices or the whims of mass sentiment, the properly advised politician was capable of learning "how to mold the mind of the voters in conformity with his own ideas of public welfare and public service" (p. 119[52]). Bernays's advice, consonant with shifting expectations of the president as a master politician, also reflected the growing influence of the social sciences in education and government, which brought principles of psychology, sociology, economics, and statistics into the public consciousness. "The whole basis of successful propaganda," Bernays wrote, "is to have an objective and then to endeavor to arrive at it through an exact knowledge of the public, modifying circumstances to manipulate and sway that public" (pp. 125–126[52]).[54]

Interestingly, Bernays observed that effective persuasion required more than verbal appeals alone, that the "emotions of oratory have been worn down through long years of overuse" (p. 116[52]). In the new era of radio broadcasting and film, a broader, more diversified media approach was needed to reach the masses—an idea embraced years earlier by the wartime Committee on Public Information.[53,54] At the heart of this appeal was an emphasis on personality. "A charming candidate is the alchemist's secret that can transmute a prosaic platform into the gold of votes" (p. 117[52]). When candidates lacked personality, well-liked personages could be associated with them. During the 1924 presidential campaign, Bernays, who began his career as a Broadway press agent, attempted such a feat by inviting Al Jolson and 40 other performers to the White House for a pancake breakfast intended to soften Calvin Coolidge's dour public image. The stunt is widely regarded as the first consultant-inspired media event orchestrated for a presidential candidate (see Blumenthal[60]).

In *Propaganda*, Bernays pitched for the creation of a new post within the president's cabinet, a secretary of public relations, to "interpret the people to the government and the government to the people" (p. 127[52]).

Although the position of presidential press secretary has not risen to the level of cabinet secretary—probably for good reason—presidents since Franklin D. Roosevelt have increasingly vested their political fortunes on the advice of pollsters, media handlers, and image consultants.[61] As political advocacy became increasingly professionalized, consultants began to bring an element of predictability to election outcomes. They did so by stretching the truth, dramatizing the issues, and going negative. Several sources[62,63,10] credit the husband–wife team of Clem Whitaker, a newsman and lobbyist, and Leone Baxter, a public relations practitioner, with setting the tone for future elections. Whitaker took a particularly jaundiced view of his target audience:

> The average American doesn't want to be educated, he doesn't want to improve his mind, he doesn't even want to work consciously at being a good citizen. But every American likes to be entertained. He likes the movies, he likes mysteries, he likes fireworks and parades. So, if you can't put on a fight, put on a show." (pp. 570–571[63])

Whitaker and Baxter emerged on the scene during a Depression-era ballot drive to halt a flood control and irrigation development in northern California, which the Pacific Gas and Electric Company considered a threat to private power. Through the shrewd use of radio and newspaper appeals, Whitaker and Baxter managed to save the Central Valley Project on a limited ($39,000) budget.[10] The next year, 1934, they were retained by Republican Governor Frank Merriam and engineered what has been described as "the campaign of the century" against socialist author Upton Sinclair's candidacy for California governor.[63] Sinclair, a crusading author and one of the original muckrakers, had won the Democratic primary, but his reform-minded ideas and championing of collectivist causes threatened the political establishment. Among Merriam's most powerful backers, and Sinclair's most fervent critics, were MGM studio head Louis Mayer and *Los Angeles Times* publisher Harry Chandler. When Sinclair swept the Democratic nomination, the *Times* denounced his victory as a national crisis and took aim at his "maggot-like horde" of supporters.[63] "As Sinclair's gubernatorial bid gathered unexpected steam, the *Times'* usual Red-baiting rhetoric accelerated to editorial screeds of breathtaking inaccuracy, warning that 'public enemy' Upton Sinclair would 'sovietize California and destroy her business and industry'" (pp. 139–140[64]). Newspapers owned by William Randolph Hearst in the northern and southern parts of the state further mocked and derided Sinclair's candidacy with only slightly less zeal. Circulars also linked Sinclair to a nonexistent Youth People's Community Party.

But the "unselling of Upton Sinclair increasingly relied on visual images" (p. 422[63]). Metro-Goldwyn-Mayer newsreels, misleadingly titled

California Election News, were shown before feature-length films in theaters, depicting Sinclair supporters (in reality, paid actors) as shifty-eyed vagrants, often speaking with feigned Russian accents. Merriam supporters, by contrast, were portrayed as well spoken and hard working: mainstream Americans. Other newsreels, distributed free to theaters and presented as objective reporting even though they would be easily recognized today as negative advertising, showed "tramps" (again, paid actors) coming off freight trains, headed for California in anticipation of a Sinclair victory.[63] Sinclair's economic plan to End Poverty in California (EPIC) was mocked on some 2,000 billboards and in editorial cartoons printed in newspapers statewide. Though vilified and lacking the endorsement of President Roosevelt, Sinclair still managed to receive 38% of the vote. Nevertheless, the campaign was a resounding endorsement of the techniques of attack politics—and the utility of image handlers.[65] The election gave rise, as Mitchell[63] noted, to the ignominious birth of media politics.

Political and religious spectacle has long featured in the national culture (see Boorstin,[66] Salmore and Salmore[47]) and, as image handling matured into a profession with the rise of television and the so-called image-is-everything presidency,[13] election campaigns took on a dramatic, visual quality. In *The Image: A Guide to Pseudoevents in America*, Boorstin[66] viewed this development with a cynical eye. "Our national politics has become a competition for images or between images, rather than between ideals," he wrote. "The domination of campaigning by television simply dramatizes this fact" (p. 149). Roosevelt was the first president to appear on television, at the 1939 World's Fair in New York, but the first television spots for a presidential campaign were not broadcast until 1952. Dwight Eisenhower hired ad man Rosser Reeves to carry out his "Eisenhower Answers America" campaign in consultation with pollster George Gallup.[67,68]

By this time, television had penetrated into some 40% of American homes.[10,69] Reeves's innovation was to produce brief spots for placement during commercial breaks *between* programs rather than sponsoring entire shows, as commercial advertisers were accustomed to, or buying costly chunks of airtime for lengthy speeches, as political candidates were in the habit of doing.[68] This strategy allowed Eisenhower to reach the national audience at a fraction of the cost of more conventional practices. The ads, which aired three weeks prior to the election in 12 battleground states,[67] featured Eisenhower responding to staged questions from ordinary looking citizens about corruption in government, the cost of living, and the Korean War, portraying the former five-star general and supreme commander of the allied forces in Europe (as well as NATO) as a Washington outsider and man of the people (for archived copies of these ads, see livingroomcandidate. org; www.pbs.org/30secondcandidate). For his television appearances

Eisenhower consulted with image handlers, actively seeking advice on lighting, makeup, set arrangements, and speech content.[10,36,69-71] Facing a $1.5 million Republican "airwar" of television advertising that year,[10] Democrats found themselves blindsided by the "new way of campaigning" and responded with sharp criticism. To the Stevenson campaign, Eisenhower had staged "a super colossal, multimillion-dollar production designed to sell an inadequate ticket to the American people in precisely the way they sell soap, ammoniated toothpaste, hair tonic, or bubble gum. They guarantee their candidates to be 99% pure; whether or not they will float remains to be seen" (George Ball, staffer for Adlai Stevenson, quoted in Sabato,[10] p. 114; see also McGinniss[72]).

Despite concerns voiced by party regulars about the growing role of political consultants in electoral politics, Eisenhower showed that image handlers could be effectively used in presidential campaigns. There was no turning back. Eisenhower kept Reeves's advertising agency, Ted Bates and Co., on retainer throughout his first term in office.[13] A survey of state party committees documented remarkable growth in the use of public relations firms for political campaigns between 1952 and 1957, with a substantial number reporting complete responsibility for campaigns.[10,73] Of course, Democrats who cried foul after Adlai Stevenson's failed bids against Eisenhower in the 1950s soon thereafter ran their own media savvy candidate, the telegenic John F. Kennedy.

During the 1960 campaign, both Nixon and Kennedy aired political spots, but their impact was greatly overshadowed by the first televised presidential debates. Nixon was widely perceived as losing the now legendary first televised debate against Kennedy, largely because he appeared unpresidential. On the day of the debate he was still recovering from a fever and hospital visit stemming from an infected knee, which he had banged against a car door; just before walking into the studio, he bumped the knee in question *again*, causing enough pain that he could not cross his legs while sitting. He also refused to wear proper makeup.[74] While Kennedy appeared rested, suntanned, athletic, and articulate, "Nixon's shadowy eyes, perspiring and brow-mopping, poor posture, inappropriate nodding, and other aspects of his appearance rather than his speech" exacted an evaluative cost in the eyes of voters (p. 104).[75] Years earlier, Nixon's vice presidential nomination had been saved with advice from the BBDO advertising agency, which carefully rehearsed a nationally televised address with him (the iconic "Checkers" speech) to explain away a secret campaign fund. In 1960, however, Nixon "rather surprisingly refused a BBDO proposal to organize his first presidential campaign around the latest media techniques" (p. 115).[10] Six days after winning the presidency, Kennedy observed, "It was TV more than anything that turned the tide" (p. 116²,).[76]

Humbled by his 1960 defeat and subsequent loss in the California gubernatorial election two years later, Nixon returned to politics in 1968 with a media-savvy campaign, allowing image handlers to rebrand him as "the New Nixon."[70,72] Color television, aggressive advertising appeals, and a series of staged question-and-answer sessions enabled Nixon to mount "one of the most remarkable comebacks in U.S. history" (p. 115[10]). Moreover, "better makeup and more frequent shavings helped to eliminate the jowly, shadowy look that had so haunted Nixon's previous television image" (p. 115[10]). The mass marketing approach to politics is ingeniously captured by the cover of the first edition of *The Selling of the President 1968* by Joe McGinnis.[72] It features the smiling face of Nixon adorning a pack of cigarettes, with the implication that if candidates were being merchandised *like* products, then why not feature their faces *on* products?

Once in office, Nixon appointed his close advisor, H. R. Haldeman, a former advertising executive and television show producer, as his chief of staff and created the White House Office of Communications to handle the press and actively shape a favorable governing image.[13] For Nixon, speech making was image making, and he, like Lyndon Johnson before him, used specific writers to evoke particular themes. "For purely political speeches, Nixon used William Safire. If, however, he wanted a more combative speech, he relied on Patrick Buchanan" (p. 117[13]). Both of these writers, who would later become influential media pundits (and Buchanan a presidential candidate), penned scorching critiques of the press that were delivered by Nixon's vice president, Spiro Agnew.[77]

Though subsequent presidents decried Nixon's Watergate-scandal ethics, they embraced his image-construction practices.[13] Following the 1976 presidential race, Democrat Jimmy Carter became the first president to appoint an outside media consultant (Gerald Rafshoon) to his full-time staff,[10] a practice that has been followed with a greater or lesser degree of formality by presidents ever since.[78] In the Reagan White House, political advisor and longtime Reagan aide Michael Deaver was appointed as deputy chief of staff, tasked with media management and responsibility for how the public perceived the president. Deaver's greatest skill, as Nancy Reagan once observed, "was in arranging what were known as good visuals—televised events or scenes that would leave a powerful symbolic image in people's minds" (p. 239[81]).

Reagan's successor, George H. W. Bush, also relied on consultant-inspired visuals to make vivid impressions, but his lasting media legacy was in the use of evocative attack advertising against opponents.[67] Roger Ailes, who had worked as a media advisor for Nixon in 1968, masterminded many of the notorious spots against Massachusetts Governor Michael Dukakis on Bush's behalf in 1988, portraying Dukakis as soft on crime, a poor steward of the environment, and weak on defense issues.[82] Widely cited as a major factor in Bush's come-from-behind victory that year, the ads "created a picture of Michael Dukakis as a friend of murderers and rapists" (Lewis, quoted in Jamieson,[67] p. 165) and sparked a searching postelection debate about the negative tenor of modern campaigns (see Bucy and Gregson[85]). The same approach by the Bush team (sans Ailes) did not work against Bill Clinton in 1992, who had assembled a rapid response team of image handlers, including James Carville, Paul Begala, Stan Greenberg, and George Stephanopoulos, who plotted strategy and countered Republican attacks out of a campaign office in Little Rock, Arkansas, that came to be mythologized in the Academy Award–nominated documentary *The War Room*.[86]

Despite Clinton's uncanny ability to communicate with political audiences,[87] he is considered by some to be the first "consultant-dependent" president (see Klein,[70] Strother[88]). Perhaps the most notorious of these advisors was Dick Morris, a scandal-plagued consultant known for working both sides of the political aisle. Clinton turned to Morris after the disastrous 1994 midterm elections, when Republicans gained control of the House and Senate for the first time in 40 years.[13] From 1995 to 1996 Morris orchestrated much of Clinton's reelection effort, sometimes unbeknownst to White House staff, writing drafts of speeches and advocating that Clinton champion conservative causes—welfare reform, balancing the federal budget, the V-chip ratings system for television—to co-opt Republican arguments and build an image of leadership. Many of Clinton's political decisions, word choices, and even vacation spots were determined by Morris-commissioned polls.[88] Although he never officially joined the White House staff, for a time Morris wielded more influence than most staffers. He saw his role not as deciding what Clinton stood for "but to figure out which of the positions he had already taken were the most popular" (p. 9[89]). Early advertising in swing states reinforced Clinton's refashioned image, even before Bob Dole secured the Republican presidential nomination. In Morris' view, "There was a vital synergy between issues and image. Rather than a presidential stand on the issues creating a desired image, the desired image was first identified, then congruent issues were selected that best promoted the new image. Image molded and directed the political agenda, not the other way around" (p. 64[13]).

The notion of keeping consultants on as staff for continuous political advice was arguably taken to new heights by George W. Bush, who appointed conservative operative and longtime Texas ally Karl Rove as his senior political advisor and deputy chief of staff. [90] As an operative in Texas, Rove was instrumental in transforming politics in the Lone Star state from an era of Democratic dominance to one of Republican ascendance.[93] With communications director Karen Hughes, Rove devised an image of Bush during the 2000 campaign as a "compassionate conservative," attempting to restyle Republican principles "in such a way that they seemed to have relevance to the new economy, the new nature of the country, and the new electorate" (quoted in Balz,[93] p. C1).

Rove's strategy won Bush about half of the popular vote and, after a contentious legal dispute ultimately decided by the Supreme Court, just enough electoral votes to take the White House.

The 2004 campaign was a different story, with Rove steering Bush back toward traditional conservative themes, particularly national security and moral values, and mobilizing the Republican base of conservative voters. Although no direct connection has been made with the Bush reelection effort, terror warnings were issued at times when John Kerry's poll ratings rose—two days after he picked John Edwards as his running mate and a few days after the end of the Democratic National Convention.[94] The timing of the alerts, a *Time* magazine columnist observed, "seemed to fall with odd regularity right on the heels of major political events."[94] Ballot amendments against gay marriage and negative attacks on Kerry's war record were also staples of the campaign. Summing up Rove's abilities, a profile in the *Atlantic Monthly* noted that "along with remarkable strategic skills, he has both an understanding of the media's unstated self-limitations and a willingness to fight in territory where conscience forbids most others."[95]

Image handlers now rank among the elite of contemporary politics, and top consultants, such as Karl Rove, James Carville, and Frank Luntz have become media celebrities[96] in their own right.[97,98] Indeed, their prestige is such that candidate viability is sometimes judged by which major-name consultant or firm a campaign has on retainer. But, as discussed in the next section, consultant-generated advice does not always suit particular candidates, and following the *wrong* advice can severely constrain a nominee's appeal and electoral success. As our analysis will show, the latter outcome has been particularly detrimental to Democrats in recent elections.

THE STRUGGLE FOR FRAME CONTROL

Classical conceptions of the press hold that the news media should serve as the public's eyes and ears, reporting on and analyzing political events, holding power holders accountable when necessary, and otherwise acting as an unbiased conduit of information.[99] In an idealized democratic system, citizens "should be concerned, cognizant, rational, and accepting of the political system," and the institutions of communication "should be comprehensive, accurate, and scrupulously fair and politically balanced" (p. 268[99]). With increased profit expectations in recent decades, the news media have been equally, if not more, driven by a need to craft stories that highlight drama and conflict in an effort to maximize audience share.[100–102] Through message shaping and image orchestration, employed with increasing sophistication since the introduction of television, politicians and their advisors continually battle journalists for frame control.

Framing is the process by which some aspects of an issue, event, or person are emphasized over others in such a way as to promote a particular causal interpretation, problem construction, or moral evaluation (see Entman[103]). In news framing of presidential campaigns, certain aspects of a candidate's issue stands, background, or voter appeal may be identified and made salient while other information is downplayed or ignored. Frames pull together the facts of a narrative, acting as the "central organizing idea for making sense of relevant events and suggesting what is at issue" (p. 157[104]). Frames consist of different narrative elements, including characteristics assigned to leading candidates in news accounts of the campaign. The extent to which candidates are framed as having ideal attributes, populist traits, or losing qualities, for instance, may limit their ability to gain momentum after a drop in the polls, or rebound from a poor debate performance or campaign crisis.

Not wanting to leave opinion formation to chance, image handlers carefully orchestrate campaign events to reinforce campaign themes, taking pains to manufacture imagery consistent with the campaign's message of the day—flags or military settings to convey patriotism and security, scenes of the great outdoors to associate the candidate with environmentally friendly positions, or appearances before enthusiastic throngs of young voters to signal popularity and change. Indeed, the primary goal of image handlers with regard to the news is to exercise control over the visual framing process by staging candidate appearances in such a way as to make it virtually impossible for television journalists to avoid the carefully choreographed production of adoring crowds, confetti showers, and message-related backdrops. Mindful of the capacity of news visuals to form impressions, they employ strategies to shape the news consistent with their desired message, regardless of its consistency with political reality. This was precisely Lesley Stahl's complaint about the Reagan campaign's news management strategy in 1984 (see Chapter 2).

In such a milieu, certain features of political coverage, including journalists' fixation on campaign strategy over policy substance and "disdaining the news,"[105] or coloring reports of events with judgmental words or phrases to demonstrate journalistic distance from their public relations purpose, can thus be regarded as attempts by news organizations to reassert editorial control over the news product.[106] "Such a publicity process," Blumler and Gurevitch[106] have noted, "is not exactly rich in vitamins for citizenship" and tends to "narrow the debate; make negative campaigning more central; foster cynicism; and, over-represent newsmaking as a field of power struggle rather than a source of issue clarification" (p. 129). Candidates and political professionals thus see themselves engaged in a competition not just with their political opponents but increasingly with the press itself.

Blumler[107] has described the constellation of persuasive efforts that attend political campaigns as the modern publicity process. In the contest for influence over popular perceptions, "leading political actors have almost to be split personalities—policy-makers and publicists—without ever being quite certain which is more important and whether the two can be reconciled" (p. 106[107]). A one-sided emphasis on either role risks projecting the wrong image, that of a cold policy wonk or hollow self-promoter, presenting voters with a choice between two undesirable options. Ultimately, leaders who have an effective communication style "can be difficult to dislodge; without it, he or she becomes vulnerable" (p. 106[107]). In his memoirs, Nixon[108] commented on the perception-management challenges facing presidents:

> Since the advent of television as our primary means of communication and source of information, modern presidents must have specialized talents at once more superficial and more complicated than those of their predecessors. They must try to master the art of manipulating the media not only to win in politics but in order to further the programs and causes they believe in; at the same time, they must avoid at all costs the charge of trying to manipulate the media. In the modern presidency, concern for image must rank with concern for substance. (p. 354)

A perception of being easily manipulated ranks high on the press's list of least desirable self-images. In fact, neither political correspondents nor politicians want to be controlled by the other.[109,110] Journalists employ a variety of measures to ward off attempts by political campaigns to manipulate them into serving as the campaign's mouthpiece. A perennial favorite is deconstructing and revealing campaign strategies to the audience, predictably followed by accusations from campaigns that the news media distort the message that candidates want conveyed to voters.[111,112] Despite this antagonism, the two sides are compelled to cooperate with each election cycle to address their mutual needs; indeed, for all the attempts at manipulation, election news is created through the *joint* efforts of journalists and candidates.[111] As Swanson[110] has observed, "politicians cannot succeed without access to the media, just as reporters cannot succeed without access to political leaders" (p. 399).

In plying their craft, political consultants take a rather formulaic approach to shaping candidate images. Typically, opinion polls and focus groups are used to identify salient issues on the minds of voters.[89,113] The next step is to assess which of these issues play to their client's advantage. A campaign strategy is then devised to prime the electorate on those issues, deploying images, symbols, and phrases that will connect the candidate to those issues in the minds of voters.[114] By asserting editorial autonomy during political campaigns, journalists

do exercise message control by way of selecting, investigating, interpreting, and regulating news stories about candidates.[115] The press may
thus construct candidate frames that contradict the image desired by
campaigns as a way of exercising their control over media content and
demonstrating their independence from campaign influence. At times
this process can produce coverage that rejects a campaign's framing
efforts or favors one candidate over another, leading to accusations of
bias or distortion (see Chapter 5).

   This struggle for frame control is captured by Entman's[103] description of a news frame as an "imprint of power—it registers the identity
of actors or interests that competed to dominate the text" (p. 53). This
battle for frame control is not an esoteric academic perspective of what
goes on—journalists and image handlers do, in fact, battle it out on the
campaign trail. As Joe Lockhart, a former press secretary for President
Clinton and senior advisor to John Kerry's 2004 presidential campaign,
summed it up, the process involves "pretty skilled manipulators, manipulating people who are very well aware of being manipulated"
(quoted in Jamieson,[116] p. 141). Political campaigns exercise substantial
control over the candidate's self-presentation during public performances, but journalists have the final say about what aspects of that
performance are conveyed to audiences and hence retain some influence over the candidate's public image. Voters integrate these filtered
campaign messages with political advertising, other campaign coverage, and their own experiences to construct a personalized candidate
image.[117,118] Voter perceptions of candidates thus depend on the interaction between campaign-supplied images, news filtering, and the feelings and cognitions voters have about those running for office.

VISUAL FRAMING

Despite the emphasis on issues that define campaigns, candidate character traits are of central interest to image handlers and journalists
alike;[19-21] they also play an important role in political impression formation.[14,122] Research has convincingly demonstrated that voters attend to
candidate images as well as issue positions to extrapolate underlying
evaluations that form the basis of voting decisions.[123-126] As an audiovisual medium that literally traffics in images, television is ideally suited
to convey character information. Indeed, most news stories may be too
short to do anything *except* present information about candidate character and personality.[123,127] Studying the visual representation of candidates during elections may therefore more accurately forecast what
viewers infer about candidates from media appearances than analyzing
the audio text of news.

   Most academic insights about framing (and framing effects), however, are derived from verbal aspects of media coverage or textual

analysis of voter discourse (e.g., Gamson;[128] Reese, Gandy, and Grant[5]). Research on visual framing has received only sporadic attention and overlooks specific investigation of candidate character, in favor of measuring broad valence frames that cast election coverage as either positive or negative, favorable or unfavorable, to particular candidates and parties.[117,129–132] While these analyses have helped to establish the concept of visual framing, they offer little insight into specific character traits that emerge in television news coverage of candidates that can be compared with the image-construction strategies of campaigns.

Another problem with coding visuals as simply positive or negative concerns the interpretation of image valence. Although an image bite might have all the markings of positive visual representation—for instance, a shot of a candidate interacting with well-wishers at a rally—a particular candidate's comfort in executing this behavior might make the image all *but* positive. Al Gore, for example, was regularly described as appearing stiff and aloof during the 2000 campaign, as was John Kerry in 2004 (see Jamieson;[133] Klein;[70] Sella;[134] Thomas, Clift, Darman, Peraino, and Goldman[135]). Images of an uncomfortable candidate mingling with crowds could hardly be counted as positive framing but would have been considered as such under a simple valence approach.

Visual analyses should move beyond the "positive versus negative" index measures and investigate more specific and nuanced character frame–building dimensions. The goal here, therefore, is to identify enduring character frames and examine the visual manifestations of these frames in election news. In support of this process we review research on verbal framing of candidate character, the aforementioned valence studies of visual framing, and experimental research on the impact that televised candidate portrayals have on audience perceptions. Insights from this literature were employed to devise coding categories (see Appendix 3) to measure visual framing of candidate character traits within the parameters of three enduring character frames: the ideal candidate, the populist campaigner, and the sure loser.[136]

The Ideal Candidate

Research on candidate images has shown that voters hold a mental picture of specific characteristics that an ideal presidential candidate should have.[138,139] Early studies found that voters value such characteristics as physical appeal, personality, candidate background and beliefs, leadership abilities, issue stands, honesty, and intelligence.[140] Other voter-perception studies have revealed traits such as compassion, honesty, sincerity, integrity, and warmth to be important evaluative criteria.[13,14,140] Assessments of job performance, including decisiveness, executive experience, competence, and speaking style, also receive mention.[9,13,140] From these qualities, the ideal candidate frame seems to coalesce around two major character themes: statesmanship (i.e., job performance dimensions) and likability.[118,139,140] Similarly, Kinder[14] reports that statesmanlike traits (competence, leadership, integrity) and compassion (empathy) form the basis of how voters evaluate candidates. We examine both of these dimensions in relation to visual coverage of elections below.

Statesmanship

Visual manifestations of statesmanship signal the mythic proportions of the presidency, projecting power, authority, control, and active leadership. To measure these character qualities visually, two television production techniques deserve consideration: associational juxtaposition and misé-en-scene. These packaging strategies also inform our explication of the populist and loser frames in subsequent sections.

Associational juxtaposition is an editing device by which qualities of one object or person are transferred to another via sequential depiction.[141] Implicit analogy often arises as the interpretive result when two unrelated scenes are brought into direct association, as when a shot of the American flag is juxtaposed with, or shown before, a shot of a candidate to communicate patriotism (see also Messaris and Abraham;[141] Messaris, Eckman, and Gumpert[143]). In a more sinister fashion, the image of a dangerous convict accused of committing additional crimes on a weekend furlough may be shown before the image of a candidate, as happened to Michael Dukakis with the infamous Willie Horton ad in 1988. The mise-en-scène (environmental context) may also transfer symbolic meaning to a political candidate. Patriotism, for example, can be symbolically transferred from the environment when the candidate appears against the backdrop of the flag or other historically potent symbols.[130] Early in his presidency, George W. Bush used the backdrop of Mt. Rushmore for an address on homeland and economic security, hoping to receive positive visual associations with the likenesses of the great presidents overlooking the scene (in one photograph posted on the White House home page, the top of Bush's head could be seen just below Thomas Jefferson's chin).

Using Messaris's[141] conceptualization of associational juxtaposition and the notion of mise-en-scène, statesmanship framing can be observed in network news coverage by measuring the occurrence of specific symbolic visual associations between the candidate and statesmanlike qualities. Appearances with high-ranking peers, for instance, serve as implied endorsements of candidates and cultivate perceptions of competence and credibility.[130,144,145] Figure 3–1 features a screen capture from general election news that illustrates the linkage to high-ranking peers. Appearances at ceremonies or campaign visits to symbolic venues such as war memorials or locations associated with economic authority (Wall Street, trade association meetings, industry conventions) or technological advancement (NASA, Silicon Valley start-ups, high-tech manufacturing plants) play on cherished principles and buttress the myth of the statesman as an emblem of national pride, economic development, and industrial progress.[10,100,146,147] Figure 3–1 presents a screen capture that exemplifies the transfer of patriotism to Bob Dole.

The celebratory pomp and spectacle of politics provokes emotional and aesthetic responses that include enthusiasm, joy, awe, and wonderment.[10,146] Linking candidates to celebratory displays such as large entourages, parades, and rallies with campaign paraphernalia (see Fig. 3–1) and confetti showers authenticate and impose reference to the power and authority of a candidate as a potential chief executive. These visual signals of statesmanship have been employed as categories in

Linked, influentials   Linked, patriotism

Bill Clinton appearing hand-in-hand with   Bob Dole amidst flag-waving supporters
Jesse Jackson at a religious service   1996
1992

Campaign paraphernalia   Wearing a suit

Bill Clinton addressing a throng of   John Kerry and George Bush after a
sign-toting supporters   televised debate
1996   2004

Figure 3–1 Screen captures from campaign coverage illustrating ideal candidate framing (statesman subdimension)

visual content analyses of candidates in newspaper photos.[148,149] Henry Kissinger[150] reveals that Nixon's image handlers intentionally blocked intersections to create traffic jams. The goal was to draw attention to the Nixon entourage to build visual evidence of popularity, authority, and diplomatic gravitas.

Performing the role of statesman also requires the use of an appropriate wardrobe. Moriarty and Popovich[131] distinguish between "dignified" attire (suit and tie) as a positive candidate portrayal and casual clothing (sportswear, shirtsleeves) as a more negative portrayal in coding candidate appearances. Kaid and Davidson[151] include a formal dress code in conceptualizing an "incumbent videostyle" compared to informal dress, which they associate with a "challenger videostyle" (p. 199). Although not articulated directly, both of these coding systems can be interpreted as drawing a distinction between a suited statesman and a casual populist campaigner (see also Trebay[152]). Figure 3–1 offers a screen capture example of statesmanlike attire from the 2004 election year.

Compassion

Once the question of competence and statesmanship is settled, voters look for evidence that the candidate is warm and compassionate.[140,153] Candidates, despite their campaign maneuverings, run as warm and benevolent personalities who should be loved and adored by voters.[127] (See also Bennett.[154]) The visual representation of political compassion can be operationalized by linking candidate behavior (e.g., affinity displays) with social symbols of compassion, such as children and families.

Baby-holding and -kissing involve perhaps the most clichéd construction of candidate compassion on the campaign trail.[145,146,155,156] Presidential candidates also have a history of surrounding themselves with their own children and grandchildren for public reinforcement of family friendliness[10,155,157] During war and in times of economic hardship children are featured more prominently in campaigns as they emphasize the softer side of a candidate, implying that decisions about war and the economy will be made with consideration of the most vulnerable among us.[10,148,155]

Linkage to children (see Figure 3–2 for an example) also supports the mythology of family, a dominant value in American culture.[145,158] In a patriarchal social environment, protecting women and children as well as honoring family and faith evoke the frame of the ideal surrogate father of the nation—a protector, provider, and moral compass.[10,148,159] During the 2008 primaries, the candidates' wives played a prominent visual role in the campaign (and in the case of Hillary Clinton, her husband). Visual analyses have utilized symbolic linkages to family to assess broader candidate images.[117,129,131,148,149] Figure 3–2

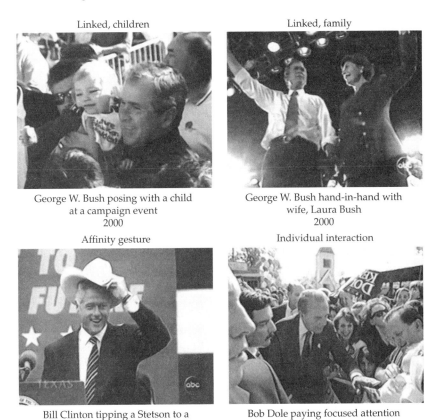

Linked, children

Linked, family

George W. Bush posing with a child
at a campaign event
2000

George W. Bush hand-in-hand with
wife, Laura Bush
2000

Affinity gesture

Individual interaction

Bill Clinton tipping a Stetson to a
Texas crowd
1996

Bob Dole paying focused attention
to a family on the rope line
1996

Figure 3–2 Screen captures from campaign coverage illustrating ideal candidate framing (compassion subdimension)

presents still images from our sample of newscasts illustrating compassion—the visual association of candidates with children, family, and admiring female supporters. Compassion and benevolence are also behaviorally signaled through personal interaction with voters and nonverbal affinity gestures, including waving, shaking hands, and paying focused attention to supporters[117,131,132,148,149] Figure 3–2 presents a visual example of a candidate affinity gesture, which signals bonding with supporters.

The Populist Campaigner

Populist narratives are built on the idea that ordinary people, a *noble troupe*, stand in opposition to an aristocratic and self-serving elite.[161,162] Since the rise of populism in the 1870s, populist appeals have been effectively invoked in American politics by diverse groups, including conservatives, liberals, neo-Nazis, civil rights organizations, and the Christian Coalition. This has led Kazin[160] to argue that populism is a "promiscuous" but persuasive impulse employed in reference to economic (bread and butter issues) and social matters (crime and drug fighting, pro-life positions, definitions of marriage, and controlling media violence; see also Stengel,[162] Wayne[163]).

Populism has also been described as a sour political tradition,[70,162] operating on the assumption that common folk can be moved to active citizenship only through low-hitting appeals that denigrate one candidate in favor of another. On television, a populist frame can be achieved through grassroots appearances and displays of mass appeal and popularity.[146,164] The aesthetics of the populism frame evolved from a log-cabin mythology in the nineteenth century to working-class symbolism in the twentieth century.[10,70] In the early stages of the 1976 presidential campaign, Jimmy Carter (not James) appeared in documentary-style advertising wearing jeans while touring his peanut farm in Plains, Georgia. On the campaign trail he remained in Plain Folks character, carrying his own garment bag and sporting cardigan sweaters to appear down to earth.[10,70] Charles Guggenheim, a documentary filmmaker employed to produce advertisements for Carter, shot Carter's campaign videos and ads in a populist style, utilizing a cinema vérité approach with little scripting.[10] The technique, which is rough and unpolished, stands in stark contrast to the slick, Madison Avenue approach of traditional advertising.

The populist frame is also observable in the evolution of political speech. Carter attempted and then Reagan perfected the populist style of television-speak by conversing with—rather than authoritatively addressing—audiences. This speech pattern includes simple and often fragmented sentences, informal transitions, and colloquial language. Bill Clinton excelled at this, especially in town hall debates.[164] In fact, the town hall format itself has a populist ring to it: candidates make appearances on televised forums with ordinary folks asking questions. "Eisenhower Answers America" was probably the first step in this direction. Eisenhower's questions were generated by his image handlers, but they were posed on camera by everyday citizens (tourists recruited from New York's Radio City Music Hall).[68,165] "While some Republican leaders worried that appearing in a commercial would diminish Eisenhower's stature, in the ad his stature is visually enhanced. At the same time the candidate is seen relating to everyday people, and offering memorable solutions to their problems."[68]

Applying a populist frame is one way for journalists to infuse excitement into a long, and at times boring, campaign process. Visual manifestations of this frame can be observed in terms of linkage and symbolic cues to two main qualities: mass appeal and ordinariness.

We specify nine categories to operationalize the visual form populism takes in news coverage of elections (see Appendix 3).

Mass Appeal

Celebrities, as symbols of populist devotion, transfer their cultural appeal to political candidates through joint appearances and endorsements.[10] Mass appeal in television news coverage also finds visual expression through linkages to large and approving crowds.[117,131,148,149] Driving the allure of these portrayals is a plain-folks bandwagon effect implying that a widely popular candidate should be seen as a man of the people—and, because the majority of people support him, all should join the bandwagon in support.[130] Indeed, speakers who are surrounded by an audience that responds positively (via affirmative head nodding, smiles, and attentive nonverbal responses) may boost their authority ratings and character dynamism compared to those shown with a disapproving audience (head shaking, frowns, and inattentiveness; Hylton[166]). Positive audience reaction shots can also make featured speakers appear more interesting and popular.[167]

Nixon's image handlers in 1968 choreographed friendly town hall–style meetings, packing the audience with supporters. Since then it has become standard procedure for political image handlers to exercise control over audiences, ensuring that candidates face an approving crowd. Both George W. Bush and Bill Clinton regulated access to campaign events by denying people entry to rallies if they did not have prior clearance from local party officials to attend.[70] Figure 3–3 features four screen captures that exemplify visual manifestations of mass appeal.

Ordinariness

The second dimension of the populist campaigner frame finds expression in visual appearances with regular folks, displays of physical activity or athletic ability, and the style of dress that candidates develop (see Figure 3–4 for screen capture examples). During the 1992, 1996, and 2000 presidential campaigns Bill Clinton and Al Gore campaigned in a suit, but without a jacket, and with their shirtsleeves rolled up. This loosened the formality of their on-stage appearances at public rallies (see Kaid and Davidson[151]). It also suggested that the candidates were subverting the formality and ceremoniousness of proper political attire. Casual and sports clothing (jeans, sports shirts, and shorts) more directly signals that a candidate is an everyday citizen. Coupled with athletic activities or depictions of physical work, populist framing establishes empathy with common folk and presents the candidate as "one of us."[10,145,160] Clinton's jogging with supporters along the campaign trail in 1992 demonstrates this point, as does Mike Huckabee's marathon training runs in the 2008 primaries. But journalists became irritated

Linked, celebrity

Al Gore high-fiving a fan during a
Tonight Show appearance with Jay Leno
2000

Large audience

Long shot linking George H. W. Bush to
a mass audience at a campaign rally
1992

Approving audience

George H. W. Bush giving a double
thumbs-up against a backdrop of adoring
supporters
1992

Crowd interaction

George W. Bush working rope-line
crowds at a campaign rally
2004

Figure 3–3 Screen captures from campaign coverage illustrating populist framing (mass appeal subdimension)

with the transparency of these image-making performances, reportedly wondering, "How many miles of this shit-eating jogging are we going to have to watch?" (p. 148[146]).

Certain athletic and work-related activities may be better suited for advancing an image of populism than others.[148] George H. W. Bush, for example, was strongly advised by his image handlers to avoid indulging in "manic rounds of his favorite elitist pastimes, golf and boating," as those visual displays would "reinforce the image of an aristocratic president out of touch with the common man" (p. 6[148]). In 2004 John Kerry arguably undermined his populist frame-building efforts by windsurfing, snowboarding, and skiing—sports that are generally regarded as elitist.

Casual dress

Sports clothes

Jeans-wearing Al Gore and Joe Lieberman addressing a crowd from the back of a pick-up truck 2000

John Kerry duck hunting in camouflage 2004

Rolled-up sleeves

Physically active

John Kerry rolling up his shirt sleeves during a town hall meeting with voters 2004

George W. Bush jogging with his Secret Service detail 2004

Figure 3–4 Screen captures from campaign coverage illustrating populist framing (ordinariness subdimension)

The Sure Loser

During general election campaigns the image of a sure loser can arise through the missteps, sudden change in fortune, or poor judgment of an otherwise leading candidate, in which case loser framing may be temporary. Alternately, a flawed nominee may endure loser framing by failing to ever emerge from a trailing position in the polls.[168] The candidacies of Democrat George McGovern in 1972 and Republican Bob Dole in 1996, which never gained traction beyond a relatively narrow base of partisan supporters, are prototypical examples of flawed nominees. Both McGovern and Dole were weak challengers running against relatively popular incumbents. In Dole's case, the presumption of failure infused media coverage (see Nagourney and Kolbert[169]) and even the candidate's own statements. During a 1996 town hall debate with Bill Clinton, Dole reinforced his losing status when, in response to a question about affirmative action, he took a self-deprecating stance highlighting his war injury and trailing position in the race: "I'm disabled. I shouldn't have a preference. I would like to have one in this race, come to think of it, but I don't get one. Maybe we can work that out. I get a 10-point spot. This is America. No discrimination."[170]

In some cases, candidates may endure unfavorable visual portrayals because they have committed a campaign blunder or otherwise provided the networks with material that cannot be ignored. Oftentimes what make the news are stories that can be readily illustrated. When George H. W. Bush glanced at his watch halfway through the second debate with Bill Clinton and Ross Perot in 1992, it became an emblem of his lack of interest in the race, a visual that communicated "Outta time. Outta here" (p. 33[171]). Loser framing may also arise from opposition attacks that target the credibility, honesty, integrity, or trustworthiness of a candidate (qualities that contribute to the ideal candidate frame), as the Bush campaign highlighted in its advertising against Gore in 2000 and Kerry in 2004. Asked why this strategy would work against Gore if it did not against Bill Clinton, Karl Rove told the *Washington Post*: "Gore lacks the redeeming charm and winning charisma of Bill Clinton."[93] Thus, a candidate's reputation coming into an election, such as Gore's aggressive debating style, inability to connect with voters, and unshakeable wooden demeanor—images that had dogged him since the 1988 Democratic primaries (see Fallows,[172] Kurtz[173])—may invite opposition attacks that frame the candidate in adverse ways and influence subsequent news coverage.

In coverage of marginalized candidates, campaign activities may be described as protest events and candidate statements made to appear false or irrelevant. This is especially true of third-party candidates who receive little coverage in relation to the major party nominees.[175] The loser frame may take on a sharp edge, referring to quixotic quests or candidate attempts to play the role of spoiler. In 2000, Ralph Nader's Green Party candidacy was portrayed largely in terms of his spoiler status, and there was considerable speculation after the election that Gore's narrow defeat was due in part to Nader's presence in the race (see Herszenhorn,[175] Magnusson[176]). The loser frame may feature calls for the fringe candidate to stop taking up valuable airtime during debates and to withdraw so that the real candidates can be heard.[177] The road back from sure loser status is almost impossible for Independent and third-party candidates to overcome. Major party nominees may also be subject to loser framing, yet they are more likely to recover, as Bill Clinton—playing the part of the Comeback Kid—showed in the 1992 election. In 2000, both Al Gore and George W. Bush were portrayed in ways that were consistent with loser framing, Gore as "a nerdy techno-crat without flash" and Bush as an inarticulate dimwit.[134] The *New York Times Magazine* highlighted this problem in a cover story about political humor, mockingly titled "The Stiff Guy vs. the Dumb Guy."[134]

Visual manifestations of the sure loser frame may emerge in opposition to the mass appeal or statesmanship dimensions of the populist campaigner and ideal candidate frames. Lukewarm responses or

Disapproving audience   Small audience

Disapproving attendees at a rally for   Long shot revealing open seats during a
George H. W. Bush   stump speech by George H. W. Bush
1992   1992

Inappropriate behavior   Defiant behavior

George W. Bush and Dick Cheney caught in   Bob Dole defiantly pointing during a
a "private" exchange facing cheering   stump-speech attack on Bill Clinton
crowds at a rally   1996
2000

Figure 3–5 Screen captures from campaign coverage illustrating loser framing

sparse attendance at campaign events would, for example, link the candidate to lack of support.[123,130,131] Signs of nonverbal audience disapproval, including head shaking, frowns, or inattentiveness, may also erode a speaker's authority and character dynamism.[166] Negative audience reaction shots can further reinforce a speaker's lackluster appeal.[167,178] Graber[123] specifically coded for hecklers and other signs of disapproving crowds to establish the incidence of negative candidate portrayals in network news coverage of the 1984 presidential race. Subsequent studies have employed similar categories to assess the valence of photographic depictions of candidates in news magazine coverage of elections (see Moriarty and Popovich[131]). Visual displays of physical weakness, defiance, and inappropriate behavior have also all been shown to undermine perceptions of leadership potential.[179,180] Figure 3–5 offers an assortment of screen capture examples to visually demonstrate the loser frame.

Specific coding categories were developed to measure the visual manifestations of the ideal candidate, populist campaigner, and sure loser frames just described (see Appendix 3). Their prevalence in network news coverage was examined across the four presidential election campaigns to assess whether visual framing by broadcast journalists reflected image handler strategies, evidenced signs of journalistic frame control, or revealed any partisan bias.

IMAGE HANDLER STRATEGIES, 1992–2004

The 1992 Election

The Bush Camp

George H. W. Bush's reelection effort was haunted by the absence of his chief strategist, Lee Atwater, who had played an instrumental role in the 1988 campaign. Atwater was diagnosed with brain cancer and passed away before the 1992 campaign started. His absence is viewed in some circles as the reason the Bush campaign was disjointed, uncoordinated, and riddled with internal conflict.[164,181–183] Three groups were involved in running the Bush reelection effort: the White House, a reelection committee, and Bush's outside consultants.[163] Without a clear market-tested strategy the team pressed on, replicating the 1988 campaign and emphasizing Bush's record as the incumbent.[154] These turned out to be poor choices. Don Sipple, who resigned as a consultant to the campaign, criticized the déjà vu quality of Bush's advertising. "You have a figure who's been president or vice president for 12 years, and the advertising is of minimal value unless you're providing new or additional information" (p. 14[181]). A source from inside the Bush camp told the *Boston Globe*, "We are in a time warp thinking that America hasn't changed and we want to run a 1988 campaign that doesn't exist" (p. 1[182]).

A study in contradictions, George H. W. Bush had embraced a strong populist frame during the 1988 election, projecting a down-home American image as a lover of pork rinds and country music. Yet he governed in an aristocratic style, showing much more concern about foreign policy than domestic affairs.[70] Bush enjoyed unprecedented approval ratings following the Gulf War, which discouraged candidates on the Democratic side from declaring their candidacies until the soft economy finally gave them reason in late 1991. Yet, despite his success in foreign policy, Bush struggled domestically to avert a recession and show that he cared about people. At one point on the campaign trail he awkwardly read off of a cue card he was supposed to expand upon extemporaneously: "Message: I care" (p. 14[183]). Bush projected the image of an upper-class statesman, not a people's president. Shots of Bush family vacations at the president's Kennebunkport estate reinforced this view. For his reelection, Bush knew that he could not run and win as the Yale-educated patrician that he was.[184]

Several blunders during the 1992 campaign illustrated how out of touch Bush was with ordinary Americans. At a grocer's convention, the president looked visibly surprised when shown a checkout-line scanner, a technology that had been operational for 20 years.[185] Moreover, he tried too hard, and awkwardly so, to use the language of common folk. In reference to Al Gore he once said: "He is way out, far out. Far out, man!" (p. 23[184]). At other times he resorted to name-calling, labeling Clinton and Gore as "these two bozos" and referring to Gore as "ozone man" and then just "ozone."[186] In speeches toward the end of the campaign he warned that a Clinton presidency, presumably focused on protecting the environment, would mean "no timber workers, only a bunch of owls," and "no farmers, only a great, big, wet hole out there somewhere if you listen to him" (quoted in Wines[187]). Besides coming across as less than presidential, these awkward attempts to connect with common folk undermined Bush's populist efforts, giving him an atonal quality, as if he were speaking out of key.

In Atwater style (but without Atwater's flair or killer instinct), Bush went on the attack against the Clinton–Gore campaign with negative advertising and a daily "fax attack" to national news media. The first of these peppery assaults charged Bill Clinton with being "the Pinocchio of the political season" (p. 1[182]). While incumbents and challengers typically stay above the fray and send out surrogates to do the dirty work of politics, Bush joined in the mudslinging, bucking the conventional wisdom that an incumbent rarely wins by direct negative campaigning.[154,163]

The Clinton Camp

Clinton also embraced a populist frame in 1992—as a down-home Arkansan from humble origins—emphasizing the themes of hope and compassion.[70,154] When Clinton won the Democratic nomination and found himself behind in the polls, his image handlers responded with a political "Manhattan Project" to refashion the image he had acquired during the campaign of a privileged Rhodes Scholar who had evaded the draft during the Vietnam War and experimented with marijuana.[70,154] Clinton was reintroduced during the Democratic National Convention as a man of the people from a town called Hope—the hardworking son of a poor, single mother.[154,159]

Clinton also hit the talk show circuit, appearing on *The Arsenio Hall Show*, *Oprah*, and *Larry King Live* and fielding questions on MTV about his small-town roots, alcoholic father, and experience of poverty.[188] So enamored were Clinton's image handlers with talk shows that he appeared on one every time his poll numbers dipped; this strategy continued from February all the way through Election Day in November.[155] Clinton was advised to keep away from economic populism that signals class warfare. Instead, he was framed as a different kind of Democrat who cared about the middle class.[154,184] Perhaps most memorably, he made the economy the central issue of his campaign, illustrated by the famous Carville slogan *It's the economy, stupid.*[184]

When the campaign turned nasty, the Clinton team called into question the leadership of the incumbent president. The Clinton team sent actors in chicken suits whenever Bush made a public appearance to visually remind voters that Bush had not yet agreed to debate. The chicken called into question Bush's bravery and willingness to face down his opponents, indirectly reprising a theme from the 1988 campaign—that Bush needed to overcome the "wimp factor." By implication, Bush was a chicken himself, rather than a bold standard-bearer of the Republican Party.[189,190] For the most part, Clinton's image handlers did the attacking through campaign advertising, leaving their candidate to talk about the issues, rally voters, and work the rope lines.

Given the image-handling efforts of the Bush and Clinton teams in 1992, we expect to see both candidates framed in a populist light. There were no strong indications of ideal candidate frame building on either side. Yet, given that compassion developed into a strategic theme for Clinton during the campaign, one would expect this dimension of ideal candidate framing to appear in news coverage. Negative campaigning on both sides is expected to show up at times as loser framing. Clearly, these expectations assume that image handlers succeeded to some extent in their efforts to bypass journalistic frame control.

Findings

As indicated in Table 3–1 and Figure 3–6, Bush was persistently portrayed as more statesmanlike than Clinton. On linkage to patriotic symbols this difference achieved statistical significance,[191] perhaps indicating a campaign strategy to present Bush as a "patriot," in contrast

Table 3–1 Means for Individual Variables and for Frames by Political Party and Election Year

| | Year/Political Party | | | | | | | | | |
| | 1992 | | 1996 | | 2000 | | 2004 | | Overall | |
Variables/Frames	D	R	D	R	D	R	D	R	D	R
Ideal Candidate	**7.60**	**7.70**	**5.79**	**7.79***	**7.11**	**6.47**	**7.75**	**8.13**	**7.07**	**7.49**
Statesman	4.83	5.39	3.33	4.71*	4.32	3.70	5.38	5.39	4.47	4.78
Linked, influentials	.68	.54	.31	.34	.66	.53	.43	.64	.52	.52
Linked, patriotism	.63	1.15*	.56	.82	.59	.47	1.53	1.62	.82	1.00†
Linked, progress	.05	.17†	.05	.08	.20	.19	.15	.15	.12	.15
Linked, entourage	.33	.39	.62	.87	.32	.21	.43	.44	.41	.47
Campaign paraphernalia	.98	.98	.49	.97*	.84	.60	.98	.89	.82	.86
Confetti shower	.08	.15	.00	.05	.14	.16	.18	.05	.10	.11
Wearing a suit	2.10	2.02	1.31	1.58	1.57	1.53	1.70	1.60	1.67	1.68
Compassionate	2.78	2.32	2.46	3.08	2.80	2.77	2.38	2.74	2.61	2.72
Linked, children	.40	.15*	.21	.34	.23	.40	.23	.28	.26	.29
Linked, family	.20	.15	.05	.08	.52	.35	.15	.54*	.24	.28
Linked, women	.43	.41	.49	.66	.32	.37	.30	.33	.38	.44
Linked, religion	.05	.00	.00	.00	.00	.00	.03	.05	.02	.01
Affinity gestures	.96	.73	.59	.89*	1.02	.93	1.18	1.13	.88	.96
Individual interaction	.25	.34	.46	.39	.34	.30	.23	.21	.32	.31
Physical contact	.73	.39†	.67	.71	.36	.42	.28	.21	.50	.43

continued

115

Table 3-1 continued

Variables/Frames	Year/Political Party									
	1992		1996		2000		2004		Overall	
	D	R	D	R	D	R	D	R	D	R
Populist Campaigner	**4.75**	**3.83**	**2.69**	**2.95**	**4.41**	**3.00***	**4.73**	**4.76**	**4.16**	**3.62†**
Mass Appeal	3.65	2.98	1.90	2.34	2.93	2.19	2.78	2.69	2.82	2.55
Linked, celebrities	.10	.12	.10	.16	.27	.19	.43	.51	.23	.24
Large audience	1.18	1.17	.69	.82	.75	.47†	.33	.36	.74	.70
Approving audience	1.35	1.17	.69	.86	1.20	.98	1.20	1.18	1.12	1.05
Crowds interaction	1.03	.51*	.41	.50	.70	.56	.83	.64	.74	.55*
Ordinariness	1.10	.85	.79	.61	1.48	.81*	1.95	2.05	1.34	1.07†
Casual dress	.20	.22	.15	.05	.64	.26*	.85	1.03	.47	.38
Sports dress	.08	.10	.13	.00*	.05	.02	.10	.15	.09	.07
Rolled sleeves	.45	.15*	.00	.00	.64	.33†	.75	.58	.47	2.62*
Linked, ordinary people	.28	.29	.41	.53	.09	.16	.08	.10	.21	.27
Physically active	.10	.10	.10	.03	.07	.05	.18	.23	.11	.10
Sure Loser	**.65**	**.95**	**.44**	**1.45***	**.73**	**.21***	**.74**	**.49†**	**.64**	**.76**
Disapproving audience	.03	.17*	.03	.03	.07	.00†	.03	.03	.04	.06
Small audience	.18	.15	.26	.42	.02	.02	.00	.00	.11	.14
Physically weak	.05	.02	.00	.42*	.00	.00	.00	.00	.01	.11*
Defiance behavior	.38	.59	.13	.58*	.64	.14*	.73	.46*	.47	.43
Inappropriate behavior	.03	.02	.03	.00	.00	.05	.00	.00	.01	.02

D = Democrat, R = Republican. *Statistically significant, †approaching statistical significance.

116

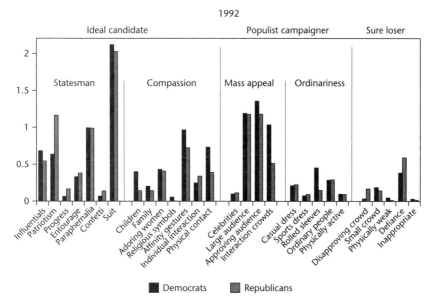

Figure 3–6 Visual framing in the 1992 election

to Clinton, the "draft dodger." Visual associations with technological and economic progress approached significance,[192] with Bush at higher levels. Overall, the composite statesman score was higher for Bush than Clinton, but the difference was not statistically significant. On the other hand, Clinton outscored Bush on the compassion dimension of the ideal candidate frame. In particular, his attention to children[193] and physical contact with constituents[194] achieved visual articulation in the news. This lines up with Clinton's image handler strategies, which emphasized the themes of hope and compassion.

Clinton's compassion also found visual traction in the populist frame, where his signature technique of working the crowds showed up significantly more than for Bush.[195] Figure 3–6 depicts a persistent pattern of Clinton's mass appeal surfacing visually in the news more prominently than for Bush. Of all presidential candidates reported on here, Clinton was shown with the highest levels of mass appeal. Campaigning in a tie, no jacket, and rolled-up sleeves added to his populist image, significantly more than for Bush.[196] Clinton also appeared more ordinary and overall more populist than Bush, but not at statistically significant levels, perhaps revealing a contest between the two campaigns' image-handling teams to consciously craft a populist image for their clients.

Although there were no significant differences between Bush and Clinton in terms of loser framing, Bush was shown significantly[197] more often among disapproving crowds. He also exhibited more defiance than Clinton.

The 1996 Election

The Clinton Camp

Early in the 1996 primaries, Clinton was generating powerful visual images on the campaign trail: enthusiastic crowds, energetic speeches, gregarious working of the rope lines, and an event-filled bus tour. But his pollsters did not see these images translate into substantially higher approval ratings. Consequently, Clinton's image handlers took him back to govern in Washington as an above-the-fray incumbent rather than portraying him as a hard-driving populist campaigner.[198] Without any challengers in the primary, Clinton could afford to stay inside the Beltway. Ceremonies such as bill signings were orchestrated to project the image of a statesman who managed to bring legislative issues such as welfare reform through the Republican-controlled Congress to a successful conclusion[199,200] Consultant Dick Morris convinced Clinton that the more he spent on advertising, the less he had to appear on the hustings. The 1984 Reagan campaign slogan, *It's Morning Again in America*, was appropriated as a campaign theme, with advertisements emphasizing Clinton's presidential achievements.[200,201] Thus, Clinton was absent from the campaign trail for much of 1996. "Right through to the Democratic convention and beyond, the Clinton campaign remained a specter, a flickering cathode ray in the suburbs" (p. 53).[202]

Although Clinton appeared politically vulnerable following the 1994 midterm losses, when he felt the need to publicly assert his constitutional relevance as president, a series of shrewd policy decisions and deftly handled responses to compelling news events facilitated the Comeback Kid's return—yet again—from the political dead.[200] Between the midterm elections and 1996 presidential campaign, Clinton's handling of military interventions in Haiti and Bosnia, the Oklahoma City bombing, and the federal government shutdowns of late 1995 and early 1996, among others, played a significant role in reviving public perceptions of the president.[200,203] By the time the campaign finally got under way, the reservoir of favorable sentiment toward Clinton may have been deep enough that nothing short of an extraordinary challenge or fatal campaign blunder could have undermined his lead. Hence, the moribund, seemingly irrelevant quality of the presidential campaign that year: the memorable news and political reactions that cemented favorable public image occurred at least a year before any ballot was cast. From this perspective, the election may have been decided before it ever started.

Throughout the lackluster fall campaign, Penn and Schoen polls identified traditional social values, specifically crime, drugs, and media violence, as salient voter issues.[70,200] As long as Clinton stood tough on these issues, his image handlers argued, voters would forgive his personal indiscretions. Incidentally, these themes were exactly what Bob Dole ran on. In essence, the Clinton team was able to co-opt and take ownership of traditionally Republican issues, positioning Dole more as an echo than a choice[200,201] The two candidates ran on essentially identical issues, one trying to sound more serious about them than the other. Lewis[202] compared Clinton and Dole to *Time* and *Newsweek*, observing that "no matter how much they claim to differ, they still run the same covers week after week" (p. 161).

The Dole Camp

Among insiders there is little disagreement that the Dole campaign of 1996 was a fiasco.[169,204,205,207] The campaign's most self-defeating elements included the lack of a clear message, Dole's weakness as a hapless campaigner, and a dysfunctional dynamic among top brass back at campaign headquarters. The campaign, for which Dole had given up his post as Senate majority leader, was characterized as a "floundering exercise in muddled messages, riven by conflict and dulled by low morale" (p. 4[200]). Teams were hired and fired as power struggles erupted among key staff.[204,208,209] There were multiple schisms but the core conflict played out between the hired guns—those who believed in focus groups and polling—and those who wanted the campaign to take a more grassroots approach, running on instinct and speeches from the heart.[208,209]

If the Dole campaign had an overarching strategy, it could be loosely characterized as securing endorsements from influentials, promoting a conservative brand of social populism, and engaging in attacks on Clinton's liberalism. Despite the campaign's disarray, Dole was supported by the Republican Party establishment, who remained at his side. In the manner of an old machine–politics campaign, Dole's press briefings became a weekly ritual that featured handlers reading off lists of organizations and people who had endorsed his candidacy.[202,204] Dole's populist appeals derived most noticeably from references to his poor upbringing in small-town America (Russell, Kansas), his long and painful recovery from a serious war injury, and (self-defeatingly) his sense of resentment for people who had not suffered like he had.[210]

On occasion Dole's campaign projected a coherent focus, but his advisors found it difficult to maneuver the candidate into a stable frame. Unlike any other candidate in our sample, Dole refused to be image-handled, rejecting teleprompters and speechwriters and refusing to stay on message. Although he received the same advice as Clinton— that the election was going to be won on social values—Dole disliked sermonizing and thought values were too personal a foundation on which to campaign.[210] Many sources have described Dole that year as an incoherent speaker who referred to himself in the third person, spoke in incomplete sentences, and delivered speeches with no main point.[200,202,207] In keeping with this incoherent image, he joked to reporters, "Don't worry very much about what I say; we're just trying to get good pictures" (p. 105).[200] By the end of the campaign Dole went negative in character attacks on Clinton. As with Bush, he came off as sour, grim, and desperate.[202,211] According to the political reporters at *Newsweek*, "If ever there was a candidate not destined to win, it was Bob Dole" (p. 199).[200]

Given the image handler strategies (or lack thereof) during the 1996 campaign, we expect Clinton to receive consistent ideal candidate framing in network news coverage while Dole is expected to appear in the populist and sure loser frames significantly more often—unless journalistic frame control intervened to take Dole's visual framing in an entirely different direction.

Findings

Ironically, Dole received robust ideal candidate framing in network news coverage of the 1996 general election. He appeared significantly more statesmanlike,[212] seemed more compassionate,[213] and displayed more ideal qualities[214] than Clinton. In fact, Dole was visually portrayed as more compassionate than any other candidate over the four elections analyzed. Dole's image handlers were also clearly fond of campaign

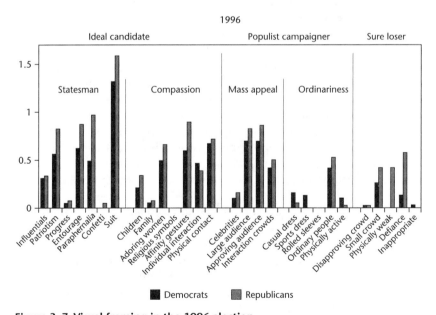

Figure 3–7 Visual framing in the 1996 election

paraphernalia when staging events[215] (perhaps something they could agree on). Overall, these findings do not align with the strategies of the two campaigns, perhaps indicating journalistic frame control.

Dole did receive more loser framing than Clinton, however.[216] Of all the candidates examined in this study, Dole was visually portrayed as the most loserlike. Images of physical weakness[217] and defiance[218] manifested in coverage of the election at statistically higher levels than for Clinton. This pattern perhaps reflects the anger and frustration of a man who was not a major optimist to begin with and whose image handlers were unable to modify his affect.

Interestingly, Clinton's trademark compassion was not reflected as strongly in network news coverage as it was during the 1992 campaign. The president's efforts to pose as a statesman also did not make it onto the news all that much, nor did his attempts at populism. Clinton did appear in athletic attire more often than Dole, mainly due to his televised jogging performances.[219] Not surprisingly, given his war injury, Dole was never seen in sports clothing. Figure 3–7 shows a consistent pattern of higher scores for Dole across variables, including those of the sure loser frame.

The 2000 Election

The Gore Camp

The Democratic races of 2000 and 2004 were masterminded by renowned consultant Bob Shrum, who despite several attempts has yet to engineer a presidential victory. Regardless of candidate, Shrum's trademark frame is economic populism, with a clear focus on health care, jobs, and social security issues.[70,97,220] Throughout the 2000 campaign season, Al Gore embraced a populist campaign slogan, *The People versus the Powerful*, and followed a strict market-tested approach to campaigning orchestrated by Shrum. This obsession with market testing backfired, however, and is widely cited as a key reason that Gore appeared stiff, unbelievable, and unlikable. Gore "shoe-horned himself inside the Message Box that had been created for him—because he had been polled and focus-grouped and dial-grouped and market-tested *literally* to the point of distraction" (p. 158[70])—and political inauthenticity.

Journalists picked up on Gore's populist phoniness and reported on it. When Gore showed up in blue jeans at a fund-raiser sponsored by the Democratic National Committee in Washington, *USA Today* ran a story that asked: "Whom did the Democrats think they were fooling with their populist pretensions at a fundraiser that raked in big bucks from trial lawyers, teachers' unions and other selfless supporters of good government?" (p. 4A[221]).

Gore's public persona was marked by inexplicable moments of awkwardness, followed by panicked after-the-fact reactions. Klein[70] (p. 139) describes Gore's peculiar behavior in 2000 as an odd oxymoron—a "panicky robot" mode of campaigning. Similar analogies were used to characterize other Gore qualities that image handlers could not control. In describing the vice president as a reactive campaigner who distrusted intuition, Marshall[222] compared Gore to a toy robot that only knows one direction once wound up. "Unless he marches straight into a brick wall he may never realize when to switch directions" (p. 2[222]). To save Gore from himself, feminist author Naomi Wolf, known for her 1991 book *The Beauty Myth*, made an entrance early in the campaign as a high-paid ($15,000 per month) consultant to offer the candidate "advice on everything from how to win the women's vote to shirt-and-tie combinations."[223] Although her exact role in the campaign was nebulous— one campaign insider described her as a "wardrobe consultant"—she successfully argued that Gore was a Beta male who needed to take on the Alpha male in the Oval Office before the public would see him as the top dog.[223] Thus, Gore's distancing from Bill Clinton during the campaign seemed to be motivated by consultant advice. Shrum and associates chafed at Wolf's role in the campaign, as they labored to keep Gore focused on poll-driven priorities.

After allowing extensive coaching and image handling, Gore gradually became frustrated with his coterie of consultants and resentful toward his critics. Over time he even simmered about responses to his stiffness and moments of public awkwardness. In preparation for the debates, identical studio sets were built and Gore's practice performances were taped and taken to dial groups to assess which answers were favorably received.[70] Gore resisted this style of preparation, and people close to him viewed his disastrous performance in the debates against Bush as a purposeful rebellion against his image handlers. During debate practice Gore's advisors pointed out that his tendency to sigh came across as arrogant and impatient. They urged him to keep his aggressive nonverbal behavior in check, even drawing a line on the preparation stage, which they made him practice not crossing. But during the televised debates, Gore—a consummate debater before the election—sighed often, particularly during the first debate, and physically approached Bush in the third debate. He also refused to remain in rehearsed character: "Three different Gores showed up: the lion, the lamb, and the stalker" (p. 156[70]). Bush showed up as himself—in a simplistic but coherent and generally likable way.

The Bush Camp

Unlike Gore, whose image handlers wrongly assumed that their candidate's character would emerge by espousing focus group–tested policy positions, Bush's handlers worked directly on framing a populist image for their candidate. In particular, Bush was presented as a caring Republican—a *compassionate conservative*, in the memorable phrase of Karl

Rove.[70,222] The Bush campaign sized up Gore's public image and constructed their populist frame as an antithesis to their opponent's persona: charitable, honest, plainspoken, and anti-Washington. What followed were consistently sharp attacks on Gore's character and reputation, tactics drawn from the playbook of Rove's mentor, the late Lee Atwater.[224]

The half-truths that Gore uttered when he was caught in panic mode were used to attack another character weakness: dishonesty, which the Bush camp used to associate Gore with Clinton—exactly what Gore was trying to avoid. Gore's verbal blunders included references to himself as the father of the Internet and claims that he and Tipper were the Harvard couple that *Love Story* was based on. These and other false assertions were publicly disproved at Gore's expense. In stark contrast, Bush's advisors promoted their candidate as someone who would restore honor, trust, and respect to the Oval Office.[36,222]

Given these tactics and contingencies, we would expect both Gore and Bush to receive populist framing during the 2000 campaign, with Gore at times more prominently cast in the loser role than Bush. Given that Bush ran on a theme of compassionate conservatism, we expect his compassion scores to be higher than Gore's. Considering the lack of strong evidence of ideal candidate image-building attempts, we do not expect either candidate to receive much ideal candidate framing, at least not along the statesman dimension of the frame.

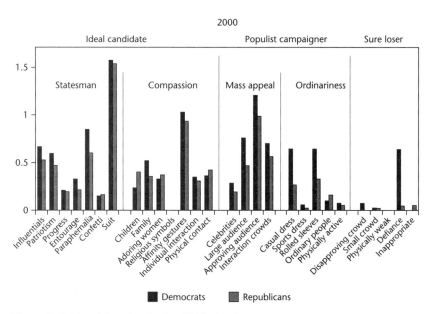

Figure 3–8 Visual framing in the 2000 election

Findings

Again, somewhat unexpectedly, Bush and Gore received noticeable and similar ideal candidate framing. Closer inspection of the two ideal candidate subframes did not reveal significant differences: Gore was visually represented as more statesmanlike than Bush on all measures, except for celebratory confetti showers (see Fig. 3–8 and Table 3–1). Bush, running as a compassionate conservative, had a slight edge on Gore for the compassion subframe. Interestingly, Gore was shown interacting with individuals on the campaign trail more than Bush, but his stiffness surfaced in the form of less physical contact with supporters. These differences were not statistically significant, however.

The populist and loser frames brought significant differences to the surface. Gore was visually represented as more populist than Bush.[225] The Shrum strategy to transform a wooden candidate into a man of the people to some extent worked. In fact, Gore outscored Bush on all mass appeal variables (see Fig. 3–8). Gore was visually linked to large crowds significantly more than Bush[226] and appeared visually more ordinary.[227] Dress variables accounted for most of this difference—Gore was featured more often in casual clothing (perhaps a result of Naomi Wolf's advice),[228] and with a tie, no jacket, and sleeves rolled up[229] more often than Bush. On some measures, such as linkages to ordinary people, Bush appeared more populist than Gore, but not at significant levels.

The analysis also revealed scattered signs of Gore's "panicky robot" mode that Klein[70] describes, particularly in the form of aggressive and defiant gestures. Gore was shown exhibiting significantly more aggression and defiance than Bush.[230] Combined with visual linkage to disapproving crowds,[231] these gestures associated Gore with the loser frame at statistically higher levels than Bush.[232] Interestingly, the Republican Party's control over friendly audiences at campaign events kept Bush at zero for the disapproving-crowds category; there simply were none for the cameras to record.

The 2004 Election

The Bush Camp

In the Rove tradition, the Bush campaign was seemingly more focused on John Kerry than on their own candidate. Polling evidence revealed that the American people considered the president a flawed but ultimately strong leader. Bush's team pursued a two-pronged attack on Kerry, focusing on two perceived character flaws, which his statements and actions kindled: his image as an elitist and as an indecisive flip-flopper.[116] Tempered by the War in Iraq and the ongoing War on Terror, the 2004 race brought to the fore voter trust of the candidates to make future decisions based on shared values (Mellman, quoted in Jamieson[116]). The need for such straight talk worked to Bush's advantage (p. 222[70]).

Perhaps the most persuasive sound bite uttered in 2004 was Bush's line, "You may not always agree with me but you'll always know where I stand." This sound bite characterized the president as a strong and straight-talking leader, in contrast to the construction of Kerry as flip-flopper (p. 151[116]). The line also upheld the populist message promoted by the Bush team, while invoking the specter of national security, another Bush strength. In Liz Cheney's words, Bush was not "running a feel-good campaign. He wasn't saying it's morning [again] in America" (quoted in Jamieson, p. 127).[116] Instead, he aimed for a different brand of certitude: that the country was at war but he was going to keep the American people safe. "This straight talk helped his credibility" (LaCivita, quoted in Jamieson, p. 216).[116]

The straight-talk motif, a reprise of John McCain's "straight-talk express" from the 2000 campaign, positioned the president as a patriarch and emphasized his concern for his larger family, the nation. Visually, this meant higher campaign visibility for the first family, since "it is a family now in the White House that deals with the nation, as opposed to just a president" (p. 179[233]). Much as Dick Morris had suggested to Bill Clinton in 1996,[13] Republican pollsters figured out that the image of the president as protector of the nation/family resonated with voters. Latinos in particular identified with Bush the family man and strong leader.[116,156] Voter connection to the human side of Bush aided in "boosting the numbers" (p. 179[233]), a campaign strategy symbolized by the infamous "Ashley" advertisement, in which a young woman whose mother died in the World Trade Center attacks recounts how President Bush comforted her at a campaign rally: "He's the most powerful man in the world and all he wanted to do is make sure I'm safe" (see http://www.youtube.com/watch?v=LWA052-B148).

The Kerry Camp

While the Bush 2004 campaign was widely described as disciplined, focused, and well organized, the Kerry campaign earned the opposite reputation. Joe Lockhart, a former Clinton press secretary and strategist who advised Kerry, said the campaign attempted to synchronize their advertising and news coverage but were not always successful. Internal divisions within Kerry's staff—reminiscent of Bob Dole's hapless run in 1996—contributed to the campaign's strategic missteps. Once again, the influence of consultant Bob Shrum, who advised Gore in 2000, was a decisive factor in the Democrats' loss.

When Shrum (and partners Mike Donilon and Tad Devine) first made overtures to assist the Kerry team, Kerry envisioned a limited role for the celebrity consultant, who had a 0-for-7 record for winning presidential campaigns. "I'll never use him as a strategist," Kerry was quoted as saying, "but I would like to have him around for speeches and debate prep" (quoted in Klein,[70] p. 186). Against the backdrop of the 2000 Gore calamity, Kerry's campaign staff worried about Shrum's reputation as an operator who would do anything to "gain absolute control over the candidate" (p. 191[70]). They also worried about a lack of focus, planning, and leadership in the campaign effort, which political reporters saw as "symptoms of the Democrats' quadrennial campaign management miasma" (p. 191[70]). Despite these concerns, Shrum eventually took charge of running the campaign.[234]

Similar to Gore, Shrum's strategy for Kerry was to turn to old populist issues: health care, education, and jobs (Donilon, quoted in Jamieson).[116] The commitment to the populist frame continued somewhat obliviously through Bush campaign and interest group (Swift Boat) attacks on Kerry's military and voting record. In fact, Kerry was advised not to go negative by defending his character but rather to stick to the populist frame of fighting for Middle America. He broke out of this frame once, in a speech on August 19, 2004, in Boston, attacking the smear campaign on his military record, but resumed his "fighting for the middle class" theme almost immediately (Cahill and Donilon, quoted in Jamieson).[116] Images of Kerry windsurfing, snowboarding, and skiing—expensive and elitist sports—did not bring credibility or visual coherence to his middle-class message. Kerry struggled to capitalize on voter anger toward the Bush administration's foreign policy adventurism and had difficulty connecting with voters. Kerry won the debates, by most accounts, not because he appeared human or caring but because Shrum thoroughly prepared him for an intellectual performance.

Given these developments, we would expect the populist frame surfacing prominently for both Bush and Kerry in 2004. Moreover, if the Bush camp succeeded in turning attention to Kerry, one would also expect to see a stronger loser frame emerging for Kerry than Bush. At the same time, Bush's ability to connect with people and the strategy to present him as a father figure is likely to be reflected in the compassion dimension of the ideal candidate frame.

Findings

Considering the networks' portrayal of Bush and Kerry as ideal candidates, they both received similar visual treatment (see Table 3–1 and Fig. 3–9). A closer look at the composite subthemes of this frame reveals that Bush was portrayed noticeably more as a statesman and as a compassionate leader than Kerry—but not at statistically significant levels. Importantly, the Bush campaign's emphasis on the president as a family man, in the post-9/11 era, made it onto the evening news at statistically higher levels than for Kerry.[235]

The Kerry campaign devoted considerably more resources on pomp and spectacle (e.g., confetti showers and campaign paraphernalia)

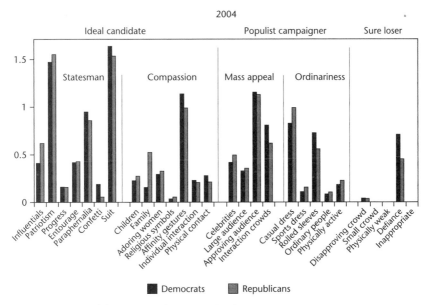

Figure 3–9 Visual framing in the 2004 election

than the Bush reelection team—or at least, these images found their way onto network news more often than for Bush. Perhaps the Bush campaign felt that the sober message of the president, that it was not "morning in America," made celebratory images in a post-9/11 election inappropriate. Instead, the campaign worked at developing a linkage between their candidate and political influentials who could help steer the nation on a desired course (see Fig. 3–9).

In terms of populist framing, the two candidates were visually depicted with almost the same amount of mass appeal and ordinariness. Given this parity, the crucial matter seems to be which candidate wore these visual frames more comfortably. According to several observers, populism suited Bush much better than it did Kerry.

The results for loser framing shed further light on campaigns' success in promoting desired images. Rove and associates managed to control defiant nonverbal behavior in Bush while their relentless campaign to frame Kerry as an unpatriotic flip-flopper probably sent Kerry into a defensive nonverbal mode, observable through statistically higher defiance scores for Kerry than for Bush.[236] These scores resulted in more loser framing for Kerry, at a level approaching statistical significance.[237] Of all eight candidates examined over these four general election campaigns, Bush in 2004 was portrayed the most prominently as both an ideal candidate and populist campaigner.

General Findings

Considering overall framing scores for all years combined, the Democratic strategy of presenting presidential candidates in a populist frame appears more frequently in network news coverage than for Republicans (see Table 3–1).[238] Images of Democratic candidates working the crowds have assumed signature status at campaign events, distinguishing their visual portrayals from Republicans.[239] Democrats also signal their ordinariness more clearly than Republicans,[240] especially by the way they dress. Campaigning in a tie and no jacket with shirtsleeves rolled up has become a Democratic candidate trademark.[241]

Republicans, by contrast, are portrayed more often than Democrats in an ideal candidate frame, with linkages to patriotic symbols.[242] Republicans also appear more often as sure losers, but not at statistically significant levels, and this finding is probably driven by Bob Dole's fall from a stage on the campaign trail in 1996 (see Table 3–1). The physical weakness scores for Dole in that election produced a higher overall loser framing score for Republicans than Democrats, at statistically significant levels.[243]

Our analysis of visual framing is motivated not by concerns about media bias (for an analysis of visual bias, see Chapter 5) but rather by the strategies employed by campaigns to promote affirmative candidate images. That said, these results do not provide evidence of systematic journalistic bias. There is no consistent pattern of favoring one political party across the four election years examined here. Ideal candidate and populist framing, which can be regarded as favorable visual representation (depending on how well the frame fits), emerged prominently for Republican and Democratic candidates during different election years. The sure loser frame also surfaced among both party's candidates across election years: George H. W. Bush in 1992, Bob Dole in 1996, Al Gore in 2000, and John Kerry in 2004. Overall, there is more evidence of positive visual framing of candidates than negative, which is consistent with findings of character coverage from previous elections (e.g., Graber[123]).

CONCLUSION

The findings from this analysis of candidate images suggest that visual frames orchestrated by image handlers do make their way into network news coverage of presidential elections, offering voters both idealized and derisive depictions of candidates. The process of visual frame construction is more nuanced than examinations of media bias or valence framing have revealed in previous research. Consideration of campaign efforts to engage in specific frame-building strategies provides a rich context for analysis and allows assessments about the role of image handlers in shaping news coverage. The struggle for frame control between these two players, journalists and image handlers, in the election drama is greatly underdocumented. Instead, researchers seem to be set on assessing ideological bias as a property of an all-powerful press that either deliver or fall short on their promise of fairness and balance. What we report here is certainly not offered as evidence of causal relationships between image handler strategies and news output; yet our data do provide some insight into how well image handler strategies match the visual outcome of candidate portrayals on the evening news.

Systematic assessments of image handler influences on television news coverage, or, as campaign consultants refer to it, *earned media*, do not exist. The work that has focused on the role of image handlers tends to take a case-study approach, revealing who these professional advocates are and how they think about their work; the focus of such studies is often on political advertisements rather than on the process of news construction. Perhaps because consultants operate largely in the shadows, away from public view, they are viewed with skepticism and have garnered considerable criticism about their role in election campaigns. Yet there are alternative views on image handling as a necessary service to candidates and officeholders. They are to politics "what attorneys are to the legal system. In an adversarial system both are duty-bound to be the best advocates they can be for their clients" (p. 77[245]). James Carville is unapologetic about his service to clients: "I am a political professional. I am paid to win races. . . . If you're looking for somebody objective, don't talk to me" (p. 76[245]).

Despite the bravado that image handlers occasionally show, suggesting they can literally sell any candidate, they clearly cannot. And they are aware of their limitations, reporting in one survey on the difficulty of marketing a mediocre candidate or one who holds unpopular views.[37] As Republican consultant Bob Goodman put it, a living candidate does not allow for the flexibility in image making that a bar of soap does (p. 144[246]). Whether image handlers admit this to their clients is not clear. The hard reality is that in every election one side will lose. Information from within campaigns and the data we report here points to a clear standard for success: an unambiguous message backed by a character frame that the candidate can wear comfortably.

For the Democrats, the frame-building efforts of the Clinton campaigns worked. Populism represented a good fit for Clinton, who embraced his humble origins as a son of Hope, Arkansas. The populist frame certainly seemed to be a more authentic match for Clinton than for George H. W. Bush, who campaigned as a people's president in 1988 but had a full term as an incumbent to remind voters that he was something other than what his campaign image had suggested. Pursuing populism again in 1992 was not a good decision for Bush. Even though we found evidence of visual linkages to the statesman subframe in our analysis, the Bush campaign ran on a populist theme, miscasting the incumbent president in an ill-fitting role.

Clinton's 1996 campaign translated into an unspectacular visual show on network news, particularly in comparison to Dole's haphazard election bid. Reinforcing these findings, a study of newspaper photographs found that Dole received more visual coverage in the *New York Times* than Clinton in 1996.[148] The Clinton campaign strategy was to keep the president in Washington as much as possible, showing how he could govern on a soft populist platform while moving to the right on values issues, thereby inoculating himself from Republican attacks. In that election, Clinton emerged as a winner perhaps more as a result of Dole's incoherent campaign strategy than his own impressiveness on the campaign trail; for a variety of reasons, the outcome that year seemed to have been determined well in advance of the actual campaign (see Bucy and Newhagen).[203]

The 2000 and 2004 campaigns represented consecutive matchups between Democratic consultant Bob Shrum and Bush strategist Karl Rove for successful populist image framing. By several accounts, the Republican campaigns were superbly disciplined, coherent, and focused on attacking the opponent's character. Our analysis presented visual evidence for both of these strategies—attacking Kerry and presenting the president as a populist campaigner. In both elections populist frames emerged prominently in network news coverage for Bush, who comfortably slipped into reassuring largely favorable crowds with his ordinariness. At the same time, Democrats were pegged in the loser frame after failing in their attempts at constructing a populism of their own. Insiders who have observed Rove describe him as a hired gun who wages psychological warfare on his opponents, turning their record into a prolonged character attack and unnerving them to the point of drifting into defensiveness, which may ultimately result in loser framing. Our findings support this observation.

Shrum's efforts at populist frame building also surfaced in network news coverage of the 2000 and 2004 presidential elections, in some ways even stronger than Rove's. But the Democrats' doggedness in pursuing populist images regardless of candidate had awkward and counterproductive outcomes for both Gore and Kerry. In essence, over two consecutive elections Shrum tried to out-Rove the Bush campaign by fitting two brainy aristocrats into a populist frame. At a post-2004 election debriefing, Bush advisor Alex Castellanos remarked to Shrum, "Your friend, James Carville, on *Meet the Press* the other day said something interesting. He said that he thought the Democratic Party had no narrative. There are lots of words we could substitute for narrative: ideology, a coherent set of beliefs, a North Star" (quoted in Jamieson, p. 137).[116]

Our data cannot confirm this charge. In fact, Democrats do seem to be—at least visually—wedded to a populist frame. But perhaps what Castellanos was trying to articulate is that Gore and Kerry did not fit comfortably into their consultant-constructed frames and, as a result, had trouble staying "in frame," as it were. Klein[70] notes that Democrats have become more dependent on image handlers than Republicans and their ability to communicate with voters has been more "uncomfortable, more opaque, more tortured" (p. 18). Shrum's choice of populist framing for Gore and Kerry was perhaps unfortunate—certainly choices that will not survive in political history as shining examples of image-handler service to political candidates. Despite Shrum's insistence, even several years after the 2004 election, that Gore and Kerry are true populists—many observers still regard them as blue-blooded elites with a social conscience. Candidates in this mold are more suited for compassionate statesman framing than populism. Marty Kaplan, a former speechwriter for Walter Mondale, observed during the 2004 election that "Gore's populism seemed more poll-generated than organic to his history and character," adding, "if populism did not quite fit Al Gore, it doesn't fit the patrician John Kerry in the least" (quoted in Auletta,[97] p. 75; see also Harris and Halperin[246]).

Shrum also underestimated the power of visual awkwardness in mouthing the words of a speechwriter. According to journalistic accounts, Shrum believes that the campaign message should focus on policies and words, in the way a debater or a speechwriter—not an image handler—might think[97] (see also Parry-Giles[248]). From this vantage point, sound and image bites are likely to signal inauthenticity, which is what our data indicate. These messages are captured through the unforgiving eye of a camera and scrutinized by an audience equipped with innate detection skills evolved over millions of years to recognize visual signs of leadership. In 2000, and again in 2004, political commentators did not fail to notice that both Al Gore and John Kerry were uncomfortable in their newly fitted populist skin. As Edelman[249] has noted, inauthentic political performances create ambivalence and skepticism about both individual leaders and the broader political process. In the words of one image handler, "[I]f someone doesn't come across as real . . . they're not going to be believable in their content either" (Carrick, quoted in Trebay).[152]

Perhaps image handler mishaps act as safety valves in the democratic process. "We're becoming a little more error free," a Republican consultant observed at the beginning of the Reagan era. "But we really don't know a great deal. If we knew more we would be dangerous" (Goodman, quoted in Sabato,[10] p. 17). Or perhaps not, as Klein[70] has argued: "Al Gore or John Kerry might have seemed more plausible as human beings if they'd had advisers who'd understood them better" (p. 234).

NOTES

1. Visual framing, as with other key terms elaborated in this book such as *image bite*, *visual bias*, and *hedonic leader display*, does not appear in prominent reference sources, such as *Safire's New Political Dictionary*.[2] Although introduced as a research term by anthropologist Gregory Bateson in 1972 and elaborated on by sociologist Erving Goffman[3] in a seminal book titled *Frame Analysis: An Essay on the Organization of Experience* a few years later (see also Gitlin[4]), framing is treated as a new term in politics. As with other aspects of political experience, the emphasis is placed on the verbal dimension of framing—how political issues, ideas, and candidates are described—rather than how they are portrayed (for an academic survey of framing research, most of which emphasizes verbal characterizations, see Reese, Gandy, and Grant;[5] for a journalistic account, see Bai[6]).

   Conservative pollster Frank Luntz[7] has helped to popularize the concept by showing how public opinion about policies or politicians shifts when different language is employed. Luntz, who worked with Newt Gingrich to formulate the Contract with America in 1994, famously recast the federal estate tax for citizens applicable at the time of death as an onerous "death tax," turning opinion against this time-honored policy. On the left, Berkeley linguist George Lakoff[8] has assumed a prominent role advising liberal candidates and groups. Lakoff's main advice is to reject conservative framing of issues, such as tax relief and family values, and instead employ arguments and phrases that tap deep-seated progressive narratives (e.g., championing *effective* government rather than *smaller* government, viewing taxes as an *investment in the common good* rather than an *unfair burden* on individuals and businesses).

   Luntz and Lakoff both assume that controlling the language of key issues will enable candidates and parties to position themselves favorably to voters. But on television, calibrating language to sell candidates and ideas is only part of the battle. As with communication researchers who ignore news imagery, neither Luntz nor Lakoff have systematically considered the impact of political visuals on candidate impression formation, although political operatives on both sides of the aisle have had an intuitive sense of visual influence at least since the Kennedy–Nixon debates of 1960.

2. Safire, William. 1993. *Safire's new political dictionary: The definitive guide to the new language of politics*. New York: Random House.

3. Goffman, Erving. 1974. *Frame analysis: An essay on the organization of experience*. Boston: Northeastern University Press.

4. Gitlin, Todd. 1980. *The whole world is watching: Mass media in the making and unmaking of the New Left*. Berkeley: University of California Press.

5. Reese, Stephen D., Oscar H. Gandy Jr., and August E. Grant. 2001. *Framing public life: Perspectives on media and our understanding of the social world*. Mahwah, NJ: Lawrence Erlbaum Associates.

6. Bai, Matt. 2005, July 17. The framing wars. *New York Times Magazine*, p. 38.

7. Luntz, Frank. 2007. *Words that work: It's not what you say, it's what people hear*. New York: Hyperion.

8. Lakoff, George. 2002. *Moral politics: How liberals and conservatives think*. 2nd ed. Chicago: University of Chicago Press.

9. Nimmo, Dan. 1976, September. Political image makers and the mass media. *Annals of the American Academy of Political and Social Science*, pp. 33–44.

10. Sabato, Larry J. 1981. *The rise of political consultants: New ways of winning elections*. New York: Basic Books.

11. Neustadt, Richard E. 1980. *Presidential power: The politics of leadership from FDR to Carter*. New York: John Wiley.

12. Cook, Corey. 2002. The permanence of the "permanent campaign": George W. Bush's public presidency. *Presidential Studies Quarterly* 32(4):753–764.

13. Waterman, Richard, Robert Wright, and Gilbert St. Clair. 1999. *The image-is-everything presidency*. Boulder, CO: Westview Press.

14. Kinder, Donald R. 1986. Presidential character revisited. In *Political cognition: The 19th annual Carnegie symposium on cognition*, ed. Richard R. Lau and David O. Sears, pp. 233–256. Hillsdale, NJ: Lawrence Erlbaum Associates.

15. Nelson, Michael. 1988. Evaluating the presidency. In *The presidency and the political system*, ed. Michael Nelson, pp. 5–28. Washington, DC: CQ Press.

16. Raichur, Arvind, and Richard W. Waterman. 1993. The presidency, the public, and the expectations gap. In *The presidency reconsidered*, ed. Richard W. Waterman, pp. 1–21. Itasca, IL: F. E. Peacock.

17. Stimson, James A. 1976. Public support for American presidents: A cyclical model. *Public Opinion Quarterly* 40:1–21.

18. Seen from the perspective of image construction, "election campaigns are fought not 'on the issues' but on the themes" (p. 55[9]), where voters respond to a political package, "not necessarily the reality behind it" (p. 11[13]).

19. Almond, Gabriel A., and Sidney Verba. 1963. *The civic culture: Political attitudes and democracy in five nations*. Princeton, NJ: Princeton University Press.

20. Lipset, Seymour Martin. 1960. *Political man: The social bases of politics*. Garden City, NY: Doubleday.

21. Kerry's campaign was heavily criticized for not initially countering the Swift Boat ads, which began airing in early August (thus violating two cardinal rules of politics: to immediately hit back when attacked, and to not allow a positive to turn into a negative), which political observers attributed to his decline in the polls.[22] In late August the campaign made a small media buy to answer the accusations but, as *Newsweek* reported, "the Kerry high command failed to see the potential for damage until it was too late" (p. 92[22]). The pattern was eerily similar to Michael Dukakis's reluctance to counter the negative attacks against him by Vice President George H. W. Bush during the 1988 campaign. The attacks on Dukakis, also launched in August, drove up the Massachusetts governor's negative ratings and eventually eroded a 17-point lead. Reflecting on the Swift Boat episode, Kerry's campaign manager, Tad Devine, later observed that "one of our big mistakes in '04 was in listening a bit too much to the swing voters who kept telling us to 'accentuate the positive . . . the consensus was that we should just let it peter out'" (quoted in Vitello).[23]

22. Thomas, Evan, and *Newsweek's* Special Project Team. 2004, November 15. How Bush did it; the vets attack. *Newsweek*, pp. 90–104.

23. Vitello, Paul. 2008, August 17. How to erase that smea . . . *New York Times*, p. WK3.

24. Stanley, Alessandra. 2008, January 29. Camelot '08 overshadows Bush speech. *New York Times*, p. A20.

25. Iyengar, Shanto, and Jennifer A. McGrady. 2007. *Media politics: A citizen's guide*. New York: W. W. Norton.

26. Miller, Joanne M., and Jon A. Krosnick. 2000. News media impact on the ingredients of presidential evaluations. *American Journal of Political Science* 44(2):295–309.

27. Druckman, James N., and Justin W. Holmes. 2004. Does presidential rhetoric matter? Priming and presidential approval. *Presidential Studies Quarterly* 34:755–778.

28. Mendelsohn, Matthew. 1996. The media and interpersonal communications. *Journal of Politics* 58(1):112–25.

29. Kornblut, Anne E. 2008, January 8. "It's not easy," an emotional Clinton says. *Washington Post*, p. A9.

30. During a nationally televised debate broadcast by ABC News the weekend before the primary, Clinton was questioned about her likability ratings among New Hampshire voters. In response to the suggestion that voters there seemed to like Obama more, Clinton quipped, "Well, that hurts my feelings . . . but I'll try to go on." Obama responded by saying, "You're likable enough, Hillary." Clinton's efforts to present herself as more likable in the last few days of the primary were apparent to political observers.[31]

31. Dowd, Maureen. 2008, January 10. Tracks of winner's tears could lead up to the Rose Garden path. *New York Times*, p. A11.

32. Givhan, Robin. 2008, January 8. A chink in the steely façade of Hillary Clinton. *Washington Post*, p. C1.

33. Powell, Michael. 2008, January 9. Retooled campaign and loyal voters add up. *New York Times*, p. A14.

34. De Vries, Walter. 1989. American campaign consulting: Trends and concerns. *PS: Political Science and Politics* 22:21–25.

35. Farrell, David M., Robin Kolodny, and Stephen Medvic. 2001. Parties and campaign professionals in a digital age. *Harvard International Journal of Press/Politics* 6(4):11–30.

36. Schultz, David A., ed. 2004. *Lights, camera, campaign! Media, politics, and political advertising*. New York: Peter Lang.

37. Thurber, James A., Candice J. Nelson, and David A. Dulio. 2000. Portrait of campaign consultants. In *Campaign warriors: The role of political consultants in elections*, ed. James A. Thurber and Candice J. Nelson, pp. 10–36. Washington, DC: Brookings Institution.

38. This last point is not trivial, given the debate over the role of money in politics (see, for example, Broder,[39] Corrado,[40] Drew[41]). Since the early 1980s, media consultants have negotiated their fees as a percentage of campaign spending on television advertising rather than settling on a flat rate or billing by the hour. Not only does this secure substantial income off of campaigns but it also camouflages consultant earnings that are reported as part of advertising budgets. From anecdotal accounts, consultants receive between 7% and 15% of campaign spending on advertising—and this figure is often supplemented by full reimbursement for production costs, a monthly consulting fee, and a postelection victory bonus.[10,42] In all, consultants receive about 20% of the average campaign budget. While

the Federal Election Commission requires campaigns to report all contributions of $200 or more, the accounting of how that money is spent is less scrutinized. Since consulting fees and television advertising spending are not separated on FEC campaign reports, there is no way to determine with any accuracy how much was paid to television stations for advertising and how much of this spending represented consulting commissions. With few exceptions (e.g., Glasser,[43] Shapiro[42]), journalists have not been particularly committed watchdogs on this matter, perhaps due to reliance on consultants as news sources.

39. Broder, David S. 2000. *Democracy derailed: Initiative campaigns and the power of money*. New York: Harcourt.

40. Corrado, Anthony. 2005. An overview of campaign finance law. In *Guide to political campaigns in America*, ed. Paul S. Herrnson, Colton C. Campbell, Marni Ezra, and Stephen K. Medvic, pp. 85–104. Washington, DC: CQ Press.

41. Drew, Christopher. 2007, December 25. Democrats try to rein in fees on consulting. *New York Times*, p. A1.

42. Shapiro, Walter. 2006, May 9. The greedy truth about media consultants. http://www.salon.com/news/feature/2006/05/09/campaign_consultants. Accessed November 24, 2007.

43. Glasser, Susan B. 2000, May 1. Winning a stake in a losing race; ad commissions enriched strategists. *Washington Post*, p. A1.

44. Friedenberg, Robert V. 1999. A prehistory of media consulting for political campaigns. In *The Manship School guide to political communication*, ed. David D. Perlmutter, pp. 11–18. Baton Rouge: Louisiana State University Press.

45. Herrnson, Paul S. 2005. The evolution of political campaigns. In *Guide to political campaigns in America*, ed. Paul S. Herrnson, Colton C. Campbell, Marni Ezra, and Stephen K. Medvic, pp. 19–36. Washington, DC: CQ Press.

46. "The rise of the political machine drastically altered the nature of political campaigns," Herrnson[45] (p. 21) has noted. "The principled discussions of the early days among elites were replaced by rallies, speeches, torchlight parades, and other popular events designed to convey a message and mobilize the masses."

47. Salmore, Stephen A., and Barbara G. Salmore. 1985. *Candidates, parties, and campaigns: Electoral politics in America*. Washington, DC: CQ Press.

48. Bush political strategist Karl Rove, who reportedly has described Hanna as his role model, compares Bush's 2004 electoral victory with McKinley's in 1896, which ushered in a long period of Republican dominance.[49] Most pundits doubt that 2004 represents a fundamental partisan realignment, however.

49. Blumenthal, Sidney. 2007, August 13. We'll go no more a-Rove-ing. *Salon.com*. http://www.salon.com/opinion/blumenthal/2007/08/13/karl_rove. Accessed February 5, 2008.

50. Beniger, James R. 1986. *The control revolution: Technological and economic origins of the information society*. Cambridge, MA: Harvard University Press.

51. Tye, Larry. 1998. *The father of spin: Edward L. Bernays and the birth of public relations*. New York: Crown.

52. Bernays, Edward. 1928/2004. *Propaganda*. Brooklyn, New York: Ig Publishing.

53. Ewen, Stuart. 1996. *PR! A social history of spin*. New York: Basic Books.

54. Bernays wrote several influential tracts on public opinion management, including *Crystallizing Public Opinion*,[55] *Propaganda*,[56] and *The Engineering of Consent*.[57] Eager to blend Freudian insights with the assumptions of crowd psychology and techniques of propaganda, Bernays favored "wrapping products in a potent symbolic aura, sneaking past the rational defenses of consumers."[58] Although Bernays, who was of Jewish descent, had snubbed Hitler and Franco as clients,[51] Hitler's chief propagandist, Goebbels, purportedly relied on his writings when formulating the Nazi campaign against the Jews in the 1930s.[59] Bernays was directly involved in several controversial campaigns for commercial clients over the years, including cigarette companies and the United Fruit Company in Central America (see Tye[51]).

55. Bernays, Edward. 1923. *Crystallizing public opinion*. New York: Boni and Liveright.

56. Bernays, Edward. 1928/2004. *Propaganda*. Brooklyn, New York: Ig Publishing.

57. Bernays, Edward. 1955. *The engineering of consent*. Norman: University of Oklahoma Press.

58. Chernow, Ron. 1998, August 16. First among flacks. *New York Times*, p. G5.

59. Bernays, Edward. 1965. *Biography of an idea: Memoirs of public relations counsel*. New York: Simon and Schuster.

60. Blumenthal, Sidney. 1980. *The permanent campaign: Inside the world of elite political operatives*. Boston: Beacon Press.

61. Grossman, Michael Baruch, and Martha Joynt Kumar. 1981. *Portraying the president: The White House and the news media*. Baltimore: Johns Hopkins University Press.

62. Johnson, Dennis W. 2000. The business of political consulting. In *Campaign warriors: Political consultants in elections*, ed. James A. Thurber and Candice J. Nelson, pp. 37–52. Washington, DC: Brookings Institution.

63. Mitchell, Greg. 1992. *The campaign of the century: Upton Sinclair's race for governor of California and the birth of media politics*. New York: Random House.

64. McDougal, Dennis. 2001. *Privileged son: Otis Chandler and the rise and fall of the L.A. Times dynasty*. New York: Perseus Books.

65. Facing little competition from other consulting firms, Whitaker and Baxter Campaigns would post a 90% success rate between 1933 and 1955, winning 70 out of 75 political campaigns they managed.[9,10] Their success inspired a host of imitators, and California soon became a major hub of campaign management.

66. Boorstin, Daniel J. 1964. *The image: A guide to pseudo-events in America*. New York: Harper and Row.

67. Jamieson, Kathleen H. 1992. *Packaging the presidency: A history and criticism of presidential campaign advertising*, 2nd ed. New York: Oxford University Press.

68. *The 30 second candidate*. 2001. Arlington, VA: PBS Online.

69. Friedenberg, Robert V. 1997. *Communication consultants in political campaigns: Ballot box warriors*. Westport, CT: Praeger.

70. Klein, Joe. 2006. *Politics lost: How American democracy was trivialized by people who think you're stupid*. New York: Doubleday.

71. Novotny, Patrick. 2000. From polis to agora: The marketing of political consultants. *Harvard International Journal of Press/Politics* 5:12–26.

72. McGinniss, Joe. 1969. *The selling of the president 1968*. New York: Trident Press.

73. Heard, Alexander. 1960. *The costs of democracy*. Chapel Hill: University of North Carolina Press.

74. Kraus, Sidney. 1996. Winners of the first 1960 televised presidential debate between Kennedy and Nixon. *Journal of Communication* 46(4):78–96.

75. Friedman, Howard S., M. Robin DiMatteo, and Timothy I. Mertz. 1980. Nonverbal communication on television news: The facial expressions of broadcasters during coverage of a presidential election campaign. *Personality and Social Psychology Bulletin* 6(3):427–435.

76. Polling data from Roper seemed to confirm this observation. Of the 4 million voters who said they based their decision on the three debates, 3 million reported voting for Kennedy, who won by 112,000 vote.[10]

77. Morrow, Lance. 1996, September 30. Naysayer to the nattering nabobs. *Time*. http://www.time.com/time/magazine/article/0,9171,985217,00.html. Accessed February 5, 2008.

78. By the early 1970s, a majority of House contenders and all but a handful of major candidates for the U.S. Senate were also employing political consultants and airing spots.[10,79] In 1969 the American Association of Political Campaign Consultants was established to formalize political consulting as a business to develop professional standards.[34,80]

79. Thurber, James A. 2000. Introduction to the study of campaign consultants. In *Campaign warriors: The role of political consultants in elections*, ed. James A. Thurber and Candice J. Nelson, pp. 1–9. Washington, DC: Brookings Institution.

80. Napolitan, Joseph. 1999. Present at the creation of modern political consulting. In *The Manship School guide to political communication*, ed. David D. Perlmutter, pp. 19–26. Baton Rouge: Louisiana State University Press.

81. Reagan, Nancy, with William Novak. 1989. *My turn: The memoirs of Nancy Reagan*. New York: Random House.

82. Ailes, now president of the Fox News Channel, worked closely with Bush campaign manager Lee Atwater, nicknamed the "happy hatchet man." Atwater is credited with innovating the technique of "push polling"—calls made to voters in the guise of a legitimate poll with the intent of influencing attitudes by spreading rumors or otherwise smearing opponents with false accusations. John McCain allegedly suffered at the hands of a push poll during the 2000 South Carolina primary, when thousands of voters were reportedly asked, "Would you be more likely or less likely to vote for John McCain for president if you knew he had fathered an illegitimate black child?" (see Davis[83]). Atwater, who died of a brain tumor in 1991, served briefly as the head of the Republican National Committee and was a mentor to Karl Rove (see Brady[84]).

83. Davis, Richard H. 2004, March 21. The anatomy of a smear campaign. *Boston Globe*, p. C12.

84. Brady, John. 1997. *Bad boy: The life and politics of Lee Atwater*. Reading, MA: Addison Wesley.

85. Bucy, Erik P., and Kimberly S. Gregson. 2001. Media participation: A legitimizing mechanism of mass democracy. *New Media and Society* 3(3):359–382.

87. Bucy, Erik P., and John E. Newhagen. 1999a. The micro- and macrodrama of politics on television: Effects of media format on candidate evaluations. *Journal of Broadcasting & Electronic Media* 43(2):193–210.

88. Strother, Raymond D. 2003. *Falling up: How a redneck helped invent political consulting*. Baton Rouge: Louisiana State University Press.

89. Morris, Dick. 1997. *Behind the Oval Office: Winning the presidency in the nineties*. New York: Random House.

90. Among other White House duties, Rove chaired prewar meetings of the White House Iraq Group, which was charged with educating the public about the threat posed by Saddam Hussein and to "set strategy for each stage of the confrontation with Baghdad."[91] In April 2007, the U.S. Office of Special Counsel launched an investigation into whether Rove or other White House aides broke federal laws by encouraging government employees to support Republican candidates. Rove left the White House a few months later.[92]

91. Gellman, Barton, and Walter Pincus. 2003, August 10. Depiction of threat outgrew supporting evidence. *Washington Post*, p. A1.

92. Labaton, Stephen, and Edmund L. Andrews. 2007, April 27. White House calls political briefings legal. *New York Times*, p. A25.

93. Balz, Dan. 1999, July 23. Team Bush; The governor's "iron triangle" points the way to Washington. *Washington Post*, p. C1.

94. Marshall, Joshua M. 2006, July 7. Toying with terror alerts? *Time*. http://www.time.com/time/nation/article/0,8599,1211369,00.html. Accessed February 5, 2008.

95. Green, Joshua. 2004, November. Karl Rove in a corner. *Atlantic Monthly*. http://www.theatlantic.com/doc/200411/green. Accessed February 5, 2008.

96. Image handlers have earned their own portmanteau: "polebrities" (p. 25).[80]

97. Auletta, Ken. 2004, September 20. Kerry's brain; annals of communications. *The New Yorker*, pp. 64–79.

98. Lemann, Nicholas. 2003, May 12. The controller: Karl Rove is working to get George Bush reelected, but he has bigger plans. *The New Yorker*, p. 68. http://www.newyorker.com/archive/2003/05/12/030512fa_fact_lemann. Accessed February 5, 2008.

99. Chaffee, Steven, H., and John L. Hochheimer. 1985. The beginnings of political communication research in the United States: Origins of the "limited effects" model. In *The media revolution in America and Western Europe*, ed. Everett M. Rogers and Francis Balle, pp. 267–296. Norwood, NJ: Ablex.

100. Bennett, W. Lance. 2006. *News: The politics of illusion*, 7th ed. New York: Longman.

101. Gans, Curtis. 1995, Fall. No magic bullets for democratic disaffection. *Social Policy* pp. 31–39.

102. Hume, Ellen. 1991. *Restoring the bond: Connecting campaign coverage to voters. A report of the campaign lessons for '92 project*. Cambridge, MA: John F. Kennedy School of Government, Harvard University.

103. Entman, Robert M. 1993. Framing: Toward clarification of a fractured paradigm. *Journal of Communication* 43(4):51–58.

104. Gamson, William A. 1989. News as framing: Commenting on Graber. *American Behavioral Scientist* 33(2):157–161.
105. Levy, Mark R. 1981. Disdaining the news. *Journal of Communication* 31(3):24–31.
106. Blumler, Jay G., and Gurevitch, Michael. 1996. Media change and social change: Linkages and junctures. In *Mass media and society*, 2nd ed., ed. James Curran and Michael Gurevitch, pp. 120–137. London: Edward Arnold.
107. Blumler, Jay G. 1990. Elections, the media, and the modern publicity process. In *Public communication: The new imperatives*, ed. Marjorie Ferguson, pp. 101–113. London: Sage.
108. Nixon, Richard M. 1978. *RN: The memoirs of Richard Nixon*. New York: Warner Books.
109. Blumler, Jay G. 1997. Origins of the crisis of communication for citizenship. *Political Communication* 14:395–404.
110. Swanson, David L. 1992. The political-media complex. *Communication Monographs* 59:397–400.
111. Blumler, Jay G., and Gurevitch, Michael. 1996. Media change and social change: Linkages and junctures. In *Mass media and society*, 2nd ed., ed. James Curran and Michael Gurevitch, pp. 120–137. London: Edward Arnold.
112. Bucy, Erik P., and Paul D'Angelo. 1999. The crisis of political communication: Normative critiques of news and democratic processes. *Communication Yearbook* 22:301–339.
113. Luntz, Frank. 2004, May. Focus group research in American politics; voices of victory, parts I and II. *The Polling Report*. http://www.pollingreport.com/focus.htm. Accessed August 21, 2008.
114. Farrell, David M., Robin Kolodny, and Stephen Medvic. 2001. Parties and campaign professionals in a digital age. *Harvard International Journal of Press/Politics* 6(4):11–30.
115. Zaller, John. 1998. The role of product substitution in presidential campaign news. *Annals of the American Academy of Political and Social Science* 560:111–118.
116. Jamieson, Kathleen H., ed. 2006. *Electing the president 2004: The insiders' view*. Philadelphia: University of Pennsylvania Press.
117. Moriarty, Sandra E., and Gina M. Garramone. 1986. A study of newsmagazine photographs of the 1984 presidential campaign. *Journalism Quarterly* 63(4):728–734.
118. Trent, Judith S., and Jimmie D. Trent. 1997. The ideal candidate revisited. *American Behavioral Scientist* 40(8):1001–1020.
119. Graber, Doris A. 1987. Kind pictures and harsh words: How television presents the candidates. In *Elections in America*, ed. Kay Lehman Schlozman, pp. 115–141. Boston: Allen and Unwin.
120. Patterson, Thomas E. 1980. *The mass media election: How Americans choose their president*. New York: Praeger.
121. Robinson, Michael J., and S. Robert Lichter. 1991. "The more things change . . .": Network coverage of the 1988 presidential nomination races. In *Nominating the president*, ed. Emmett H. Buell Jr. and Lee Sigelman, pp. 196–212. Knoxville: University of Tennessee Press.
122. Lau, Richard R. 1986. Political schema, candidate evaluations, and voting behavior. In *Political cognition: The 19th annual Carnegie symposium on*

cognition, ed. Richard R. Lau and David O. Sears, pp. 95–126. Hillsdale, NJ: Lawrence Erlbaum Associates.

123. Graber, Doris A. 1987. Kind pictures and harsh words: How television presents the candidates. In *Elections in America,* ed. Kay Lehman Schlozman, pp. 115–141. Boston: Allen and Unwin.

124. Lang, Kurt, and Gladys Engel Lang. 1968. *Politics and television.* Chicago: Quadrangle Books.

125. Popkin, Samuel L. 1994. *The reasoning voter: Communication and persuasion in presidential campaigns,* 2nd ed. Chicago: University of Chicago Press.

126. Rosenberg, Shawn W., Lisa Bohan, Patrick McCafferty, and Kevin Harris. 1986. The image and the vote: The effect of candidate presentation on voter preference. *American Journal of Political Science* 30(1):108–127.

127. Keeter, Scott. 1987. The illusion of intimacy: Television and the role of candidate personal qualities in voter choice. *Public Opinion Quarterly* 51(3):344–358.

128. Gamson, William A. 1992. *Talking politics.* New York: Cambridge University Press.

129. Coleman, Renita, and Stephen Banning. 2006. Network TV news' affective framing of the presidential candidates: Evidence for a second-level agenda-setting effect through visual framing. *Journalism & Mass Communication Quarterly* 83(2):313–328.

130. Grabe, Maria Elizabeth. 1996. The SABC's coverage of the 1987 and 1989 elections: The matter of visual bias. *Journal of Broadcasting and Electronic Media* 40(1):1–27.

131. Moriarty, Sandra E., and Mark N. Popovich. 1991. Newsmagazine visuals and the 1988 presidential election. *Journalism Quarterly* 68(3):371–380.

132. Waldman, Paul, and James Devitt. 1998. Newspaper photographs and the 1996 presidential election: The question of bias. *Journalism and Mass Communication Quarterly* 75(2):302–311.

133. Jamieson, Kathleen H., ed. 2006. *Electing the president 2004: The insiders' view.* Philadelphia: University of Pennsylvania Press.

134. Sella, Marshall. 2000, September 24. The stiff guy vs. the dumb guy. *New York Times Magazine,* pp. 72–80, 102.

135. Thomas, Evan, Eleanor Clift, Jonathan Darman, Kevin Peraino, and Peter Goldman. 2005. *Election 2004: How Bush won and what you can expect in the future.* New York: Public Affairs.

136. For an earlier, qualitative articulation of visual character framing, see Bucy, D'Angelo, and Gregson.[137]

137. Bucy, Erik P., Paul D'Angelo, and Kimberly S. Gregson. 2005. *Real news biases: Character coverage and the winnowing of presidential candidates.* Paper presented to the annual convention of the National Communication Association, Political Communication Division, Boston, MA.

138. Hellweg, Susan A. 1995. Campaigns and candidate images in American presidential elections. In *Candidate images in presidential elections,* ed. Kenneth L. Hacker, pp. 1–17. Westport, CT: Praeger.

139. Trent, Judith S., Paul A. Mongeau, Jimmie D. Trent, Kathleen E. Kendall, and Ronald B. Cushing. 1993. The ideal candidate. *American Behavioral Scientist* 37(2):225–250.

140. Nimmo, Dan, and Robert L. Savage. 1976. *Candidates and their images: Concepts, methods, and findings.* Pacific Palisades, CA: Goodyear.

141. Messaris, Paul. 1991. *Visual "literacy": What is it? How do we measure it?* Paper presented at the Fifth Visual Communication Conference, Breckenridge, CO.

142. Messaris, Paul, and Linus Abraham. 2001. The role of images in framing news stories. In *Framing public life: Perspectives on media and our understanding of the social world,* ed. Stephen D. Reese, Oscar H. Gandy Jr., and August E. Grant, pp. 215–226. Mahwah, NJ: Lawrence Erlbaum Associates.

143. Messaris, Paul, Bruce Eckman, and Gary Gumpert. 1979. Editing structure in the televised versions of the 1976 presidential debates. *Journal of Broadcasting* 23(3):359–369.

144. Bennett, W. Lance. 1977. The ritualistic and pragmatic bases of political campaign discourse. *Quarterly Journal of Speech* 63(3):219–238.

145. Rudd, Robert. 1986. Issues as image in political campaign commercials. *Western Journal of Speech Communication* 50(1):102–118.

146. Erickson, Keith V. 2000. Presidential rhetoric's visual turn: Performance fragments and the politics of illusionism. *Communication Monographs* 67(2):138–157.

147. Valence studies have coded the presence of flags as campaign props as evidence of positive candidate associations.[130,132,148,149]

148. Glassman, Carl, and Keith Kenney. 1994. Myths and presidential campaign photographs. *Visual Communication Quarterly* 49(10):4–7.

149. Lee, Tien-tsung, William E. Ryan, Wayne Wanta, and Kuang-Kuo Chang. 2004. Looking presidential: A comparison of newspaper photographs of candidates in the United States and Taiwan. *Asian Journal of Communication* 14(2):121–139.

150. Kissinger, Henry. 1979. *White House years.* Boston, MA: Little, Brown.

151. Kaid, Lynda L., and Dorothy K. Davidson. 1986. Elements of videostyle. In *New perspectives on political advertising,* ed. Lynda Lee Kaid, Dan Nimmo, and Keith R. Sanders, pp. 184–209. Carbondale: Southern Illinois University Press.

152. Trebay, Guy. 2007, July 22. Campaign chic: Not too cool, never ever hot. *New York Times,* p. ST1.

153. Nimmo, Dan. 1995. The formation of candidate images during presidential campaigns. In *Candidate images in presidential elections,* ed. Kenneth L. Hacker, pp. 51–63. Westport, CT: Praeger.

154. Bennett, W. Lance. 1995. The clueless public: Bill Clinton meets the new American voter in Campaign '92. In *The Clinton presidency: Campaigning, governing, and the psychology of leadership,* ed. Stanley A. Renshon, pp. 91–112. Boulder, CO: Westview Press.

155. Sherr, Susan A. 1999. Scenes from the political playground: An analysis of the symbolic use of children in presidential campaign advertising. *Political Communication* 16(1):45–59.

156. Wolf, Naomi. 2004, September 27. Female trouble. *New York Magazine.* http://nymag.com/nymetro/news/columns/thesexes/9911/. Accessed October 31, 2007.

157. Schlesinger, Arthur M. 1965. *A thousand days: John F. Kennedy in the White House*. Boston: Houghton Mifflin.

158. Nimmo, Dan, and James E. Combs. 1980. *Subliminal politics: Myths and myth-makers in America*. Englewood Cliffs, NJ: Prentice-Hall.

159. Parry-Giles, Shawn J., and Trevor Parry-Giles. 2002. *Constructing Clinton: Hyperreality and presidential image-making in postmodern politics*. New York: Peter Lang.

160. Kazin, Michael. 1995. *The populist persuasion*. New York: Basic Books.

161. Spragens, Thomas A. 2007. Populist perfectionism: The other American liberalism. *Social Philosophy and Policy* 24:141–163.

162. Stengel, Richard. 1988, November 7. A dose of old time populism. *Time*. http://www.time.com/time/magazine/article/0,9171,968836,00.html?iid=chix-sphere. Accessed November 24, 2007.

163. Wayne, Stephen J. 1996. *The road to the White House 1996: The politics of presidential elections*. New York: St. Martin's Press.

164. Denton, Robert E. 2002. The form and content of political communication. In *Shades of gray: Perspectives on campaign ethics*, ed. Candice J. Nelson, David A. Dulio, and Stephen K. Medvic, pp. 185–214. Washington, DC: Brookings Institution.

165. Schultz, David A., ed. 2004. *Lights, camera, campaign! Media, politics, and political advertising*. New York: Peter Lang.

166. Hylton, Cal. 1971. Intra-audience effects: Observable audience response. *Journal of Communication* 21(3):253–265.

167. Duck, Stephen W., and John Baggaley. 1975. Audience reaction and its effect on perceived expertise. *Communication Research* 2(1):79–85.

168. Negative framing of candidates as losers particularly applies to third-party and, during primary campaigns, lower tier candidates, whose poll ratings remain mired in the single digits. Just as often, these candidates are simply ignored. Lacking a large professional staff and team of image consultants, losing candidates find all too often that unrehearsed and unplanned political performances can backfire and expose them to negative image framing by journalists and opponents in ways that cultivate doubt and mistrust.[146]

169. Nagourney, Adam, and Elizabeth Kolbert. 1996, November 8. Anatomy of a loss: How Bob Dole's dream was dashed. *New York Times*, p. A1.

170. Commission on Presidential Debates. 1996. *Debate transcript, October 16, 1996: The second Clinton-Dole presidential debate*.

171. McDaniel, Ann. 1992, October 26. White House: Mourning in America. *Newsweek*, p. 33.

172. Fallows, James. 2000, April 6. The fascination of what's "obvious." *The Atlantic Monthly*. http://www.theatlantic.com/unbound/fallows/jf2000-04-06.htm. Accessed February 5, 2008.

173. Kurtz, Howard. 1999, June 25. In race for 2000, a tortoise and hare start; media portray Gore hobbled by baggage and running out of points behind Bush. *Washington Post*, p. A8.

174. Burkum, Larry G. 1994, August. *Marginalizing Perot: Visual treatment of the candidates in the 1992 presidential debates*. Paper presented to the annual convention of the Association for Education in Journalism and Mass Communication, Atlanta, GA.

175. Herszenhorn, David M. 2000, November 17. Public lives; this green isn't blue about Nader or Gore. *New York Times*, p. B2.

176. Magnusson, Paul. 2000, November 20. The punishing price of Nader's passion. *Business Week*, p. 44.

177. Rosenstone, Steven J., Roy L. Behr, and Edward H. Lazarus. 1984. *Third parties in America: Citizen responses to major party failure.* Princeton, NJ: Princeton University Press.

178. Wiegman, Oene. 1987. Attitude change in a realistic experiment: The effect of party membership and audience reaction during an interview with a Dutch politician. *Journal of Applied Social Psychology* 17:37–49.

179. Bucy, Erik P. 2000. Emotional and evaluative consequences of inappropriate leader displays. *Communication Research* 27(2):194–226.

180. Masters, Roger D., and Dennis G. Sullivan. 1989. Nonverbal displays and political leadership in France and the United States. *Political Behavior* 11:121–153.

181. Bereke, Richard L. 1992, July 22. The 1992 campaign: The media; Bush camp plans pre-convention ads to aid sagging image. *New York Times*, p. A14.

182. Kranish, Michael. 1992, July 30. Bush campaign is riven by debate over new strategy, economic plan. *Boston Globe*, p. 1.

183. Rosenthal, Andrew. 1992, January 24. The 1992 campaign: White House leader and salesman; Bush turns to power of incumbency and tries to defuse revolt in party. *New York Times*, p. A14.

184. Glad, Betty. 1995. How George Bush lost the presidential election of 1992. In *The Clinton presidency: Campaigning, governing, and the psychology of leadership*, ed. Stephen A. Renshon, pp. 11–35. Boulder, CO: Westview Press.

185. Kurtz, Howard. 1992, February 19. The story that just won't check out. *Washington Post*, p. C1.

186. Lewis, Anthony. 1992, November 2. Abroad at home; Foul words and falsehoods. *New York Times*, p. A19.

187. Wines, Michael. 1992, October 22. The 1992 campaign; the Republicans; President, after 10 cool months, is catching fire as a campaigner. *New York Times*, p. A1.

188. Ridout, Christine F. 1993. News coverage and talk shows in the 1992 presidential campaign. *PS: Political Science & Politics* 26(4):712–716.

189. Cavanaugh, John W. 1993. *Media effects on voters: A panel study of the 1992 presidential elections.* Lanham, MD: University Press of America.

190. Zakahi, Walter R., and Kenneth L. Hacker. 1995. Televised presidential debates and candidate images. In *Candidate images in presidential elections*, ed. Kenneth L. Hacker, pp. 51–63. Westport, CT: Praeger.

191. $t(79) = -2.77, p = 0.007$.

192. $t(79) = -1.74, p = 0.086$.

193. $t(79) = 1.92, p = 0.05$.

194. $t(79) = 1.83, p = 0.072$.

195. $t(79) = 3.12, p = 0.003$.

196. $t(79) = 2.79, p = 0.007$.

197. $t(79) = -2.24, p = 0.028$.

198. Klein, Joe. 1997. Foreword to *Back from the dead: How Clinton survived the Republican revolution*, by Evan Thomas, Karen Breslau, Debra Rosenberg,

Leslie Kaufman, and Andrew Murr, pp. vii–xii. New York: Atlantic Monthly Press.

199. Dover, Edwin D. 1998. *The presidential election of 1996: Clinton's incumbency and television*. Westport, CT: Praeger.

200. Thomas, Evan, Karen Breslau, Debra Rosenberg, Leslie Kaufman, and Andrew Murr. 1997. *Back from the dead: How Clinton survived the Republican revolution*. New York: Atlantic Monthly Press.

201. Ceaser, James W., and Andrew E. Busch. 1997. *Losing to win: The 1996 elections and American politics*. Lanham, MD: Rowman and Littlefield.

202. Lewis, Michael. 1997. *Trail fever*. New York: Alfred Knopf.

203. Bucy, Erik P., and John E. Newhagen. 1999b. The emotional appropriateness heuristic: Processing televised presidential reactions to the news. *Journal of Communication* 49(4):59–79.

204. Kolbert, Elizabeth, and Adam Nagourney. 1996, September 15. Behind the campaign; staff turmoil seems a staple of Dole's management style. *New York Times*, p. A1.

205. Lichter, S. Robert, Richard E. Noyes, and Lynda L. Kaid. 1999. New news or negative news: How the network nixed the 1996 campaign. In *The electronic election: Perspectives on the 1996 campaign communication*, ed. Lynda L. Kaid and Diane G. Bystrom, pp. 3–13. Hillsdale, NJ: Lawrence Erlbaum Associates.

206. Nagourney, Adam, and Elizabeth Kolbert. 1996, November 8. Anatomy of a loss: How Bob Dole's dream was dashed. *New York Times*, p. A1.

207. Stengel, Richard, and Eric Pooley. 1996, November 18. Masters of the message. *Time*. http://205.188.238.109/time/magazine/article/0,9171,985538,00.html. Accessed November 24, 2007.

208. Mundy, Alicia. 1996, November 11. Legend of the fall guys: The story of Dole's serpentine run for president may best be told by the ads that never ran. *Mediaweek*. Lexis-Nexis *Academic*. Accessed October 31, 2007.

209. Seelye, Katharine Q. 1996, September 6, 1996. Dole replaces 2 aides to sharpen message. *New York Times*, p. B10.

210. Woodward, Bob. 1997. *The choice: How Clinton won*. New York: Simon and Schuster.

211. Dowd, Maureen. 1996, October 10. Liberties; Bill be limbo. *New York Times*, p. A33.

212. $t(75) = -2.48, p = 0.015$.

213. *n.s.*

214. $t(75) = -2.22, p = 0.029$.

215. $t(75) = -3.34, p = 0.001$.

216. $t(75) = -5.09, p = 0.001$.

217. $t(75) = -4.39, p = 0.001$.

218. $t(75) = -3.68, p = 0.001$.

219. $t(75) = 2.33, p = 0.022$.

220. Glasser, Susan B. 2000, May 1. Winning a stake in a losing race; ad commissions enriched strategists. *Washington Post*, p. A1.

221. Shapiro, Walter. 2000, May 26. Simple bluejeans, pockets stuffed with cash. *USA Today*, p. 4A.

222. Marshall, Joshua M. 2000, April, 25. *Al Gore's campaign stagnates*. http://archive.salon.com/politics2000/feature/2000/04/25/quiet/index.html. Accessed October 31, 2007.

223. Duffy, Michael, and Karen Tumulty. 1999, November 8. Gore's secret guru. *Time.* http://www.time.com/time/magazine/article/0,9171,992464,00. html. Accessed February 5, 2008.

224. Von Drehle, David. 2000. Lee Atwater, the specter of South Carolina. *Washington Post,* p. C1.

225. $t(85) = -2.00, p = 0.048$.

226. $t(85) = 1.68, p = 0.096$.

227. $t(85) = 2.13, p = 0.036$.

228. $t(85) = 2.46, p = 0.016$.

229. $t(85) = 1.76, p = 0.081$.

230. $t(85) = 4.42, p = 0.001$.

231. $t(85) = 1.75, p = 0.083$.

232. $t(85) = 3.62, p = 0.001$.

233. Dowd, Maureen. 2005. *Bushworld: Enter at your own risk.* New York: Berkley Books.

234. When Kerry's campaign manager, Jim Jordan, became more frustrated and frank with Kerry about his indecisiveness, Shrum provided unconditional support and praise. He also warmed up to Kerry's family, especially Teresa Heinz Kerry, and turned Kerry against Jordan.[70] Kerry soon fired Jordan and replaced him with Mary Beth Cahill. By late March of 2004, Jim Margolis, who was widely credited for the advertising campaign that won Kerry the Democratic Party nomination, left the campaign. Shrum and associates were, from that point on, effectively in charge of the campaign operation, which is exactly what John Kerry had told friends would not happen.[70]

235. $t(77) = -3.32, p = 0.001$.

236. $t(77) = 1.96, p = 0.05$.

237. $t(77) = 1.83, p = 0.072$.

238. $t(321) = 1.73, p = 0.085$.

239. $t(321) = 2.41, p = 0.016$.

240. $t(321) = 1.80, p = 0.073$.

241. $t(321) = 2.72, p = 0.007$.

242. $t(322) = -1.84, p = 0.067$.

243. $t(322) = -3.28, p = 0.007$.

244. Nelson, Candice J., Stephen K. Medvic, and David A. Dulio. 2002. Hired guns or gatekeepers of democracy? In *Shades of gray: Perspectives on campaign ethics,* ed. Candice J. Nelson, David A. Dulio, and Stephen K. Medvic, pp. 75–97. Washington, DC: Brookings Institution Press.

245. Sabato, Larry J. 1991. *Feeding frenzy: How attack journalism has transformed American politics.* New York: Free Press.

246. Halperin, Mark, and John F. Harris. 2006. *The way to win: Taking the White House in 2008.* New York: Random House.

247. Parry-Giles, Trevor. 1999. Speechwriting. In *The Manship School guide to political communication,* ed. David D. Perlmutter, pp. 11–18. Baton Rouge: Louisiana State University Press.

248. Edelman, Murray J. 1988. *Constructing the political spectacle.* Chicago, IL: University of Chicago Press.

4

Facing the Electorate

The press sometimes in the television age focuses a little bit more on style and a little bit less on substance than the American people would actually like. . . . This campaign is not about the, the gestures I make in an interview. The campaign is about [the issues]. Not style—substance.

—Al Gore on *20/20*, June 1999

Despite former Vice President Al Gore's claims to the contrary—and his personal struggle to appear comfortable in front of the camera during the 2000 presidential campaign—political campaign practices moved onto a visual footing with the rise of television as the dominant mode of campaign communication.[1] The nationally televised Kennedy–Nixon debates of 1960 in particular stirred considerable interest in the relationship between television, nonverbal communication, and political behavior—and compelled subsequent candidates to assign more priority to their on-camera appearance and behavior. "A common response to a speech on television," Meyrowitz[2] rightly noted, "is to think about the speaker rather than the speech" (p. 95). In the era of 24-hour news channels and high-definition broadcasts, television coverage focuses attention on the expressive behavior of presidential candidates like never before, highlighting particularly masterful performances as well as conspicuous moments when norms of interaction and expected codes of conduct are violated (see Clayman[3] and Kurtz[4]).

The impact that the 1960 debates had on viewers, especially the perceived differences between those who viewed the debates on television and those who listened by radio, has inspired a voluminous literature about the political effects of television (see Druckman[5] and Kraus[6]) and rhetorical strategies candidates employ in their mediated communications.[7,8] Absent from most studies of the debates, or content analyses of political news generally, however, are detailed assessments of the candidates' nonverbal behavior. Although the visual emphasis of contemporary politics has been recognized and practiced with increasing sophistication since the Kennedy era, its repercussions at the individual and social level are not fully understood. In *Processing Politics*, Graber[9] aptly observed that "most social scientists have ignored pictures in their television content analyses, treating the messages as if they consisted only of verbal texts. . . . Similarly, [they] have rarely used pictures as stimuli to test people's attitudes" (p. 93).

Nonverbal communication is politically important because expressive displays have been shown to have considerable persuasive influence.[10,11] Unlike attractiveness and other more or less stable aspects of appearance, facial displays are highly variable and reveal important moment-to-moment information about the emitter's internal state. Given their capacity to influence emotional, cognitive, and evaluative responses in observers,[12-14] candidate expressions are an important component of political influence that merit closer scrutiny. Indeed, Masters[15] has characterized televised leader displays as "microlevel phenomena that form the elements underlying more diversified and elaborate political processes" (p. 234).

Given the tendency of candidates to appear in image bites more than sound bites, the nonverbal behavior of presidential nominees takes on added significance. In this chapter we argue that facial displays are influential elements within image and sound bites, and we examine the character of televised candidate displays shown on the evening news. To structure the analysis, we draw on the literature of biopolitics (see Masters and Sullivan[10] and Somit and Peterson[16]) that has identified three classes of displays relevant to the study of televised political behavior.

EXPRESSIVE DISPLAY TYPES

Studies of the televised nonverbal behavior of political leaders has identified three general categories of expressive displays recognized for their social significance: anger/threat, fear/evasion, and happiness/reassurance.[17] These categories draw on research from primate and human ethology, which has found that different patterns of display behavior are associated with distinct roles in rivalry for dominance (see Masters et al.[18]). As composite terms, anger/threat, fear/evasion, and happiness/reassurance reflect the duality of the emotion being expressed and correspond to the behavioral intentions of attack, flight (or submission), and bonding. Far from having trivial impacts, leader displays hold evolutionary significance for social organization and, by conveying emotion and transmitting important nonverbal cues, are instrumental in regulating status and power relationships.[10]

Although these three display types are categorically distinct, they can be grouped according to two broader styles of interaction important to social organization and attention structure—agonic and hedonic (see Chance[19] and Kortmulder and Robbers[20]). Whereas agonic interactions are characterized by competitive behaviors, namely, displays of threat and submission (or appeasement), hedonic interactions feature conciliatory gestures and reassuring expressions. Agonic encounters function largely to establish and regulate power relations; hedonic encounters, which are more relaxed and playful, tend to reinforce social status. Such expressive patterns apply to interactions of both adults and children, in which "the leader is more likely to exhibit reassuring displays, whereas second-ranking individuals—and, particularly in groups of children, those marginal to the group—more frequently engage in aggressive behavior"[18] (p. 122). Thus, facial displays and other nonverbal behaviors index what ethologists refer to as dominance hierarchies, with anger/threat and fear/evasion representing an agonic style of interaction and happiness/reassurance a hedonic style.

The human repertoire of expressive displays is much more variable and nuanced than in other primates, owing in large part to the interplay in *Homo sapiens* between gestures, language, and culture. "Human communication is extraordinarily complex because spoken messages are accompanied by nonverbal cues, not only of the face and body, but also of the voice"[21] (p. 99). Just focusing on expressive displays, research in nonverbal communication has documented considerable variation between individuals in the performance of similar gestures.[22] Indeed, political candidates differ widely in the effectiveness of their nonverbal behavior, an observation borne out by experimental tests of Reagan and Mondale's happiness/reassurance displays on viewers.[23] Variations in display intensity and in the ability to communicate positive emotion, which is central to reassuring others and bonding citizens to leaders, seem to be particularly important.[23] More than a leader's capacity to emote effectively in the abstract, it is the observation of competitive contests by third parties—and the *observer's response* to nonverbal behavior—that determines social status.[21]

Analyses of network news broadcasts from the 1980s have documented how each of the three major display types, as widely visible instances of nonverbal leader behavior, occurs in presidential election coverage.[24,25] Each display type can be reliably classified and documented using distinct coding criteria (see Ekman[26] and Sullivan et al.[27]), which facilitates systematic measurement of candidate portrayals in election news through visual content analysis techniques. In this chapter, we adapt coding criteria employed in earlier biopolitical research to assess the nonverbal display repertoires of presidential candidates during general election contests. Our investigation focuses on the relationship between the display types shown in network election coverage, the context in which the displays are shown, and candidate standings in the polls. Beyond facial displays, the analysis also takes into consideration the verbal tone of candidate sound bites as well as the hedonic or agonic quality of hand gestures and physical embraces. The defining characteristics of each facial display are summarized in Table 4–1 and described below.

Happiness/reassurance. Characterized by a smile or relaxed mouth position, happiness/reassurance displays are relatively fluid, smooth, and flexible. In these expressions, the eyes may be wide open, normal, or just slightly closed. Also evident are raised eyebrows and visible upper, or upper and lower, teeth.[28] Eye contact may be brief, followed by a cut-off or change of gaze to avoid staring. In addition, crow's-feet wrinkles may appear around the eyes and the candidate's head might be tilted to the side, back, or in a nodding position. Functionally, happiness/reassurance displays facilitate a hedonic or friendly mode of social interaction and in most situations lower the probability of an aggressive or agonic encounter.[27,29]

Table 4–1 Criteria for Classifying Facial Displays

	Display Type		
	Anger/threat	Fear/evasion	Happiness/ reassurance
Eyelids	Opened wide	Upper raised/lower tightened	Wide, normal, or slightly closed
Eyebrows	Lowered	Lowered and furrowed	Raised
Eye orientation	Staring	Averted	Focused then cut off
Mouth corners	Forward or lowered	Retracted, normal	Retracted and/ or raised
Teeth showing	Lower or none	Variable	Upper or both
Head motion			
Lateral	None	Side-to-side	Side-to-side
Vertical	Upward	Up-down	Up-down
Head orientation			
To body	Forward from trunk	Turned from vertical	Tilted from vertical
Angle to vertical	Down	Down	Up

From Roger D. Masters, Dennis G. Sullivan, John T. Lanzetta, Gregory J. McHugo, and Basil G. Englis. 1986. "Facial displays and political leadership." *Journal of Biological and Social Structures* 9:330. Copyright 1986. Reprinted with permission from Elsevier. As modified by Roger D. Masters (1996, p. 141).

Anger/threat. A more rigid pattern of facial tendencies characterizes anger/threat displays, which may include a fixed stare; vertical head orientation; raised upper, and tightened lower, eyelids; brows that are pulled down and drawn together; lower or no teeth showing; and lowered mouth corners.[28] In such displays the lips may be pressed firmly together or squared and tightened. The expression overall has a negative or tense quality about it and is coupled with a hostile communicative intent. Functionally, anger/threat displays are associated with agonic encounters, aggressive behavior, social rivalry, and challenges to dominance hierarchies. Whereas challengers and rivals are frequently aggressive, "the leader is usually the focus of attention, often engaging in hedonic or reassuring behavior" (p. 64[30]). As Howard Dean learned after his infamous scream in 2004, leading candidates who exhibit too much anger/threat may, as the focus of intense media attention, quickly find their behavior characterized as non-presidential.[4]

Fear/evasion. Expressions that feature furrowed brows and gaze aversion; a lowered head position, abrupt movement, and, at times, side-to-side head turning are indicative of fear/evasion displays.[27] In some cases, the emitter's eyelids will be raised, as with the "deer caught in the headlights" look. Other times, the brows might be slightly furrowed and wrinkles may form in the middle of the forehead, suggesting worry; the lips may also stretch horizontally and the chin may be lowered.[28] An evasive expression communicates an intention to avoid confrontation. Functionally, fear/evasion displays are also associated with agonic encounters, but instead of indicating aggression they signal subordination, avoidance, and inferior status. Candidates who are forced to respond to allegations or difficult questions, who are reported to be trailing badly in the polls, or who are asked to justify contradictory statements might exhibit fear/evasion. Representative examples of hedonic and agonic candidate displays, captured from news coverage analyzed for this study, appear in Figures 4–1A and 4–1B.

In analyzing nonverbal displays and political leadership, it is important to distinguish between the stimulus characteristics or objective features of the displays themselves and their impressive significance as elicitors of emotional responses in others.[27] A given display does not have the same effects in all viewers but rather interacts with prior attitudes, the viewing context, and short-term perceptions to influence emotional, evaluative, and attitudinal outcomes.[10,14] Candidate nonverbal behavior may also influence voting intention; indeed, as a forecasting tool, reviewer ratings of short video clips from gubernatorial debates (shown in 10-second slices, with the sound off) outperform a range of more conventional predictors of election outcomes.[31,32] In this way, facial displays convey considerable social meaning and significance, depending on the context in which they are seen.[27,33] Taking these factors into account, a substantial body of experimental research has

Hedonic Displays (Happiness/Reassurance)

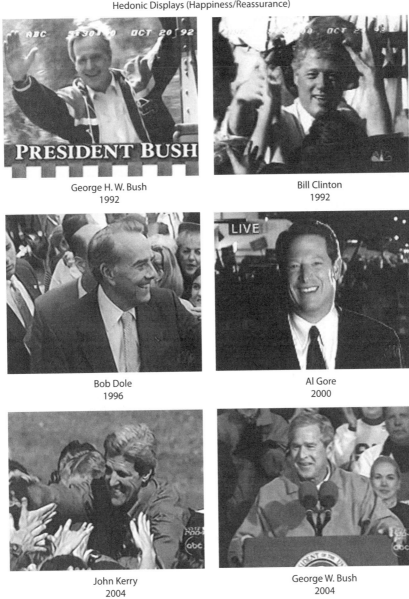

Figure 4–1A Screen captures from presidential campaign coverage showing hedonic displays

Agonic Displays (Anger/Threat and Fear/Evasion)

George H. W. Bush
1992

George H. W. Bush
1992

Bob Dole
1996

George W. Bush
2000

Al Gore
2000

George W. Bush
2004

Figure 4–1B Screen captures from presidential campaign coverage showing agonic displays

documented the political effects of televised leader displays on viewers in both the United States and Europe across numerous election and crisis communication contexts.

THE SIGNIFICANCE OF TELEVISED LEADER DISPLAYS

For viewers, televised leader displays serve as a heuristic, or judgmental shortcut, for assessing presidential performance[25,27] and have been shown to predict election outcomes.[31] Recent studies of candidate photographs from U.S. Senate and congressional races[34] and videotaped excerpts of gubernatorial candidates[31] have demonstrated the ability of viewers to accurately identify election winners based on "thin slice" exemplars of expressive behavior, which tend to be highly predictive of reactions to much longer exposures (see Ambady and Rosenthal[35]). Interestingly, hearing the candidates speak only confuses matters: when excerpts of gubernatorial debates were shown to viewers with the sound on, the ability to predict electoral outcomes actually *declined* in comparison to a filtered (inaudible) sound condition and visual-only condition that showed the candidates with no sound.[31] By contrast, when participants were allowed to hear the candidates speak (i.e., to briefly discuss policy positions), their ability to guess party membership significantly improved over the silent and filtered conditions.

Similarly, a common finding in the biopolitics literature is that the impact of different display types depends on the specific presentation modality. Image-only presentations elicit stronger responses, particularly to happiness/reassurance displays, than those accompanied by sound, that is, those featuring the candidate's articulation of issue positions and policy information.[23,30] These effects are evident in self-report questionnaires as well as psychophysiological measures of emotion, including facial electromyography (EMG), which provides a real-time readout of facial muscle activation (see Bucy and Bradley[13] and Lanzetta et al.[17]). When facial displays of leaders are seen without sound, the smiling activation (zygomatic muscle) reactions of viewers are greatly amplified—negatively for agonic expressions and positively for hedonic expressions.[21]

Leader displays may also be evaluated for the personality or communicative traits they reveal about the source, including how appropriate, honest, credible, trustworthy, and potent (i.e., efficacious) viewers consider them to be.[12,36] This is particularly true when candidates are portrayed in close-up shots that promote emotional involvement and establish social proximity between televised subjects and viewers (see Chapter 5). By minimizing the psychological distance between viewing audiences and actors on the political stage, television prompts viewers to regard candidates in personal terms, fostering familiarity and trust.[37] Focus group responses to Bill Clinton shown in different communication settings during the 1992 campaign (e.g., a close-up interview and televised town hall meeting) support the notion that production techniques may significantly affect candidate evaluations.[33] As one voter commented upon viewing footage from the campaign, "the closeness of Bill Clinton almost filling the entire screen with his face" invited identification with the candidate. "He was making eye contact. I'd vote for the man based on that. You sat there and watched the man and you're not even listening to his answer" (quoted in Bucy and Newhagen,[33] p. 205).

However, too much familiarity may breed contempt. By bringing candidates in close for visual inspection, the camera lowers the political hero to the level of the people.[2] Prior to television, "the nonelectronic communication environment favored candidates who appeared powerful and forceful at a distance. The president's minute facial expressions and appearance mattered little" (p. 279[2]). The camera, by bringing a rich range of expressive information to the contemporary audience, exalts telegenic communicators and performances—but is just as likely to expose human frailty. Television routinely invades the personal space of politicians, erasing distinctions between public and private behavior. "It watches them sweat, sees them grimace at their own ill-phrased remarks. It coolly records them as they succumb to emotions," Meyrowitz[2] commented (p. 271). "'Greatness' is an abstraction, and it fades as the image of distant leaders comes to resemble an encounter with an intimate acquaintance" (p. 273[2]).

Compared to institutions and other political structures that are difficult to visualize, images of leaders "are easily recognized and function as effective information processing cues" (p. 378[24]). The communicative efficiency of expressive displays derives from the extraordinary sensitivity humans, beginning in infancy, show to differences in the facial behavior they observe.[38] As an individual matures, "nonverbal behavior and especially facial displays play a critical role in the development of interaction with peers" (p. 42[21]). The face, more than any other expressive feature, serves as the primary channel of emotional communication, conveying the affective state and behavioral intention of the communicator while transmitting important social signals to observers.[13] "Since the capacity to decode and respond to facial displays is functionally necessary for normal social behavior, it should not be surprising that the facial displays of political leaders can influence observers' emotions and attitudes" (Masters,[21] p. 46).[39] This applies to both mediated (i.e., televised) and nonmediated contexts.

Whether different displays will have political influence depends on at least two qualities of candidates themselves—political status and expressive ability.[41] High-status leaders are said to have an attention-binding quality that draws continued observance by other members of the social group, who monitor dominant individuals for motivational cues (see Chance[19]). In campaign settings, front-runners typically enjoy advantages over candidates who are trailing in the polls, including heightened media attention, greater name recognition, and enhanced fund-raising ability. A candidate's expressive ability also plays an important role. In American politics, candidates who are able to emit convincing displays of happiness/reassurance are generally regarded as effective communicators—"happy warriors," in the memorable phrase of Sullivan and Masters[23]—while those without much evocative ability last only briefly on the national stage or experience low approval ratings while in office.

Presidential advisor David Gergen attributed a major part of Ronald Reagan's *political* success to his *expressive* success, observing that his "sense of humor and smile, when dealing with the press on television, [were] worth a million votes" (quoted in Hertsgaard,[44] p. 46). Meyrowitz[2] also commented on the performance genius of Reagan, which seemed to win over members of the press and the public—even if they disagreed with his policies. "Reagan's communications are often mundane, sometimes incomprehensible, but they are frequently salvaged by a voice that chokes with emotion or by eyes that fill with tears or by a playful grin—all perfectly timed and coordinated" (p. 304).

The allure of Barack Obama during the 2008 Democratic primaries, with his optimistic brand of "Yes, We Can" politics, drew on this evocative ability to inspire.[45] Obama's appeal reflected a "charisma mandate"[46] strong enough to attract the endorsement of influential members of the Kennedy family (Ted and Caroline) and for Obama to be dubbed the "son of Camelot" by *ABC World News* while nostalgic images of President John F. Kennedy lifting his son John-John filled the screen.[47] "Waiting to hear what Obama has to say—win, lose, or tie—has become the most anticipated event of any given primary night," Klein[45] observed after the Super Tuesday contests. "The man's use of pronouns (never *I*), of inspirational language, and of poetic meter—'WE are the CHANGE that we SEEK'—is unprecedented in recent memory" (p. 18).

As with the 2008 election, the candidates featured in Sullivan and Masters' happy-warriors study displayed varying degrees of communicative ability. In particular, there were marked differences in the capacity of Ronald Reagan's smile to elicit strong positive emotions and favorable postexposure attitudes compared to Walter Mondale (Reagan's opponent in the 1984 presidential campaign), whose happiness/reassurance displays "neither transmitted warm feelings nor contributed to post-test attitudes" (p. 361[23]). To explain the difference, they noted how the facial displays of Mondale were perceived as blended—partially positive but diluted by subtle signs of other expressive qualities—and not capable of evoking much enthusiasm or positive emotion. Compared to unblended expressions, displays perceived as mixtures of distinct cues and that evidence "leakage" tend to elicit weaker emotions, are less likely to activate favorable opinions, and produce less attitude change.[48] Interestingly, the greater the perceived difference between a leader's neutral and happiness/reassurance displays, that is, the more distinct each display appears, the more that reassurance displays enhance emotional responses.[49]

During the 1984 Democratic primaries, Mondale was more likely than his rivals to exhibit fear/evasion in his speeches and was less effective in communicating warm emotions to reinforce the support of favorably disposed viewers.[18,23] Even though he managed to win the Democratic nomination over Gary Hart and Jesse Jackson, Mondale "failed to secure the focus of attention usually reserved for the winner [and] never successfully united the traditional Democratic constituencies" (pp. 128–129[18]). In the general election debates with Reagan, the younger Mondale was rated as less expressive and less physically attractive than Reagan and exhibited a high rate of blinking—more than once per second, on average[11]—indicating nervousness and tension (see Exline[50]). Bob Dole similarly exhibited a high blinking rate and was viewed as sour and visually unappealing in the 1996 presidential debates against Bill Clinton.[51]

Consistent with the ethological observation that the challenger or second-ranking individual is frequently more aggressive than the leader,[18,30] candidates who are ahead in the polls can be expected to exhibit more happiness/reassurance displays than candidates who are trailing. During the 1984 primaries, Jackson evidenced more anger/threat than either Hart or Mondale, reflecting his position as an outsider challenging the political establishment.[18,52] In competitive contexts, "threat displays characterize a lower status individual, whereas the successful leader uses them only as a last resort" (p. 127).[18] On the other hand, we would expect leading candidates, as the primary focus of social attention, to be depicted more often engaging in hedonic or reassuring behavior, since increased popularity has been associated with a greater frequency of happiness/reassurance displays in both photographic and television coverage of presidential campaigns.[18,31] Varying amounts of hedonic and agonic expressive behavior should be evident in our election sample, as human behavior is distinguished by the relative fluidity between these different modes of social interaction.[30]

FINDINGS FOR FACIAL DISPLAYS

The starting point for this analysis is the "happy warriors" forecast that leading candidates would be shown engaging in more hedonic behavior, both visually and in sound bite tone, than trailing candidates. Appendix 4 provides details on the coding instrument and how we assessed leading and trailing candidates. Investigating this question involved a series of t-test comparisons between front-runners and trailing candidates, as determined by daily tracking polls, across four groups of variables. As shown in Table 4–2, the means overall (all years combined) are very similar with front-runners shown slightly more in hedonic displays than trailing candidates, but the difference is not statistically significant. Looking at the four hedonic variables individually (facial displays during sound and image bites, the verbal tone of sound bites, reassuring hand signals, and bonding embraces) also did not produce significant results for all years combined. Yet hedonic tone in sound bites

Table 4–2 Hedonic and Agonic Representation of Front-runners and Trailing Candidates

Candidate Behavior	Front-runner			Trailing Candidate			df	t	p
	N	M	SD	N	M	SD			
Overall									
Hedonic									
All years combined	261	3.18	3.39	267	3.16	3.44	526	.08	.939
1992	67	3.07	3.97	62	2.40	2.86	127	1.09	.276
1996	50	2.90	2.02	57	3.47	3.42	92	−1.06	.288*
2000	70	3.14	3.68	75	3.02	3.36	143	.20	.843
2004	74	3.50	3.32	73	3.68	3.90	145	−.31	.758
Agonic									
All years combined	261	1.49	2.38	267	2.31	3.12	497	−3.36	.001*
1992	67	1.01	2.24	62	2.22	4.18	91	−2.02	.046*
1996	50	.34	.79	57	2.56	2.70	66	−5.91	.000*
2000	70	1.37	1.81	75	1.86	2.51	134	−1.36	.174*
2004	74	2.82	3.04	73	2.63	2.94	145	.39	.695
Facial Display									
Hedonic Face									
All years combined	261	1.64	1.83	267	1.64	1.72	526	−.03	.977
1992	67	1.56	1.85	62	1.25	1.50	127	1.04	.302
1996	50	1.28	.90	57	1.61	1.54	92	−1.38	.169*
2000	70	1.55	2.01	75	1.61	1.75	143	−.18	.858
2004	74	2.01	2.05	73	2.01	1.92	145	.00	1.00
Agonic Face									
All years combined	261	.79	1.32	267	1.11	1.55	526	−2.54	.011
1992	67	.38	.62	62	1.03	1.94	87	−2.34	.021*
1996	50	.20	.49	57	1.16	1.34	72	−4.99	.000*
2000	70	.67	1.07	75	.92	1.44	143	−1.17	.243
2004	74	1.67	1.72	73	1.34	1.42	140	1.27	.203*

continued

Table 4–2 continued

Candidate Behavior	Front-runner			Trailing Candidate					
	N	M	SD	N	M	SD	df	t	p
Verbal Tone									
Hedonic Bite Tone									
All years combined	261	.36	.68	267	.27	.58	510	1.76	.079*
1992	67	.38	.83	62	.21	.60	120	1.39	.165*
1996	50	.34	.59	57	.15	.41	86	1.81	.072*
2000	70	.34	.65	75	.32	.61	143	.21	.829
2004	74	.39	.63	73	.35	.65	145	.33	.738
Agonic Bite Tone									
All years combined	261	.48	.83	267	.71	1.06	503	−2.84	.005*
1992	67	.31	.67	62	.62	1.21	93	−1.79	.075*
1996	50	.04	.19	57	.82	1.19	59	−4.87	.000*
2000	70	.54	.77	75	.62	.92	143	−.58	.557
2004	74	.85	1.09	73	.78	.96	145	.41	.679
Candidate Gestures									
Hedonic Hand Display									
All years combined	261	.77	1.12	267	.92	1.26	526	−1.42	.156
1992	67	.48	.97	62	.77	1.15	127	−1.58	.116
1996	50	.52	.64	57	.94	1.02	105	−2.53	.013
2000	70	.97	1.35	75	.74	.97	143	1.15	.250
2004	74	1.10	1.17	73	1.19	1.67	145	−.74	.455
Agonic Hand Display									
All years combined	261	.25	.65	267	.50	.97	464	−3.45	.001*
1992	67	.31	.87	62	.56	1.36	127	−1.25	.212
1996	50	.10	.30	57	.57	.88	70	−3.83	.000
2000	70	.15	.36	75	.32	.64	119	−1.89	.060*
2004	74	.37	.77	73	.56	.94	145	−1.29	.199
Hedonic Contact									
All years combined	261	.43	.94	267	.35	.76	526	1.03	.304
1992	67	.64	1.41	62	.16	.45	80	2.64	.010*
1996	50	.76	.93	57	.75	1.05	105	.03	.977
2000	70	.27	.61	75	.34	.79	143	−.63	.527
2004	74	.14	.45	73	.19	.54	145	−.52	.604

*Homogeneity of variance assumption violated, equal variances not assumed procedure used.

approached significance, in the predicted direction, that is, a reassuring tone was more evident in coverage of front-runners than trailers.

We next examined whether trailing candidates (irrespective of political party) would be presented in more agonic depictions, both visually and in verbal tone, than leading candidates, for all years combined. As summarized in Table 4–2, trailers were shown exhibiting agonic behavior significantly more often than front-runners. To identify where these differences were located, facial display, sound bite tone, and agonic gesture variables were isolated for further analysis. All means were in the expected direction. Differences between front-runners and trailing candidates were statistically significant for all analyses.

Together these findings offer strong support for the idea that trailing candidates emit more agonic displays, or at least journalists present more coverage of them in this competitive state, than front-runners. Counter to theoretical expectations, hedonic displays were not clearly associated with front-runners.

Given these results, the data call for further parsing along election years to determine whether these trends are stable over time. Table 4–2 presents year-by-year results for front-runners and trailers. Notably, in 1992 the front-runner was depicted significantly more often in hedonic contact with supporters than the trailing candidate. Coverage of the 1996 election featured front-runners speaking in a hedonic sound bite tone more often than trailing candidates, at a near-significant level. In the same year, contrary to expectation, the trailing candidate (Bob Dole) was shown significantly more often using hedonic hand displays, such as waving or giving a thumbs-up. These few points of statistical difference are not enough to overturn the general conclusion pointing to a lack of strong association between hedonic behavior and front-runner or trailing status, however. Additional perspective on this question is revealed below in the analyses by political party.

Agonic displays varied significantly between front-runners and trailing candidates in two out of our four election years. Looking at individual agonic categories separately it becomes clear that competitive behaviors are more clearly associated with trailers than hedonic behaviors are with front-runners. Findings for agonic displays are quite stable across elections, with the 1992 and 1996 election years statistically most prominent in setting the overall pattern of agonic association with trailing candidates (see Table 4–2).

To examine the hedonic and agonic display behaviors of front-runners and trailers in greater detail, we next consider partisan differences. This analysis is motivated less by concerns about biased portrayals across party lines than differences in the campaigning styles of Republicans and Democrats. Whereas Republicans are associated with law and order and national defense issues, Democrats commonly campaign on domestic issues, such as job security and health care. According to Lakoff,[53] liberals and conservatives approach politics in a way that corresponds to their moral stands or worldviews: conservatives as upholders of authority and protectors from external evil (a "strict father" morality), liberals as nurturing and empathetic, protective of those who need assistance (a "nurturant parent" approach). Applied to expressive behavior on the campaign trail, these differences in issue emphasis and campaigning styles may give rise to a sterner, more agonic presentation mode for Republican candidates and a softer, more hedonic mode for Democrats. And, since trailing candidates are more likely to go on the attack regardless of party affiliation, we would expect these differences to be more apparent for front-runners than trailers. In any event, there are reasons to suspect that Democrats and Republicans may indeed behave differently on the campaign trail, which should be apparent in network news coverage.

Because candidates from both parties did not appear as front-runners and trailers in every election, the year (1992, 1996, 2000, 2004) by party (Democrat, Republican) by poll status (front-runner, trailer) matrix had a number of empty cells. Hence, the analysis could not be performed individually for each election year. For all election years combined, however, several party-by-poll-status interactions were significant (see Table 4–3). Figures 4–2 through 4–4 visually represent the key interactions.

The significant interaction shown in Figure 4–2 indicates, somewhat ironically, that Democrats are more hedonic in their behavior as trailers than front-runners. Republicans, on the other hand, are depicted more hedonically as front-runners than trailers. Thus, it appears that Republicans fit the overall prediction for hedonic behavior—that front-runners would emit more hedonic displays than trailing candidates—while Democrats

Table 4–3 Interactions for Political Party by Poll Status (all election years combined)

Candidate Behavior	df	F	p	Partial η^2
Overall				
Hedonic	1	3.53	.061	.007
Agonic	1	17.61	.001	.033
Facial Display				
Hedonic face	1	6.27	.013	.012
Agonic face	1	26.69	.001	.048
Verbal Tone				
Hedonic bite tone	1	2.49	.120	.005
Agonic bite tone	1	11.38	.001	.021
Candidate Gestures				
Hedonic hand display	1	13.95	.001	.026
Agonic hand display	1	.59	.442	.001
Hedonic contact	1	15.59	.001	.029

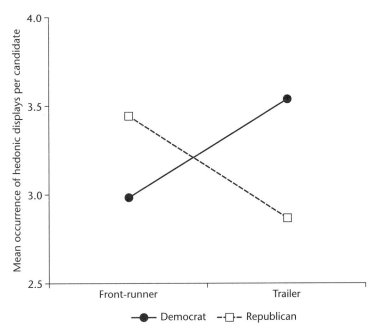

Figure 4–2 Interaction for political party and poll status on all hedonic behavior

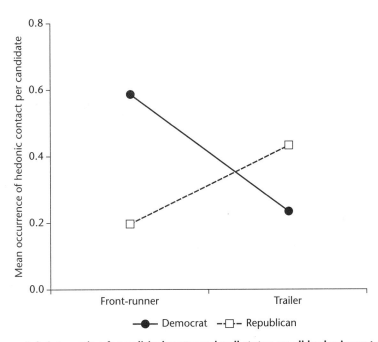

Figure 4–3 Interaction for political party and poll status on all hedonic contact

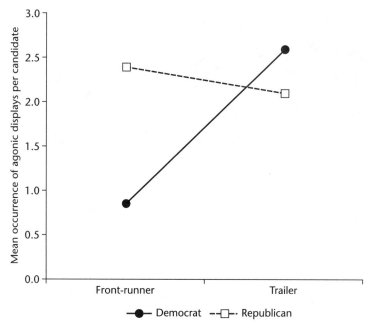

Figure 4–4 Interaction for political party and poll status on all agonic behavior

do not. In fact, Democrats display the opposite behavior: when they are behind in the polls they tend to behave more hedonically (or at least they are portrayed that way in the news). The exception to this trend is the hedonic contact variable that measured physical contact with supporters on the campaign trail. As Figure 4–3 indicates, Democrats engage in more handshaking and hugging when they are ahead in the polls than when they are behind. Republicans, on the other hand, engage in less physical contact when they are front-runners than trailers.

Examining the means for the significant agonic interactions reported in Table 4–3 reveals an interesting pattern. While Republicans generally engage in slightly more agonic behavior as front-runners than trailers, their agonic behavior shows little variation across front-running and trailing conditions (see Fig. 4–4). Democrats, on the other hand, engage in dramatically more agonic behavior when they are behind in the polls, reserving attacks for times in the campaign when they find themselves in the underdog role. As front-runners, Democrats seem to engage in considerably less agonic behavior than Republicans, perhaps displaying the nurturing, empathetic style Lakoff suggests is typical of Democrats. These differences in front-runner behavior confirm expectations for ideologically driven communication styles: When trailing in the polls, Democrats display more agonic behavior than Republicans. In this sense, Democrats fulfill normative expectations of engaging in noticeably more agonic behavior when behind, while Republicans are more apt to do so when leading in the polls.

Considering these findings across political parties, Republicans confirm expectations for hedonic displays while Democrats confirm expectations for agonic displays. When Republicans are ahead in the polls they engage in more hedonic behavior; when Democrats are behind in the polls they express themselves more agonically—but also exhibit more hedonic behavior. This finding for trailing candidates could send a mixed message to voters that although Democrats will engage in competitive behaviors when trailing, they are also more content than Republicans to be trailing in the polls. By contrast, when Democrats are ahead in the polls, they are less expressive than Republicans. Republicans visually attack regardless of whether they are leading or trailing, but act more hedonically when they are leading.

Critical Events

Performances in nationally televised presidential debates, potentially critical campaign events where rivals for power square off for an extended period of time on the same stage, offer an important window of evaluation for undecided voters and weak partisans who are wavering in their support for a particular candidate. In instances when a clear debate winner (or loser) emerges, shifts in public opinion in favor of the winner or against the loser usually follow. After the first debate between John Kerry and George W. Bush in 2004, in which Bush came across as awkward and inarticulate, Kerry emerged from the encounter with a generally more favorable image and managed to overcome an 8-point deficit to tie Bush in the polls.[54] Bush, however, was still seen as more likable and believable and as a stronger leader than Kerry. In 2000, Bush saw his numbers go up after he performed better than expected in the first and second debates against Al Gore. He also gained ground among likely voters who saw the straight talking governor as more honest, likable, and able to lead than Gore.[55] Following these shifts in poll standings and voter perceptions, we would expect an increase in hedonic portrayals of recognized debate winners and agonic depictions of recognized debate losers.

As mentioned, analysis of candidate photographs in print media has shown that increased popularity during campaigns is reflected by a greater occurrence of hedonic portrayals.[31,56] A similar pattern was found in network news coverage of the 1984 Democratic primaries, where political success was generally associated with an increase in happiness/reassurance depictions and losing status with a tendency for candidates to be shown exhibiting more anger/threat.[18] Assuming that network campaign coverage has continued to cover leading candidates in a positive light and trailing candidates in a negative light, we expect debate winners to be shown exhibiting more hedonic behavior (both visually and in verbal tone) than losers, and debate losers to be shown exhibiting more agonic behavior (both visually and in verbal tone) than winners.

Findings for Critical Events

Hedonic variables were subjected to a "critical events" analysis, defined as general election debates in which there were clear perceived

Table 4–4 Hedonic and Agonic Representation of Debate Winners and Losers

Candidate Behavior	Winner			Loser			df	t	p
	N	M	SD	N	M	SD			
Overall									
Hedonic									
All years combined	143	3.81	3.97	149	3.18	3.28	290	1.46	.144
1992	32	3.88	4.82	31	2.29	2.54	61	1.62	.110
1996	20	3.40	3.10	22	2.91	2.89	40	.53	.599
2000	34	3.41	3.30	41	3.17	3.33	73	.31	.755
2004	57	4.18	4.14	55	3.81	3.67	110	.46	.647
Agonic									
All years combined	143	1.63	2.53	149	2.56	2.99	285	2.86	.005*
1992	32	1.38	2.77	31	2.23	3.12	61	−1.14	.258
1996	20	.35	.74	22	3.05	3.24	23	−3.79	.001*
2000	34	1.59	2.09	41	2.46	2.70	73	−1.54	.127
2004	57	2.26	2.86	55	2.63	3.08	110	−.66	.508
Facial Display									
Hedonic Face									
All years combined	143	1.87	1.93	149	1.73	1.77	290	.63	.532
1992	32	1.97	2.19	31	1.26	1.50	61	1.49	.140
1996	20	1.25	1.20	22	1.27	1.27	40	−.06	.953
2000	34	1.62	1.90	41	1.78	1.72	73	−3.88	.699
2004	57	2.19	1.98	55	2.16	2.02	110	.08	.938
Agonic Face									
All years combined	143	.87	1.46	149	1.30	1.63	288	2.32	.021*
1992	32	.56	1.13	31	1.10	1.77	61	−1.42	.159
1996	20	.20	.52	22	1.32	1.39	27	−3.50	.002*
2000	34	.82	1.24	41	1.14	1.52	73	−.99	.325
2004	57	1.32	1.81	55	1.51	1.73	110	−.57	.565

Table 4–4 continued

Candidate Behavior	Winner			Loser			df	t	p
	N	M	SD	N	M	SD			
Verbal Tone									
Hedonic Bite Tone									
All years combined	143	.45	.76	149	.34	.69	290	1.15	.251
1992	32	.47	.84	31	.10	.39	44	2.25	.029*
1996	20	.45	.68	22	.09	.42	31	2.01	.053*
2000	34	.47	.78	41	.37	.69	73	.61	.544
2004	57	.42	.75	55	.58	.83	110	−1.07	.286
Agonic Bite Tone									
All years combined	143	.52	.87	149	.78	1.11	279	2.17	.031*
1992	32	.41	.79	31	.65	.95	61	−1.08	.283
1996	20	.05	.22	22	.91	1.57	21	−2.53	.019*
2000	34	.64	.91	41	.75	1.04	73	−.47	.636
2004	57	.68	.98	55	.81	1.05	110	−.70	.489
Candidate Gestures									
Hedonic Hand Display									
All years combined	143	1.04	1.47	149	.91	1.16	290	.79	.431
1992	32	.78	1.26	31	.77	1.08	61	.02	.981
1996	20	.75	.85	22	.91	.92	40	−.58	.565
2000	34	1.03	1.33	41	.78	1.12	73	.87	.385
2004	57	1.30	1.79	55	1.11	1.31	110	.64	.527
Agonic Hand Display									
All years combined	143	.28	.71	149	.52	.83	286	2.61	.010*
1992	32	.41	1.13	31	.48	.85	61	−3.07	.760
1996	20	.10	.30	22	.82	.95	25	−3.33	.003*
2000	34	.12	.32	41	.56	.77	55	−3.32	.002*
2004	57	.37	.67	55	.38	.80	110	−.09	.924
Hedonic Contact									
All years combined	143	.45	1.05	149	.23	.64	231	2.07	.040*
1992	32	.66	1.73	31	.16	.52	36	1.54	.131*
1996	20	.95	1.14	22	.63	1.20	40	.95	.350
2000	34	.29	.57	41	.24	.62	73	.36	.721
2004	57	.25	.60	55	.11	.45	104	1.34	.183*

*Homogeneity of variance assumption violated, equal variances not assumed procedure used.

winners and losers, as determined by postdebate polls and media coverage of the debates. Details about the coding instrument and how debate winners and losers were identified are provided in Appendix 4. Table 4–4 summarizes the findings of postdebate analyses between winners and losers, showing differences in hedonic and agonic depictions. All means are in the expected direction: clear debate winners, for all years combined, were featured in more hedonic displays than losers. However, only the test for hedonic contact was statistically significant. This lends weak support for the idea that debate winners will be shown exhibiting more hedonic behavior than losers.

A critical events analysis was next performed comparing the level of agonic behavior between debate winners and losers. The results for all years combined, summarized in Table 4–4, show significant differences between debate winners and losers for each variable analyzed. This delivered a strong pattern of significant results that confirms expectations for agonic behavior.

To assess the stability of these patterns, analyses were performed for each election year individually. Among hedonic variables, significant differences between debate winners and losers surfaced for sound bite tone in 1992 and 1996. The means were in the predicted direction: in each year the debate winner (Bill Clinton) was shown in a greater number of hedonic sound bites than the debate losers (George H. W. Bush and Bob Dole). No other significant differences were found, lending no additional support to the expectation that debate winners will emit more hedonic behavior than losers.

The pattern associated with agonic variables was consistent across election years. The 1996 election emerged as a strong case in point. Winner/loser tests were significant for every agonic variable, and in the predicted direction. In the 2000 election, Al Gore, the debate loser, was shown using agonic hand displays significantly more than the debate winner, George W. Bush. Overall, this pattern is stable across election years when looking at the direction of means, but with few statistically significant differences.

There were no significant differences between debate winners and losers across political parties, as the results of a party (Democrat, Republican) by debate outcome (winner, loser) analysis of variance indicate (see Table 4–5). Year-by-year analyses could not be performed because Democrats and Republicans were not both clear winners and/or losers of debates in each election year.

Communication Setting

Different communication settings may also influence the expressive behavior of presidential candidates. In particular, speeches—a formal and somewhat impersonal mode of address—are likely to

Table 4–5 Interactions for Political Party by Debate Outcome (all election years combined)

Candidate Behavior	df	F	p	Partial η^2
Overall				
Hedonic	1	.31	.277	.001
Agonic	1	.07	.788	.001
Facial Display				
Hedonic face	1	.31	.578	.001
Agonic face	1	.42	.516	.001
Verbal Tone				
Hedonic bite tone	1	.07	.787	.001
Agonic bite tone	1	.23	.632	.001
Candidate Gestures				
Hedonic hand display	1	.34	.561	.001
Agonic hand display	1	.53	.469	.002
Hedonic contact	1	.65	.420	.002

contain more anger/threat displays than interviews, whereas interviews, a more personal and intimate form of communication, are more likely to feature reassuring and upbeat candidate behavior.[18] From a dramaturgical perspective, the difference between speeches and interviews can be explained in terms of what sociologist Erving Goffman[57] referred to as front-region and back-region behavior. The former pertains to carefully crafted on-stage activities that an individual performs for public consumption, while playing out an idealized conception of a social role.[2] Traditionally front-region roles, including actor, waiter, professor, and politician, adhere to prescribed modes of interaction that clearly demarcate between on-stage and off-stage behaviors. Back-region roles and activities, on the other hand, refer to more private, unguarded, and candid conduct—the behind-the-scenes interactions that take place in the kitchen, smoke-filled room, private office, or after party. "In 'back regions' the individual and those who share his performance relax, discuss strategies, and analyze front region occurrences" (p. 134[58]).

With the rise of electronic media in politics, a new middle region of exposure has come into view, which reveals aspects of both front- and back-region behaviors (Meyrowitz, 1977).[58] The zoom lens and sensitive microphone now capture the intimate personal style of candidates for all to see and hear—the momentary hesitation before giving an answer, the offhand comment uttered to an aide, rope-line supporter, or running mate, the doubts that surface in spontaneous facial expressions.

In this way, front-region activities may reveal cues about what goes on backstage. The television camera also records more—and demands more—than other forms of media, invading the candidate's personal life, eroding once-accepted boundaries, and weakening the ability of candidates to perform a purely front-region role. "We see a politician address a crowd of well-wishers then greet his wife and children 'in private.' We join a candidate as he speaks with his advisors, and we sit behind him as he watches conventions on television," Meyrowitz[58] (p. 135) noted. "Now visible backstage, the hero has less time to rehearse . . . and build up his own confidence" (p. 140).

This new reality of middle-region exposure becomes evident in televised interviews, which demand a "behavioral style that is neither private conversation nor public proclamation" (p. 289[2]). If, as the anthropologist Edward Hall[59] argued, conversational tone, facial expression, and choice of language are often determined by the physical distance between people, with a more intimate style at close range and a more formal style with increased distance, we would expect candidates to exhibit more hedonic behavior in interviews than in speech settings. Physical closeness between an interviewer and interviewee dictates a certain sociability and agreeableness. Consequently, the television interview "generally turns away from oratory and 'ideas' and moves toward the chatty and the personal" (p. 290).[2]

During the 1984 Democratic primaries (the only election for which related findings are available), both leading candidates—Walter Mondale and Gary Hart—were twice as likely to be shown in close-up shots exhibiting happiness/reassurance displays when being interviewed than when delivering speeches.[18] Both were also pictured expressing anger/threat behavior almost exclusively in speeches. Anecdotally, Hillary Clinton's style in the 2008 presidential primaries personified this change in tone across communication settings. At the close of a sit-down conversational debate with Barack Obama in Austin, Texas, on February 21, she adopted an air of collegiality: "You know, no matter what happens in this contest," she said, turning to Obama to finish the sentence, "I am honored, I am honored to be here with Barack Obama." She then shook his hand and continued: "I am absolutely honored . . . whatever happens, we're going to be fine." The *New York Times* described the moment as "the night's most memorable grace note,"[60] which left voters with a gentle final impression. Two days later, in speech mode and behind a podium at a news conference in Cincinnati, Ohio, Clinton angrily denounced her opponent over two mailings she said misrepresented her views. In a scolding tone of voice, she admonished her rival: "Shame on you, Barack Obama. It is time you ran a campaign consistent with your messages in public. That's what I expect from you. Meet me in Ohio. Let's have a debate about your tactics and your behavior in this campaign."[61]

Assuming these communication patterns are consistently associated with different settings and are not just anecdotal occurrences, we expect presidential candidates in our sample years to be shown engaging in more agonic behavior in speeches than in interviews. Conversely, presidential candidates should be shown engaging in more hedonic behavior in interviews than in speeches.

Findings for Communication Setting

Categories employed in this part of the investigation are described in Appendix 4. For the analysis, sound bites from personal interviews and

Table 4–6 Hedonic and Agonic Representation in Speeches and Interviews

Candidate Behavior	Speeches			Interviews			df	t	p
	N	M	SD	N	M	SD			
Overall									
Agonic Sound Bites									
All years combined	267	2.02	2.08	47	1.85	2.23	266	1.35	.177
1992	62	1.55	2.08	14	.93	1.73	61	2.34	.230
1996	53	1.74	1.99	8	1.00	1.19	52	2.69	.010
2000	67	1.84	1.63	21	2.76	2.62	66	−4.64	.001
2004	85	2.64	2.3	4	2.00	1.63	84	2.77	.007
Hedonic Sound Bites									
All years combined	267	.87	1.20	47	1.43	1.79	266	−7.69	.001
1992	62	.84	1.24	14	.71	.99	62	.82	.418
1996	53	.79	1.11	8	1.25	.88	52	−2.99	.004
2000	67	.93	1.13	21	1.90	2.23	66	−7.04	.001
2004	85	.88	1.29	4	1.75	2.36	84	−6.22	.001
Facial Displays									
Agonic Face in Bites									
All years combined	267	1.00	1.18	47	1.00	1.42	266	.00	1.00
1992	62	.76	1.11	14	.50	1.16	62	.06	.955
1996	53	.83	.91	8	.75	.88	52	.64	.526
2000	67	.85	1.00	21	1.43	1.74	66	−4.72	.001
2004	85	1.40	1.39	4	1.00	.81	84	2.64	.010
Hedonic Face in Bites									
All years combined	267	.35	.60	47	.72	1.21	266	−9.98	.001
1992	62	.29	.55	14	.29	.47	61	.01	.996
1996	53	.42	.60	8	.75	.70	52	−4.05	.001

continued

Table 4–6 continued

Candidate Behavior	Speeches			Interviews			df	t	p
	N	M	SD	N	M	SD			
2000	67	.33	.58	21	.95	1.59	66	−8.66	.001
2004	85	.36	.66	4	1.00	1.41	84	−8.74	.001
Verbal Tone									
Agonic Bite Tone									
All years combined	267	1.02	1.07	47	.85	.95	266	2.63	.009
1992	62	.79	1.10	14	.43	.65	61	2.57	.013
1996	53	.91	1.21	8	.25	.46	52	3.94	.001
2000	67	.99	.84	21	1.33	1.06	66	−3.35	.001
2004	85	1.29	1.08	4	1.00	.81	84	2.52	.014
Hedonic Bite Tone									
All years combined	267	.52	.76	47	.70	.83	266	−3.90	.001
1992	62	.55	.95	14	.43	.64	61	.98	.332
1996	53	.38	.59	8	.50	.53	52	−1.50	.140
2000	67	.60	.71	21	.95	.97	66	−4.02	.001
2004	85	.52	.74	4	.75	.95	84	−2.86	.005

stump speeches were segmented from press conferences and debates. The means for agonic and hedonic behaviors for all years combined, in both interview and speech settings, were then compared using one-sample *t*-tests. As summarized in Table 4–6, agonic tone indeed occurred significantly more often in speeches than in interviews. This was the only significant difference, however. Agonic facial displays occurred with the exact same frequency in speeches and interview settings.

Based on previous findings for communication setting, we expected that presidential candidates would emit more hedonic displays in interviews than in speeches. The same procedure was followed to test for differences in hedonic behaviors for all years combined. The results from Table 4–6 indicate strong support for this idea. Tests for all three hedonic behaviors (facial displays, verbal tone, and overall hedonic behavior) produced statistically significant results in the anticipated direction. Candidates were clearly shown exhibiting more hedonic displays in interviews than in speeches.

The next step involved assessing the findings for hedonic and agonic behavior across election years. For the agonic dimension, the overall pattern was relatively stable. Means for three of the four elections were in the predicted direction and, for 1996 and 2004, candidates evidenced significantly more agonic behavior in speeches than in interviews. The 2000 election bucked this trend, however. In particular, Al Gore exhibited more agonic behavior in interviews than in speeches. A more detailed look at two agonic variables—verbal tone and facial displays in sound bites—reveals that Gore was also seen significantly more often in agonic facial expressions and was heard significantly more often in agonic verbal tone during his personal interviews than during his speeches, perhaps driving the nonsignificant findings for all years combined.

At times, Gore was on the attack. At other times, however, he clearly emitted signs of evasiveness. In an awkward live exchange with Tom Brokaw on November 3, a few days before the election, Gore was asked about George W. Bush's D.U.I. conviction decades earlier: "Do you think than an arrest 24 years ago will have any impact on the governor's ability to lead the country if, in fact, he's elected president?" Gore initially said he didn't have a comment on this piece of breaking news, then offered a hesitant reply, distancing himself from the issue. During his reply, however, Gore appeared visibly uncomfortable, gazing downward, shrugging his shoulders, moving his head from side to side, and avoiding direct eye contact with the camera—classic signs of fear/evasion (see Figure 4–1B). In answering the question, Gore acted as if *his* behavior was in question. "All I know is this," Gore offered, "our campaign had absolutely nothing to do with it."

Other election years produced support for the overall expectation that candidates would emit more agonic behavior in speeches than in interviews. Indeed, except for the 2000 election, all means for individual agonic variables were in the predicted direction. For facial displays, the test for 2004 was significant, while tests for agonic verbal tone were significant in 1992, 1996, and 2000, matching expectations.

Year-by-year examination of hedonic displays in speeches and interviews points to the 1992 election as an outlier. It is the only election year in which differences between speeches and interviews were not significant. Moreover, the means for 1992 ran counter to expectations: interviews were associated with less hedonic behavior than speeches, particularly for sound bite tone. All other election years support the prediction that candidates tend to display more hedonic behavior in interviews. All but one statistical test (for hedonic sound bite tone in 1996) was significant, offering strong support for the idea that interviews are associated with a happy/reassuring communication style.

Analysis of partisan differences across speech and interview settings produced several noteworthy findings, particularly for Republicans.[62] As shown in Figure 4–5, Democrats exhibited little variation in hedonic behavior across speech and interview settings (see also Tables 4–7 and

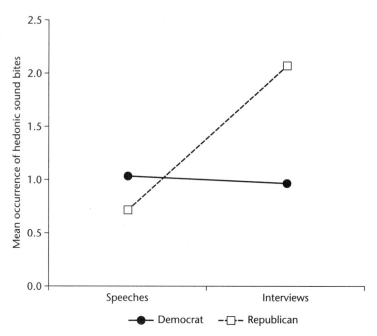

Figure 4–5 Interaction for political party and speech setting for hedonic sound bites

4–8). Republicans, on the other hand, clearly displayed more hedonic behavior in interviews than speeches, perhaps driving the overall findings we have reported for tests of hedonic behaviors. For agonic behaviors, there were no significant differences between Republicans and Democrats for any of the analyses (see Tables 4–7 and 4–8).

Display Repertoires over Time

Finally, we analyzed the breadth of candidate display repertoires over time. Masters et al.[18] found in their analysis of primary news that the Democratic candidates' expressive behaviors varied at different points in the campaign. After the New Hampshire primary, for example, both Walter Mondale and Gary Hart became more expressive, whereas Jesse Jackson evidenced the most display variation in speeches. As the campaign progressed, Mondale's anger/threat displays became much less frequent—and his happiness/reassurance displays more common. In the final phase of the primary campaign leading up to the Democratic National Convention, Mondale's facial expressions in speeches were largely neutral (perhaps in an effort to avoid mistakes), even though his interviews continued to feature happiness/reassurance displays frequently (p. 127[18]). If the same logic can be applied to over-time analyses of the general election, we would expect agonic displays to decrease while hedonic displays increase in frequency during the run-up to Election Day.

Findings for Over-Time Changes in Display Repertoires

Considering candidate nonverbals at different points in time, we expected agonic displays to decrease and hedonic displays to increase as Election Day approached. For this analysis, the three time periods constructed for comparison (see Appendix 4) were used as levels of an independent variable in one-way analysis of variance tests for

Table 4–7 Hedonic and Agonic Representation in Speeches by Political Party

Candidate Behavior	Democrats			Republicans			df	t	p
	N	M	SD	N	M	SD			
Overall									
Agonic sound bites	123	1.95	2.18	144	2.08	1.99	265	−.52	.606
Hedonic sound bites	123	1.03	1.27	144	.72	1.11	265	2.12	.035
Facial Displays									
Agonic face in bites	123	1.05	1.34	144	.96	1.01	265	.62	.533
Hedonic face in bites	123	.38	.62	144	.32	.59	265	.84	.403
Verbal Tone									
Agonic bite tone	123	.90	.98	144	1.13	1.13	265	−1.69	.091
Hedonic bite tone	123	.65	.85	144	.40	.66	227	2.61	.010*

*Homogeneity of variance assumption violated, equal variances not assumed procedure used.

Table 4–8 Hedonic and Agonic Representation in Interviews by Political Party

Candidate Behavior	Democrats			Republicans			df	t	p
	N	M	SD	N	M	SD			
Overall									
Agonic sound bites	27	1.89	2.60	20	1.80	1.67	45	.13	.895
Hedonic sound bites	27	.96	1.28	20	2.05	2.18	45	−2.14	.038
Facial Displays									
Agonic face in bites	27	1.00	1.64	20	1.00	1.12	45	.00	1.000
Hedonic face in bites	27	.33	.55	20	1.25	1.61	22	−2.43	.024*
Verbal Tone									
Agonic bite tone	27	.88	1.08	20	.80	.76	45	.31	.756
Hedonic bite tone	27	.62	.88	20	.80	.76	45	−.69	.494

*Homogeneity of variance assumption violated, equal variances not assumed procedure used.

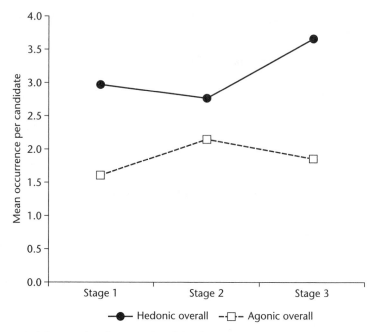

Figure 4–6 Interaction for emotional displays and campaign stages

agonic and hedonic behaviors. The overall (all years combined) pattern across variables revealed an increase in televised portrayals of hedonic behaviors and decrease in agonic depictions over the course of the election. These results confirm expectations.

Figure 4–6 illustrates the over-time increase in hedonic and decrease in agonic depictions for all four election years combined. As this figure shows, hedonic displays were more or less stable, dipping slightly from stage 1 to stage 2, but then sharply increased from stage 2 to Election Day. Agonic displays, on the other hand, increased from stage 1 to stage 2, then declined toward Election Day. Post hoc tests confirmed this finding. Dunnett C tests (not assuming equal variance) revealed a statistically significant ($p = 0.05$) difference between stages 1 and 3 for hedonic displays. There were no significant differences between stage pairs for agonic displays or for the overall one-way comparison (see Table 4–9).

Closer scrutiny of individual variables revealed a consistent pattern of hedonic displays—facial expressions, sound bite tone, and hand gestures—increasing toward Election Day. Physical contact between candidates and citizens was the only hedonic behavior that did not steadily increase over time. Instead, these behaviors became less apparent in the debate period and then experienced a resurgence in the final stretch of the campaign. Post hoc Dunnett C tests showed that both the initial decrease and ensuing increase toward Election Day were significant ($p = 0.05$). These analyses also identified a significant ($p = 0.05$) increase in hedonic sound

Table 4–9 Hedonic and Agonic Representation over Time

Candidate Behavior	Stage 1		Stage 2		Stage 3		df	F	p
	M	SD	M	SD	M	SD			
Overall									
Hedonic									
All years combined	2.97	3.39	2.77	3.09	3.66	3.73	2	3.54	.030
1992	2.51	3.00	2.85	3.21	3.13	4.06	2	.54	.582
1996	3.81	3.26	2.39	2.19	3.25	3.15	2	2.16	.120
2000	3.51	4.18	2.30	2.54	3.33	3.43	2	1.21	.303
2004	2.33	2.69	3.23	3.70	4.68	3.98	2	6.42	.002
Agonic									
All years combined	1.59	2.40	2.13	3.11	1.86	2.78	2	1.91	.150
1992	.98	1.95	2.05	4.28	1.67	3.11	2	2.07	.130
1996	1.60	2.25	1.06	1.53	1.77	2.83	2	.92	.403
2000	1.04	1.62	1.67	2.24	2.04	2.50	2	3.83	.024
2004	3.30	3.14	3.11	2.99	1.85	2.83	2	3.98	.021
Facial Display									
Hedonic Face									
All years combined	1.49	1.83	1.53	1.72	1.84	1.82	2	2.47	.086
1992	1.25	1.74	1.78	2.12	1.48	1.55	2	1.22	.298
1996	1.79	1.48	1.21	1.05	1.28	1.30	2	2.30	.105
2000	1.69	2.13	1.17	1.14	1.75	1.90	2	1.04	.356
2004	1.35	1.80	1.74	1.92	2.58	1.99	2	6.11	.003
Agonic Face									
All years combined	.78	1.28	1.13	1.69	.91	1.44	2	2.96	.052
1992	.43	.96	.90	2.07	.76	1.29	2	1.97	.134
1996	.72	1.18	.61	.99	.78	1.19	2	.20	.816
2000	.51	1.08	.833	1.26	.97	1.39	2	2.40	.094
2004	1.74	1.56	1.81	1.73	1.05	1.73	2	3.55	.031
Verbal Tone									
Hedonic Bite Tone									
All years combined	.23	.55	.34	.59	.40	.78	2	4.02	.018
1992	.17	.59	.34	.65	.33	.76	2	1.32	.272
1996	.30	.51	.12	.33	.28	.61	2	1.34	.266

continued

Table 4–9 continued

Candidate Behavior	Stage 1		Stage 2		Stage 3				
	M	SD	M	SD	M	SD	df	F	p
2000	.30	.61	.37	.55	.40	.77	2	.92	.677
2004	.19	.43	.45	.67	.54	.90	2	3.91	.022
Agonic Bite Tone									
All years combined	.51	.82	.61	.97	.60	1.03	2	.87	.420
1992	.32	.73	.61	1.09	.43	.83	2	1.48	.230
1996	.53	.85	.21	.48	.55	1.29	2	1.45	.240
2000	.63	1.04	1.03	1.60	1.40	2.09	2	2.40	.094
2004	.93	1.04	.85	1.06	.66	.97	2	1.00	.369
Candidate Gestures									
Hedonic Hand Display									
All years combined	.79	1.07	.71	1.22	1.00	1.25	2	3.13	.045
1992	.59	1.05	.56	.92	.76	1.17	2	.51	.600
1996	.81	1.02	.52	.66	.86	.93	2	1.49	.230
2000	1.07	1.19	.60	.85	.92	1.27	2	1.69	.188
2004	.74	.91	1.01	1.73	1.37	1.40	2	2.94	.056
Agonic Hand Display									
All years combined	.31	.70	.38	.94	.39	.81	2	.71	.492
1992	.23	.58	.54	1.45	.48	1.13	2	1.69	.187
1996	.35	.71	.24	.56	.44	.80	2	.70	.499
2000	.14	.35	.20	.40	.38	.68	2	3.80	.024
2004	.63	1.03	.45	.82	.31	.65	2	2.08	.128
Hedonic Contact									
All years combined	.47	.88	.22	.56	.44	1.00	2	4.49	.012
1992	.49	.87	.17	.49	.57	1.50	2	1.91	.151
1996	.91	1.06	.55	.86	.83	1.10	2	1.24	.294
2000	.45	.96	.17	.53	.27	.60	2	1.73	.181
2004	.09	.29	.08	.27	.27	.69	2	3.04	.051

Stage 1 runs from Labor Day to the day of the first debate of each election year; stage 2 from the day after the first debate to a few days after the last debate; and stage 3 encompasses the final stretch to Election Day.

bite tone between stages 1 and 3. Tukey tests (since the data met the homogeneity of variance assumption) showed the same increase at near-significant levels ($p = 0.07$) for hedonic facial displays and hand gestures.

Depictions of agonic displays, on the other hand, increased from the opening phase of the campaign to the debate period and then dropped off as Election Day approached. The drop-off in the last stage of the campaign supports the expectation that expressive behavior would be more positive and less varied over time, with the added nuance that agonic displays increased in the debate period before tapering off. Of all the Dunnett C post hoc paired comparisons, only one was significant ($p = 0.05$)—an increase in agonic facial displays from stage 1 to stage 2. The reported pattern for hedonic behaviors remained remarkably stable across our three election stages and election years. In fact, looking at the directions of means, the last stage (leading up to Election Day) was consistently associated with the highest hedonic scores.

The "all years combined" pattern for agonic variables was not stable across election years. In fact, agonic candidate behavior seems to be quite specific to individual election years (see Table 4–9). The elections of 2000 and 2004 deserve closer scrutiny because they produced a number of significant differences between time periods. Overall, these two elections are mirror opposites of each other. In 2000, agonic displays increased significantly toward Election Day, while in 2004 agonic displays decreased significantly as the election progressed. These trends hold up for several individual agonic behaviors, including facial displays, sound

Table 4–10 Interaction Effects for Political Party and Campaign Stages

Candidate Behavior	df	F	p	Partial η^2
Overall				
Hedonic	2	.43	.653	.001
Agonic	2	1.27	.282	.004
Facial Display				
Hedonic face	2	.14	.871	.001
Agonic face	2	.23	.792	.001
Verbal Tone				
Hedonic bite tone	2	.12	.890	.001
Agonic bite tone	2	.39	.681	.001
Candidate Gestures				
Hedonic hand display	2	.29	.752	.001
Agonic hand display	2	2.27	.104	.007
Hedonic contact	2	1.11	.332	.004

bite tone, and agonic hand gestures. Not all variables are significant, but this pattern is noticeable.

Finally, to assess partisan differences, a party (Democrat, Republican) by campaign stages (early, debate period, final stretch) analysis of variance was run. There were no significant interactions (see Table 4–10). Given the conflicting findings for agonic behaviors in 2000 and 2004, these two election years were isolated and subjected to further analysis. All variables, agonic and hedonic, were included in each ANOVA model; however, only the test for agonic hand gestures produced significant findings, for both election years[63] (see Figs. 4–7 and 4–8). Together, these figures show that George W. Bush, in both elections, displayed the expected agonic behavior curve: a peak in stage two, around the presidential debates, with lower points at stages 1 and 3.

The two Democratic candidates, on the other hand, exhibited a wildly different over-time pattern. In 2000, Gore's agonic hand gestures increased sharply after the debates and into the home stretch of the campaign, following the expected model for hedonic—not agonic—nonverbal behavior. Gore's behavior may have been indicative of what we reported in Chapter 3 about the anatomy of that election's image handling. Gore became increasingly frustrated with his image handlers as Election Day neared, ignoring advice that his televised nonverbal be-

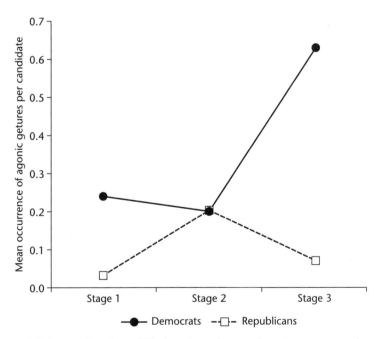

Figure 4–7 Interaction for political party and campaign stages on agonic hand gestures during the 2000 election

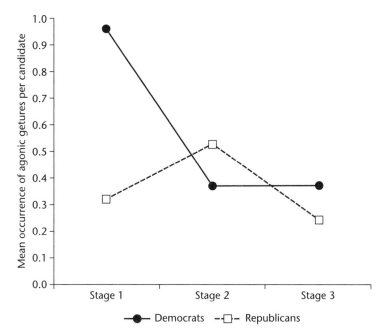

Figure 4–8 Interaction for political party and campaign stages on agonic hand gestures during the 2004 election

havior had an unsettling quality about it. Kerry, on the other hand, was shown in 2004 using dramatically more agonic hand gestures during the early stage of the general election campaign than in either the debate period, where one would expect to find it, or the final stretch. This curve again contradicts expectations for agonic behavior, which George W. Bush exemplified in his own way as an almost model nonverbal campaigner.

DISCUSSION

Presidential candidates elicit feelings from potential voters in different ways—by distinctive rhetorical styles, through citizen responses to positive or negative policy outcomes, and by hedonic and agonic display repertoires communicated via television news.[27,64] This chapter investigated the mediated aspects of this phenomenon, systematically examining the different modes of candidate behavior shown on network news and how coverage differs for individual candidates over time.[7,23] Summarizing the prevailing attitude against studying news visuals, Graber[65] has observed that "television's detractors have argued that the visual components of the story are trivial, adding very little to the substantive content" (p. 91). The argument that audiovisuals carry scant political meaning or electoral significance, however, simply cannot be sustained in light of existing research.

Inferences drawn from televised leader displays are particularly informative and affect partisans and undecided voters alike. Happiness/reassurance and anger/threat displays have larger effects on supporters than critics,[27] indicating the close scrutiny that candidate behavior receives. Supporters tend to respond positively to hedonic displays of an admired leader and, in some cases, instances of aggression. Agonic behavior can be effective in bonding followers to leaders but is not reassuring to critics.[66] Instead, critics tend to respond negatively to anger/threat displays and are likely to report neutral or no emotional responses after viewing the smiling face of an unliked leader. Happiness/reassurance displays are thus capable of neutralizing the negative feelings of critics, a quality that agonic expressions lack. Fear/evasion displays, by contrast, elicit negative feelings from supporters and critics alike.[17,25] Interestingly, the largest lasting effects of televised leader displays have been found for politically neutral viewers,[25] that undecided swath of voters who determine close elections.

Departing from conventional approaches that investigate the verbal aspects of news coverage, the results of this analysis confirm and extend what we know about media portrayals of presidential candidates. Hedonically, there were few differences between front-runners and trailing candidates from 1992 to 2004, with the exception that clear debate winners were shown engaging in significantly more physical embraces with supporters in the period following their commanding performance. Such a subtle form of favorable news coverage would scarcely register verbally, if at all, in a text-based content analysis but is readily apparent when coded visually. But as a visual cue, hedonic contact signals support and admiration. For the most part, the major party nominees were shown in roughly the same number of happiness/reassurance displays, as well as positive sound bites and upbeat gestures—a tendency that increased in the final stretch of the campaign. In the general election, candidates indeed came across as happy warriors. This was especially true in interview settings, which featured significantly more hedonic depictions than formal speeches.

Agonic displays were slightly less prominent in news coverage overall but were associated with trailing candidates and debate losers significantly more than front-runners and debate winners. Candidates, in other words, who were behind in the polls were more often shown exhibiting anger/threat (or fear/evasion), making defiant gestures, and delivering statements that were negative in tone or hostile in intent than candidates who were ahead. This behavioral pattern is consistent with ethological observations that have documented aggression in second-ranking individuals or challengers to power. Agonic displays increased during the debate period, due to increased competitive behaviors and attacks by trailing candidates, but then decreased in the final stretch of the campaign when the strategic goal is to maximize the candidate's popular appeal. The decrease in aggression and embrace of a more positive, hedonic style of campaigning in the last few weeks of the election suggests that candidates become much more focused on building their prestige with the electorate than dominating the opponent after the debate period. A certain amount of competitive (agonic) behavior persists to Election Day, but the competition becomes more focused on building public support and less on direct political rivalry.

Examined by party, over-time analyses of candidate displays revealed some dramatic differences in the campaigning styles of Democrats and Republicans. Republicans are appropriately most feisty around debate time, when facing a formal encounter with the opposition, and grow more hedonic toward Election Day, appearing leaderlike and victorious. Democrats, on the other hand, are most hedonic in the heated debate period, when they should perhaps be most confrontational, and become progressively more agonic toward Election Day, appearing defeated and perhaps desperate. As with any analysis of mean tendencies, there are some notable exceptions to these trends, but overall Republicans seem to be more effective than Democrats at utilizing expressive behavior at key junctures in the campaign.

The aggregate trends documented by this analysis support the ethological notion that contests for leadership or dominant status can be characterized by the display repertoires of leading candidates. Differences between parties are again telling. Ethological theory would predict more happiness/reassurance expressed by winners and incumbents, and more anger/threat exhibited by trailers and challengers. But the televised displays of Republicans and Democrats are decisively divergent when faced with the environmental realities of winning and losing in the polls. Democrats emote most—hedonically and agonically—when they are *trailing* in the polls; Republicans, by contrast, show more emotion when they are *winning* the horse race.

Being seen as a happy and aggressive loser is arguably less leaderlike than being portrayed as a reassuring and aggressive front-runner— that is, a happy warrior. The Republican tactic of going on the attack when in a position of strength suggests a well-planned strategy. Even at the microlevel of nonverbal behavior, candidates might be executing image-handler advice. Indeed, displays of aggression can be effective in rallying one's base of core supporters and bonding leaders to followers. The contrary pattern for Democrats, the "angry and happy loser" phenomenon, sends a mixed message of being simultaneously pleased with and desperate to overcome their subordinate status. This display ambivalence places candidates in a double bind: angry losers are unlikely to emerge as leaders, while being content with losing appears Pollyannaish and weak.

Democrats also fail to capitalize on the potential to connect hedonically with voters in the context of the personalized interview setting. Instead, they save their reassuring and upbeat messages for the big stage, during speeches. Republicans, either intuitively or perhaps due to clever image handling, use the one-on-one conversational setting of the interview to clearly signal optimism and reassurance. Considering that close-up shots are more likely to be used in interviews and long shots more for speeches, Republicans have thus placed themselves in a much better visual position than Democrats to emotionally connect with viewers through the intimacy-enhancing qualities of the sit-down interview. At the same time, G.O.P. candidates save their competitive flourishes or agonic behavior—which could be tough to take in the close-up interview format—for the longer shots that are more commonly used in speeches.

Sullivan and Masters[23] have argued that emotional reactions to facial displays and other nonverbal behaviors play an important role in producing the "momentum" that candidates develop over the course of an election. Although a candidate's status derives from numerous factors, such as political reputation, fund-raising ability, popularity, and elite opinion, televised portrayals play an influential role in regulating the esteem with which a candidate or officeholder is held. This analysis cannot answer why expressive displays vary—whether it is because candidates behave differently or because news framing is applied unevenly—but we would argue that the final news product represents an interplay between candidate tendencies (i.e., their communication style) and the political narrative that emerges for individual candidacies. Regardless of causality, the way in which leaders are depicted on television shapes and indexes their status such that political power in the contemporary era can no longer be fully understood without regard for television coverage.[24]

With the rise of television, a close-up medium, as the primary channel of political communication, the effects of expressive leader displays have become increasingly important to consider. Indeed, the communicative behavior of public figures has become central to evaluations of political effectiveness. Rivals for power who appear weak and overwhelmed on the one hand, or overly aggressive on the other, are politically disadvantaged. Consistent with this argument, unfavorable visual portrayals are now recognized as central to accusations of media bias (see Grabe[67,68]), a point we consider thoroughly in Chapter 5.

Without question, new media technology adds to the growing centrality of visuals in election news. The diffusion of widescreen and high-definition television sets that offer enhanced visual resolution and, through the use of home theater systems, audio fidelity augurs an era of even *closer* viewer scrutiny of candidate behavior. Compared to a standard televised presentation, campaign coverage broadcast in high definition (HDTV), where the communication style and expressive displays of leaders are seen with up to six times the image resolution of conventional broadcasts, should have a noticeably stronger evaluative impact. Indeed, an experimental investigation comparing HDTV (with 1,080 lines of vertical resolution) to a standard-resolution broadcast (with 480 lines) found a marked increase in self-reported social presence for the high-definition condition.[69] In particular, viewers of high definition reported being able to observe facial expressions and body movement significantly better than those who observed the same scenes in the standard-resolution condition.[70] Given the fine-grained detail of today's cameras, candidates would do well to assume they are *always* being broadcast in high definition and shown on a big screen TV or high resolution computer display.

Because expressive displays of highly recognizable political figures within newscasts are capable of evoking a range of cognitive and emotional responses, both favorable and unfavorable, that affect viewer attitudes and serve as dispositions to action, they warrant our continued attention. On television, these effects hold whether the leader's voice is heard, filtered, or overlaid with a reporter's audio narration.[10,12,32,37] Thus, *how* presidential candidates communicate, and the quality of coverage they receive in national broadcast media, matters. News visuals are deceptive in the sense that they are processed with little conscious effort on the part of the viewer. Yet in electoral campaigns, as in the exercise of political office, leadership is closely associated with the capacity to capture and hold the attention of audiences.[24] Candidates who are effective nonverbal communicators have the advantage of utilizing this attention to affect the quality of news coverage they receive, thereby improving their political prospects.

NOTES

1. Ansolabehere, Stephen, Roy Behr, and Shanto Iyengar. 1993. *The media game: American politics in the television age.* New York: Macmillan Publishing.

2. Meyrowitz, Joshua. 1985. *No sense of place: The impact of electronic media on social behavior.* New York: Oxford University Press.

3. Clayman, Steven E. 1995. Defining moments, presidential debates, and the dynamics of quotability. *Journal of Communication* 45(3):118–146.

4. Kurtz, Howard. 2004, January 23. Reporters shift gears on the Dean bus; Iowa vote and outburst rewrite the campaign sage. *The Washington Post,* p. C1.

5. Druckman, James N. 2003. The power of television images: The first Kennedy-Nixon debate revisited. *Journal of Politics* 65(2):559–571.

6. Kraus, Sidney. 1996. Winners of the first 1960 televised presidential debate between Kennedy and Nixon. *Journal of Communication* 46(4):78–96.

7. Jamieson, Kathleen H. 1988. *Eloquence in an electronic age: The transformation of political speechmaking.* New York: Oxford University Press.

8. Perloff, Richard M. 1998. *Political communication: Politics, press, and public in America.* Mahwah, NJ: Lawrence Erlbaum Associates.

9. Graber, Doris A. 2001. *Processing politics: Learning from television in the Internet age*. Chicago: University of Chicago Press.

10. Masters, Roger D., and Dennis G. Sullivan. 1993. Nonverbal behavior and leadership: Emotion and cognition in political information processing. In *Explorations in political psychology*, ed. Shanto Iyengar and William J. McGuire, pp. 150–182. Durham, NC: Duke University Press.

11. Patterson, Miles L., Mary E. Churchill, Gary K. Burger, and Jack. L. Powell. 1992. Verbal and nonverbal modality effects on impressions of political candidates: Analysis from the 1984 presidential debates. *Communication Monographs* 59:231–242.

12. Bucy, Erik P. 2000. Emotional and evaluative consequences of inappropriate leader displays. *Communication Research* 27(2):194–226.

13. Bucy, Erik P., and Samuel D. Bradley. 2004. Presidential expressions and viewer emotion: Counterempathic responses to televised leader displays. *Social Science Information/Information sur les Sciences Sociales* 43(1):59–94.

14. Masters, Roger D. 2001. Cognitive neuroscience, emotion, and leadership. In *Citizens and politics: Perspectives from political psychology*, ed. James H. Kuklinski, pp. 68–102. New York: Cambridge University Press.

15. Masters, Roger D. 1991. Primate politics and political theory. In *Primate politics*, ed. Glendon Schubert and Roger D. Masters, pp. 221–247. Carbondale: Southern Illinois University Press.

16. Somit, Albert, and Steven A. Peterson. 1998. Biopolitics after three decades: A balance sheet. *British Journal of Political Science* 28:559–571.

17. Lanzetta, John T., Dennis G. Sullivan, Roger D. Masters, and Gregory J. McHugo. 1985. Emotional and cognitive responses to televised images of political leaders. In *Mass media and political thought: An information-processing approach*, ed. Sidney Kraus and Richard M. Perloff, pp. 85–116. Beverly Hills, CA: Sage.

18. Masters, Roger D., Dennis G. Sullivan, Alice Feola, and Gregory J. McHugo. 1987. Television coverage of candidates' display behavior during the 1984 Democratic primaries in the United States. *International Political Science Review* 8(2):121–130.

19. Chance, Michael R. A. 1976. Attention structures as the basis of primate rank orders. In *The social structure of attention*, ed. Michael R. A. Chance and Ray R. Larson, pp. 11–28. New York: John Wiley & Sons.

20. Kortmulder, Koenraad, and Yuri Robbers. 2005. *The agonic and hedonic styles of social behaviour*. London: Edwin Mellen Press.

21. Masters, Roger D. 1989. *The nature of politics*. New Haven: Yale University Press.

22. Rozelle, Richard M., Daniel Druckman, and James C. Baxter. 1986. Nonverbal communication. In *A handbook of communication skills*, ed. Owen Hargie, pp. 59–94. New York: New York University Press.

23. Sullivan, Dennis G., and Roger D. Masters. 1988. "Happy warriors": Leaders' facial displays, viewers' emotions, and political support. *American Journal of Political Science* 32(2):345–368.

24. Masters, Roger D., Siegfried Frey, and Gary Bente. 1991. Dominance and attention: Images of leaders in German, French, and American TV news. *Polity* 25:373–394.

25. Sullivan, Dennis G., and Roger D. Masters. 1994. Biopolitics, the media, and leadership: Nonverbal cues, emotions, and trait attributions in the evaluation of leaders. In *Research in biopolitics*, vol. 2, ed. Albert Somit and Steven A. Peterson, pp. 237–273. Greenwich, CT: JAI Press.

26. Ekman, Paul. 1982. *Emotion in the human face.* New York: Cambridge University Press.

27. Sullivan, Dennis G., and Roger D. Masters, with John T. Lanzetta, Gregory J. McHugo, Basil G. Englis, and Elise F. Plate. 1991. Facial displays and political leadership: Some experimental findings. In *Primate politics*, ed. Glendon Schubert and Roger D. Masters, pp. 188–206. Carbondale: Southern Illinois University Press.

28. Masters, Roger D., Dennis G. Sullivan, John T. Lanzetta, Gregory J. McHugo, and Basil G. Englis. 1986. Facial displays and political leadership. *Journal of Biological and Social Structures* 9:319–343.

29. The exception is counterempathy, in which case a smile or other hedonic signal conveyed by a disliked other, for example a reviled politician or tormenting superior, may evoke a negative response in the observer (see Bucy and Bradley[13]).

30. Masters, Roger D. 1981. Linking ethology and political science: Photographs, political attention, and presidential elections. *New Directions for Methodology of Social and Behavioral Science* 7:61–80.

31. Benjamin, J. Daniel, and Jesse M. Shapiro. 2006. *Thin-slice forecasts of gubernatorial elections.* NBER Working Paper No. 12660. Cambridge, MA: National Bureau of Economic Research. http://home.uchicago.edu/~jmshapir/thinslice102306.pdf. Accessed February 9, 2007.

32. The persuasive influence of televised leader displays depends, of course, on a host of contextual, attitudinal, dispositional, and perceptual factors,[25] including "the nature of the display, the relationship between the viewer and the leader, and characteristics of the viewer" (p. 355[23]). Masters[14] has proposed a neuroscientific model of viewer responses to leaders that includes four classes of variables impinging on leader evaluations: the quality of the display or communication (stimulus features), viewer characteristics, political predispositions, and short-term perceptions or episodic emotions evoked by the presentation. The associated news context also influences audience responses to leader displays (Bucy[12,36] and Bucy and Bradley[13]).

33. Bucy, Erik P., and John E. Newhagen. 1999. The micro- and macrodrama of politics on television: Effects of media format on candidate evaluations. *Journal of Broadcasting & Electronic Media* 43(2):193–210.

34. Todorov, Alexander, Anesu N. Mandisodza, Amir Goren, and Crystal C. Hall. 2005. Inferences of competence from faces predict election outcomes. *Science* 308(10):1623–1626.

35. Ambady, Nalini, and Robert Rosenthal. 1992. Thin slices of expressive behavior as predictors of interpersonal consequences: A meta-analysis. *Psychological Bulletin* 111(2):256–274.

36. Bucy, Erik P. 2003. Emotion, presidential communication, and traumatic news: Processing the World Trade Center attacks. *Harvard International Journal of Press/Politics* 8(4):76–96.

37. Zettl, Herbert. 2007. *Sight, sound, motion: Applied media aesthetics*, 5th ed. Belmont, CA: Wadsworth.

38. Babchuk, Wayne A., Raymond B. Hames, and Ross A. Thompson. 1985. Sex differences in the recognition of infant facial expressions of emotion: The primary caretaker hypothesis. *Ethology & Sociobiology* 6:89–101.

39. During both primary and general election settings, Sullivan and Masters[23] found that changes in viewer attitudes are more likely to be influenced by emotional responses to happiness/reassurance displays than party identification, issue agreement, or assessments of leadership ability. Of course, poll standings and presidential approval ratings depend on a host of other important factors, both foreign and domestic, of which communication ability is but one (see Brody[40]).

40. Brody, Richard A. 1991. *Assessing the president: The media, elite opinion, and political support*. Stanford: Stanford University Press.

41. Whether owing to their personal appeal or image management strategies, some candidates and officeholders seem better able to attract and maintain favorable news coverage while others stumble in the national spotlight (see Hayden[42] and Moore[43]). Hertsgaard[44] (pp. 4–5), in his examination of the extraordinarily positive press coverage of the Reagan administration, contended that Reagan's "personal gifts—an amiable personality, sincere manner, perfect vocal delivery, and photogenic persona" made attacks on the president basically "unthinkable."

42. Hayden, Joseph. 2001. *Covering Clinton: The president and the press in the 1990s*. Westport, CT: Praeger.

43. Moore, Mark P. 1992. "The Quayle quagmire": Political campaigns in the poetic form of burlesque. *Western Journal of Communication* 56(2): 108–124.

44. Hertsgaard, Mark. 1989. *On bended knee: The press and the Reagan presidency*. New York: Schocken Books.

45. Klein, Joe. 2008, February 18. Inspiration vs. substance. Obama's flights of rhetoric are the stuff of legend. But Clinton simply knows more. What this nail biter of a Democratic primary may come down to. *Time* 18–19.

46. Zernike, Kate. 2008, February 17. The charisma mandate. *The New York Times*, p. WK1, 4.

47. Stanley, Alessandra. 2008, January 29. Camelot '08 overshadows Bush speech. *The New York Times*, p. A20.

48. Masters, Roger D., and Dennis G. Sullivan. 1989. Nonverbal displays and political leadership in France and the United States. *Political Behavior* 11:121–153.

49. McHugo, Gregory J., John T. Lanzetta, and Lauren K. Bush. 1991. The effect of attitudes on emotional reactions to expressive displays of political leaders. *Journal of Nonverbal Behavior* 15:19–41.

50. Exline, Ralph V. 1985. Multichannel transmission of nonverbal behavior and the perception of powerful men: The presidential debates of 1976. In *Power, dominance, and nonverbal behavior*, ed. Steve L. Ellyson and John F. Dovidio, pp. 183–206. New York: Springer-Verlag.

51. Nyhan, David. 1996, October 9. Dole's blinkmanship. *The Boston Globe*, p. A27.

52. The frequency of Jackson's aggressive displays in speeches (and even in interviews before the New Hampshire primary) "could be attributed to

his status as a candidate with a low probability of winning, who sought to strengthen the attachment of his constituency rather than to reassure his critics" (p. 127[18]).

53. Lakoff, George. 1996. *Moral politics: How liberals and conservatives think.* Chicago: University of Chicago Press.

54. Stevenson, Richard W., and Janet Elder. 2004, October 5. Poll finds Kerry assured voters in initial debate. *The New York Times*, p. A1.

55. Fineman, Howard. 2000, October 23. Too close for comfort. *Newsweek*, p. 39.

56. Masters, Roger D. 1976. The impact of ethology on political science. In *Biology and politics*, ed. Albert Somit, pp. 197–233. The Hague: Mouton.

57. Goffman, Erving. 1959. *The presentation of self in everyday life.* New York: Doubleday Anchor Books.

58. Meyrowitz, Joshua. 1977. The rise of "middle region" politics. *Et cetera: A review of General Semantics* 34(2):133–144.

59. Hall, Edward. 1966. *The hidden dimension.* New York: Doubleday.

60. Healy, Patrick, and Jeff Zeleny. 2008, February 22. Debate takes on contentious air for Democrats. *The New York Times*, p. A1.

61. Bosman, Julie. 2008, February 24. Clinton criticizes Obama over fliers on trade sent to voters in Ohio. *The New York Times*, p. A21.

62. Year-by-year comparisons for Democrats and Republicans across interviews and speeches produced cell sizes that were too small for reliable statistical analysis.

63. For 2000: $F(2, 164) = 3.96$, $p < 0.021$, partial $\eta^2 = 0.05$; for 2004: $F(2, 166) = 3.26$, $p < 0.041$, partial $\eta^2 = 0.04$.

64. Roseman, Ira J., Robert P. Abelson, and Michael F. Ewing. 1986. Emotion and political cognition: Emotional appeals in political communication. In *Political cognition: The 19th annual Carnegie Symposium on Cognition*, ed. Richard R. Lau and David D. O. Sears, pp. 279–294. Hillsdale, NJ: Lawrence Erlbaum Associates.

65. Graber, Doris A. 1996. Say it with pictures. *Annals of the American Academy of Political and Social Science* 546:85–96.

66. Sullivan, Dennis G. 1996. Emotional responses to the nonverbal behavior of French and American political leaders. *Political Behavior* 18:311–325.

67. Grabe, Maria Elizabeth. 1996. The SABC's coverage of the 1987 and 1989 elections: The matter of visual bias. *Journal of Broadcasting & and Electronic Media* 40(1):1–27.

68. Grabe, Maria Elizabeth. 2007, May. *The liberal bias accusation against journalism: Contradictory evidence from a visual perspective.* Paper presented at the annual meeting of the International Communication Association, Visual Communication Division, San Francisco, CA.

69. Bracken, Cheryl C. 2005. Presence and image quality: The case of high-definition television. *Media Psychology* 7(2):191–205.

70. Social presence in this study was measured with two questions: "During the media experience, how well were you able to observe the facial expressions of the people you saw/heard?" and "During the media experience, how well were you able to observe the body language of the people you saw/heard?"[69]

The Pew Research Center for the People and the Press. (2000). *The tough job of communicating with voters.* Retrieved on January 15, 2006, from: http://peoplepress.org/reports/. Accessed January 15, 2006.

5

Visual Bias

Grousing about the news media is a central and historically persistent part of American political discourse.[1-4] Indeed, the very idea of cataloging praise for the media's role in elections seems anachronistic, a vestige of a bygone era of high trust in government and the media. Criticism of the press springs from several sources, including partisan accusations of purported biases in news coverage of politics, campaign and image-handler complaints about candidate portrayals in news, and metacoverage of media performance that journalists inflict upon themselves.

Candidates might be smeared by opponents and occasionally ambushed by aggressive news reporting but they at least face cheers of support on the campaign trail. Image handlers, because they remain to a large degree under the public radar, face little sustained scrutiny. Citizens—despite their documented apathy—are civically unassailable. Of the four major players in the election process, journalists arguably receive the bulk of blame for imperfections in the system. Indeed, with the increasing influence of media in politics journalism has become a popular target of criticism. Complaints about liberal media bias in news have grown in frequency and force over the past three decades as a staple theme of this rhetorical ritual, most predictably as accusations from conservative politicians and interest groups during presidential elections. Academics and political commentators have also become fond of hammering the news media about the quality of coverage, accusing the press of trivializing political discourse and weakening the accountability of public officials,[6,7] and of being overly intrusive, interpretive, and evaluative,[2] elitist, self-serving, and arrogant,[7] fixated on conflict and mired in a tabloid culture that specializes in prediction rather than assessment,[7-9] carnivorous,[10] and producers and purveyors of bad new.[11-15]

Journalists themselves compound this criticism by playing the role of "suicidal messengers" who, through self-coverage about media performance, contribute to the erosion of public confidence in the news as an institution.[16] In recent years, right-leaning reporters have further added to the public alarm about media bias, issuing late-career mea culpas or writing insider exposés about a hidden liberal bias in television newsrooms (e.g., Goldberg[17,18] and Stossel[19]). Andy Rooney of *60 Minutes* reinforced this view in one of his commentaries during the 2004 election, remarking: "I know a lot of you believe that most people in the news business are liberal. Let me tell you, I know a lot of them, and they were almost evenly divided this time. Half of them liked Senator Kerry; the other half hated President Bush" (quoted on *60 Minutes*, November 7, 2004).

Perhaps not surprisingly, then, polling data show that an increasing number of citizens believe there is an ideological slant to news content.[20] Between 1992 and 2007, according to Roper polls, the percentage of the public who felt news media were exhibiting a liberal bias grew from 27% to 38%. Yet popular discussions and even some academic research about media bias are characterized by contradictory and equivocal claims. In fact, empirical studies of news, whether analyzing news content or the personal political views of reporters, produce ambiguous results. One meta-analysis of 59 media bias studies of presidential news coverage since 1948 found no significant differences in how favorably Democrats and Republicans were treated in print media, and small but probably insubstantial differences in airtime and journalistic commentary favoring Democrats in studies of network news.[21]

Despite repeated efforts, scholarly investigations of liberal bias have not exhausted all avenues of inquiry, largely ignoring visual analyses of television news content. The bastions of elite print media, particularly the *New York Times* and *Washington Post*, are regarded as more worthy of investigation. The unarticulated assumption in this research is that detecting bias in venerated print outlets might be more harmful to democracy than the transgressions of television journalists. Even when television coverage is investigated, it is largely analyzed without regard for the visual component of the medium. Instead, the overall volume of coverage and narrative content (audio track) of television news are examined. The few times that researchers have paid attention to visual manifestations of bias, they have looked mostly at the content of candidate appearances (e.g., symbolic backgrounds, dress, posture, interaction with voters), which reveal more about the advice of image handlers than decisions made by news organizations (see Chapter 3).

To clarify this muddled area of research and analysis—and recast the contentious yet stale public debate over media bias—we introduce a new approach to measuring bias based on the visual aspects of broadcast news. Unlike the candidates' verbal statements and self-presentation style, the indicators of visual bias we employ fall more squarely under the control of editors and producers than candidates and their consultants. To explain the persistence of the liberal bias charge against journalism as a political theme, we trace the rise of partisan attacks on the press in recent decades. Accusations aside, questions concerning media favoritism represent a serious challenge to the credibility of the press (and hence the informational basis of democratic decision making) and deserve careful examination. If news workers are skewing coverage, assessments of bias must be able to pinpoint journalistic favoritism and rule out competing explanations, such as campaign orchestration of the news.

When the visual packaging of general election news is carefully considered, it becomes clear that the networks have in fact systematically favored one party over another. Contrary to the liberal bias accusation against mainstream media, our data show that visual coverage has consistently favored Republican presidential candidates while Democrats have endured less favorable treatment in each of the four general election contests we examined. This chapter explains how and suggests a few reasons for why this trend exists, including the idea that journalists sometimes unwittingly surrender control over visual portrayals to campaign image handlers.

THE STORIED HISTORY OF THE MEDIA BIAS ACCUSATION

Before proceeding with our analysis, we briefly consider the history of the media bias accusation against journalism, a difficult-to-substantiate charge made politically relevant in the 1948 presidential election. As mentioned, accusations of press bias have been a more or less stable feature of public life since the earliest days of the republic. Until the advent of a professionalized and commercially independent press in the mid-1800s, such charges were largely misplaced given that most newspapers were owned by or closely affiliated with political parties or organizations.[22] Even as advertising revenues freed the press from overt political control, the Progressives in the early 1900s saw in journalism the opportunity for mass edification and criticized news organizations for pursuing commercialism over a higher-minded democratic mission (see West[22]). The rise of sensationalism, early consolidation within the media industries, and growing concerns about authoritarian uses of the press surrounding the world wars led to a thoroughgoing examination of media performance in the late 1940s by the Hutchins Commission on the Freedom of the Press. Recommendations in the commission's report, *A Free and Responsible Press*,[23] were later elaborated as *Four Theories of the Press* by Siebert, Peterson, and Schramm[24] and articulated a social responsibility role for American journalism to steer a public service path around a government-run, party-controlled, or exclusively market-driven press.

Ironically, given the predominant accusation of a *liberal* media bias in today's political discourse, it was a Democrat who first made press influence in presidential politics a campaign issue. In October of 1948, when it appeared that Harry Truman faced almost certain defeat at the hands of Republican Thomas E. Dewey (the polls were so one-sided that *Life* magazine had declared Dewey the next president a week before the election), Truman set out on a historic coast-to-coast whistle-stop tour with two centerpiece issues: the "do nothing" Republican Congress and the "one party press"—by which he meant a conservatively leaning press.[3] Truman's accusation against the news media was grounded in the fact that most newspapers in the 1948 election (65%, according to an *Editor & Publisher* poll) endorsed Dewey for president—a trend that continued with Eisenhower's elections in the 1950s.[3] Of course, editorial page *endorsements*, which represent the political beliefs of media owners and editors, are not the same as biased *coverage*,[25-27] but this was largely a moot point: Truman had, in the eyes of many observers, successfully turned the press into a campaign issue.

Democratic presidential nominee Adlai Stevenson turned up the heat over what he perceived as unfair press coverage following his losses to Eisenhower in 1952 and 1956, but the issue crescendoed on both sides of the political aisle during the contentious 1960 election between John F. Kennedy and Richard Nixon.[3] Following protests of press favoritism by Democrats *and* Republicans that year, some 13 separate studies of newspaper bias were conducted, none of which confirmed these partisan concerns.[28] With the ascendance of liberal ideas and policies in the 1960s and no effective means for conservative, monied interests "to comprehend, much less quell or combat, the social and political turmoil then engulfing the whole of American society" (p. 33[29]), accusations of media bias began to veer in a left-leaning direction. Indeed, following the election of Nixon in 1968, criticism of the press resurfaced in a more virulent, cultural form, taking on an almost ideological fervor against the fabled East Coast intellectual establishment.[29] The new look of liberal media criticism was unveiled in the fall of 1969 by Nixon's vice president, Spiro T. Agnew, in a series of addresses written by then–White House speechwriters William Safire and Patrick Buchanan (who later became national media personalities in their own right). Exhorting citizens to register their complaints on bias to the networks directly, Agnew (1969/1987) characterized television news anchors, commentators, and decision makers as

[T]his little group of men who not only enjoy a right of instant rebut-
tal to every presidential address, but more importantly, wield a free
hand in selecting, presenting, and interpreting the great issues of our
nation. . . . We would never trust such power over public opinion in
the hands of an elected government—it is time we questioned it in
the hands of a small and unelected elite. (quoted in Ryan[30] p. 214)

The following year, still railing against the administration's per-
ceived antagonists, including the media and opponents of the Vietnam
War, Agnew (1970) famously observed in an address to the California
Republican state convention that "in the United States today, we have
more than our share of the nattering nabobs of negativism" (quoted in
Morrow[31]).

Around the same time, several right-leaning policy institutes and
think tanks were formed to propagate a conservative message, partly
in response to the cultural upheaval and political unrest of the times,
which some conservatives felt threatened the very fabric of society and
even the free enterprise system itself (see Lapham[29]). The 1970s were a
period of robust growth and reinvigoration of conservative policy institutes and politically oriented religious movements. The decade witnessed the establishment of the Heritage Foundation, Cato Institute,
and Business Roundtable, the revival of the American Enterprise Institute, and formation of Jerry Falwell's Moral Majority, among others. In
what came to be known as the intellectual counterrevolution that eventually brought Ronald Reagan to office, a consistent effort was made to
challenge the liberal consensus that had forged Roosevelt's New Deal
during the Depression and helped pass Johnson's Great Society programs during the civil rights era. Integral to this effort, according to
Lapham,[29] was "the demonization of the liberal press" (p. 35).

Ironically, and perhaps strategically, accusations of liberal media
bias took hold and gained popularity among conservative politicians at
roughly the same time that conservative lawmakers repealed the Fairness Doctrine, which required broadcasters to give balance to opposing
viewpoints in opinion programming.[32] The doctrine provided a mechanism for achieving at least rudimentary political balance on television
and radio but was roundly criticized by conservatives as a means of
keeping their views from being expressed in the media or as a way to
deliberately cut their available airtime in half.[33] Before the doctrine's
abolition in 1987, on-air editorials were integrated into broadcast news
content with access granted to the opposing side. The Fairness Doctrine also effectively postponed the rise of politically oriented talk radio
and cable news channels, which became plausible only after the rule's
repeal.

By the end of Ronald Reagan's second term in office, an estimated $100
million a year was being spent, in a more or less coordinated fashion,

by extragovernmental organizations on promoting a conservative message of antiliberal policy objectives.[29] Exhortations for further deregulation of the broadcast news environment have been central to this effort.[32] Amplifying this perspective today is a $300 million "message machine" that gives voice to conservative causes and ideas through cable television networks and discussion shows, talk radio programs, and both print and online publishing ventures,[29] including media monitoring organizations that keep a close eye on political coverage.[32,34,35] Perhaps as a consequence of all this ideological activity, "the basic American consensus has shifted over the last thirty years from a liberal to a conservative bias" in which government is viewed as the problem, not the solution; the social contract a dead letter; and the free market the answer to most of society's ills (Lapham,[29] p. 32). In this political milieu, accusations of liberal media bias by Republican candidates and politicians have picked up in frequency and force—a trend documented by empirical research of recent elections (see Watts et al.[22]).

VOLUME OF COVERAGE

Since the 1960s, a continuous stream of research literature, including the work of media monitoring organizations, has searched for,[28,36] purportedly found,[37–40] and also refuted claims of a liberal slant in American journalism that favors Democrats over Republicans.[21,41–44] Surveys of journalists show that a slight majority are voting Democrats, although not strongly liberal in ideological orientation.[45,46] As with editorial page endorsements of newspapers, the *voting behavior* of individual journalists cannot be taken as evidence of liberally biased *coverage*, which is subject to competitive pressures, professional norms, real-time reporting constraints, and a host of other institutional and organizational influences.[1] Moreover, the measures employed for conventional tests of partisan bias in election coverage are quite limited in scope.

The most basic and widely used measure of journalistic bias is volume of coverage.[47–52] Volume in this context refers to how much media attention a particular party or candidate received. Variance in volume of coverage across candidates of different parties is taken as a sign of bias, with the candidate who receives the most coverage identified as the beneficiary of media bias. The underlying argument here is that greater prominence in the news, achieved through a higher volume of coverage, could lead to agenda-setting outcomes in which some candidates will stand out to voters as more important and worthy of consideration than others. Volume of coverage thus corresponds to the news media's surfacing and winnowing functions, in which the power to grant or deny coverage is regarded as politically consequential, particularly for lesser known candidates (see Trent and Friedenberg[53]).

To quantify volume, studies of print media typically measure column inches or total number of stories dedicated to particular candidates,[36,54–56] whereas broadcast news studies conventionally measure the total amount of airtime candidates receive.[57] Some investigators assess volume of coverage by scrutinizing the amount of time candidates are featured speaking on air, which falls into analysis of sound bites (see D'Alessio and Allen,[21] Druckman and Parkin,[27] and Lowry and Shidler[49]). As reported in Chapter 2, the average length of Republican sound bites was longer than those of Democrats in 1992 and 1996 but shrank dramatically in 2000 and 2004, comparing unfavorably to Democrats in those elections years. Contra the liberal-bias accusation, there seems to be an inverse relationship between sound bite length and election outcomes—namely, the years in which Democrats won the White House featured longer sound bites from Republicans, whereas the years in which Republicans took the presidency featured longer sound bites from Democrats. These correlations are statistically investigated in Chapter 6.

The idea of having access to or voice in media coverage has long been equated with individual and political empowerment.[24,58–60] Interestingly, most empirical studies show little or no inequality (i.e., bias) in the total amount of coverage allotted to the major party candidates.[21,49] Because volume of coverage forms the cornerstone of most inquiries into media bias, we examined it longitudinally to compare our findings with existing research. Specifically, we gathered data to assess whether the *amount of coverage* for major party nominees reveals any systematic tendencies (or biases) when examined over time.

Findings for Volume of Coverage

A multiprong approach was used to assess volume of coverage. First, single-party stories that focused exclusively on the Democratic or Republican ticket were identified and comparisons across parties were performed. Appendix 5 contains detailed descriptions of our categories, definitions, and measures. Chi-square analyses were not significant either overall or for any of our four election years. Yet, overall and in each election year except 1992, there were more single-party stories featuring Republicans than Democrats (see Table 5–1).

The second prong of assessing volume of coverage involved calculating the duration, or length in seconds, of single-party stories. As with the number of stories, no significant differences emerged. Looking at the direction of means, Republicans received more single-party coverage in 1996 and 2004, whereas Democrats received more in 1992 and 2000. Again, no pattern of favoritism was evident. Overall, in single-party stories Democrats ($M = 109$) received about one second more airtime

Table 5–1 Trends in Volume of Coverage across Election Years and Political Parties

	Party Affiliation									
	Republicans					Democrats				
Volume of Coverage	'92	'96	'00	'04	Overall	'92	'96	'00	'04	Overall
Single-Party Stories										
Percentage	46.8	58.9	51.4	54.5	53.1	53.2	41.1	48.6	45.5	46.9
Mean duration	95.91	94.85	136.61	126.0	108.36	108.04	85.61	145.59	104.80	109.24
SD	55.72	52.03	40.57	27.72	50.68	65.01	44.05	81.15	44.31	63.95
Dominance in Multiple-Party Stories										
Percentage	66.7	55.6	44.4	43.2	50.5	33.3	44.4	55.6	56.8	49.5

Durations are represented in seconds.

on average than Republicans ($M = 108$). This extra second represents a negligible amount of time.

The third prong of investigating potential bias in the volume of coverage involved analyzing campaign stories that featured candidates from more than one party to assess who was given more prominent coverage. Over half (56.8%, $n = 138$) of all multiple-party stories featured candidates from different parties with the same prominence. Among the multiple-party stories that were identified as favoring one party, Republicans were more prominent than Democrats in the 1992 and 1996 elections, while Democrats dominated in the 2000 and 2004 elections. Once again, the relationship between prominence in coverage and election outcomes appears to be negative and systematic bias against Republicans is unsubstantiated.

Considering these three different sets of findings for volume, there is no persistent trend of partisan bias toward candidates of either party over the four election cycles examined, let alone a consistent liberal slant to the news. Durations of single-party stories are graphically represented in Figure 5–1. On a few points, gaps between Democrats and Republicans are observable, but there is neither statistical support nor a consistent pattern of favoritism toward either party.

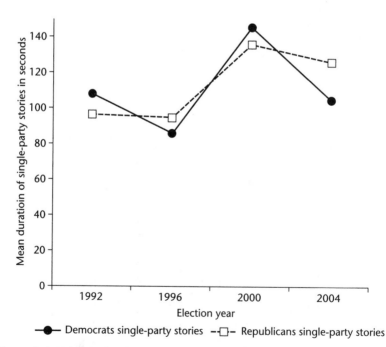

Figure 5–1 Volume of coverage for Republicans and Democrats in single-party stories over time

LIBERATING THE STUDY OF MEDIA BIAS FROM
THE GUTENBERG LEGACY

As other researchers have rightly noted, visual analysis is a sorely ne-glected mode of media investigation.[61] Although attempts have been made to study the visual component of television[62-65] and even news-paper and Web coverage of elections,[66-69] when visuals are studied the emphasis is often on content—not the packaging of content.[68-70] This is somewhat problematic for research on bias because the visual content of candidate portrayals, such as facial expressions, candidate behavior (e.g., embracing supporters, shaking hands with high-status figures and celebrities, hugging babies), or appearances adorned with patriotic symbols, is likely to be under the control of the candidates or their image handlers (see Chapter 3). As Lesley Stahl learned while covering Ronald Reagan's 1984 presidential campaign, there is not much journal-ists can do to avoid the artful staging of a candidate as heroic, patriotic, athletic, kind to children, and revered and supported by celebrities.

But reporters do exercise control over production decisions. In fact, the internal structure of news stories—their placement in the news-cast; editing techniques; and manipulations related to camera angles, shot lengths, eyewitness perspectives, and zoom movements—is at the volition of news workers, free of the influence of image handlers. These packaging maneuvers, also known as the structural or formal features of broadcast news, have been shown to impact evaluations of sources independent of image content.[71] Moreover, the specific ways in which packaging techniques transform content are part of for-mal journalism training—and constitute the core knowledge among media workers who employ visual images in storytelling. Therefore, to isolate journalistic agency or volition from nebulous claims about partisanship, it seems appropriate to define and measure visual bias in terms of news *packaging*, rather than—or at least in addition to—news *content*.

In our view, visual bias in news packaging can be observed at two distinct levels. First, at a broad structural level the visual weight (*not* the volume of coverage) assigned to stories about competing candidates should be compared for emphasis and assigned importance; and sec-ond, at a microlevel, camera and editing techniques employed to pack-age news about candidates must be scrutinized for evenhandedness.

Visual Weight

We conceptualized visual weight in terms of two dimensions: story type or architecture, and placement in the newscast (see Appendix 5 for further explication and description of how these dimensions were measured). Together these packaging features assign visual importance to a candidate with the potential for visual agenda setting.

As for story architecture, television news stories can be organized into five types that vary in visual weight:

1. The least amount of time and substance is assigned to stories called *readers*. These are reports that feature the anchor on camera reading live from the teleprompter, looking into the camera. No full-motion video material of the candidate is presented. At most, a still image of a candidate might appear in a graphic box to the left side of the anchor.

2. A *voice-over* (VO) is a report in which visual material of the candidate is shown while the anchor reads the script live in the studio. In essence, a VO is a reader with full motion visuals of candidates.

3. A *voice-over-sound-on-tape* (VO/SOT) story consists of a voice-over read by the anchor with accompanying visual material, or B-roll. It also includes one sound bite from a news source, which marks the difference between a VO/SOT and VO.

4. A *package* is a story in which the anchor reads an introduction, live, on camera. This is followed by a prerecorded independent report compiled and narrated by a reporter who appears aurally in voice narration and often also visually in a stand-up address to the camera, complete with a closing wrap-up and verbal "toss back" to the anchor.

5. An *interview* is an exchange between the reporter (or anchor) and candidate either in the studio or on location, such as the candidate's campaign bus or home.

Because they require a reporter and camera operator to be sent out into the field, packages, interviews, and VO/SOTs represent a large investment of time and resources in covering candidates during a campaign. Consequently, these story types carry the most visual weight—and prestige—among reporters. In addition, these news formats are typically longer than readers and VOs. Industry conventions about the varying visual weight of story architectures are supported by arguments from within the Gutenberg legacy camp about the shrinking sound bite. VO/SOT, package, and interview formats literally give voice to candidates—to be seen speaking admits the speaker into the domain of public discourse. And although we are arguing for enhanced consideration of visuals, the idea that verbal access to the airwaves empowers political actors and other news sources has long been central to conceptions of the media's idealized democratic role.[24,48]

The positioning of stories in the newscast also signals visual weight.[54] A lead story airs at the top of the newscast, immediately following the program logo and headline promotions, and is considered the most prominent and important development of the day. All stories that appear before the first commercial break, referred to as the first block, are considered more important than stories appearing in subsequent blocks of airtime between commercials. Nisbett and Ross[72] (p. 62) argue that this kind of perceptual prominence creates a "vividness bias" with potent consequences for persuasion. By experimentally testing the influence of story placement, Iyengar and Kinder[73] found that the lead position makes news stories seem more important and influential than placement in the middle of the newscast. A week after exposure, participants listed issues that appeared in lead stories as among the most important problems facing the nation.

Based on this research and the television news industry conventions identified above, story architecture and placement within the newscast are regarded as two dimensions of *visual weight* that can be conceptually justified and systematically observed. Moreover, as products of editorial decision making, these elements of political news are under the direct control of news workers, not presidential candidates or their image handlers. To examine the visual weight assigned to candidates, we performed a longitudinal analysis and made comparisons across political parties.

Findings for Visual Weight

Results related to visual weight are summarized in Table 5–2.[74] Overall, Republicans received the most favorable treatment, appearing

Table 5–2 Trends in Visual Weight across Election Years and Political Parties

Visual Weight Variables	Party Affiliation									
	%					%				
	Republicans					Democrats				
	'92	'96	'00	'04	Overall	'92	'96	'00	'04	Overall
Type of Story										
Reader	9.1	0	0	0	2.4	12.0	4.3	0	0	5.4
VO	13.6	9.1	0	10	8.5	16.0	17.4	6.3	10	13.5
VO/SOT	9.1	21.2	0	0	11.0	0	8.7	0	20	5.4
Package	63.6	69.7	94.1	80	74.4	68.0	69.6	75.0	60	68.9
Interview only	4.5	0	5.9	10	3.7	4.0	0	18.8	10	6.8
Story Position										
Lead	19.0	12.1	11.1	10	13.4	8.3	4.3	12.5	0	6.8
Before 1st beak	52.4	48.5	66.7	90	58.5	66.7	47.8	75.0	100	67.1
After 1st break	28.6	39.4	22.2	0	28.0	25.0	47.8	12.5	0	26.0

least often in readers and voice-overs (VOs) and most often in voice-over-sound-on-tape (VO/SOT) stories and packages. Democrats benefited, though, by appearing in more interviews. A closer look at each election year reveals that these findings remained fairly stable over time. Figure 5–2 illustrates these trends graphically. To reveal more general patterns, the weightier story types (VO/SOTs, packages, and interviews) were combined and averaged for each party and plotted alongside the lighter story types (readers and VOs) across election years. Except for the 2004 election, the trend line representing visual weight for Republicans is consistently higher than the line for Democrats, whereas the line representing lighter story types is consistently lower for Republicans than Democrats. Thus, with the exception of the 2004 election, Republicans seem to have benefited from the manner in which news about their campaigns was covered, with more substantial story types associated with coverage of G.O.P. candidates. Despite these trends, however, the differences between parties were not statistically significant.

The other visual weight variable, story position in the newscast, produced low counts in some cells; consequently, the Chi-square statistic

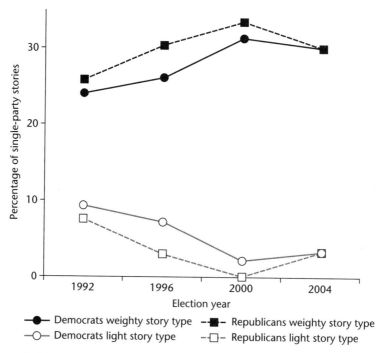

Figure 5–2 Visual weight (story type) of coverage for Republicans and Democrats over time

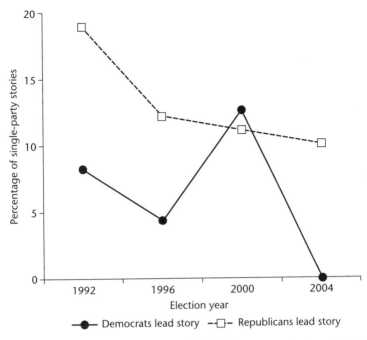

Figure 5–3 Visual weight (lead story position) of coverage for Republicans and Democrats over time

was not applied in cross-tabulation comparisons. Yet notable patterns emerged, some in line with the results for story type (see Table 5–2). Overall, Republicans were featured in lead stories about twice as often as Democrats. Republican dominance in lead single-party stories held up for all election years examined except 2000, when Democrats were featured in the lead position the most. Figure 5–3 represents this trend visually. At the same time, Democrats received more coverage in the first block (before the first commercial break) and less coverage deeper into the newscast than Republicans.

Packaging Techniques

Visual weight provides a unique perspective on potential agenda-setting outcomes. In this section we examine more microlevel visual packaging trends that might influence how candidate character traits are perceived. Among media professionals there are widely held conventions about the use of editing and camera techniques, which are thought to shape perceptions of news sources subjected to their application. Since we are primarily concerned with journalistic agency (i.e., editorial decisions) in the construction of broadcast news, visual packaging techniques can serve as a reliable standard on which assessments of visual bias can be made (see Appendix 5 for a detailed account of the coding instrument). In most instances, experimental findings from media research bolster journalistic intuition about the influence of different presentation techniques on audience perceptions of candidates.

Editing: Last Say and Lip Flap

In line with our conceptualization of visual bias as journalist centered, we assume that editing techniques are under the exclusive control of editors and producers; moreover, their application has perceptual consequences, either beneficial or detrimental, for candidates.

Last say, or the so-called *Goldilocks effect*, is a comparative technique thought to have beneficial consequences, which has been identified and employed in research on news bias in the South African Broadcasting Corporation's coverage of elections during the Apartheid era (see Grabe[62] and Van Vuuren et al.[75]). Van Vuuren et al.[75] describe the perceptual benefit of having the last say in stories that feature candidates from multiple parties by arguing that having the first say is a little too hot, the second a little too cold, but the last say is just right and tends to leave the strongest, most favorable impression. This reasoning is in line with research in political communication that favors recency (the last thing heard or seen) over primacy (the first thing heard or seen). Ample evidence exists for the idea that information about candidates or other sources presented later in a news report has more influence on opinion formation and is remembered better than information presented first (see Bositis, Baer, and Miller[76]; McGraw, Lodge, and Stroh[77]; and Newhagen and Reeves[78]).

Lip flap refers to the overlay of a reporter narration on corresponding video of a candidate who appears to be mouthing the words of a speech or spoken comment. The awkward outcome is visual representation of a candidate speaking while the audio of his or her voice remains inaudible. Instead, the viewer hears the reporter's narration. In effect, the reporter is using a candidate in sound bite mode as visual material to cover voice-over narration. This phenomenon, though relatively easy to find in news coverage of elections, is generally viewed as a violation of professional television news production standards that has detrimental consequences. Not only is lip flap unflattering for the candidate who appears in this presentation mode but it also distracts from the reporter's narration because viewers focus attention on making sense of what the lip flapper appears to be saying.[79] Moreover, lip flap is a type of audiovisual incongruency, which has been shown experimentally to prompt tune-out of the verbal channel (the reporter's voice) and tune-in of the visual channel.[80,81] Visual scenarios where attention is drawn to a candidate who appears voiceless but is awkwardly mouthing words cannot be taken as neutral coverage.

Findings for Editing Techniques

To examine the Goldilocks effect, stories in which Republicans and Democrats were both featured speaking (n = 243) were selected and subjected to analysis. Overall, Republicans had the last say in a slight majority (51.6%) of these stories. Looking at election years individually, G.O.P. candidates were favored in terms of having the last say in all but the 2004 election. The gaps between Republicans and Democrats fluctuated in size across election years. In 1992, the difference was notable, with Republicans having the last say 57.9% of the time. The 1996 election produced the starkest discrepancy: Republicans were accorded more than *eight times* (89.5%) as many last-say opportunities as Democrats. The difference between the two parties was small in 2000 but Republicans again emerged as the beneficiaries with 53% of last-say opportunities. Democrats were accorded 65% of last-say opportunities in 2004, making it the only year in which they were the beneficiaries of the Goldilocks effect.

Statistical tests were conducted to compare the duration of last-say sound bites for Republicans and Democrats (see Table 5–3). Overall, Republican last-say opportunities were significantly longer than those of Democrats.[82] Year-by-year analyses revealed that the mean durations of these sound bites were higher in every year for Republicans. Despite this clear pattern, only the differences for 1996 were statistically significant.[83] In terms of lip flap, Republicans were presented less often in this unflattering mode than Democrats—for each individual election year and all election years combined. However, none of these differences was statistically significant (see Table 5–3).

Given the pattern of findings for these editing variables, it is reasonable to conclude that the networks have given a persistent advantage to Republicans over Democrats. Yet statistical support for this claim is spotty.

Camera Maneuvers: Length, Angle, Movement

Several camera operations effectively illustrate the degree of reporter-controlled fairness in reporting. These can be organized along three dimensions: shot length, camera angle, and camera movement.

Shot length. Close-up shots are widely understood to create intimacy between the portrayed object/person and the viewer. The medium shot establishes a comfortable neutral distance, and the long shot creates distance and detachment between the portrayed person and the viewer.[84–86] Meyrowitz[87] discusses the relevance of shot lengths in terms of their paraproxemic function. The term paraproxemic refers to the perceptual similarities between face-to-face and mediated interaction with subjects who are presented through varying shot lengths. The relative size of news sources, including political candidates, on a television screen serves to index the perceived distance between the viewer and person depicted. Television close-ups in particular promote the illusion of face-to-face interaction and may even advance a parasocial relationship between the viewer and broadcast persona, or television personality (see Horton and Wohl[88]).

Yet close-up shots can also be *too* close for comfort, violating conventions analogous to personal space in face-to-face interaction. In news circles, these oversized shots are known as *extreme close-ups* and present an underdistanced perspective that emphasizes physical flaws or nervousness with the potential to repel viewers or provoke emotional discomfort that they would likely retreat from in person. In our analysis, extreme close-ups were treated as a scrutinizing perspective that reveals or emphasizes unflattering physical characteristics (e.g., a bad complexion) or unleaderlike emotional responses such as nervousness or stress (e.g., sweat on the upper lip, a twitching eye). Operationally, an extreme close-up was defined as a shot in which the viewer sees only the candidate's face without the shoulder or chest area visible. In such tightly framed shots, the candidate's chin and/or forehead are visually cut off.

Close-ups, which are seen as a means of establishing intimacy with viewers without violating conventions of comfortable personal space, reveal the candidate's full head and shoulders and a small portion of the chest area (well above the waist and elbows). A medium shot is viewed among news professionals as the most neutral shot, revealing the candidate's full head, shoulders, and waist area but not full body. A long (or establishing) shot reveals the full body and might include other objects and/or people on either side of the candidate.

The notion that different shot lengths moderate the level of perceived intimacy between the viewer and candidate is frequently applied in studies of news content. In an analysis of the 1976 televised presidential debates, Tiemens[65] found that Carter was the overall beneficiary of coverage because he appeared in more close-up shots than Ford. In media production circles, the implications of shot length are central to news editors' and producers' visual vocabulary.[79,86] Experimental research confirms the impact of varying shot lengths on viewer perceptions and evaluations. Whereas audience members generally express more positive attitudes toward objects or people portrayed in close-ups, long shots tend to decrease subjective involvement and result in less favorable evaluations because attention is diverted to the detail surrounding the object or person (Bucy and Newhagen[89] and Kepplinger and Donsbach[90]; see also Salomon[91,92]). Figure 5–4 shows representative screen captures of different shot lengths of Bill Clinton drawn from our 1992 election sample.

Camera angle.   Among media workers and film theorists there is a high level of agreement on the implications of using different camera

Table 5–3 Means for Visual Presentation Techniques across Election Years and Political Parties

Structural Features of News Coverage	Republicans					Democrats				
	'92	'96	'00	'04	Overall	'92	'96	'00	'04	Overall
Editing										
Last say	10.23	9.67	8.64	8.60	9.30	7.27	5.50*	7.94	7.29	7.39*
SD	6.52	4.36	4.25	2.58	4.67	4.02	.70	4.20	3.69	3.80
Lip flap	1.87	.90	2.25	3.13	2.11	2.38	.98	2.72	3.73	2.60
SD	4.08	2.70	3.66	5.73	4.36	5.23	2.17	4.24	6.60	5.08
Camera Maneuvers										
Low angle	.90	1.32	1.43	1.69	1.33	.76	.67	1.00	1.25	.94†
SD	2.15	2.79	3.36	2.88	2.81	2.28	1.76	2.90	2.64	2.49
High angle	1.00	.79	1.06	.95	.96	1.98*	1.27	1.78	.98	1.55*
SD	2.12	2.61	2.22	2.25	2.27	3.94	2.53	4.54	2.33	3.58
Extreme close-up	.19	.25	0	.04	.11	.48	.15	.02	.30	.25
SD	1.80	1.19	0	.24	1.10	2.14	1.10	.21	2.34	1.73
Close-up	4.40	5.31	7.48	6.18	5.82	5.19	2.69†	6.62	5.32	5.20
SD	8.83	9.85	10.18	13.87	10.91	8.38	5.05	9.31	11.51	9.19
Medium shot	18.44	22.67	20.14	25.13	21.49	18.21	14.54*	24.09	26.47	21.41
SD	17.19	18.53	26.95	18.73	20.72	18.70	12.51	48.18	22.76	30.47
Long shot	5.43	2.54	3.81	6.36	4.71	3.31*	2.88	7.20	6.30	5.12
SD	8.30	4.28	5.53	6.93	6.74	5.46	3.99	2.59	7.66	12.65
Zoom in	2.86	3.57	3.25	4.31	3.48	2.63	2.43	3.31	3.07	2.91
SD	5.34	6.55	8.93	8.80	7.55	4.45	4.44	5.68	5.89	5.21
Zoom out	2.02	2.49	1.00	1.25	1.66	2.38	1.69	1.69	1.57	1.86
SD	4.11	5.27	2.21	2.70	3.69	4.08	3.96	3.21	2.82	3.52
Eyewitness	1.87	3.52	3.40	.35	2.17	1.66	1.35*	2.62	.31	1.53†
SD	5.04	6.00	5.71	1.33	4.94	4.04	5.17	5.94	1.26	4.49

Durations are represented in seconds. *Statistically significant difference between Democrats and Republicans for a given year. †Differences between Democrats and Republicans for a given year approached statistical significance.

Figure 5–4 Screen captures from Bill Clinton's campaign coverage in 1992 showing varying shot lengths and camera angles

angles in filming people. The eye-level shot is viewed as the most fair and balanced perspective, whereas the low-angle view (looking upward) is believed to attribute power, dominance, and stature to a photographed subject.[84,86] Edmonds[85] argues that low-angle shots simulate the visual perspective of children during the period in which they first become socialized into power relationships with parents and other adults. The physical reality of a child looking up at adults is often portrayed in children's drawings of adults with long legs, large bodies, and disproportionately small heads. When the camera simulates this perspective, the argument goes, the audience is figuratively placed in a view reminiscent of childhood memories of gazing up at adults, activating early conceptions of authority. Inversely, the high-angle perspective (looking downward) attributes diminished stature or weakness to portrayed objects or sources.[85,86] Researchers have employed the conventional meaning of camera angles in content analyses to assess fairness in visual coverage of politicians around the world.[62,63,65,68,69]

Consistent with research on close-up and long shots, studies have demonstrated more favorable perceptions for persons depicted in low-angle than high-angle shots.[90,93,94] In one study that manipulated camera angle along with facial displays of fictional political candidates, high-angle portrayals were rated less favorably in terms of perceived character, fitness for office, and voter preference.[95] Figure 5–4 shows representative screen captures of Bill Clinton appearing in low and high camera angles, drawn from the 1992 material in our election sample.

Camera and lens movement. Action induced by camera activity, particularly zoom movements, also influences perceptions of news sources.[84,86] The evaluative effects of camera movements are similar to impressions formed by variable shot lengths. Like close-ups, zoom-in lens movements are thought to increase the viewer's involvement with a subject, whereas zoom-out movements presumably decrease involvement with the subject.[86,96] Salomon[91,92] has argued that zoom-in camera movements facilitate attention and learning; through continuous lens movement, the zoom seamlessly performs the transformation from a longer to a closer shot, not unlike approaching an object of interest in real life. By contrast, an abrupt *cut* from a long shot to a close-up is more demanding because it requires mental effort and visualization to connect two disjointed parts into a continuous whole. News production texts and content analyses documenting the prevalence of zoom movements in television and film reveal general agreement about the meaning of these camera operations (see Hellweg and Phillips,[63] Kepplinger,[64] Tiemens,[65] Shook,[78] Zettl,[86] and Kervin[97]).

Finally, the *eyewitness camera* perspective deserves consideration among camera techniques that might signal visual bias. This camera perspective assumes the position of the viewer as the camera is placed on the camera operator's shoulder to subjectively pursue the action. Eyewitness news—a decades-old marketing slogan for some local newscasts—literally refers to a "you are there" approach to television journalism.[98,99] Because the eyewitness view assumes the perspective of the audience, it has the potential to draw viewers into the content, enhancing paraproxemic experiences. Although there is little experimental evidence to support this notion, the eyewitness perspective is employed in television news circles to attract viewer attention, arouse curiosity, and make viewers feel closer to the action. Table 5–4 presents a visual dictionary summarizing the definitions and referential meanings of the aforementioned shot lengths, camera angles, camera movement, and video editing techniques.[100]

Table 5–4 Visual Dictionary: Elements of Bias in Television News

Camera/Editing Technique	Definition	Referential Meaning
Video Editing Techniques		
Goldilocks	Final speaking turn	Authority
Lip flap	Mouthing words with no sound	Awkward, unworthy of being heard
Shot Length		
Extreme close-up	Face only fills the screen	Personal space violation
Close-up	Face and shoulders fill the screen	Visual intimacy
Medium shot	Face and torso fills the screen	Personal relationship
Long shot	Full body, broader setting, other actors visible on screen	Personal distance
Camera Angle		
Low angle shot	Upward camera angle	Power, authority
High angle shot	Downward camera angle	Diminished stature, weakness
Camera Movement		
Zoom-in	Lens moves closer in	Emphasis, intimacy
Zoom-out	Lens moves farther out	De-emphasis, distance
Eyewitness camera	Subjective position of the viewer	"You are there" proximity and immediacy

The research literature related to camera and editing techniques offers convincing evidence that television's structural features are an effective means of influencing political evaluations. The question more pertinent for this analysis of visual bias, however, is whether candidates of different parties receive equal visual treatment in network news coverage of presidential campaigns. To answer this question, we examined whether the application of camera and editing techniques in general election coverage revealed any systematic tendencies or biases when looked at longitudinally.

Findings Related to Camera Maneuvers

Across all nine categories examining fairness in the use of camera perspective, including camera angle, shot length, and lens movement variables, Republicans received more favorable treatment than Democrats. Not all categories yielded statistically significant differences between parties, but the overall pattern provides evidence to declare Republicans the unmistakable beneficiaries of visual presentation techniques across the four general elections studied.

Findings for camera angle clearly illustrate the Republican advantage. Overall, Republican candidates were covered in more low-angle[101] and fewer high-angle shots[102] than Democrats. Analyses by election year revealed a consistent, though not always significant, pattern of results. In 1992, a year in which these differences were statistically significant,[103] Democrats were almost twice as likely to be portrayed in high-angle shots than Republicans (see Table 5–3).

Shot length followed a pattern similar to that of camera angle. Republicans were seen least through the scrutinizing and unflattering perspective of an extreme close-up. This was the case overall and for all election years except 1996 (see Table 5–3). None of the mean comparisons achieved statistical significance, however. The Republican advantage continued in the findings for close-ups. Overall and for each of the four election years except 1992, Republicans visually benefited by appearing in more close-up shots that facilitate intimacy with viewers than Democrats. These differences were particularly pronounced in 1996, approaching statistical significance.[104]

Overall, the medium shot—regarded by television news editors as the most neutral camera length—was applied almost equally to Democrats and Republicans (see Table 5–3). There was some fluctuation over time, however. In 2000 and 2004 Democrats appeared more often in medium shots than Republicans, while the inverse was true for 1992 and 1996. Visual coverage of the 1996 election again stood out, with Republicans appearing significantly more often in this neutral camera length than Democrats.[105] Long shots, which are *not* conducive to establishing rapport between candidates and viewers, were more evident in coverage of Democrats than Republicans overall, but not at statistically significant levels. In 1992, the reverse was true—George H. W. Bush and Dan Quayle were presented in significantly more long shots than Bill Clinton and Al Gore.[106]

The durations of zoom movements in visual portrayals were next subjected to comparison. Overall, Republicans benefited from longer zoom-in and shorter zoom-out portrayals but not at statistically significant levels. Year-by-year analyses showed that the overall trend persisted with two exceptions: during the 2000 election Democrats were shown for a longer period of time in zoom-in movements, and in 1996 Republicans were subjected to more zoom-out portrayals. Overall, application of the favorable you-are-there eyewitness camera perspective was heaviest for Republicans, at a near-significant level.[107] This pattern persisted for each election year individually, and in 1996, once again, the difference was significant (see Table 5–3).[108]

For a comprehensive look at the application of visual presentation techniques across election years and political parties, a composite *visual benefit* score was constructed by summing the durations of the following variables: last say, low angle, close-up, zoom in, and eyewitness

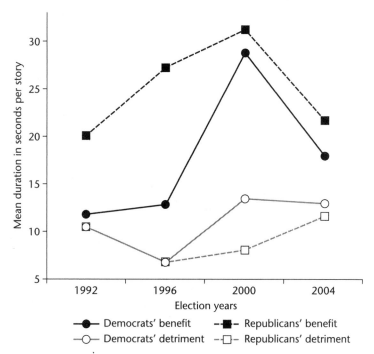

Figure 5–5 Durations for beneficial and detrimental visual packaging over time

camera perspective. Similarly, a summative *visual detriment* score was computed using the variables lip flap, high angle, extreme close-up, long shot, and zoom out. Tests of mean differences performed on these composite scores showed Republicans (M = 24.68) with a significantly higher benefit score than Democrats (M = 19.18).[109] At the same time, Republicans (M = 9.54) evidenced a lower detriment score than Democrats (M = 11.44).[110] Year-by-year analyses showed this trend to be stable. In all years of our analysis, Republicans were visually depicted more favorably and less detrimentally than Democrats. Not all tests were significant, but in 1992 Republicans (M = 20.15) benefited from a significantly higher visual benefit score than Democrats (M = 11.92).[111] For the 2000 election, the detriment score for Republicans (M = 8.14) was noticeably lower than for Democrats (M = 13.43), approaching significance.[112] Figure 5–5 illustrates these visual packaging patterns.

The short answer to our question about the application of visual presentation techniques to general election coverage of presidential candidates is this: the data show a persistent pattern of visual benefit (positive bias) for Republicans and visual detriment (negative bias) for Democrats. These findings run counter to the liberal bias accusation against mainstream news.

DISCUSSION

As the analyses in this chapter have shown, *more* network news coverage does not necessary mean more *favorable* coverage. Although Republicans and Democrats received nearly equal amounts of coverage across the four elections examined, Republicans emerged as the primary beneficiaries of visual weight in all elections except 2000 and clearly benefited from the application of visual packaging techniques under journalistic control in all elections.

Taking a closer look at visual coverage patterns across the four general election cycles in terms of volume, visual weight, and packaging, a notable pattern emerges. In 1992, Democrats were covered slightly more than Republicans but Republicans were visually more prominent in coverage; they also received both more favorable *and* less unfavorable camera and editing treatment than Democrats. In 1996—a near-landslide election year for Bill Clinton—the networks' preferential treatment of Republicans (i.e., the Dole campaign) reached the highest level with consistent visible gaps between the two parties in terms of volume of coverage, visual weight, and visual packaging. This pattern is prominent and persistent enough to call network news coverage of the 1996 campaign biased. Not only did the networks favor Republican candidates in terms of volume but they also facilitated more positive visual representations of the Dole-Kemp ticket. That Clinton won both the 1992 and 1996 elections despite this unfavorable visual treatment testifies to the former president's uncanny ability to connect with viewers through televisual media.[89]

During the 2000 election, Al Gore and Joe Lieberman profited from more coverage but less visual prominence in newscasts than George W. Bush and Dick Cheney. In terms of visual benefits bestowed by the networks, Democrats were again shortchanged. Republicans emerged that year with both more advantageous and less disadvantageous visual representation than Democrats. Gore's struggle to connect with voters during the campaign is widely viewed as a key factor in his forfeiting the election to Bush (see Sella[113]). As elaborated in Chapter 3, Gore often appeared impersonal and uncomfortable in his televised appearances. Network news packaging of Democrats that year certainly did not help Gore to build rapport with viewers but rather compounded his difficulty with communicating nonverbally.

During the 2004 election, Republicans received more coverage and were again favored in visual weight and visual packaging. There was a notable drop in visual benefits for Republican candidates between the 2000 and 2004 elections, but they were still favored by the networks in 2004. John Kerry, similar to Gore, was considered aloof and somewhat cerebral—characteristics not known for bonding candidates to undecided and persuadable voters. Network news coverage did not help Kerry in overcoming these shortcomings. At the same time, Bush enjoyed more favorable treatment via camera and editing techniques that advanced the appearance of power and leadership. He also received less *un*favorable camera and editing treatment than Kerry.

Although it is interesting to consider these findings in the context of election outcomes, it is not possible to claim effects on the audience based on the analyses reported here. In Chapter 6 we parse out potential effects of visual packaging on candidate standings in the polls. What can be concluded from these data is that there is a persistent pattern of visual bias in network news coverage of presidential candidates and that this slant clearly disfavors Democrats. Indeed, the patterns observed here (although mindful that not every comparison in our analysis is statistically significant) point in one direction: Republican candidates consistently received preferential camera treatment and editing constructions of their network news appearances in each presidential election from 1992 to 2004. Journalistic favoritism toward Republicans is evident not only in the amount of beneficial visual treatment they received but also in the persistent tendency to present Democrats in an unfavorable light.

Given these findings, an important question to ask is how much visual bias is necessary to declare news coverage of elections clearly biased. Some would argue that only statistically significant differences between political parties should count. This approach seems appropriate in making assessments in one-shot studies of single election years. However, when persistent patterns emerge after examining multiple elections, even if all point-by-point comparisons are not statistically significant, it seems justifiable and important to report these patterns as general tendencies. In our analysis, the overwhelming pattern of findings points to evidence of visual bias in favor of Republican candidates.

Whether these observed biases were *intended* by the networks cannot be resolved with this content analysis. Yet, given common knowledge of the consequences of various packaging techniques among television news professionals, our findings do suggest that network news workers bear responsibility for the unequal visual representation of Democrats and Republicans. A conspiracy among news professionals in favor of conservative candidates seems unlikely. Too many news workers, across three nationally competitive networks, participate in the daily coverage of presidential elections to synchronize editorial efforts. Coordination at that level simply does not seem plausible.

Our observations of visual bias cut against the long-standing accusations of liberal media bias leveled during campaigns. Two explanations, one rooted in practice and the other in media ownership, deserve consideration here. First, because there is a long history of publicly accusing the media of liberal bias, journalists may overcompensate by remaining hesitant to present Democrats in a visually favorable light; at the same time, on account of this pressure they might be reluctant to apply unfavorable visual packaging to Republicans. Most likely, this happens at low levels of awareness and explains the subtle but persistent pattern of favoritism toward Republicans.

If this explanation is valid, it is necessary to consider candidate and image handler influences on the news packaging process, terrain that traditionally has been the province of journalists. Given the long shelf life of the liberal bias accusation, it is indeed plausible that conservative pressure groups have succeeded in moderating the coverage that Republican candidates receive. Through an unrelenting decades-old campaign of accusing journalists of unfairness—the very thing that news reporters are most sensitive to—Republicans have perhaps set in motion a state of media self-censorship that has become part of political journalists' internalized news values.[114] With the exception of Gerald Ford, Republican presidential candidates since Richard Nixon have consistently charged the mainstream news media with liberal bias.[115] As outlined earlier in this chapter, the liberal media bias accusation lodged by conservatives—fully evident in speeches delivered at the 2008 Republican National Convention—has evolved into a political strategy of sorts. During the 1992 presidential election, Republican Party Chair Rich Bond as much as stated this when he compared journalists to sports referees: "If you watch any great coach, what they try to do is 'work the refs.' Maybe the ref will cut you a little slack next time."[116]

This strategy of working journalists by accusing them of unfair treatment seems to have been successful in the context of this study's findings. Moreover, surveys of news workers show that a substantial percentage (41%) report awareness of self-censorship[117] and consider their audiences to be more conservative than they are. About three in ten journalists also believe that some news stories are ignored because they might conflict with the financial interests of their news organizations or advertisers. This tendency to ignore issues that are considered detrimental to corporate media owners might extend to the way presidential elections are covered. Thus, a second possible explanation for the observed bias in favor of Republicans might be located in the realm of media ownership.

The political leanings of media owners, publishers, and upper management are more likely than the political views of working journalists to delimit the ideological landscape of network news organizations. In this regard, McChesney[32] provides compelling evidence that the political leanings of the networks' corporate owners line up with the economic policies and priorities of the Republican Party. The news, as Epstein[118] commented, "is not the product of a group of willful or biased or political men, but of an organization striving to meet the regularities needed to survive" (p. 267). Given the conservative political sensibilities that define media ownership and the durable campaign to construct the mainstream news media as liberal and pro-Democratic, visual bias in favor of the G.O.P. can be described in functional terms as an adaptive response among news workers to a perceived survival threat.

AFTERWORD: THE LIBERAL BIAS ACCUSATION, REVISITED

Beyond the rough and tumble of presidential politics, charges of media bias are deeply rooted in wide-ranging criticisms of press performance, amounting to what media scholars have described as a crisis of communication for citizenship (see Blumler and Gurevitch[119]). Television occupies a central role in this crisis.[120] Unfortunately, when it comes to claims about political coverage, "discussions of news media faults too often fail to distinguish criticisms based on unsystematic observation from those based on more solid evidence" (p. 127[121]). Indeed, the very idea of bias places efforts to study media content on a normative or evaluative footing, evoking questions about what ought to be, of which there is no shortage of available opinion.

Although rarely articulated in research, normative assumptions about the ability of the press to meet the demands of an idealized democratic system has driven much political communication scholarship since the early voting studies.[122] According to the assumptions of this system, as articulated by the Hutchins Commission on the Freedom of the Press, the news media should provide a truthful, comprehensive, and intelligent account of the day's events in a context that gives them meaning; serve as a forum for the exchange of comment and criticism; and project a representative picture of the constituent groups in society (pp. 21–28[23]). Concerns about representativeness invoke the journalistic values of fairness and balance, which are central to investigations of media bias. But their measurement, as detailed in this chapter, has been problematic, and most academic studies of bias, which have asserted null findings, have not had a noticeable impact on public debate. Instead the accusation persists among elites and has gained currency with the public, as evidenced by poll results that have shown eroding citizen trust in the news media.[22]

Although it drowns out other discussions about media performance, partisan bias is but one of several forms of distortion the press is accused of perpetuating. Bennett,[123] for example, views obsession over ideological forms of bias as a distraction and a relatively trivial problem facing citizens compared to more pressing *information* problems, including declining space for hard news and the growing popularity of soft news formats and infotainment programs; a growing consumerist outlook by corporate owners intent on pursuing ratings at the expense of informing; and dwindling space for international news in American media. Various authors have also identified *institutional* forms of media bias, including news routines and practices, such as pack journalism, that result in narrowed and repetitive depictions of events; technological biases that privilege image trafficking over issue discussion; and journalistic preference for clear-cut issues over diffuse policy debates (see Bucy and D'Angelo[1]).

In addition to the visual evidence presented in this chapter, any sober discussion about media bias should reference the classic sociological analyses and newsroom ethnographies of American journalism, including in-depth studies of newsmagazines and television network news. These analyses, which began appearing at roughly the same time that Edith Efron's skewed view of the news, *The News Twisters* (1971), was published, have generally concluded that "the news is not so much liberal or conservative as it is reformist" (p. 68[58]). In *Deciding What's News*, Gans[58] observed that mainstream American journalism was guided by a para-ideology of enduring values, notably responsible leadership and individualism, which operated within conventional political boundaries and descended from the reformist ethos of turn-of-the-twentieth-century Progressivism. Despite such careful and politically uncommitted scholarly analyses, the time period surrounding Richard Nixon's 1968 and 1972 presidential elections also gave birth to the perennial conservative accusation of liberal media bias.

Of course, none of the classic newsroom studies directly contradicts the possibility that the personal biases of journalists and editors—particularly their personal political views—infiltrate the news production process at *some* level. But again, just as political coverage differs from a media organization's official editorial position, so the news product cannot be equated with the personal beliefs of correspondents. In a cross-national survey of newspaper and broadcast journalists from Germany, Great Britain, Italy, Sweden, and the United States, Patterson and Donsbach[45] found that news workers' beliefs are "accurately characterized as slightly left of center rather than as unambiguously liberal" (p. 465). Rather than corroborate the oft-cited and largely unchallenged media elite argument that journalists who work for the prestige press constitute a new class of effete liberals bent on ideological influence (see, for example, Lichter, Rothman, and Lichter[40]), these authors[45] instead support Gans's conclusion that "journalists hold 'progressive' but 'safe' views" (p. 465).

Ironically, perhaps because charges of and (apparently) beliefs about liberal media bias are so widespread, ideological bias has been discounted by research.[42,119] The orchestration of journalists by political handlers and the press's obsession with horse-race or strategy-based news are seen as larger problems than questions about partisan slants to the news.[124–126] As with other careful analysts of the news, Entman[127] concludes that "liberal ideological bias has a less persistent and politically significant framing impact than other biases that, unlike liberalism, are embedded with—and legitimated by—professional journalistic practice" (p. 78). Information biases and problematic institutional practices, summarized above, are thus regarded as pressing concerns that transcend political favoritism.

By impeding political understanding through accepted but limiting constraints on coverage, news reporting of politics may discourage active, informed citizenship.[127] To some (e.g., Tuchman[128]), this fateful result is due to the *conservatizing* pressures of newsgathering—in which journalists and editors are induced to work in lockstep with official sources—rather than any partisan bias of newsgatherers. Indeed, Bennett and colleagues[129] have recently shown how the press failed its watchdog mission in the case of the Iraq War by relying too heavily on official sources. But this is beyond the scope of our analysis.

NOTES

1. Bucy, Erik P., and Paul D'Angelo. 1999. The crisis of political communication: Normative critiques of news and democratic processes. *Communication Yearbook* 22:301–339.
2. Patterson, Thomas E. 1993. *Out of order*. New York: Knopf.
3. Stempel, Guido H. 1991. Where people really get most of their news. *Newspaper Research Journal* 12(4):2–9.

4. Complaints about the press are as old as the republic itself. During his presidency, Thomas Jefferson grew especially strident in his observations about newspapers, observing in 1803 that the Federalists, "having failed in destroying the freedom of the press by their gag law, seem to have attacked it in the opposite form . . . by pushing its licentiousness and its lying to such a degree of prostitution as to deprive it of all credit" (p. 364[5]).

5. Levy, Marion J. 1966. *Modernization and the structure of societies: A setting for international affairs*. Princeton, NJ: Princeton University Press.

6. Iyengar, Shanto. 1996. Framing responsibility for political issues. *Annals of the American Academy of Political and Social Science* 546:59–70.

7. Postman, Neil. 1986. *Amusing ourselves to death: Public discourse in the age of show business*. New York: Penguin Books.

8. Fallows, James. 1996, February. Why Americans hate the media. *Atlantic Monthly*. http://www.theatlantic.com/doc/199602/americans-media. Accessed February 29, 2008.

9. Kurtz, Howard. 1993. *Media circus: The trouble with America's newspapers*. New York: Times Books.

10. Kurtz, Howard. 1996. *Hot air: All talk, all the time*. New York: Times Books.

11. Patterson, Thomas E. 1994. Legitimate beef: The presidency and a carnivorous press. *Media Studies Journal* 8(2):21–26.

12. This criticism has not gone unnoticed by the press. As *Washington Post* columnist Richard Harwood[13] has observed: "The academic community, once smitten with the media [during the Vietnam and Watergate eras], has gone revisionist, producing books and tracts in great numbers denouncing the press for cynicism, ignorance, and mindless arrogance that endanger democracy and the political process. We are also capitalist tools, as Noam Chomsky and Ralph Nader frequently remind us" (p. A23).

13. Harwood, Richard. 1996, September 6. Deconstructing Bob Woodward. *Washington Post*, p. A23.

14. Patterson, Thomas E. 1996a. Bad news, period. *PS: Political Science & Politics*, 29:17–20.

15. Patterson, Thomas E. 1996b. Bad news, bad governance. *Annals of the American Academy of Political and Social Science*, 546:97–108.

16. Fan, David P., Robert O. Wyatt, and Kathy Keltner. 2001. The suicidal messenger: How press reporting affects public confidence in the press, the military, and organized religion. *Communication Research* 28:826–852.

17. Goldberg, Bernard. 2001. *Bias: A CBS insider exposes how the media distort the news*. Washington, DC: Regnery Publishing.

18. Goldberg, Bernard. 2003. *Arrogance: Rescuing America from the media elite*. New York: Warner Books.

19. Stossel, John. 2004. *Give me a break: How I exposed hucksters, cheats, and scam artists and became the scourge of the liberal media*. New York: HarperCollins.

20. Watts, Mark. D., David Domke, Dhavan V. Shah, and David P. Fan. 1999. Elite cues and media bias in presidential campaigns: Explaining public perceptions of a liberal press. *Communication Research* 26:114–175.

21. D'Alessio, Donald, and Michael Allen. 2000. Media bias in presidential elections: A meta-analysis. *Journal of Communication* 50(4):133–156.

22. West, Darrell M. 2001. *The rise and fall of the media establishment*. Boston: Bedford/St. Martin's.

23. Leigh, Robert D. 1947. *A free and responsible press: A general report on mass communications—newspapers, radio, motion pictures, magazines, and books.* Commission on Freedom of the Press. Chicago: University of Chicago Press.

24. Siebert, Fred S., Theodore Peterson, and Wilbur Schramm. 1956. *Four theories of the press: The authoritarian, libertarian, social responsibility, and Soviet communist concepts of what the press should be and do.* Urbana: University of Illinois Press.

25. On this point, however, Kahn and Kenney[26] and Druckman and Parkin[27] have provided compelling evidence from Senate campaigns that endorsements may influence the tenor of newspaper coverage in favor of the candidate endorsed on the editorial page and that voters evaluate endorsed candidates more favorably than those who lack newspaper endorsements.

26. Kahn, Kim Fridkin, and Patrick J. Kenney. 2002. The slant of the news: How editorial endorsements influence campaign coverage and citizens' views of candidates. *American Political Science Review* 96(2):381–394.

27. Druckman, James N., and Michael Parkin. 2005. The impact of media bias: How editorial slant affects voters. *Journal of Politics, 67*(4), 1030–1049.

28. Highbie, Charles, E. 1961. 1960 election studies show broad approach, new methods. *Journalism Quarterly* 38:164–170.

29. Lapham, Lewis H. 2004, September. Tentacles of rage. The Republican propaganda mill, a brief history. *Harpers*, pp. 31–41.

30. Agnew, Spiro T. 1969/1987. Television news coverage. In *American rhetoric from Roosevelt to Reagan*, 2nd ed., ed. Halford Ross Ryan, pp. 212–219. Prospect Heights, IL: Waveland Press.

31. Morrow, Lance. 1996, September 30. Naysayer to the nattering nabobs. *Time.* http://www.time.com/time/magazine/article/0,9171,985217,00.html. Accessed July 20, 2006.

32. McChesney, Robert W. 2004. *The problem of the media.* New York: Monthly Review Press.

33. Koppelman, Alex. 2007, April 16. Is Rush Limbaugh next? Conservatives fear that Don Imus is the first casualty in a liberal-led media purge to force right-wing talkers off the air. *Slate.* http://www.salon.com/news/feature/2007/04/16/fairness_doctrine/. Accessed February 29, 2008.

34. Although these organs exist on the left, they are not as well funded or popular. The liberal critique of mainstream media—that news coverage rarely challenges the status quo and largely reflects the social, economic, and political interests of the corporations that own the media—has thus not gained much traction (see Alterman[35] and McChesney[32]).

35. Alterman, Eric. 2003. *What liberal media? The truth about bias and the news.* New York: Basic Books.

36. Stempel, Guido H. III, and John W. Windhauser. 1991. Newspaper coverage of the 1984 and 1988 campaigns. In *The media in the 1984 and 1988 presidential campaigns*, ed. Guido H. Stempel III and John W. Windhauser, pp. 13–66. New York: Greenwood.

37. Dalton, Russell J., Paul A. Beck, and Robert Huckfeldt. 1998. Partisan cues and the media: Information flows in the 1992 presidential election. *American Political Science Review* 92(1):111–126.

38. Groseclose, Tim, and Jeff Milyo. 2003. *A measure of media bias.* http://64.233.161.104/search?q=cache:tCEKSNVWOYJ:mason.gmu.edu/

~ataba rro/MediaBias.doc+Groseclose+Milyo&hl=en&gl=us&ct=clnk&cd=
4&client=firefox-a. Accessed July 20, 2006.

39. Kuypers, Jim A. 2002. *Press bias and politics: How the media frame controversial issues.* Westport, CT: Praeger.

40. Lichter, S. Robert, and Stanley Rothman, with Linda S. Lichter. 1986. *The media elite: America's new power brokers.* Bethesda, MD: Adler and Adler.

41. Arterton, F. Christopher. 1984. *Media politics: The news strategies of presidential campaigns.* Lexington, MA: Lexington Books.

42. Buchanan, Bruce, 1991. *Electing a president: The Markle Commission research on campaign '88.* Austin: University of Texas Press.

43. Hofstetter, C. Richard. 1976. *Bias in the news: Network television coverage of the 1972 election campaign.* Columbus: Ohio State University Press.

44. Robinson, Michael J., and Margaret A. Sheehan. 1983. *Over the wire and on TV: CBS and UPI in Campaign '80.* New York: Russell Sage Foundation.

45. Patterson, Thomas E., and Wolfgang Donsbach. 1996. News decisions: Journalists as partisan actors. *Political Communication* 13:455–468.

46. Weaver, David H., Randal A. Beam, Bonnie J. Brownlee, Paul S. Voakes, and G. Cleveland Wilhoit. 2006. *The American journalist in the 21st century: U.S. news people at the dawn of a new millennium.* Mahwah, NJ: Lawrence Erlbaum Associates.

47. A few studies investigating the verbal *tone* of coverage have found evidence of bias, whereas analyses of *volume* generally have not. Tone usually refers to the verbal valence frame within which a candidate is presented in the news. Most studies use positive, negative, neutral, or undetermined/ mixed options[27,48] to code tone and look for evidence of it in the voice of the journalist,[44] the content of candidate sound bites, or even in sound bites of journalists talking about candidates.[49] The measurement of tone is somewhat problematic in that researchers do not always carefully operationalize and clearly discuss the particulars of what constitutes different valence dimensions, although reported coder reliability figures on tone assessments appear sound.

Computer-assisted content analysis has also been employed to code tone from text-only accounts of news content (e.g., Domke et al.[50]). This method seems particularly problematic given Conway's[51] findings about the irreconcilable differences between human and computer coding in election coverage. Studies of tone focus on verbal content, even when the medium under investigation is television.[44,48,49,52]

48. Hallin, Daniel C. 1992. Sound bite news: Television coverage of elections, 1968–1988. *Journal of Communication* 42(2):5–24.

49. Lowry, Dennis T., and Jon A. Shidler. 1995. The biters and the bitten: An analysis of network TV news bias in campaign '92. *Journalism and Mass Communication Quarterly* 69(2):341–361.

50. Domke, David, Mark D. Watts, Dhavan V. Shah, and David P. Fan. 1999. The politics of conservative elites and the "liberal media" argument. *Journal of Communication* 49(4):35–59.

51. Conway, Mike. 2006. The subjective precision of computers: A methodological comparison with human coding. *Journalism and Mass Communication Quarterly* 83(1):186–200.

52. Benoit, William L. 2003. Topic of presidential campaign discourse and election outcome. *Western Journal of Communication* 67(1):97–112.

53. Trent, Judith S., and Robert V. Friedenberg. 2004. *Political campaign communication: Principles and practices*. 5th ed. Westport, CT: Praeger.

54. Fico, Fred, and William Cote. 1999. Fairness in the structural characteristics of newspaper stories in the 1996 presidential election. *Journalism and Mass Communication Quarterly* 76(1):124–137.

55. Mantler, Gordon, and David Whitemen. 1995. Attention to candidates and issues in newspaper coverage of the 1992 presidential campaign. *Newspaper Research Journal* 16(3):14–28.

56. Stovall, James Glen. 1988. Coverage of 1984 presidential campaign. *Journalism Quarterly* 65(2):443–449, 484.

57. Doll, Howard, and Bert Bradley. 1974. A study of the objectivity of television news reporting of the 1972 presidential campaign. *Central States Speech Journal* 25(4):254–263.

58. Gans, Herbert. 1979. *Deciding what's news*. New York: Pantheon.

59. Parenti, Michael. 1986. *Inventing reality: The politics of the mass media*. New York: St. Martin's Press.

60. Schudson, Michael. 1978. *Discovering the news: A social history of American newspapers*. New York: Basic Books.

61. Graber, Doris A. 2001. *Processing politics: Learning from television in the Internet age*. Chicago: University of Chicago Press.

62. Grabe, Maria E. 1996. The SABC's coverage of the 1987 and 1989 elections: The matter of visual bias. *Journal of Broadcasting and Electronic Media* 40(1):1–27.

63. Hellweg, Susan A., and Steven L. Phillips. 1981. A verbal and visual analysis of the 1980 Houston Republican primary debate. *Southern Speech Communication Journal* 47(1):23–38.

64. Kepplinger, Hans Mathias, 1982. Visual biases in television campaign coverage. *Communication Research* 9(3):432–446.

65. Tiemens, Robert K. 1978. Television's portrayal of the 1976 presidential debates: An analysis of visual content. *Communication Monographs* 45(4):362–370.

66. Bucy, Erik P. 2004. Second generation Net news: Interactivity and information accessibility in the online environment. *The International Journal of Media Management* 6(1–2):102–113.

67. Bucy, Erik P., and Robert B. Affe. 2006. The contributions of Net news to cyber democracy: Civic affordances of major metropolitan newspaper sites. In *Internet newspapers: The making of a mainstream medium*, ed. Xigen Li, pp. 227–242. Mahwah, NJ: Lawrence Erlbaum Associates.

68. Moriarty, Sandy E., and Mark N. Popovich. 1991. Newsmagazine visuals and the 1988 presidential election. *Journalism Quarterly* 68(3):371–380.

69. Waldman, Paul, and James Devitt. 1998. Newspaper photographs and the 1996 presidential election: The question of bias. *Journalism and Mass Communication Quarterly* 75(2):302–311.

70. Verser, Rebecca, and Robert H. Wicks. 2006. Managing voter impressions: The use of images on presidential candidate Web sites during the 2000 campaign. *Journal of Communication* 56(1):178–197.

71. Grabe, Maria E., Annie Lang, and Xiaoquan Zhao. 2003. News content and form: Implications for memory and audience evaluation. *Communication Research* 30(4):387–413.

72. Nisbett, Richard E., and Lee Ross. 1980. *Human inference: Strategies and shortcomings of social judgment.* Englewood Cliffs, NJ: Prentice-Hall.

73. Iyengar, Shanto, and Donald R. Kinder. 1987. *News that matters.* Chicago: University of Chicago Press.

74. Some cells of the political party by story type cross-tabulation had fewer than five cases, making the Chi-square statistic unreliable.

75. Van Vuuren, Daan, J., Lawrence Schlemmer, Hendrik C. Marais, and Jo Latakgomo. 1987. *South African election 1987: Context, process and prospect.* Pinetown, South Africa: Owen Burgess.

76. Bositis, David A., Denise L. Baer, and Roy E. Miller. 1985. Cognitive information levels, voter preferences, and local partisan political activity: A field experimental study on the effects of timing and order of message presentation. *Political Behavior* 7(3):266–284.

77. McGraw, Kathleen M., Milton Lodge, and Patrick Stroh. 1990. On-line processing in candidate evaluation: The effects of issue order, issue importance, and sophistication. *Political Behavior* 12(1):41–58.

78. Newhagen, John E., and Byron Reeves. 1992. This evening's bad news: Effects of compelling negative television news images on memory. *Journal of Communication* 42(2):25–41.

79. Shook, Fredrick. 2005. *Television field production and reporting,* 4th ed. Boston: Allyn and Bacon.

80. Drew, Dan G., and Thomas Grimes. 1987. Audio-visual redundancy and TV news recall. *Communication Research* 14(4):452–461.

81. Lang, Annie. 1995. Defining audio/video redundancy from a limited capacity information processing perspective. *Communication Research* 22(1):86–115.

82. $t(138) = -2.7, p = 0.008.$

83. $t(15) = -3.38, p = 0.005.$

84. Baggaley, Jon, Philip Brooks, and Margaret Ferguson. 1980. *Psychology of the TV image.* New York: Praeger.

85. Edmonds, Robert. 1982. *The sights and sounds of cinema and television: How the aesthetic experience influences our feelings.* New York: Teachers College Press.

86. Zettl, Herbert. 2007. *Sight, sound, motion: Applied media aesthetics,* 5th ed. Belmont, CA: Wadsworth.

87. Meyrowitz, Joshua. 1986. Television and interpersonal behavior: Codes of perception and response. In *Intermedia: Interpersonal communication in a media world,* ed. Gary Gumpert and Robert Cataract, pp. 253–272. New York: Oxford University Press.

88. Horton, Donald, and R. Richard Wohl. 1956. Mass communication and para-social interaction: Observations on intimacy at a distance. *Psychiatry* 19(3):215–229.

89. Bucy, Erik P., and John E. Newhagen. 1999. The micro-and macrodrama of politics on television: Effects of media format on candidate evaluations. *Journal of Broadcasting and Electronic Media* 43(2):193–210.

90. Kepplinger, Hans Mathias, and Wolfgang Donsbach. 1987. The influence of camera perspectives on the perception of a politician by supporters,

opponents, and neutral viewers. In *Political Communication Research: Approaches, studies, assessments,* ed. David Paletz, pp. 63–71. Norwood, NJ: Ablex.

91. Salomon, Gavriel. 1972. Can we effect cognitive skills through visual media? *Audiovisual Communications Review* 26:133–168.

92. Salomon, Gavriel. 1979. *Interaction of media, cognition, and learning.* San Francisco: Jossey-Bass.

93. Kraft, Robert N. 1987. The influence of camera angle on comprehension and retention of pictorial events. *Memory and Cognition* 15(4):291–307.

94. Mandell, Lee M., and Donald L. Shaw. 1973. Judging people in the news—unconsciously: Effect of camera angle and bodily activity. *Journal of Broadcasting* 17(3):353–362.

95. Rosenberg, Shawn W., and Patrick McCafferty. 1987. The image and the vote: Manipulating voters' preferences. *Public Opinion Quarterly* 51(1):31–47.

96. Millerson, Gerald. 1976. *Effective television production.* New York: Hastings House.

97. Kervin, Denise J. 1985. Reality according to television news: Pictures from El Salvador. *Wide Angle* 7(4):61–70.

98. Dominick, Joseph R., Alan Wurtzel, and Guy Lometti. 1975. Television journalism vs. show business: A content analysis of eyewitness news. *Journalism Quarterly* 52(2):213–218.

99. Hofstetter, C. Richard, and David M. Dozier. 1986. Useful news, sensational news: Quality, sensationalism and local TV news. *Journalism Quarterly* 63(4):815–820, 853.

100. Table inspired by Berger, Arthur Asa. 1981. Semiotics and TV. In *Understanding Television,* ed. Richard Adler, pp. 91–114. New York: Praeger.

101. $t(617) = -1.80, p = 0.073$.

102. $t(615) = 2.43, p = 0.015$.

103. $t(176) = 2.08, p = 0.039$.

104. $t(111) = -1.73, p = 0.086$.

105. $t(111) = -2.68, p = 0.008$.

106. $t(176) = -2.01, p = 0.046$.

107. $t(617) = -1.68, p = 0.089$.

108. $t(111) = -2.05, p = 0.043$.

109. $t(140) = -2.03, p = 0.044$.

110. $t(613) = 1.67, p = 0.097$.

111. $t(33) = -2.15, p = 0.039$.

112. $t(162) = 1.81, p = 0.072$.

113. Sella, Marshall. 2000, September 24. The stiff guy vs. the dumb guy. *New York Times Magazine,* pp. 72–80, 102.

114. In conducting research about political influence, academics also run the risk of self-censorship, in the same way that journalists might respond to Republican accusations of bias. The academe could be described as a social institution almost as often accused of liberal bias as mainstream news. Safeguarding academic freedom, including rigorous investigations of political bias in all its guises, seems critical at a time when ideological criticism of the academe is on the rise and government funding of higher education at record lows.

115. Shafer, Jack. 2003. The varieties of media bias, part 1: Who threw the first punch in the press bias brawl? *Slate*. http://www.slate.com/id/2078200/. Accessed May 12, 2006.

116. Grove, Lloyd. 1992, August 20. Media to the left! Media to the right! The GOP, shooting the messengers. *Washington Post*, p. C1.

117. Pew Center for the People and the Press. 2000a. *The job of communicating with voters*. http://peoplepress.org/reports/display.php3?PageID=242. Accessed May 15, 2006.

118. Epstein, Edward J. 1973. *News from nowhere: Television and the news*. New York: Random House.

119. Blumler, Jay G., and Michael Gurevitch, 1995. *The crisis of public communication*. London: Routledge.

120. Kellner, Douglas. 1990. *Television and the crisis of democracy*. Boulder, CO: Westview Press

121. McLeod, Jack M., Gerald M. Kosicki, and Douglas M. McLeod. 1994. The expanding boundaries of political communication effects. In *Media effects: Advances in theory and research*, ed. Jennings Bryant and Dolf Zillmann, pp. 123–162. Hillsdale, NJ: Lawrence Erlbaum.

122. Chaffee, Steven H., and John L. Hochheimer. 1985. The beginnings of political communication research in the United States: Origins of the "limited effects" model. In *The media revolution in America and Western Europe*, ed. Everett M. Rogers and Francis Balle, pp. 267–296. Norwood, NJ: Ablex

123. Bennett, W. Lance. 2007. *News: The politics of illusion*. 7th ed. New York: Pearson Longman.

124. Cappella, Joseph N., and Kathleen Hall Jamieson. 1997. *Spiral of cynicism: The press and the public good*. New York: Oxford University Press.

125. Kerbel, Mathew R. 1994. *Edited for television: CNN, ABC, and the 1992 presidential campaign*. Boulder, CO: Westview.

126. Kerbel, Matthew R. 1995. *Remote and controlled: Media politics in a cynical age*. Boulder, CO: Westview.

127. Entman, Robert M. 1996. Reporting environmental policy debate: The real media biases. *Press/Politics* 1(3):77–92.

128. Tuchman, Gaye. 1978. *Making the news: A study in the construction of reality*. New York: The Free Press.

129. Bennett, W. Lance, Regina G. Lawrence, and Steven Livingston. 2007. *When the press fails: Political power and the news media from Iraq to Katrina*. Chicago: University of Chicago Press.

6

Visual Influence

The preceding chapters have built a theoretical and data-driven case for why news visuals in general and image bites in particular should be considered for their persuasive influence and taken more seriously in election news research. The scaffolding for our longitudinal content analysis of presidential campaign news has been assembled in a cross-disciplinary fashion with contributions from communication research, neuroscience, cognitive and evolutionary psychology, behavioral biology, sociology, and political science, among other areas. The patterns of candidate coverage we have identified are therefore interpretable in light of existing research evidence and theory about media influences from a variety of perspectives. In this chapter we examine our content analysis findings in relation to public opinion data to assess the potential influence of network news coverage on candidate support. Specifically, we investigate the relationship between tracking poll data and visual, verbal, and volume of coverage variables for each election year (for a list of variables in the analysis, see Appendix 6).

VOTER SUPPORT AND MEDIA CONTENT: BIVARIATE CORRELATIONS

Key content analysis variables from each chapter were subjected to bi-variate correlations with polling data for Democratic and Republican candidates for each election year. Results are reported here by sets of variables relevant to each chapter's content analysis findings, offering insight into (1) the relative reliability of categories as we have conceptualized them, and (2) the statistical associations with candidate standings in the polls. In the final section, we put our categories to the test in a series of regression models designed to predict candidate support.

Sound and Image Bites

In our analysis of sound and image bites (Chapter 2), we reported three notable differences between Republicans and Democrats in terms of sound bite size and total amount of sound bite time. In the 1996 election, Republican candidates were allotted more bite time per news story than Democratic candidates, at a near-significant level. In 2004, the networks reversed this tack. On average, Republican sound bites were significantly shorter than those of Democrats. Moreover, the total amount (i.e., volume) of sound bite time per story was shorter for G.O.P. candidates than for Democrats.

Although sound bite durations in 1996 and 2004 seem lopsided, first in favor of Republicans and then in favor of Democrats, these imbalances were not significantly associated with candidate support. As Table 6–1 indicates, longer speaking opportunities for Republicans in 1996 were not meaningfully related to poll standings. Moreover, in 2004 neither party's standing in the polls was statistically related to sound bite size or total sound bite time. In fact, bite size and volume evidenced only sporadic associations with polling data across parties and election years. Just three instances of weak association emerged.[1]

The lack of statistical association and inconsistent direction of the few near-significant correlations between the polling data and sound bite size and volume variables lead us to reemphasize arguments about measuring media bias (see Chapter 5). Namely, sound bite size and volume are overstated and overused as measures of political information. Being heard more and in longer bite sizes does not seem to either inspire or weaken support for candidates during the general election—a conclusion supported by regression analyses reported below.[2] Consequently, more speaking time does not translate into more favorable views of candidates among voters. Indeed, as we will discuss in more detail later, sound bite volume contributed to predictive models by explaining *declines* in voter support for two Republican candidates. Against the backdrop of these findings, research primarily focused on average sound bite length or the total sound bite time allotted to candidates as measures of fairness in reporting would seem to explain little.

Consistent with visual primacy theory, image bite volume produced stronger associations with voter support for candidates than either the sound bite size or volume variables (see Table 6–1). However, the visual analyses reported in Chapter 2 revealed no significant differences in image bite coverage between Democrats and Republicans for any of our election years. The statistical associations between image bite

Table 6-1 Correlations between Polling Data and Sound/Image Bite Variables from Chapter 2

Sound/Image Bite Measures	1992				1996				2000				2004			
	Dem		Rep		Dem		Rep		Dem		Rep		Dem		Rep	
	r	p	r	p	r	p	r	p	r	p	r	p	r	p	r	p
Size																
Sound bite	.273	.065†	.155	.179	-.321	.055†	.194	.128	-.083	.314	.124	.243	.206	.110	-.142	.202
Volume																
Sound bite	-.111	.273	-.109	.260	-.247	.112	.001	.497	-.220	.098†	.212	.114	.096	.286	-.091	.295
Image bite	-.315	.024*	-.340	.015*	-.053	.377	.011	.474	-.236	.064†	.289	.031*	.262	.098†	.040	.424
Sound Bite Content																
Issue	.361	.011*	.168	.147	-.297	.033*	.023	.446	-.129	.202	.128	.208	-.088	.294	-.120	.233
Rally the troops	-.365	.010*	-.108	.250	-.127	.220	-.198	.117	-.199	.098†	.202	.097†	.405	.005*	.266	.051†
Defense	-.164	.155	-.040	.403	-.131	.213	-.091	.294	.022	.444	-.060	.351	—	—	-.043	.397
Attack	-.111	.248	-.095	.277	-.104	.264	.167	.158	-.261	.044*	.225	.074†	-.047	.387	-.312	.026*

*Correlations with poll data that are statistically significant at the $p < .05$ level. †Correlations with poll data approaching statistical significance at the $p < .10$ level.

variables and the polling data therefore have weak contextual linkage to our content analysis findings. In 1992, significant negative correlations between image bite coverage and support for candidates of both parties suggested an adverse effect of visual coverage volume on voter preference. But with virtually equal amounts of image bite coverage for Democrats and Republicans that year, it appears that image bite volume did not benefit either party's slate of candidates.

In 2000, image bite coverage was negatively related to voter support for Democrats at a near-significant level while the popularity of Republicans positively and significantly correlated with visual coverage volume. Perhaps Al Gore's difficulties connecting with voters through television on the one hand, and successful image bite management of the Bush election team on the other, were partially at play in these associations. Content analysis findings show nonsignificant differences but slightly more coverage for Bush than Gore. In this regard more visual coverage might have been beneficial to Bush and detrimental to Gore, which again raises questions about the validity of treating volume of coverage—visual or verbal—as a valid indicator of media favoritism since more network attention seems to have an adverse effect on some candidates.

The final image bite correlation worth mentioning is a weak but positive association with John Kerry's 2004 poll data. Interestingly, this association resurfaces in a regression model as a predictor of support for Kerry. Image bites also played a role in predictive models for Republicans, especially in 1996. Yet, as reported below, image bite volume made an unimpressive showing in the regression analyses.

Sound Bite Content

The next set of analyses tested correlations between our sound bite content variables and candidate polling data for each election year. As summarized in Table 6–1, three content variables—issue statements, calls to rally the troops, and attacks on opponents—produced significant, or near-significant, associations with the polling data. Defensive rhetoric was inconsequential. Indeed, in 2004 John Kerry was not featured in a single defensive sound bite in our sample of network news from Labor Day to Election Day. No noteworthy relationships between defensive sound bite occurrences and candidate polling data for any presidential ticket emerged for any election year analyzed.

Issue bites produced significant correlations in 1992 and 1996 for Democrats but with varying directional associations. In 1992 Clinton's issue bites were positively correlated with his voter support but in 1996 the association was negative. By most accounts the 1992 race was heated, especially turning on domestic concerns, which perhaps offered Clinton an opportunity to impress voters with his verbal command of the issues. Four years later, Clinton defended his incumbency in a campaign that was widely described as lackluster, with few sharp policy differences between the two presidential candidates and a hapless, undisciplined opponent in Bob Dole. Issue bites produced no interesting associations with Republican poll data. Moreover, our earlier content analysis findings showed similar amounts of issue bite coverage for Republicans and Democrats across election years (see Chapter 2).

When it comes to rallying supporters on the campaign trail, Republicans seem to be more effective than Democrats. In fact, John Kerry was the only Democrat with a significant positive correlation between rallying sound bites and tracking poll numbers. For all other Democrats the coefficients were negative—significantly so for Clinton in 1992 and nearly significant for Gore in 2000. For Republicans, on the other hand, especially George W. Bush, the coefficients were positive and approached significance in both 2000 and 2004. In our content analysis findings for rallying sound bite occurrences, there were no significant differences between political parties for any election year.

Attack bites produced notable associations with polling data in the 2000 election. From the analysis reported in Chapter 2, we observed slightly longer attack bites from Gore (an average of 13.05 seconds per

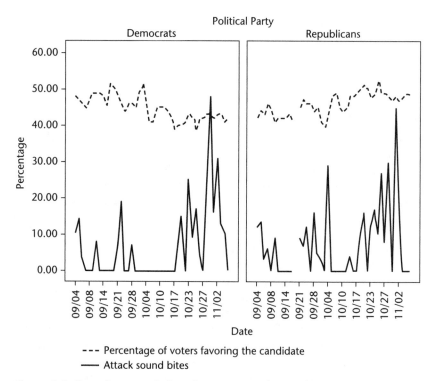

Figure 6–1 Over-time correlations between attack sound bites and polling data for 2000

story) than Bush (12.23 seconds per story). This agonistic approach did not seem to benefit Gore: the bivariate analysis yielded a significant *negative* correlation with Gore's polling numbers and a *positive*, near-significant correlation with Bush's numbers. In fact, the 2000 election illustrates how verbal attacks may boomerang in the polls. Judging by Figure 6–1, which shows the over-time correlations between attack sound bites and polling data for 2000, Gore and Bush engaged in the most verbal aggression during the last two weeks of the race. During that period Bush was able to launch attacks from a position of strength as the front-runner, whereas Gore attacked as a candidate on the ropes after weeks of declining poll numbers.

Circumstances changed in 2004 when Bush's attack bites were significantly and negatively correlated with his standing in the polls. Voter support for Kerry was also negatively correlated with attack bites but not significantly so. Earlier we reported a significantly higher volume of attack bites for Kerry than Bush, reinforcing Kerry's challenger status (see Chapter 2). Bush faced more verbal attacks from opponents than what he personally doled out[3] and his polling data evidenced inconsistent relationships with attack discourse across the

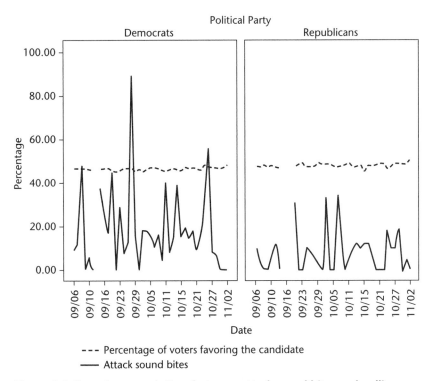

Figure 6–2 Over-time correlations between attack sound bites and polling data for 2004

two elections. Figure 6–2 shows the over-time correlations between attack sound bites and polling data for the 2004 election. Most noticeably, Kerry's attack bites (shown in the left panel) spiked just before the first presidential debate on September 30—a finding consistent with the facial display analysis from Chapter 4 that showed how agonic behavior increases during the debate period.

For all of Kerry's aggressive posturing and verbal attacks in 2004, his poll numbers were flat-lined and statistically unassociated with his tendency to go on the offensive. Bush, on the other hand, might have made a tactical mistake going negative around the debates in late September and early October in a somewhat weakened position since he generally performed poorly in those encounters against Kerry. As elaborated in Chapter 4, attacks work best when launched from a position of strength.

Sound bite content was more likely to be associated with candidate support than sound bite size or volume. These findings affirm the impotency of total airtime (without regard for content) as a measure of favorable coverage. More sophisticated analyses that rely on the care and precision of human coders to assess the nuances of bite content seem to have more measurement validity. From our analyses, it appears that going on the attack while trailing in the polls or shortly after losing a debate is not conducive to popularizing one's candidacy. As we report below, sound bite content seems to have played a significant role in predicting the outcomes of the 1992, 1996, and 2004 elections. Yet bite content is but one dimension of political news coverage. Visual framing, televised leader displays, and forms of visual bias may affect voter support as well. The influence of each of these visual forms is considered next.

Visual Framing

Visual framing was more consequential for Democrats than Republicans (see Table 6–2). The ideal candidate frame, consisting of the compassion and statesmanship subdimensions, might have worked against Clinton in 1992, with a significant negative correlation, and again in 1996, with a negative but not significant association, when his image handlers set out to construct him as a compassionate statesman. In 1992, Clinton received about the same amount of ideal candidate framing as George H. W. Bush. But the efficacy of this strategy may have been diluted given the difficulty of a folksy candidate, famously viewed as the Comeback Kid, to muster public support by symbolically appearing presidential next to an incumbent president. As we reported in Chapter 3, journalists exercised stringent frame control on Clinton in 1996, heavily filtering his intended ideal candidate construction in network news coverage. Oddly enough, Bob Dole as the challenger was visually presented as more statesmanlike than Clinton, the incumbent.

Table 6–2 Correlations between Polling Data and Visual Framing Variables from Chapter 3

Visual Frames	1992 Dem		1992 Rep		1996 Dem		1996 Rep		2000 Dem		2000 Rep		2004 Dem		2004 Rep	
	r	p	r	p	r	p	r	p	r	p	r	p	r	p	r	p
Ideal candidate	-.349	.014*	-.187	.121	-.048	.385	.093	.289	-.216	.080[†]	.216	.082[†]	.211	.095[†]	.191	.126
Populist campaigner	-.343	.015*	-.186	.123	.054	.372	.118	.240	-.294	.027*	.146	.175	-.057	.363	.072	.335
Sure loser	-.177	.137	-.103	.261	-.083	.307	.015	.464	-.213	.082[†]	.146	.175	-.117	.239	-.158	.168

*Correlations with poll data that are statistically significant at the $p < .05$ level. [†]Correlations with poll data approaching statistical significance at the $p < .10$ level.

231

Although not significant, Dole's ideal candidate scores were positively correlated with his polling numbers.

Political observers have widely speculated that Al Gore would have been more successful in 2000 had he proactively embraced the image of a statesman or ideal candidate rather than running as an ill-suited populist. The results of our analysis from Chapter 3 showed slightly higher ideal candidate scores for Gore compared to Bush, but counter to pundit speculations, the correlation test produced a near-significant *negative* association with Gore's polling numbers. More statesmanship might not have delivered a boost for Gore after all. Perhaps his visual framing performances for the news cameras were on the whole poorly executed. Consultant and image-handler interventions reportedly wore on him toward the end of the campaign, possibly making his on-camera behavior stilted or out of sync with who he was as a person, re-gardless of frame content. Ironically, Bush walked away with a positive and near-significant correlation between his ideal candidate scores and standing in the polls.

By many accounts, John Kerry projected natural ideal candidate character qualities, much like Gore. Kerry's total package appeal might be reflected in the positive, near-significant correlation between

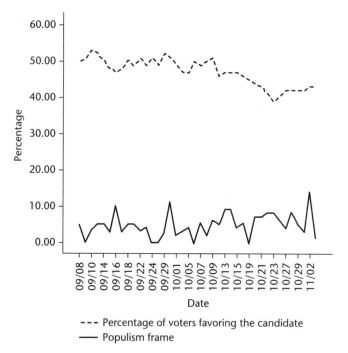

Figure 6–3 Over-time correlations between populist framing and polling data for Bill Clinton in 1992

this frame and his voter support. Yet, as reported in Chapter 3, Kerry received slightly less ideal candidate framing than Bush in 2004. Unlike Gore four years earlier, more visual statesmanship and compassion might have benefited Kerry's electoral prospects.

Despite all the documented strategies to present Democrats in a populist mold during the four elections analyzed, their poll standings were negatively correlated with populist framing in each election year except 1996. In 1992, Clinton's campaign worked vigorously, in a behind-the-scenes effort code-named the Manhattan Project, to play up their candidate's humble origins in small town Hope, Arkansas. Our content analysis showed that Clinton's image handlers achieved a small edge in manifesting this frame in network news coverage over George H. W. Bush's image handlers, who also pursued a populist frame. Yet, Clinton's populist framing scores were significantly and *negatively* associated with his poll data in 1992. As shown in Figure 6–3, the emphasis on Clinton's populist appeal intensified gradually from mid-October to Election Day, a period that coincided with a more than 10-point drop in voter support.

George H. W. Bush was no more successful in this frame in 1992—but the correlation with his polling data was not significant. In fact, there were

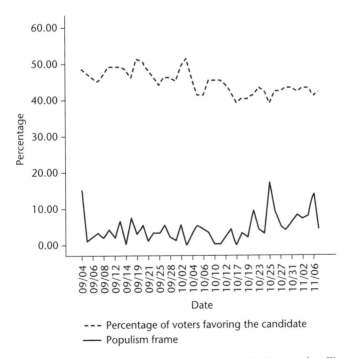

Figure 6–4 Over-time correlations between populist framing and polling data for Al Gore in 2000

no statistically significant correlations between voter support for Republicans and populist framing in any election year. Even so, George H. W.
Bush was the only Republican whose voter support stood in negative
association with his populist framing. Although populism is a favored
theme among Democratic consultants, correlational tests for Republicans more often produced positive coefficients for this frame.

The 2000 election was particularly telling with regard to visual
framing. Al Gore's image handlers won the framing battle in news
coverage that reflected populist themes but lost the election, some have
argued, because this frame was a poor fit for their candidate. Indeed,
as we reported in Chapter 3, Gore received significantly more populist
image framing than Bush, but the correlation analysis showed a
significant negative relationship between populist campaign images
and candidate support. As Figure 6–4 illustrates, Gore's populist
framing increased from mid-October to Election Day, similar to Clinton's
in 1992, corresponding with a decrease in his poll standings. Together
these findings point to the fickleness of populist image construction and
the importance of "fit" in dressing candidates in a particular frame.

As one would expect, the loser frame was negatively related to
polling data in a majority of analyses. Only in 2000, however, did the

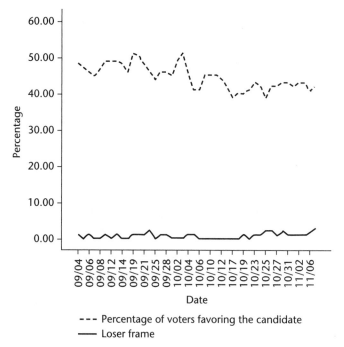

Figure 6–5 Over-time correlations between loser framing and polling data for
Al Gore in 2000

negative association approach significance. That year's network news coverage cast Gore significantly more often in the loser frame than Bush (see Chapter 3). Figure 6–5 shows how the loser frame, although low in prominence, increased for Gore during the final weeks of the race. Combined with declining voter support, this scenario certainly did not help Gore's electoral prospects. Interestingly, the loser frame was *positively* correlated with Bush's poll standings, but not at a significant level.

Of all the candidates included in our analyses, Bob Dole received the most loser framing. Yet, his poll numbers were positively associated with this frame, albeit at a nonsignificant level. Perhaps voters were reacting to Dole with a type of sympathy response.

From these correlational findings, we can conclude that visual framing of candidates seems to have affected support for Democrats more clearly and negatively than support for Republicans. As we report in the regression results below, visual framing variables were instrumental in driving predictive models in 2000 and 2004. In particular, the populist frame was a potent predictor of support for both Gore and Kerry.

Facing the Electorate

The analysis of televised leader displays in Chapter 4 reported stark differences between the hedonic and agonic nonverbal communication of winning and trailing candidates. When trailing in the horse race, Democrats were more emotive (both hedonically and agonically) than when leading. Republicans, to the contrary, displayed a wider range of hedonic and agonic behavior when they were ahead in the polls. We speculated that the timing of these different modes of communication might give Republicans, who avoided projecting an image of happy losers, an edge over Democrats. Voter support for Democrats was, perhaps not surprisingly, negatively correlated with both modes of nonverbal behavior—agonic and hedonic alike (see Table 6–3). Except for John Kerry's hedonic displays in 2004, which were positively but not significantly associated with his polling data, this pattern was persistent.

Examining these relationships in more detail, Bill Clinton's hedonic and agonic displays were negatively correlated with voter support in 1992. Closer inspection reveals that Clinton emoted with heightened intensity toward the final stage of the election when his support among voters was flagging. Despite widely held views about his nonverbal skills and telegenic ability to connect with voters, Clinton's expressive behavior in the final weeks of the campaign was not enough to shore up weakening public support (see Figure 6–6). The 1996 election did not feature any significant correlations between polling data and nonverbal display variables for Clinton or Dole. In 2000, Gore's agonic behavior was significantly associated with a downward trend in his voter support. An increase in agonic displays in the final weeks of the election,

Table 6–3 Correlations between Polling Data and Facial Display Variables from Chapter 4

Display Types	1992 Dem		1992 Rep		1996 Dem		1996 Rep		2000 Dem		2000 Rep		2004 Dem		2004 Rep	
	r	p	r	p	r	p	r	p	r	p	r	p	r	p	r	p
Agonic	−.321	.022*	−.198	.108	−.140	.198	−.118	.241	−.336	.013*	.186	.117	−.114	.241	.022	.448
Hedonic	−.307	.027*	−.187	.121	−.207	.103	.165	.160	−.044	.389	.107	.248	.107	.225	.287	.038*

*Correlations with poll data that are statistically significant at the $p < .05$ level. †Correlations with poll data approaching statistical significance at the $p < .10$ level.

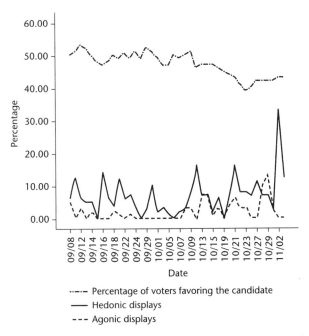

Figure 6–6 Over-time correlations between nonverbal behavior and polling data for Bill Clinton in 1992

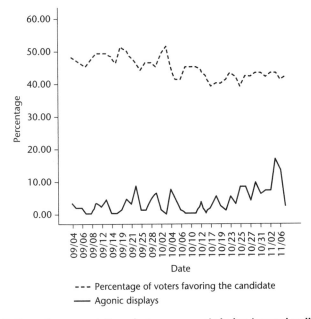

Figure 6–7 Over-time correlations between agonic behavior and polling data for Al Gore in 2000

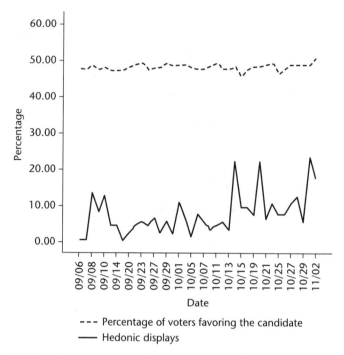

Figure 6–8 Over-time correlations between hedonic behavior and polling data for George W. Bush in 2004

combined with weakening support, did not make for a winning trajectory (see Figure 6–7).

Unlike support for Democrats, support for Republican candidates was mostly positively associated with emotional displays—both hedonic and agonic. The exception is George H. W. Bush. His nonverbal behavior, like Bill Clinton's in 1992, was negatively associated with his poll standings, although not at statistically significant levels. The 1996 and 2000 elections featured no significant correlations for Republicans but in both years their nonverbal displays were positively associated with voter support (except for Dole's agonic behavior). In the post-9/11 election of 2004, the reassuring hedonic behavior of George W. Bush might explain the significant and positive correlation with his polling data, since effective leadership has been associated with the social bonding evoked by happiness/reassurance displays (see Chapter 4). Figure 6–8 depicts this trend in Bush's hedonic behavior, revealing an increase toward Election Day that sustained him in a bumpy but winning course toward the end of the race.

In sum, it appears that Republicans were more effective than Democrats in influencing voter support through nonverbal displays—a trend reinforced by our findings from the regression analyses reported below.

Visual Bias

In Chapter 5 we identified a pattern of visual bias, most pronounced in camera and editing packaging that favored Republicans. In that analysis we employed three sets of variables—volume, weight, and packaging—which we include in correlation analysis with polling data here. The volume of coverage variable assessed the total amount of single-party stories in which individual news items were fully dedicated to one party's candidate. Results from Chapter 5 indicated that candidates of both parties received roughly the same amount of single-party story coverage. In 1992, Bill Clinton was featured slightly more often in single-party stories than George H. W. Bush, yet his polling numbers were *negatively* associated with this coverage. The same scenario materialized for Clinton in 1996. Although he received marginally less single-party coverage than Dole, again, there was a *negative* correlation with his polling numbers. Dole's volume of single-party spotlight coverage, on the other hand, was *positively* correlated with his standing in the polls.

Single-party correlation results for 2000 mirrored the 1996 election. Support for Democratic candidates, who received slightly more exclusive coverage, was *negatively* associated with single-party coverage while for Republicans exclusive coverage *positively* and significantly correlated with their polling data. The 2004 election, in which John Kerry received less single-party coverage than George W. Bush, featured the only positive and significant correlation between single-party coverage and poll standings for any Democratic candidate. In short, more exclusive coverage of Democrats was not, with the exception of Kerry in 2004, associated with higher levels of support. On the other hand, there were a few indicators that more solo coverage was positively associated with Republican poll standings. Overall, single-party coverage was not a consistent correlate of polling outcomes (see Table 6–4).

Earlier we advised caution in treating the total amount of sound and image bite news coverage allocated to candidates as a reliable standard for detecting media bias. Here, with another volume of coverage variable, single-party stories, we reported more statistical association but inconsistent direction in correlations with polling data. More coverage was not necessarily beneficial, at least not to Democratic candidates; hence, more or less media attention should not automatically be taken as evidence of helping or hurting candidates. At the same time, the amount of single-party stories a candidate received was influential in regression analyses reported below. In fact, the amount of single-party coverage was a significant predictor of support for both parties' candidates in all election years except 2000. Thus, in relation to other,

Table 6–4 Correlations between Polling Data and Measures of Visual Bias from Chapter 5

Measures of Visual Bias	1992 Dem r	1992 Dem p	1992 Rep r	1992 Rep p	1996 Dem r	1996 Dem p	1996 Rep r	1996 Rep p	2000 Dem r	2000 Dem p	2000 Rep r	2000 Rep p	2004 Dem r	2004 Dem p	2004 Rep r	2004 Rep p
Volume																
Single-party coverage	−.230	.077†	.038	.408	−.219	.090†	.217	.095†	−.216	.079†	.390	.005*	.430	.003*	−.088	.298
Packaging																
Visual weight	−.271	.045*	−.098	.270	−.318	.024*	.140	.201	−.250	.051†	.378	.006*	.423	.003*	−.192	.120
Detrimental	−.424	.003*	−.325	.019*	−.148	.184	−.077	.323	−.210	.086†	−.121	.221	−.209	.098†	−.090	.292
Beneficial	.083	.306	.204	.101	.112	.135	.230	.082†	.151	.164	.325	.017*	.061	.354	.087	.299

*Correlations with poll data that are statistically significant at the $p < .05$ level. †Correlations with poll data approaching statistical significance at the $p < .10$ level

more nuanced content variables, the amount of single-party stories a candidate receives becomes a catalyst for beneficial poll outcomes. This suggests that the *content* of what is covered in single-party news coverage trumps sheer volume as an influence on candidate support, further pointing to the questionability of treating volume alone as a test of fair coverage.

Our argument that visual weight, or prominence of coverage, might be a better indicator of bias than measures of volume, received some support from the correlation analyses. As with single-party coverage, more visual weight did not necessarily translate into higher poll ratings, especially for Democrats (see Table 6–4). In every election except 2004, the more visual weight Democrats received, the lower was their standings in the polls. A significant positive correlation between Kerry's visual weight and voter support in 2004 was the exception to the pattern. Visual weight was less consequential for Republicans, with just one significant, positive correlation—for George W. Bush in 2000.

The expectation that candidates who received more visual weight or prominence in news coverage would benefit in the polls was not consistently supported. Support for Democrats was actually hurt by more prominent coverage. This trend of negative association between voter support and visual weight scores merits closer consideration. Either the content of network news coverage was unfavorable to Democrats or increases in coverage paled in comparison to the media attention Republicans were receiving, making Democratic candidates appear less important than their Republican opponents. In Chapter 5 we reported that Republicans were assigned more visual prominence and were more often featured in the lead story position than Democrats. In view of these findings, the negative correlations for Democrats on the combined visual weight measure used in the correlation analyses (story type plus placement in the newscast) suggest that their lack of visual emphasis compared to Republicans might have undermined voter support. Kerry, again the exception to this trend, was assigned roughly the same news prominence as Bush during the 2004 election, at least in terms of story type, and he was the only Democrat with a significant positive association between his polling numbers and visual weight scores.

Closer visual scrutiny of the data shows that Democrats received the most visual weight during the critical last few days of the race when their voter support was typically not at a high point (see Figure 6–9). Indeed, John Kerry was the only Democratic presidential candidate from 1992 to 2004 whose polling numbers were not in noticeable decline shortly before Election Day, which explains why his case might be exceptional. Democrats rarely overshadowed Republicans in visual prominence. As shown in Figure 6–9, Democrats were assigned more prominence at a few points close to Election Day in 1992 and 1996 when their voter support was flagging. In 2000 and 2004 Democrats started out low then

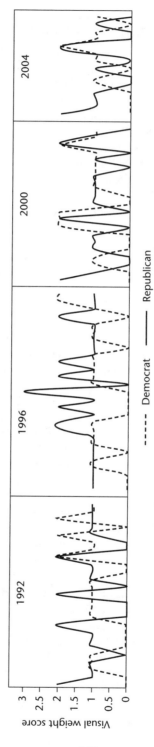

Figure 6–9 Over-time visual weight scores for Democrats and Republicans, 1992–2004

alternated with Republicans for peaks of prominence throughout the campaign. The indicators here are that visual weight might have influence depending on the status of the horse race and the comparative visual weight of the opposition's coverage. When candidates are leading, that is, doing well in the polls or in debates, measures of visual weight seem to have a positive association with voter support.

Our conceptualization of visual bias detectable in camera and editing techniques was validated by associations found in the polling data. What we termed beneficial packaging (low-angle camera perspectives, close-up shots, zoom-in movements, last say speaking turns, etc.) correlated positively with candidate support; detrimental packaging (lip flap, high-angle camera perspectives, zoom-out movements, long shots, etc.), on the other hand, correlated negatively with candidate polling data. Not all correlations were significant. Yet the coefficients were all in the expected direction, supporting our conceptualization of the packaging measures. Not only can one make a strong argument, based on experimental evidence, that these production techniques facilitate beneficial and detrimental perceptions of candidates but also that public opinion data here tangibly demonstrates the influence of the production features.

Year-by-year correlation analyses of beneficial and detrimental packaging scores for Republicans and Democrats produced a number

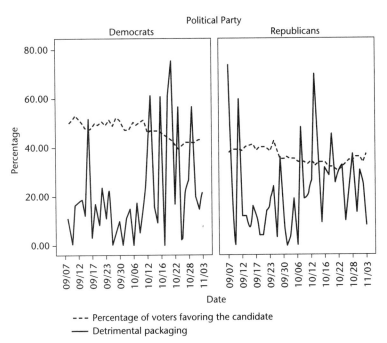

Figure 6–10 Over-time correlations between detrimental packaging and polling data for Bill Clinton and George H. W. Bush in 1992

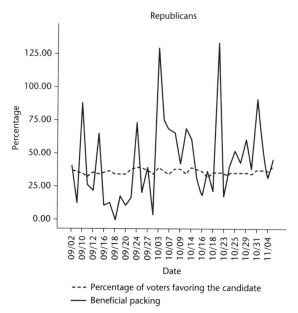

Figure 6–11 Over-time correlations between beneficial packaging and polling data for Bob Dole in 1996

of notable findings (see Table 6–4). As reported in Chapter 5, Republican candidates were the beneficiaries of favorable camera and editing applications in 1992. Yet they also received as much detrimental packaging as Democratic candidates. Tests of association with polling data show significant negative correlations for both parties with detrimental packaging and positive, but not significant, correlations with beneficial packaging. Thus, if packaging techniques impacted candidates in 1992, it was to the detriment of both parties (see Figure 6–10).

In 1996 beneficial packaging variables were positively associated with voter support for Dole at a near-significant level. Our content analysis findings indicated substantial variation in the application of beneficial packaging between parties, with Dole receiving more beneficial coverage than Clinton. The correlation with polling data for Dole suggests that the positive visual packaging he received might have added to an upward trend in his public support (see Figure 6–11).

In 2000, public support for Gore was negatively associated with detrimental packaging at a near-significant level, whereas George W. Bush's polling numbers were positively and significantly correlated with beneficial packaging features. Our content analysis from Chapter 5 found that Bush received more beneficial and less detrimental visual packaging in network news coverage than Gore. The correlations suggest that Bush might have benefited not only from more favorable

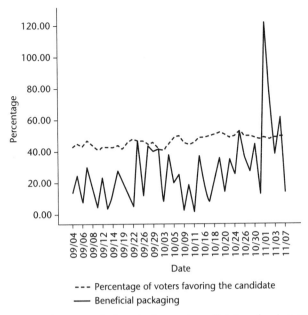

Figure 6–12 Over-time correlations between beneficial packaging and polling data for George W. Bush in 2000

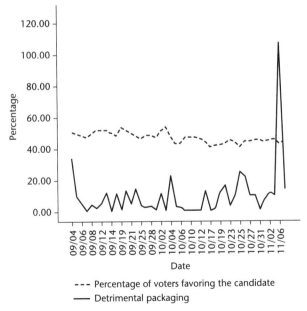

Figure 6–13 Over-time correlations between detrimental packaging and polling data for Al Gore in 2000

visual portrayals but also from the negative influence of Gore's detrimental packaging scores on his public support. Figures 6–12 and 6–13 show these trends visually. A similar dynamic emerged in 2004, when Kerry (like Gore) received slightly more detrimental packaging than Bush, and public support for Kerry was negatively correlated with his detrimental packaging scores.

Given the persistent associations between visual packaging and public support for presidential candidates from 1992 to 2004, investigations of media favoritism would be well served to consider visual forms of bias in addition to the tenor and volume of coverage—operationalizations that have dominated past research. As the following discussion of our regression results shows, measures of visual bias—both beneficial and detrimental—play a consequential role in predictive models of candidate support, especially for Republicans.

MODELS OF CANDIDATE SUPPORT: REGRESSION ANALYSES

Moving beyond bivariate associations between content analysis variables and polling data, linear regression was employed to examine the influence of our visual, verbal, and volume of coverage measures on public support for the candidates in a series of multivariate models. The backward method of entering variables into the analysis was employed to prevent suppressor effects, which emerge when one variable affects the outcome of interest (or dependent variable, such as candidate support) positively through an intervening variable, and negatively through another. As a result, it may seem at first that the two predictors do not influence (i.e., have a significant relationship with) the dependent variable and may be excluded from the model under the forward inclusion procedure.[4-6]

The logic behind the backward inclusion procedure was to enter the content analysis variables into the structure and allow them to compete with each other in producing significant models for predicting candidate support. In this way, the relative potency of different kinds of variables could be assessed comparatively. This approach is consistent with the nature of our data, which are continuous and the fact that our measures have not been previously used in predictive models. Their statistical behavior is, as yet, unknown. Variables included in these models are listed in Appendix 6. Results are reported below for each election year and candidate slate.

The 1992 Election

Democrats

Nine models—all statistically significant—were generated in predicting support for Bill Clinton in 1992. As Table 6–5 shows, models 8 and 9 predicted the largest amount of variance in candidate support with

Table 6–5 Regression Models Predicting Support for Democrats in 1992

Models	Adjusted R^2	df	F	p
Model 1	.372	16	2.44	.025
Model 2	.397	15	2.71	.014
Model 3	.420	14	3.02	.008
Model 4	.440	13	3.36	.004
Model 5	.458	12	3.74	.002
Model 6	.469	11	4.14	.001
Model 7	.478	10	4.58	.001
Model 8	.487	9	5.11	<.001
Model 9	.487	8	5.63	<.001

Bolded variables indicate statistically significant standardized beta values, with the direction of the correlation included in parentheses.

Model 1 = detrimental packaging, beneficial packaging, visual weight, **agonic displays (–)**, hedonic displays, ideal candidate framing, populist framing, **loser framing (+)**, **issue sound bites (+)**, rally the troops sound bites, defensive sound bites, **attack sound bites (+)**, single-party story volume, sound bite size, sound bite volume, image bite volume.

Model 2 = detrimental packaging, beneficial packaging, visual weight, **agonic displays (–)**, hedonic displays, ideal candidate framing, populist framing, **loser framing (+)**, **issue sound bites (+)**, rally the troops sound bites, defensive sound bites, **attack sound bites (+)**, single-party story volume, sound bite size, image bite volume.

Model 3 = detrimental packaging, beneficial packaging, visual weight, **agonic displays (–)**, hedonic displays, ideal candidate framing, populist framing **loser framing (+)**, **issue sound bites (+)**, rally the troops sound bites, defensive sound bites, **attack sound bites (+)**, single-party story volume, sound bite size.

Model 4 = detrimental packaging, beneficial packaging, **visual weight (–)**, **agonic displays (–)**, hedonic displays, ideal candidate framing, populist framing, **loser framing (+)**, **issue sound bites (+)**, rally the troops sound bites, **attack sound bites (+)**, single-party story volume, sound bite size.

Model 5 = detrimental packaging, **visual weight (–)**, **agonic displays (–)**, hedonic displays, ideal candidate framing, populist framing, **loser framing (+)**, **issue sound bites (+)**, rally the troops sound bites, **attack sound bites (+)**, single-party story volume, sound bite size.

Model 6 = **visual weight (–)**, **agonic displays (–)**, hedonic displays, ideal candidate framing, populist framing, **loser framing (+)**, **issue sound bites (+)**, rally the troops sound bites, **attack sound bites (+)**, single-party story volume, sound bite size.

Model 7 = **visual weight (–)**, **agonic displays (–)**, ideal candidate framing, populist framing, **loser framing (+)**, **issue sound bites (+)**, rally the troops sound bites, **attack sound bites (+)**, **single-party story volume (+)**, sound bite size.

Model 8 = **visual weight (–)**, **agonic displays (–)**, **ideal candidate framing (–)**, **loser framing (+)**, **issue sound bites (+)**, rally the troops sound bites, **attack sound bites (+)**, **single-party story volume (+)**, sound bite size.

Model 9 = **visual weight (–)**, **agonic displays (–)**, **ideal candidate framing (–)**, **loser framing (+)**, **issue sound bites (+)**, rally the troops sound bites, **attack sound bites (+)**, **single-party story volume (+)**.

eight and nine variables, respectively. The more parsimonious of the two, model 9, will be discussed here in more detail. Included in this model were sound bite content, framing, facial display, volume of coverage, and visual packaging variables (see Table 6–6).

Closer inspection of the standardized beta values shows that three sound bite content variables significantly predicted support for Clinton.

Table 6–6 Content Analysis Variables for Model 9 Predicting Support for Democratic Candidates in 1992

Variables	Standardized ß	t	p
Issue sound bites	.43	3.34	.002
Rally the troops sound bites	−.25	−1.71	.098
Attack sound bites	.57	3.37	.002
Ideal candidate framing	−.55	−3.06	.005
Loser framing	.61	3.17	.003
Agonic displays	−.68	−3.95	<.001
Single-party story volume	.75	2.30	.029
Visual weight	−1.03	−3.06	.004

Verbal attacks and issue statements were significantly and positively associated with his polling data, whereas sound bites that featured calls to rally the troops bore a near-significant negative relationship with the data.

In terms of visual framing, the ideal candidate frame emerged as a negative predictor of support for Clinton, while the loser frame made a positive contribution to the regression model (both were significant). This outcome seems counterintuitive. Yet, these two findings are consistent with the way Clinton's competing Comeback Kid and Slick Willy personas may have impacted his support. The image of a statesmanlike ideal candidate who could seemingly deflect almost any accusation leveled against him (i.e., Slick Willy) contradicted Clinton's more inspiring image as the underdog challenger to an incumbent president (i.e., the Comeback Kid). Thus, public support for Clinton emerged more vividly when the losing underdog frame was invoked than when he appeared as a polished, ideal politician. These results suggest that the loser frame provided public space for Clinton to showcase his ability to overcome adversity and in the process strengthen support among voters. The ideal candidate frame, to the contrary, contradicted his tenacity as a fighter and apparently undermined some of his support. Indeed, it might have been unbecoming for a challenger, fighting a political battle against an incumbent president, to visually assume a statesmanlike position prematurely.

Another contextual matter might be relevant here. Clinton's loser frame scores quite possibly could be the result of the vigorous negative campaign George H. W. Bush was running toward the end of the election. A strategy of fierce attack on the opponent, initially engineered for Bush by Lee Atwater and used with much success in the 1988 campaign against Michael Dukakis, might have backfired when unleashed against Clinton. As mentioned in Chapter 3, Atwater passed away before the 1992 campaign and the Bush camp struggled to execute an Atwater-style campaign without his guidance and supervision. The ferocity with which Bush participated in attacking the Democrats might have helped to invoke the loser frame for his opponent but with the unintended consequence of evoking support for Clinton. Indeed, these are the only loser frame scores across four elections and eight candidates that were statistically associated with deepening public support.

Clinton's agonic displays also contributed significantly to the model, negatively impacting his poll numbers. Interestingly, we reported earlier that agonic *verbals* (attack sound bites) were positively correlated with Clinton's polling data but agonic *visuals* (primarily, anger/threat displays) were negatively related. Broadly considered, Clinton was more effective in connecting with voters through aggressive verbal than nonverbal behavior. Indeed, in line with theoretical arguments reported in Chapter 4, agonic nonverbal behavior exhibited by a challenger was not conducive to building voter support.

The length of single-party stories, featuring Democratic candidates only, contributed positively to Clinton's poll standings. Thus, in this case more exclusive coverage meant more voter support. Given the public's relative unfamiliarity with Clinton in 1992 compared to his main opponent, incumbent President Bush, more single-party coverage seems to have worked to his advantage. Yet, visual weight, the measure of a candidate's visual prominence in coverage, negatively impacted Clinton's poll standings. As with bivariate correlations reported earlier, visual prominence negatively influenced support for Clinton in the regression analysis. However, the conflicting coefficients for visual weight and single-party coverage, some negative and some positive, suggest that visual prominence may not be a more reliable measure of beneficial coverage than volume.

Notably, model 9 significantly predicted almost half (49%) of the variance in Clinton's poll standings. This is not, by social science standards, a small percentage. Of the eight variables in the model, four indexed visual dimensions of coverage: agonic displays, the ideal candidate and sure loser framing, and visual weight in packaging. The visual aspects of network news clearly held their own in relation to Clinton's sound bite content and single-party coverage in predicting public support.

Republicans

The poll fluctuations of George H. W. Bush were predicted by six of 15 regression models in our analysis of the 1992 campaign. Table 6–7 summarizes findings for all models. Among the significant models, number 11 predicts the largest chunk of variance (around 20%) in Bush's poll standings, employing six variables. Standardized beta coefficients for this model are reported in Table 6–8 and are discussed here in more detail.

Table 6–7 Regression Analysis Predicting Support for Republicans in 1992

Models	Adjusted R^2	df	F	p
Model 1	−.047	16	.89	.590
Model 2	−.006	15	.98	.498
Model 3	.032	14	1.10	.406
Model 4	.065	13	1.21	.323
Model 5	.095	12	1.35	.247
Model 6	.124	11	1.51	.180
Model 7	.145	10	1.68	.132
Model 8	.166	9	1.89	.091
Model 9	.187	8	2.15	.059
Model 10	.200	7	2.43	.040
Model 11	.201	6	2.68	.031
Model 12	.199	5	2.99	.024
Model 13	.168	4	3.02	.030
Model 14	.152	3	3.40	.028
Model 15	.126	2	3.89	.029

Bolded variables indicate statistically significant standardized beta values, with the direction of the correlation included in parentheses. Models 1 through 9 = *n.s.*

Model 10 = detrimental packaging, beneficial packaging, issue sound bites, single-party story volume, sound-bite size, sound-bite volume, image-bite volume.

Model 11 = detrimental packaging **beneficial packaging (+)**, issue sound bites, single-party story volume, sound-bite volume, image-bite volume.

Model 12 = **detrimental packaging (–)**, **beneficial packaging (+)**, issue sound bites, single-party story volume, sound-bite volume.

Model 13 = **detrimental packaging (–)**, beneficial packaging, issue sound-bites, single-party story volume.

Model 14 = **detrimental packaging (–)**, beneficial packaging, single-party story volume.

Model 15 = **detrimental packaging (–)**, beneficial packaging.

Table 6–8 Content Analysis Variables for Model 11 Predicting Support for Republican Candidates in 1992

Variables	Standardized β	t	p
Sound-bite volume	−.21	−1.20	.239
Image-bite volume	−.21	−1.04	.307
Issue sound bites	.26	1.56	.129
Single-party story volume	.31	1.94	.061
Detrimental packaging	−.31	−1.60	.118
Beneficial packaging	.35	2.26	.030

Two volume of coverage variables from our content analysis, sound and image bite volume, appeared in model 11, but neither had significant beta values. The coefficients for both variables were negatively associated with voter support for Bush. Issue-oriented sound bite content was positively, but again not significantly, associated with Bush's polling numbers. Thus, the three bite variables identified in Chapter 2 contributed to model 11, but not at significant levels. Neither did these variables feature at significant levels in models 10 or 12, which explained similar amounts of variance.

Single-party coverage volume was a positive predictor of support for Bush, as it was for Clinton. Indeed, during the 1992 election more exclusive coverage seemed to have had positive outcomes for both candidates' poll standings. The beta coefficient for detrimental packaging was negative but not significant, whereas for beneficial packaging techniques the coefficient was positive and significant. The directions of these beta values, again, line up with the conceptualization and measurement of detrimental and beneficial visual packaging techniques discussed in Chapter 5. Moreover, these two visual packaging variables were the strongest predictors of public support for Bush in 1992. In fact, as the last model (number 15) demonstrates, these two variables alone accounted for around 13% of the variance in the polling data. In this sense they were central in driving significant models that predicted support for Bush.

Given that Bush received significantly more beneficial packaging in network news coverage than Clinton in 1992 (see Chapter 5), one can argue, with requisite caution, that journalistic bias in the form of visual packaging techniques helped his standings in the horse race.

The 1996 Election

Democrats

In the regression models for Democrats from the 1996 election, seven of 15 models that emerged in the analysis were significant predictors of candidate support. Model 11 predicted the largest amount of fluctuation in the polls (see Table 6–9). Six variables accounted for almost a quarter of the variance in support for Clinton. Among these were two sound bite content measures, a volume of coverage variable, and three visual content/packaging variables.

Closer inspection of the standardized beta coefficients reveals that most variables negatively influenced support for Clinton at significant or near-significant levels (see Table 6–10). Attack and issue sound bites both adversely affected Clinton's polling numbers in 1996, as did his hedonic displays—despite his widely admired ability to connect with voters through evocative nonverbal behavior. These results are

Table 6–9 Regression Models Predicting Support for Democrats in 1996

Models	Adjusted R^2	df	F	p
Model 1	−.007	16	.98	.505
Model 2	.036	15	1.10	.411
Model 3	.076	14	1.22	.321
Model 4	.112	13	1.37	.241
Model 5	.144	12	1.53	.175
Model 6	.174	11	1.73	.121
Model 7	.201	10	1.95	.080
Model 8	.209	9	2.11	.061
Model 9	.227	8	2.39	.040
Model 10	.231	7	2.63	.029
Model 11	.232	6	2.92	.022
Model 12	.191	5	2.80	.032
Model 13	.174	4	3.00	.032
Model 14	.157	3	3.36	.029
Model 15	.129	2	3.82	.031

Bolded variables indicate statistically significant standardized beta values, with the direction of the correlation included in parentheses. Models 1 through 8 = *n.s.*

Model 9 = beneficial packaging, **visual weight (–)**, **hedonic displays (–)**, issue sound bites, defensive sound bites, attack sound bites, **single-party story volume (+)**, sound- bite size.

Model 10 = beneficial packaging, **visual weight (–)**, **hedonic displays (–)**, issue sound bites, attack sound bites, **single-party story volume (+)**, sound-bite size.

Model 11 = beneficial packaging **visual weight (–)**, hedonic displays, issue sound bites, attack sound bites, **single-party story volume (+).**

Model 12 = beneficial packaging, visual weight, hedonic displays, issue sound bites, single-party story volume.

Model 13 = beneficial packaging, visual weight, issue sound bites, single-party story volume.

Model 14 = beneficial packaging **visual weight (–)**, single-party story volume.

Model 15 = **visual weight (–)**, single-party story volume.

Table 6–10 Content Analysis Variables for Model 11 Predicting Support for Democratic Candidates in 1996

Variables	Standardized β	t	p
Issue sound bites	−.30	−1.88	.069
Attack sound bites	−.26	−1.66	.107
Hedonic displays	−.32	−1.80	.081
Single-party story volume	1.02	2.04	.049
Visual weight	−1.01	−2.07	.046
Beneficial packaging	.25	1.73	.094

somewhat puzzling given that Clinton, an incumbent president and front-runner throughout the 1996 election, was expected to benefit from his much talked about ability to connect with voters (see Chapter 4).

As in 1992, the volume of single-party coverage significantly influenced support for Clinton in a positive direction. By contrast, the amount of visual weight allotted to his candidacy negatively impacted his standings in the polls. Consistent with trends from 1992, these findings show that more exclusive coverage, rather than visual emphasis, had the capacity to move public opinion. Both of these variables emerged as important predictors of Clinton's poll data in 1996. The last model in the regression analysis, number 15, which predicted 13% of the variance in voter support for Clinton, featured visual weight and single-party coverage only.

Although Clinton received substantially less beneficial packaging than Dole in 1996, his polling numbers responded positively to this relative scarcity. The coefficient was not significant, however. Perhaps more favorable visual packaging of Clinton, somewhere close to Dole's level, would have had more robust impact on his voter support.

Republicans

Support for Dole in 1996 was significantly predicted by six of 12 regression models generated by the analysis (see Table 6–11). Model 10 accounted for the most variance, with seven variables—including three measures of visual influence—explaining 28% of the fluctuation in Dole's polling numbers. Standardized beta coefficients for this model are presented in Table 6–12.

Sound and image bite volume were significantly and negatively related to Dole's standing in the polls. Moreover, given the former Senate majority leader's struggle to connect with voters, it was not surprising to see negative coefficients for both a hedonic sound bite category (calls to rally the troops) as well as his agonic nonverbal displays. Effectively appealing for voter support without front-runner status probably requires exceptional verbal talent and nonverbal ability—qualities Dole simply did not display during the campaign. Moreover, given Dole's status in 1996 as a chronic also-ran and hapless campaigner, his agonic appearances held little potential for building enthusiasm among all but the most diehard partisans (see Chapter 4).

As was the case for Clinton, exclusive coverage positively influenced Dole's polling numbers while visual weight had no impact. These results further erode the case for visual weight as a more reliable measure of favorable coverage than volume. Indeed, the content of prominent news coverage, combined with the timing of visual prominence in the election cycle, appears to drive support more than story type and placement in the newscast. Finally, the beneficial visual packaging that Dole

Table 6–11 Regression Models Predicting Support for Republicans in 1996

Models	Adjusted R^2	df	F	p
Model 1	.066	16	1.16	.367
Model 2	.108	15	1.30	.281
Model 3	.147	14	1.45	.206
Model 4	.180	13	1.62	.147
Model 5	.206	12	1.80	.104
Model 6	.230	11	2.00	.071
Model 7	.253	10	2.25	.046
Model 8	.260	9	2.44	.034
Model 9	.277	8	2.78	.021
Model 10	.281	7	3.07	.015
Model 11	.278	6	3.38	.011
Model 12	.270	5	3.74	.009

Bolded variables indicate statistically significant standardized beta values, with the direction of the correlation included in parentheses. Models 1 through 6 = *n.s.*

Model 7 = **beneficial packaging (+)**, visual weight, agonic displays, ideal candidate framing, populist framing, issue sound bites, **rally the troops sound bites (-)**, **single-party story volume (+)**, **sound-bite volume (-)**, **image-bite volume (–)**.

Model 8 = **beneficial packaging (+)**, visual weight, agonic displays, ideal candidate framing, issue sound bites, **rally the troops sound bites (-)**, **single-party story volume (+)**, **sound-bite volume (–)**, **image-bite volume (–)**.

Model 9 = **beneficial packaging (+)**, visual weight, agonic displays, issue sound bites, **rally the troops sound bites (-)**, **single-party story volume (+)**, **sound-bite volume (–)**, **image-bite volume (–)**.

Model 10 = **beneficial packaging (+)**, visual weight, agonic displays, **rally the troops sound bites (-)**, **single-party story volume (+)**, **sound-bite volume (–)**, **image-bite volume (–)**.

Model 11 = **beneficial packaging (+)**, visual weight, **rally the troops sound bites (-)**, **single-party story volume (+)**, **sound-bite volume (–)**, **image-bite volume (–)**.

Model 12 = **beneficial packaging (+)**, **rally the troops sound bites (-)**, **single-party story volume (+)**, **sound bite volume (–)**, **image-bite volume (–)**.

Table 6–12 Content Analysis Variables for Model 10 Predicting Support for Republican Candidates in 1996

Variables	Standardized β	t	p
Sound-bite volume	−.56	−2.49	.018
Image-bite volume	−.56	−2.53	.017
Rallying sound bites	−.38	−2.50	.018
Agonic displays	−.17	−1.07	.294
Single-party story volume	.69	2.69	.012
Visual weight	−.28	−1.17	.252
Beneficial packaging	.94	3.65	.001

received seemed to have been gainful. The regression coefficient was positive and significant, whereas Clinton's beneficial packaging produced a weaker, near-significant result.

Overall, the model for Dole again demonstrated that visual influences were integral to predicting candidate support.

The 2000 Election

Democrats

Just one of the 15 models generated by the analysis for Gore significantly predicted voter support in 2000. Model 15 contained just two visual variables, hedonic displays and populist framing, accounting

Table 6–13 Regression Models Predicting Support for Democrats in 2000

Models	Adjusted R^2	df	F	p
Model 1	−.020	16	.96	.530
Model 2	.030	15	1.07	.434
Model 3	.075	14	1.20	.342
Model 4	.116	13	1.35	.257
Model 5	.150	12	1.52	.189
Model 6	.175	11	1.68	.140
Model 7	.180	10	1.77	.120
Model 8	.186	9	1.89	.099
Model 9	.173	8	1.91	.099
Model 10	.149	7	1.88	.112
Model 11	.129	6	1.86	.122
Model 12	.129	5	2.04	.101
Model 13	.113	4	2.12	.103
Model 14	.130	3	2.75	.059
Model 15	.121	2	3.41	.045

Bolded variables indicate statistically significant standardized beta values, with the direction of the correlation included in parentheses. Models 1 through 14 = *n.s.* Model 15 = hedonic displays, **populist framing (–)**.

Table 6–14 Content Analysis Variables for Model 15 Predicting Support for Democratic Candidates in 2000

Variables	Standardized β	t	p
Populist framing	−.59	−2.61	.014
Hedonic displays	.40	1.79	.082

for 12% of the variation in Gore's polling numbers (see Table 6–13). Whereas volume of coverage and sound bite content featured prominently in the regression models for both parties in 1992 and 1996, the significant model for Gore in 2000 consisted of visual influences only.

Most notably for Gore, his attempts at campaigning as a populist—a prominent but ill-fitting frame for the sitting vice president—seemed to have had an injurious impact on his poll standings. As shown in Table 6–14, the regression coefficient was significant and negative, suggesting the populist frame was primarily driving the model that predicted voter support. The other visual influence, Gore's hedonic displays, was positively but not significantly associated with his polling data.

Republicans

In the regression analysis for George W. Bush in 2000, six of 16 regression models predicting voter support were significant (see Table 6–15). Model 12, employing five visual variables, explained the most variance, accounting for close to 17% of the variation in Bush's polling numbers (see Table 6–16).

In contrast to Gore, the populist frame was a positive but not significant predictor of voter support for Bush. These contrasting findings for Bush and Gore deserve discussion. As reported in Chapter 3, both party's image handlers set out to build populist images of their clients in 2000. There was criticism of this strategy for Gore, and the populist frame negatively influenced his public support. The positive impact of populist framing on support for Bush suggests the former Texas governor was more comfortable and convincing in projecting this homespun, man of the people image than Gore. Perhaps, as we argued in Chapter 3, Democratic consultant Bob Shrum erred in trying to "out-Rove" the Bush campaign by force-fitting a brainy aristocrat into a populist frame. Our data indicate that the Bush team won the populist framing contest among voters and, perhaps at least in part because of that, a close election.

Visual packaging of the candidates also influenced voter support during the 2000 election. Bush received more visual weight in coverage than Gore, and the impact on his poll data was positive. Moreover, as we reported in Chapter 5, Bush received more favorable and less unfavorable packaging than Gore. In the regression model, beneficial packaging was positively and detrimental packaging negatively associated with support for Bush. Thus, Bush seemed to profit from visual forms of bias.

In summary, regression results from 2000 showcase the capacity of visual variables to affect candidate support. Based on this evidence, it appears that the election outcome might have turned in part on the damaging consequences of fitting Gore into a populist frame, combined with subtle yet favorable visual packaging of George W. Bush's

Table 6–15 Regression Models Analysis Predicting Support for Republicans in 2000

Models	Adjusted R^2	df	F	p
Model 1	−.055	16	.86	.613
Model 2	−.019	15	.95	.528
Model 3	.015	14	1.05	.440
Model 4	.044	13	1.15	.361
Model 5	.070	12	1.26	.289
Model 6	.093	11	1.39	.226
Model 7	.105	10	1.49	.187
Model 8	.126	9	1.67	.135
Model 9	.144	8	1.88	.096
Model 10	.157	7	2.12	.067
Model 11	.163	6	2.37	.050
Model 12	.168	5	2.66	.038
Model 13	.158	4	2.98	.031
Model 14	.165	3	3.82	.017
Model 15	.133	2	4.24	.021
Model 16	.122	1	6.83	.012

Bolded variables indicate statistically significant standardized beta values, with the direction of the correlation included in parentheses. Models 1 through 10 = *n.s.*

Model 11 = **detrimental packaging (–)**, beneficial packaging, visual weight, hedonic displays, populist framing, loser framing.

Model 12 = **detrimental packaging (–)**, beneficial packaging, visual weight, hedonic displays, populist framing.

Model 13 = detrimental packaging, beneficial packaging, visual weight, populist framing.

Model 14 = detrimental packaging, beneficial packaging, visual weight.

Model 15 = beneficial packaging, visual weight.

Model 16 = **visual weight (+)**.

Table 6–16 Content Analysis Variables for Model 12 Predicting Support for Republican Candidates in 2000

Variables	Standardized β	t	p
Populist framing	.27	1.26	.215
Hedonic displays	−.22	−1.14	.263
Visual weight	.28	1.77	.085
Detrimental packaging	−.37	−2.06	.047
Beneficial packaging	.30	1.71	.096

appearances on the nightly news. Clearly, the coverage in 2000 was not all one-sided—detrimental packaging exercised a tempering influence on support for Bush, for instance—but the net result of visual

Table 6–17 Regression Models Predicting Support for Democrats in 2004

Models	Adjusted R^2	df	F	p
Model 1	.329	15	2.28	.035
Model 2	.356	14	2.54	.020
Model 3	.380	13	2.84	.011
Model 4	.403	12	3.19	.006
Model 5	.423	11	3.60	.003
Model 6	.442	10	4.09	.001
Model 7	.459	9	4.67	.001
Model 8	.472	8	5.37	.001
Model 9	.481	7	6.17	.001
Model 10	.476	6	6.91	.001
Model 11	.475	5	8.06	.001

Bolded variables indicate statistically significant standardized beta values, with the direction of the correlation included in parentheses.

Model 1 = **detrimental packaging (–)**, beneficial packaging, visual weight, agonic displays, hedonic displays, ideal candidate framing, populist framing, loser framing, issue sound bites, rally the troops sound bites, attack sound bites, single-party story volume, Sound-bite size, Sound-bite volume, image-bite volume.

Model 2 = **detrimental packaging (–)**, beneficial packaging, agonic displays, hedonic displays, ideal candidate framing, populist framing, loser framing, issue sound bites, rally the troops Sound-bites, attack Sound-bites, **single-party story volume (+)**, Sound-bite size, Sound-bite volume, image-bite volume.

Model 3 = **detrimental packaging (–)**, beneficial packaging, agonic displays, ideal candidate framing, populist framing, loser framing, issue sound bites, rally the troop sound bites, attack sound bites, **single-party story volume (+)**, Sound-bite size, Sound-bite volume, image-bite volume.

Model 4 = **detrimental packaging (–)**, beneficial packaging, agonic displays, ideal candidate framing, populist framing, issue sound bites, rally the troops sound bites, attack sound bites, **single-party story volume (+)**, Sound-bite size, sound- bite volume, image-bite volume.

Model 5 = **detrimental packaging (–)**, beneficial packaging, agonic displays, ideal candidate framing, populist framing, issue sound bites, rally the troops sound bites, attack sound bites, **single-party story volume (+)**, sound- bite size, image-bite volume.

Model 6 = **detrimental packaging (–)**, agonic displays, ideal candidate framing, **populist framing (–)**, issue sound bites, rally the troops sound bites, attack sound bites, **single-party story volume (+)**, Sound-bite size, **image-bite volume (+)**.

Model 7 = **detrimental packaging (–)**, agonic displays, **populist framing (–)**, issue sound bites, rally the troops sound bites, attack sound bites, **single-party story volume (+)**, Sound-bite size, **image-bite volume (+)**.

Model 8 = **detrimental packaging (–)**, agonic displays, **populist framing (–)**, issue sound bites, rally the troops sound bites, attack sound bites, **single-party story volume (+)**, **image-bite volume (+)**

Model 9 = **detrimental packaging (–)**, **populist framing (–)**, issue sound bites, rally the troops sound bites, attack sound bites, **single-party story volume (+)**, **image-bite volume (+)**.

Model 10 = **detrimental packaging (–)**, **populist framing (–)**, rally the troops sound bites, attack sound bites, **single-party story volume (+)**, **image-bite volume (+)**.

Model 11 = **detrimental packaging (–)**, **populist framing (–)**, rally the troops sound bites, **single-party story volume (+)**, **image-bite volume (+)**.

portrayals of both campaigns seemed to hinder Gore (largely for self-inflicted reasons) and promote Bush.

The 2004 Election

Democrats

All 11 models generated in the regression analysis predicting support for Kerry were significant. Similar to the results for Clinton in 1992, this particular set of models explained large amounts of variance (see Table 6–17). Indeed, models 8 to 11 all explain more than 47% of variance in the poll data for Kerry. Model 9, which explains the most, is relatively parsimonious in employing seven variables. Given that Kerry's poll numbers were practically flat-lined across our sample period (see Figure 6–2), the fact that small fluctuations were highly predictable is striking. Table 6–18 presents the standardized beta coefficients for this model, which include three significant visual predictors of candidate support plus single-party coverage volume.

The amount of image bite coverage Kerry received was positively and significantly related to his standings in the polls.[7] Model 9 also offers insight into two visual variables that have been central to our content analysis findings: populist framing and detrimental packaging techniques. As with Al Gore in 2000, the populist frame (again, courtesy of Bob Shrum) was an equally poor choice for John Kerry—but one that featured prominently in network news coverage. The regression analysis showed populist framing significantly and negatively influenced Kerry's poll standings. Detrimental visual packaging techniques, which were applied more generously to Kerry than Bush in 2004, further eroded support for Kerry, as indicated by the significant negative coefficient in Table 6–18.

Finally, the volume of single-party coverage had a significant and positive impact on Kerry's poll data. Thus, Kerry profited from exclusive focus on his campaign.

Table 6–18 Content Analysis Variables for Model 9 Predicting Support for Democratic Candidates in 2004

Variables	Standardized β	t	p
Image-bite duration	.48	2.97	.001
Issue sound bites	.15	1.15	.261
Rallying sound bites	.20	1.50	.144
Attack sound bites	−.20	−1.37	.180
Populist framing	−.41	−2.79	.009
Single-party story volume	.69	4.74	.001
Detrimental packaging	−.36	−2.92	.006

Republicans

In the regression analysis predicting support for George W. Bush in 2004, eight of 11 models were significant (see Table 6–19). Model 9, employing eight variables, accounted for the largest portion of variance, just over 36%. Examination of the regression coefficients shows that visual variables, both in terms of content and packaging, were once again prominent (see Table 6–20).

In terms of verbal influence, attack sound bites significantly and negatively influenced support for Bush—and rightly so. As argued

Table 6–19 Regression Models Predicting Support for Republicans in 2004

Models	Adjusted R^2	df	F	p
Model 1	.187	16	1.55	.169
Model 2	.222	15	1.73	.116
Model 3	.255	14	1.93	.076
Model 4	.284	13	2.16	.048
Model 5	.303	12	2.37	.032
Model 6	.327	11	2.68	.018
Model 7	.339	10	2.95	.012
Model 8	.353	9	3.31	.007
Model 9	.361	8	3.68	.004
Model 10	.349	7	3.91	.004
Model 11	.360	6	4.57	.002

Bolded variables indicate statistically significant standardized beta values, with the direction of the correlation included in parentheses. Models 1 through 3 = *n.s.*

Model 4 = detrimental packaging, beneficial packaging, visual weight, **agonic displays (+)**, hedonic displays, ideal candidate framing, populist framing, **loser framing (–)**, issue sound bites, **attack sound bites (–)**, single-party story volume, Sound-bite size, Sound-bite volume.

Model 5 = detrimental packaging, beneficial packaging, **visual weight (–)**, **agonic displays (+)**, hedonic displays, ideal candidate framing, populist framing, **loser framing (–)**, issue sound bites, **attack sound bites (–)**, single-party story volume, Sound-bite size.

Model 6 = detrimental packaging, beneficial packaging, **visual weight (–)**, **agonic displays (+)**, hedonic displays, ideal candidate framing, populist framing, **loser framing (–)**, **attack sound bites (–)**, single-party story volume, Sound-bite size.

Model 7 = detrimental packaging, **visual weight (–)**, **agonic displays (+)**, hedonic displays, ideal candidate framing, **populist framing (+)**, **loser framing (–)**, **attack sound bites (–)**, single-party story volume, Sound-bite size.

Model 8 = detrimental packaging **visual weight (–)**, **agonic displays (+)**, hedonic displays, ideal candidate framing, **populist framing (+)**, **loser framing (–)**, **attack sound bites (–)**, **single-party story volume (+)**.

Model 9 = **visual weight (–)**, **agonic displays (+)**, hedonic displays, ideal candidate framing, **populist framing (+)**, **loser framing attack sound bites (–)**, **single-party story volume (+)**.

Model 10 = **visual weight (–)**, **agonic displays (+)**, hedonic displays, **populist framing (+)**, **loser framing (–)**, **attack sound bites (–)**, **single-party story volume (+)**.

Model 11 = **visual weight (–)**, **agonic displays (+)**, **populist framing (+)**, **loser framing (–)**, **attack sound bites (–)**, **single-party story volume (+)**.

Table 6–20 Content Analysis Variables for Model 9 Predicting Support for Republican Candidates in 2004

Variables	Standardized β	t	p
Attack sound bites	−.44	−2.71	.001
Ideal candidate framing	−.29	−1.26	.217
Populist framing	.44	2.38	.024
Loser framing	−.55	−2.85	.008
Agonic displays	.74	3.60	.001
Hedonic	.30	1.36	.184
Single-party story volume	1.32	2.66	.012
Visual weight	−1.60	−3.17	.003

in Chapter 4, an incumbent president is perhaps best advised to stay above the fray and let surrogates attack the opposition.

All three framing variables appeared in model 9. Ideal candidate framing, surprisingly, was negatively related to support for Bush. The coefficient was not significant, but a sitting president, appearing compassionate and statesmanlike, was expected to make a positive impression on voters. Findings for populist framing were similar to the results for 2000. Once again, the populist frame played well for Bush. A positive and significant relationship between populist framing and Bush's polling numbers testifies to this. As was the case in 2000, Bush projected more visual appeal than Kerry in his ability to wear the populist frame convincingly. Loser framing also surfaced in the model as a significant negative predictor of Bush's polling data—but was not very prominent in his coverage overall.

Another class of variables, televised leader displays and sound bite content, were differentially related to support for Bush depending on the communication modality. Agonic displays significantly and *positively* influenced his standing in the polls, while attack bite content—the verbal instantiation of agonic behavior—had a significant but *negative* influence. Subtle agonic nonverbal displays were thus more effective in bonding supporters to Bush than explicit verbal attacks. Hedonic displays were positively but not significantly related to candidate support. Given the positive associations between Bush's televised displays and his support among voters, he can be singled out as the candidate who had the most success in moving public opinion through nonverbal communication.

Both single-party coverage (positively related to his polling numbers) and visual weight in coverage (negatively related to polling numbers), were significant predictors of support for Bush. Together, these findings again suggest that caution should be taken in treating visual weight as a reliable measure of partisan bias. Overall, the predictive model for Bush was dominated by visual variables. Of the eight variables included, six consisted of visual content or packaging measures while the other two represented sound bite content and volume of coverage.

CONCLUDING CONSIDERATIONS

Given some unavoidable limitations, a *mea culpa* on the statistical short-comings of our tests to predict candidate support from content analysis data is in order. At the risk of a mawkish analogy, the very pursuit of these statistical associations is reminiscent of the old Danish folk story, *The Princess and the Pea*. It seems unlikely that the pea (i.e., the predictive value of our content variables) could be directly detected through layers of statistical "mattresses" (i.e., uncontrolled and unaccounted influences). Indeed, many moderating influences may have prevented our content measures from being statistically observed as directly affecting candidate support. First, we have no indication of how much respondents in the polling data viewed presidential campaign coverage during the sample period—Labor Day to Election Day of each election year. Neither do we know how much exposure respondents had to other media outlets from which they obtained election information or the extent to which they engaged in political discussions that might have influenced their opinions.

Second, we have no sociodemographic data on the poll respondents. Individual characteristics such as age, gender, education, and socioeconomic status are often highly correlated with media effects.[8-10] Third, we have no account of respondents' political orientations or attitudes, which play a major role in determining candidate preference (see Iyengar and McGrady[11]). Thus, the statistical associations and predictive outcomes that have emerged in our analyses should be taken as exploratory evidence in need of replication.

Yet, despite the imprecision of the polling data used in these analyses, a multitude of significant bivariate correlations and regression models, explaining between 12% and 48% of the variance in voter support for the candidates, emerged in association with our content analysis variables. Due to lack of control, our findings should be considered more suggestive than absolute. Indeed, much work, employing more detailed respondent information (e.g., the demographic characteristics and political orientations of viewers) in relation to visual content variables is needed to develop a comprehensive understanding of the influence of visual packaging, visual framing, televised nonverbal displays, and volume of coverage variables on candidate support and election outcomes.

Bearing this caution in mind, our data nevertheless support a well-founded case for visual influence. The analysis found noticeable increases

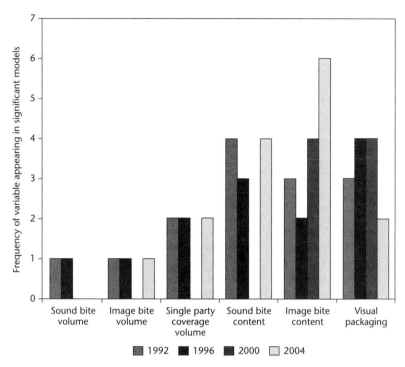

Figure 6–14 Frequency of image and sound bite content, packaging, and volume variables over time in significant regression models

in image bite coverage over time and a palpable shift away from sound bite content to visual variables in predictive models for each election. Figure 6–14 shows the relative stability by election year for key variables in the analysis: sound and image bite volume and content (emotional displays and visual frames combined), single-party coverage volume, and visual packaging (including both visual weight and formal features). Measures of image bite content and visual packaging were the most stable contributors to significant models predicting candidate support across election years. By contrast, the brute duration of sound and image bites appears to be the *least* stable set of variables for predicting candidate support. The behavior of variables that drove our predictive models provides compelling evidence that visual measures, including both content and packaging, can no longer be ignored in research that purports to study the political impact of televised election coverage.

Of the four elections analyzed, the influence of visual framing was strongest and most noticeable in 2000 and 2004. In particular, populist framing wields considerable influence over candidate support. Against the backdrop of known image-handler strategies, this frame's manifestation in network news coverage is of particular importance. Bob Shrum, the chief consultant for both Gore and Kerry, strongly favored populist framing for both of these blue-blooded candidates. So did Karl Rove, for George W. Bush, in both elections. The content analysis findings reported in Chapter 3 show how Shrum won the contest to present his clients most prominently in the populist campaigner frame for the evening news. In the process, however, he might have lost the elections for both of his clients. Our regression analyses confirmed that populist framing significantly and negatively contributed to models that predicted voter support for the 2000 and 2004 Democratic nominees. George W. Bush, on the other hand, was associated with models that produced positive statistical relationships between his populist framing scores and poll standings, especially in 2004.

In line with ethological and nonverbal communication theory reviewed in Chapter 4, it behooves presidential candidates to stay above the fray when they are behind in the polls or put on weak debate performances. Aggression in the final stage of the campaign also does not seem to move public opinion favorably. Both Clinton and George W. Bush demonstrated negative relationships between their agonic behavior and polling numbers in the final stretch to Election Day.

Visual weight turned out to be a particularly finicky variable, showing up regularly in significant associations but acting rather unpredictably across candidates and elections. Story type and placement within the newscast are overlooked aspects of news coverage that certainly deserve more attention. Studies in the agenda-setting tradition should incorporate this visual variable into predictive models to assess its role as a prominence cue with the potential to affect issue salience.

Visual packaging variables that have been identified in experimental studies as influential in shaping candidate perceptions also surfaced in our regression models as significant predictors of voter support—all in the expected direction. The camera and editing techniques we explicated in Chapter 5 as beneficial or detrimental to candidate portrayals found firm validation in their association with the public opinion data we tested them against.

Together, these correlational and predictive analyses produced robust support for the idea of visual influence and amplify the call for further research on the visual component of television news. If scholars and students of political communication are indeed interested in understanding the forces that shape election outcomes in our mediated age, campaign news visuals simply cannot be ignored. On an encouraging note, a small number of innovative studies are beginning to document the influence of news visuals, some of which are just now appearing in the literature. These studies are discussed in the final chapter as exemplars for future work.

NOTES

1. Sound bite size was positively but not significantly associated with support for Democrats in 1992. In 1996, however, the (near-significant) correlation for sound bite size was negative. Results for sound bite volume were equally unspectacular. In 2000 there was a weak negative correlation between total sound bite time and voter support for Democrats.
2. Across all elections and candidates, entailing eight regression analyses in total, sound bite volume emerged twice in significant predictive models while sound bite size did not appear in any significant models. In 1992 and 1996, sound bite volume was *negatively* associated with Republican polling data.
3. Of course, this does not include attacks on Al Gore and John Kerry by independent conservative interest groups, most notoriously the Swift Boat Veterans for Truth, which in 2004 denigrated Kerry's military record and anti–Vietnam War pronouncements from the 1970s.
4. Lewis, Jerry W. 1986. Suppression and enhancement in bivariate regression. *The Statistician* 35(1):17–26.
5. Lynn, Henry S. 2003. Suppression and confounding in action. *The American Statistician* 57(1): 58–61.
6. Smith, Richard L., Ager, Joel W. Jr., and Williams, David L. 1992. Suppressor variables in multiple regression/correlation. *Educational and Psychological Measurement* 52(1):17–29.
7. Sound bite content variables appeared in this model but not at significant levels. Defensive sound bites were excluded from the analysis because Kerry was not featured in this bite mode in our sample of newscasts.
8. Bennet, Earl S. 2002. Predicting Americans' exposure to political talk radio in 1996, 1998, and 2000. *International Journal of Press/Politics* 7(1):9–22.
9. Mutz, Diana C., & Martin, Paul S. 2001. Facilitating communication across lines of political difference: The role of mass media. *American Political Science Review* 95(1):97–114.
10. Sotirovic, Mira, and McLeod, Jack M. 2001. Values, communication behavior, and political participation. *Political Communication* 18(3):273–300.
11. Iyengar, Shanto, and Jennifer A. McGrady. 2007. *Media politics: A citizen's guide*. New York: W. W. Norton.

7

Taking Television Seriously

*Television's detractors have argued that the visual components of the story are trivial,
adding very little to the substantive content. In particular, they argue that audiovisual
[content] carries little political meaning. They are wrong.*

—Political Scientist Doris Graber
Annals, July 1996

Over the past four decades, television news has become the primary
source of political information for a majority of Americans and, as that
reliance has grown, the most credible, appealing, interesting, and
believable source as well.[1-3] These trends are not without reason, as
audiovisual media more effectively complement human information-
processing abilities than any other message platform. Politically, television connects candidates with voters and provides a visual record of
campaign events. Just as newspapers of record deliver the first draft of
written history, network news provides the equally important first draft
of *visually recorded* history.[4] It is the significance of this latter point that
intellectuals and other self-appointed guardians of the public sphere
have difficulty acknowledging. The irony of taking television seriously
stems from the research community's stubborn refusal to grant the medium best positioned to fulfill mass communication's great promise
its due.

Although consistent with culturally defined priorities reviewed in
the introduction, this neglect is out of step with biologically based principles of how humans process information. As we have highlighted
throughout this book, the nonverbal communication that news visuals
convey forms the basis of political impressions and evaluations as well
as more elaborate decisional processes up to and including vote choice.
Appreciating this observation, however, requires at least a basic understanding of the efficiency, complexity, and evolutionarily motivated
foundations of visual processing, particularly of socially important
stimuli. "The human brain is far more adept at extracting information

from audiovisual stimuli than from purely verbal information," Graber[1] has observed. "One quick glance at complex visual scenes suffices to identify situations that words would describe with far less fidelity" (p. 86)—in a much more cumbersome and cognitively demanding fashion. Audiovisuals thus offer the best hope for mitigating the problem of information overload endemic to an "unlimited" media environment, where the amount of available information far exceeds the audience's limited time and capacity to process it.

REVISITING THE INFORMATIONAL CONSEQUENCES OF TELEVISION NEWS

Before jumping on the denunciatory bandwagon, critics of media and politics would do well to heed some of the more consequential findings from the emerging interdisciplinary science of image processing and reconsider television news from a visual perspective. Converging results from political psychology, neuroscience, public opinion research, and even economics are difficult to dismiss—and worth a closer look. New and ongoing studies are showing how (1) viewers of television news are as politically informed and motivated as readers of newspapers and other print media revered by the word culture; (2) visual forms of political knowledge equalize gender, race, and educational differences—and may more effectively predict voter turnout than traditional measures of verbal knowledge; and (3) thin-slice exemplars of political stimuli, namely, candidate photographs and 10-second image bites, provide viewers with enough social information to make reliable inferences about candidate competence and electoral suitability. Except perhaps for concerns about the quality of political discourse, these findings effectively neutralize criticism that television does not perform a useful civic duty.

Informing and Motivating

Despite several high-profile assaults on television's purported corrosive effect on civic participation, political discourse, and the overall health of the public sphere (see Cappella and Jamieson,[5] Hart,[6] Kellner,[7,8] Patterson,[9] Postman,[10] Putnam[11]), empirical research has been quietly documenting a positive and persistent relationship between network news viewing and political learning. The consistency and robustness of these findings—based on measures of *verbal knowledge*, interestingly enough— suggest that the role of television news in cultivating an informed electorate, after all the criticism, is woefully misunderstood. But news of these studies goes largely unnoticed precisely because the findings do not fit the prevailing critical fashion, popular among academics and politicians, of inveighing against the only true medium of the masses.

Contradicting the hypothesis that media use inevitably leads to voter apathy, ignorance, and alienation, a series of political learning studies conducted by David Weaver and Dan Drew of Indiana University has consistently found television news viewing to predict voter knowledge of candidate issue stands.[12] Similar findings have been reported by other survey and experimental researchers (see Chaffee, Zhao, and Leshner,[13] Kleinnijenhuis,[14] Norris,[15] Sotirovic and McLeod,[16] Zhao and Chaffee[17]), some of whom argue that television is particularly suited to providing information about the personal qualities of candidates important to leadership and electability (see Chaffee and Frank,[18] Kinder,[19] Lowden et al.[20]).[21] This work lines up well with our content analysis findings, which validated network news as a rich source of information about candidate character, visually manifested through the ideal candidate, populist campaigner, and sure loser frames.

Television also contributes alongside other forms of hard news use—newspapers, radio, the Web, and televised debates—as a predictor of campaign interest.[12] For those low in political interest, television news has the capacity to "break the attention barrier" that otherwise obscures low-salience issues (p. 114[23]) and produce the most issue knowledge gain among the least interested voters.[24] Yet, even when interest in specific news topics is statistically controlled, experimental research shows that television news has the upper hand over print media and the Web in facilitating knowledge gain among lower education groups.[25]

Leveling the Playing Field

Our discussion of the stratifying character of print culture in the first chapter highlighted the tendency of social practices that require high levels of literacy to promote rather than flatten social hierarchies. Verbal tests of knowledge show large disparities in political information levels based on education, gender, race, and other demographic markers.[26] On the other hand, we argued that visual media have the capacity to transcend the inequities associated with cognitive barriers to learning from the written word and shrink the gap between information haves and have-nots.

Experimental work on the knowledge gap between citizens of lower and higher socioeconomic status, using verbal memory measures that test for factual information comprehension and retention over time, shows that television news reduces differences between high and low education groups to statistically insignificant levels. Newspapers and online news sites, on the other hand, exacerbated the cleavage between the two groups (Grabe, Kamhawi, Yegiyan,[25] in press). The question remains what consequences *visual* memory measures might have in such a study. Indeed, Graber contends that ignoring visual information biases our estimates of political knowledge in the electorate.[1,2,27,28] Because visual measures are not included in most research, citizens appear less knowledgeable and civically engaged than they actually are. In fact, they may be quite informed, just not from a traditional word or fact-based perspective. Ongoing research again corroborates this view.

In an innovative and revealing inquiry into visual political knowledge, Markus Prior of Princeton University asked whether knowledge improves when the same questions use visual cues rather than words alone.[29-31] In this research, a series of experimental manipulations were embedded in a representative online opinion survey, alternating between the names of political actors (the verbal condition) and pictures of their faces (the visual condition).[32] In the verbal condition, knowledge levels were sharply divided along gender, education, and racial lines, with men, white respondents, and college graduates scoring significantly higher on measures of political knowledge than women, minorities, and non–degree holders. Most studies would end here, lamenting the persistence of demographic disparities in knowledge and attributing the gap to historical conditions and continuing inequalities in access to resources that stifle political integration (Delli-Carpini and Keeter,[26] p. 204). In the case of gender, Prior observes, we are left with the unsatisfying conclusion that politics is a "man's game" and that the gender gap seems to "reflect a genuine difference in the taste for politics" (p. 1064[33]).

Add visual measures to the mix and not only does the gender gap suddenly disappear but so do differences based on education and race. Without visual cues, men answered correctly more often than women on every knowledge question asked (52.1% on average, compared to 40.7% for women). In the visual condition, however, the correct response rate levels to 46.2% for women and 47.6% for men—an insignificant difference—and on four of the 10 questions asked women were *more* likely to be correct than men. The number of "don't know" responses also flattens in the visual condition. Verbal knowledge scales, he finds, reward learning from verbal news sources, namely print media and radio (even after controlling for education, cognitive skills, and news preferences), and appear to underestimate the impact of television news viewing as a mode of political learning. In the visual condition, the effects of both gender and race disappear completely, while in the verbal condition the demographic disparities persist. These differences for gender and education on traditional measures of knowledge have been replicated many times over in other research (see Drew and Weaver,[12] Gaziano,[34] and Gunter[35]).

In addition to revealing a greater degree of political knowledge in the electorate, visual knowledge is equally effective, if not better, at predicting civic competence (measured as opinion consistency on issues of spending and taxation) than verbal knowledge.[29-31] The most visually knowledgeable respondents, for example, are more likely than the most verbally knowledgeable to recognize that government cannot simultaneously cut taxes and provide universal health care without harmful budgetary consequences. Sophistication in the electorate may not be entirely the province of the politically interested "highly literate" if the consequences of visual knowledge are considered. Visual knowledge, which Prior argues is associated with a sense of civic duty, also seems to be a slightly better predictor of voter turnout in congressional and presidential elections than verbal knowledge.

While traditional verbal measures of information point to disparities in knowledge, a host of democratically desirable outcomes appear to be associated with visual knowledge. These findings await further confirmation, but the preliminary results speak to substantial, as yet unappreciated contributions of broadcast news to informing the electorate. Another positive effect of television news viewing is political learning, which cross-channel comparisons of media use have tracked for some time. Indeed, a preference for viewing national network news is positively associated with both visual *and* verbal forms of knowledge.[31]

Inferring Viability

Much learning and reasoning draw on the tendency to make logical inferences to reach conclusions from incomplete or partial information. In fact, most decision making (including political evaluations and choices) occurs under conditions of uncertainty or incomplete information since obtaining full information about any topic, even if known and familiar, is practically impossible.[36] Inferences drawn from close-ups of human faces are particularly accurate and predictive of candidate viability, serving as a heuristic or judgmental shortcut in the political evaluation process.[1,37-39] This applies to mediated portrayals of candidates on full-color television as well as simple black and white headshots. When candidates for political office are shown on screen, viewers use dynamic visual presentations, including facial expressions and body language, to infer personality traits such as competence, integrity, leadership, and empathy.[1,40] But reliable inferences of competence—one of the key trait attributes relevant to political leadership and success—may also be derived from very brief exposures to still photographs.

In one such study, remarkable for its predictive simplicity, inferences of competence based solely on 1-second exposures to black-and-white headshots of major party candidates for Congress predicted actual election outcomes with almost 70% accuracy.[39] In a series of experiments involving candidates from the 2000, 2002, and 2004 elections, viewers who were naïve to the candidates' identity were shown multiple photographic pairs of winners and losers and were asked to assess them along several trait attributes, including competence, trustworthiness, and likability, as well as personality dimensions.[41] Ratings of competence were the most predictive. The candidate who was perceived as more competent by viewers actually won in 71.6% of Senate races and

66.8% of House races. Inferences of competence were also positively related to the margin of victory.[42]

A similar finding was reported by Benjamin and Shapiro[43] in a study involving 10-second video clips of gubernatorial debates from 37 different states between 1988 and 2002. With no other information except a silent videotaped excerpt, that is, a 10-second image bite, naïve viewers correctly identified the winning candidate 57% of the time. When the sound was turned on, that is, when the clip was converted into a sound bite (images plus sound), predictive accuracy decreased, even though viewers' confidence in their prediction increased.[44] Adding policy information—in other words, turning the sound on—only seems to worsen judgment while cultivating a false sense of certainty. The confusion introduced by verbal information reflects the plight of pundits and other expert forecasters who, though well-versed in policy debates, are often found to perform no better than chance in predicting election outcomes (Benjamin and Shapiro[43]; see also Tetlock[45]).

Given these findings, does the predictive accuracy of first impressions from such thin-slice exposures to political candidates render the campaign process unnecessary and obsolete? Not entirely, since a substantial percentage of election winners were still wrongly classified in the above studies and individual voting decisions are based on multiple information sources, both endogenous and exogenous to the campaign.[46] But it does suggest that the current length of the election drama is excessive from the point of view of making a vote choice; that rapid evaluations of potential leaders based solely on visual information provide substantial predictive accuracy in forecasting election outcomes; and that intense elite focus on policy debates (or complaints about the amount of policy coverage in news) may be misguided. Even if the number of televised presidential debates increased by a factor of 10 and the campaign remained focused on policy issues only, voters would still base their decisions in large part on seeing candidates on television or in person.

In light of existing research on voter learning, visual knowledge, and thin slice forecasts, television news clearly functions as a highly efficient form of political information that viewers rely on to form judgments and make inferences. A review of the empirical literature on television surmised over a decade ago that "a general rehabilitation of the reputation of television news has been building in the literature for some years" (p. 53[18]), even if it is not reflected in public debate. Considering the research described in this chapter and reported throughout the book, it becomes evident that the charges leveled against network news of mindlessly trafficking in irrelevant images and imparting little of civic value are rooted in opinion, not fact.[47] However, representing television as a serious source of political information "runs contrary to much previous scholarly criticism" (p. 49[18]) and remains a difficult argument to make. The changed thinking of Harvard political scientist Robert Putnam on this very topic offers an interesting case in point.

Putnam, noted for his "bowling alone" thesis,[48] initially asserted that the introduction of television into American society in the 1950s was a major factor in the subsequent decline of social capital, defined as a nexus of social trust, networks of association, and participation in civic organizations. Across educational level, Putnam initially found a negative association between television exposure and the level of reported social trust and number of groups an individual belongs to.[11] Without regard to type of programming (i.e., news or entertainment, nonfiction or fiction), he presented television use as the "800-pound gorilla" of leisure time and accused it of displacing social activities outside the home, "especially social gatherings and informal conversations" (p. 679[11]). Thus, he argued that the country's supply of social capital had eroded. But then, faced with new data that clearly showed the contribution of television news to political knowledge, Putnam revised his views considerably.

In *Bowling Alone*,[49] his book-length treatment of the idea, Putnam relied on new data and distinguished between news and entertainment programming, crediting news exposure with *increased* civic involvement. No longer standing by his earlier blanket indictment of television, he conceded that "as a technical matter, the extraordinary power of television can encourage as well as discourage civic involvement" (p. 410[49]). Both in earlier work and in *Bowling Alone*, newspaper reading receives no such criticism. Instead, time spent with print media is associated with high levels of social capital and is positively related to social trust and group membership. In Putnam's reformulation of the bowling alone thesis, newspapers still occupy a privileged position over television—with the twist that television news coverage is now held in higher esteem than entertainment programming. Even as reformulated, however, the argument represents an elitist view about what constitutes valid information. News visuals, the most important element of television news, are scarcely mentioned.

VISUALS AS INFORMATION

Consistent with the arguments and data we have presented throughout this book, visual stimuli serve an informational purpose. When the stimulus happens to be an image of a major party nominee during a presidential election, visuals convey information on multiple levels. Facial displays and other aspects of expressive behavior form the basis of inferences about more enduring candidate qualities, especially character and electoral viability, influencing support among voters. As our analyses have shown, it is not just the type of display but the timing of different modes of nonverbal behavior (agonic versus hedonic) that makes a difference in building or weakening voter support. Aggression, for example, is not conducive to rallying support when a candidate is behind in the polls or after a poor debate performance. Al Gore's intensifying agonic behavior during the final three weeks of the 2000 election shows how exhibiting too much anger/threat in the context of dwindling public support can have an injurious result. George W. Bush, on the other hand, demonstrated how emphasizing positive displays of happiness/reassurance toward Election Day can sustain a candidate in a tight race.

Moreover, how camera angles and other packaging features are employed in newscasts can greatly transform the content and embedded meaning of campaign news stories. Our analysis revealed positive correlations between tracking poll data and beneficial packaging features for Bob Dole in 1996 and George W. Bush in 2000, and negative correlations for detrimental packaging of Bill Clinton and George H. W. Bush in 1992, Al Gore in 2000, and John Kerry in 2004. If persistently applied, visual packaging can affect candidate support by either enhancing or undermining perceptions of leadership and momentum. We also found evidence showing how visual framing can dampen candidate appeal, as it did for the polling numbers of George H. W. Bush, Al Gore, and John Kerry.

More often than not, however, political visuals are discounted or simply overlooked in analyses of news and politics. To Graber[1] (1996) and others (e.g., Prior[31]) negligence of news visuals stems from a cultural bias favoring the type of knowledge that literacy allows (see also Graff[50,51]). Historically, printed messages have been equated with sophistication, intelligence, and rationality. "To be literate has meant to be able to learn and communicate via the written word. The notion of building knowledge and achieving wisdom through audiovisual literacy has been an unfamiliar concept. Considering the unique capabilities of audiovisuals to inform average people, the time is ripe for changing that badly outdated view of human learning" (p. 96[1]).

Understanding visuals as a type of information important to political decision making will require assessing and then altering engrained assumptions about what knowledge *is* as well as appreciating the capacity of different media to facilitate knowledge acquisition. Viewing politics as primarily geared toward verbal articulation of issues places knowledge and expertise on a path toward verbal indicators of competence: being politically sophisticated means having the motivation and capacity to debate issues as framed in the print press or as represented on discussion programs. From a psychological perspective, however, inferences made from visual depictions of candidates occur rapidly, if not automatically, influencing subsequent information processing about candidates even if not consciously contemplated (p. 1623[39]).

Visual portrayals, in this sense, may prime later judgments about political viability and shape the criteria by which candidates are evaluated, including their policy positions. Hence, visual information complements verbal knowledge—and vice versa.

As suggested by the image bite analysis from Chapter 2, evocative candidate displays may act as heuristic cues that are regarded by observers as predictive of future behavior, whether in a positive or a negative sense; that is, either as an iconic moment or a damaging gaffe. Hillary Clinton's repeated verbal claims during the 2008 presidential primaries of being under sniper fire at the Tuzla Air Base in Bosnia during a visit in 1996 found powerful visual contradiction when archival video footage of her arrival aired on *CBS News*. Authoritative as documentary evidence, these images instantly rendered the claim of sniper fire as a gaffe, since they clearly showed Clinton and daughter Chelsea comfortably strolling down the tarmac, greeting troops, and interacting with children. Instead of a definitive video clip, a verbal contradiction that recounted for the media who was present at the event arguably would not have turned this incident into a defining moment of exaggeration or faulty recollection; it simply would have been characterized as a difference of opinion or recollection.

In addition to priming subsequent evaluations, visuals serve as a foundation for decision making in their own right. Visual information from thin slice exposures of political candidates seems to function effectively as a forecasting tool, predicting electoral outcomes on par with more conventional measures such as retrospective evaluations of the incumbent or economic conditions.[43] Visual knowledge as indexed by candidate photographs is both demographically equalizing and associated with political competence, predicting voter turnout in congressional and presidential elections. Even on measures of verbal knowledge, network news viewing has been consistently associated with political learning and works in conjunction with other hard news use to generate interest in the campaign. None of these effects would occur if news visuals truly made no appeal to reason and merely served as visual decoration for verbal narratives.

When considering visuals as information, a distinction needs to be made between factual knowledge and social information of the kind that news visuals provide. Table 7–1 compares factual and social information types in relation to four key contextual dimensions: the media that are associated with them, biological predispositions to attend to them, cognitive competence to process them, and social constructions of their informational status in society. Clearly, these information types are not as cleanly separated as we have listed here for comparative purposes. Yet, the comparison illustrates how elites have managed to construct the information offered in print media as the acme of civic knowledge—despite the biological and cognitive predisposition of humans to absorb social information from visual-based media.

Table 7–1 Comparison of Factual and Social Information Types

	Information Types	
	Factual	Social
Media	Word-based	Visually based
	Dependent on literacy	Independent of literacy requirements
	Biased toward print media	Biased toward television, visual media
	Present in audio track of television news	Present in video track of television news
Biology	Developed late in hominoid evolution	Developed early in hominoid evolution
	No specialized brain centers for reading	Specialized brain centers for visual processing
	Emerges within cognitive band of processing (500 msec and above)	Emerges within biological band of processing (50 msec and above)
Cognition	Difficult to recall	Easy to recall
	Requires extensive rehearsal for memory	Requires minimal rehearsal for memory
	Most useful with a political schema	Not dependent on a political schema
	Permits slow inferences of politically relevant traits	Enables quick inferences of politically relevant traits
	Overriden by compelling visuals	Assigned priority over spoken words
Culture	Viewed as a marker of intellect	Viewed as a marker of "idiocy"
	Culturally constructed as rational	Culturally constructed as emotional
	Associated with elites, sophistication	Associated with nonelites, lack of sophistication
	Socially stratifying, exclusionary	Socially equalizing, inclusionary

The point-by-point comparisons between factual and social information leave little room to doubt the arbitrariness of crowning print media, and their dissemination of facts, as democratizing. Indeed, if democratic theory and practice truly valued the participation of *the people*, especially citizens from lower levels of the social strata, the recognition that visuals impart valuable political knowledge would be better integrated into public debate and the research agendas of scholars. The devaluation of political images on which a majority of citizens rely casts doubt on the sincerity of scholarly and journalistic pronouncements that the democratic ideal of an informed and participating citizenry is a high priority.

Rationality as it is usually discussed implies the deployment of factual knowledge into an elaborated political schema, or semantic memory network, upon which citizens are assumed to base reasoned decisions. This is a limited view of voter competence. As work on visual knowledge documents, memory associations derived from news visuals provide an equally potent foundation for decision making—for a vast proportion of the electorate. Indeed, visuals are highly efficient conduits of information that highlight inconsistencies and facilitate connections between candidates, their political stances, and voter evaluations. Moreover, visuals handily outperform the written and spoken word in tests of both long- and short-term memory.

We have asked, and perhaps gotten, all that we can from newspapers and other print media. Perhaps the time is right to reconsider the value of television to informing voters. Indeed, television news appears to have a more positive relationship with democracy than previously acknowledged. Since news visuals convey substantive social information and influence candidate support, they should be regarded as indices of political knowledge that work in conjunction with verbal messages to cultivate civic competence. The visually informed voter uses a varying combination of factual and social information from media and other sources to assess political developments and arrive at intelligent decisions. Visually informed voters may not possess extensive procedural knowledge of institutional processes or an encyclopedic memory for the names of important public figures but they may be remarkably adept at recognizing the faces of those figures and knowing what policies the person behind the name stands for.

With the growing availability of and access to full-motion images in the online environment, the arbitrary devaluation of visuals may begin to reverse course. The separation between factual and social forms of information might also be bridged by a new generation of citizens whose use of social networking, file-sharing, and online news sites to share, consume, and produce media content can be seen as part of a multichannel process of media participation in civic and political life (see Bucy and Gregson[52]). There is reason for cautious optimism in this regard, as 40% of citizens between 18 and 29 routinely turn to online sources, including social networking sites, not only to share files but also to learn about politics and engage in debate.[53]

Just as control of knowledge had to be wrested from the medieval monasteries to open new intellectual vistas and allow the slow democratization of society, so an emerging medium might compel a reconsideration of print culture standards for defining knowledge. Likewise, just as Latin was replaced by common dialects such as English and German to advance liberty and human emancipation, so a converged medium might help change and eventually overturn the rationalist paradigm's insistence that verbal language is paramount to or the sole standard of an informed and participating citizenry. Despite its declining market share and, some would say, likely extinction, network news has played a fundamental but underappreciated role in realizing these transformations with inordinate speed.

NOTES

1. Graber, Doris A. (1996). Say it with pictures. *Annals of the American Academy of Political and Social Science*, 546:85–96.
2. Graber, Doris A. (2001). *Processing politics: Learning from television in the Internet age.* Chicago: University of Chicago Press.
3. Project for Excellence in Journalism. (2008). The state of the news media. Retrieved May 5, 2008 from, http://www.stateofthenewsmedia.com/2008/narrative_networktv_intro.php?cat=0&andmedia=6. Accessed May 5, 2008.
4. The availability of network news transcripts on the Lexis-Nexis information database and existence of the Vanderbilt Television News Archive (http://tvnews.vanderbilt.edu), which maintains a comprehensive video archive of network news dating back to 1968, speaks to the lasting cultural value that is placed on network news, despite elite criticism.
5. Cappella, Joseph N., and Kathleen Hall Jamieson. (1997). *Spiral of cynicism: The Press and the public good.* New York: Oxford University Press.
6. Hart, Roderick P. (1999). *Seducing America: How television charms the modern voter,* 2nd ed. Thousand Oaks, CA: Sage.
7. Kellner, Douglas. (1990). *Television and the crisis of democracy.* Boulder, CO: Westview Press.
8. Kellner, Douglas. (2005). *Media spectacle and the crisis of democracy: Terrorism, war, and election battles.* Boulder, CO: Paradigm Publishers.
9. Patterson, Thomas E. (1993). *Out of order.* New York: Knopf.
10. Postman, Neil. (1986). *Amusing ourselves to death: Public discourse in the age of show business.* New York: Penguin Books.
11. Putnam, Robert D. (1995). Tuning in, tuning out: The strange disappearance of social capital in America. *PS: Political Science &and Politics,* 28: 664–683.
12. Drew, Dan D., and Weaver, David H. (2006). Voter learning in the 2004 presidential election: Did the media matter? *Journalism and Mass Communication Quarterly,* 83(1):25–42.
13. Chaffee, Steven H., Xinshu Zhao, and Glenn Leshner. (1994). Political knowledge and the campaign media of 1992. *Communication Research,* 21:305–324.
14. Kleinnijenhuis, Jan. (1991). Newspaper complexity and the knowledge gap. *European Journal of Communication,* 6(4):499–522.
15. Norris, Pippa. (2000). *A virtuous circle: Political communications in postindustrial societies.* Cambridge: Cambridge University Press.
16. Sotirovic, Mira, and Jack M. McLeod. (2004). Knowledge as understanding: The information processing approach to political learning. In *Handbook of political communication research,* ed. Lynda Lee Kaid, (Ed.), *Handbook of political communication research* (pp. 357–394). Mahwah, NJ: Lawrence Erlbaum Associates.

17. Zhao, Xinshu, and Steven H. Chaffee. (1995). Campaign advertisements versus television as sources of political issue information. *Public Opinion Quarterly,* 59:41–65.

18. Chaffee, Steven, and Stacey Frank. (1996). How Americans get political information: Print versus broadcast news. *Annals of the American Academy of Political and Social Science,* 546:48–58.

19. Kinder, Donald R. (1986). Presidential character revisited. In *Political cognition: The 19th annual Carnegie symposium on cognition,* ed. Richard R. Lau and David O. Sears, (Eds.), *Political cognition: The 19th annual Carneigie symposium on cognition* (pp. 233–256). Hillsdale, NJ: Lawrence Erlbaum Associates.

20. Lowden, Nancy, B., Peter A. Andersen, David M. Dozier, and Martha M. Lauzen. (1994). Media use in the primary election: A secondary medium model. *Communication Research,* 21(3):293–304.

21. Attention to television news does not account for all of the explained variance in these models but works in conjunction with other media as well as interpersonal discussion networks to broaden political knowledge and stimulate campaign interest (Drew and Weaver,[12] Eveland et al.,[22] Chaffee and Frank[18]). Statistically, this produces a substantial amount of multicollinearity and variable interdependence, which requires careful controls and conceptual modeling. Given the diverse media diets of news consumers, "most people who watch television news also see candidates' television ads, and many read newspapers as well"[18] (p. 51).

22. Eveland, William P., Jr., Andrew F. Hayes, Dhavan V. Shah, and Nojin Kwak. (2005). Understanding the relationship between communication and political knowledge: A model comparison approach using panel data. *Political Communication,* 22:423–446.

23. Neuman, W. Russell, Marion Just, and Ann N. Crigler. (1992). *Common knowledge: News and the construction of political meaning.* Chicago: University of Chicago Press.

24. Patterson, Thomas E. (1980). *The mass media election: How Americans choose their president.* New York: Praeger Publishers.

25. Grabe, Maria Elizabeth, Rasha Kamhawi, and Narine Yegiyan. (in press). Informing citizens: How people with different levels of education process television, newspapers, and Web news. *Journal of Broadcasting &and Electronic Media.*

26. Delli-Carpini, Michael X., and Scott Keeter. (1996). *What Americans know about politics and why it matters.* New Haven, CT: Yale University Press.

27. Graber, Doris A. (1988). *Processing the news: How people tame the information tide,* 2nd ed. New York: Longman.

28. Graber, Doris A. (1990). Seeing is remembering: How visuals contribute to learning from television news. *Journal of Communication,* 40:134–155.

29. Prior, Markus. (2002, August). *More than a thousand words? Visual cues and visual knowledge.* Paper presented at the Annual meeting of the American Political Science Association, Boston, MA.

30. Prior, Markus. (2004, September). *Visual political knowledge: A better measure of what people know?* Paper presented at the Annual meeting of the American Political Science Association, Chicago, IL.

31. Prior, Markus. (2008). *Visual political knowledge.* Working paper, Department of Politics and Woodrow Wilson School of Public and International Affairs, Princeton University.

32. The studies featured four different question designs, beginning with the "who is" and "which office" designs. In the "who is" design, participants in the visual condition were asked to name the position held by a depicted politician based on an identifying photograph but with no name cue (e.g., What position is currently held by the person shown in this picture?). In the verbal version, politicians' names were used instead of their images (e.g., What position is currently held by Alan Greenspan?).

In the "which office" design, participants were asked to identify the office held by depicted politicians either with a visual cue or verbal cue present, that is, either with four photographs or the names of four likely political figures (e.g., Who is the current Senate majority leader?). A third design asked participants to indicate the party of four politicians (Tom Daschle, Christine Todd Whitman, Howard Dean, and Ralph Nader) identified either by name or by photograph.

The fourth design required participants to mark all correct answers (out of four) in response to a question about a series of politicians who were represented either by their names or pictures (e.g., Which of these politicians has/have announced they will run for the Democratic nomination for president in 2004?). The response options were Joe Lieberman, Hillary Clinton, Al Gore, and John Edwards.

In each of the four designs, multiple-choice questions were asked of all participants but randomly varied as to whether they were posed verbally or visually.

33. Verba, Sidney, Nancy Burns, and Kay Lehman Schlozman. (1997). Knowing and caring about politics: Gender and political engagement. *Journal of Politics,* 59:1051–1072.

34. Gaziano, C. (1997). Forecast 2000: Widening knowledge gaps. *Journalism and Mass Communication Quarterly,* 74(2):237–264.

35. Gunter, Barry. (1987). *Poor reception: Misunderstanding and forgetting broadcast news.* Hillsdale, NJ: Lawrence Erlbaum Associates.

36. Tversky, Amos, and Daniel Kahneman (1974). Judgment under uncertainty: Heuristics and biases. *Science,* 185, 1124–1131.

37. Masters, Roger D. (2001). Cognitive neuroscience, emotion, and leadership. In *Citizens and politics: Perspectives from political psychology,* ed. James H. Kuklinski (Ed.), *Citizens and politics: Perspectives from political psychology* (pp. 68–102). New York: Cambridge University Press.

38. Masters, Roger D., and Dennis G. Sullivan. (1993). Nonverbal behavior and leadership: Emotion and cognition in political information processing. In *Explorations in political psychology,* ed. Shanto Iyengar and William J. McGuire (Eds.), *Explorations in political psychology* (pp. 150–182). Durham, NC: Duke University Press.

39. Todorov, Alexander, Anesu N. Mandisodza, Amir Goren, and Crystal C. Hall. (2005). Inferences of competence from faces predict election outcomes. *Science,* 308(10):1623–1626.

40. Bucy, Erik P. (2000). Emotional and evaluative consequences of inappropriate leader displays. *Communication Research,* 27(2):194–226.

41. Recognized faces were discarded from analysis. Thus, "all findings are based on judgments derived from facial appearance in the absence of prior knowledge about the person" (Todorov et al.[41] p. 1624).

42. The accuracy of the predictions was not affected by the candidates' race or sex, and statistical controls ruled out the possibility that age, attractiveness, or familiarity accounted for the relationship between competence judgments and election outcomes (Todorov et al.[41]; see also Martin, D. S. [1978]. Person perception and real-life electoral behavior. *Australian Journal of Psychology*, 30[3]:255–262).

43. Benjamin, Daniel J., and Jesse M. Shapiro. (in press). Thin-slice forecasts of gubernatorial elections. *Review of Economics and Statistics*, 90.

44. Participant estimates of election winners were highly correlated with actual vote shares across the 58 elections analyzed and their contribution to the predictive model survived controls for candidate race, gender, and height as well as a range of economic predictors. The predictions accounted for over one-fifth of the overall variation in two-party vote shares.[44]

45. Tetlock, Philip E. (1999). Theory driven reasoning about plausible pasts and probably futures in world politics: Are we prisoners of our preconceptions? *American Journal of Political Science*, 43(2):335–366. 37.

46. Although aggregate studies of election outcomes demonstrate that elections can be explained by a few key political and economic variables before the campaign even begins (namely, the strength of partisan identification in the electorate, retrospective evaluations of the incumbent, and measures of economic performance), there is ample evidence to suggest that campaigns—and the information generated by media coverage during the election—do matter (see Holbrook, Thomas M. 1996. *Do campaigns matter?* Thousand Oaks, CA: Sage; and Popkin, Samuel. 1994. *The reasoning voter: Communication and persuasion in presidential campaigns.* 2nd ed. Chicago: University of Chicago Press).

47. A growing body of research on the information role of soft news and political entertainment shows, particularly *The Daily Show* on the Comedy Central cable network, has demonstrated learning effects from these human interest and comedy formats (see Baum, Matthew A. 2003. *Soft news goes to war: Public opinion and American foreign policy in the new media age.* Princeton: Princeton University Press; Baum, Matthew A. 2005. Talking the vote: Why presidential candidates hit the talk show circuit. *American Journal of Political Science* 49[2]:213–234; and Young, Dannagal G., and Russell M. Tisinger. 2006. Dispelling late-night myths: News consumption among late-night comedy viewers and the predictors of exposure to various late-night shows. *Harvard International Journal of Press/Politics* 11[3]:113–134). Surely if there are positive outcomes associated with daytime talk show and entertainment news viewing, the networks remain influential in their own right. Notably, the success of political entertainment and mock news programs rely on the reporting, visual framing, and video footage provided by the networks.

48. Among other things, the bowling alone thesis holds that growing use of mass media and changing lifestyle patterns since World War II have substantially contributed to declining levels of citizen engagement in civic affairs, evidenced in part by the rising number of people who are bowling alone rather than in teams (see Putnam).[49]

49. Putnam, Robert D. (2000). *Bowling alone: The collapse and revival of American community*. New York: Simon &and Schuster.

50. Graff, Harvey J. (1987). The legacies of literacy: Continuities and contradictions in western culture and society. Bloomington, IN: Indiana University Press.

51. Graff, Harvey J. (1991). The literacy myth: Cultural integration and social structure in the nineteenth century. New Brunswick, NJ: Transaction Publishers.

52. Bucy, Erik P., and Kimberly S. Gregson. (2001). Media participation: A legitimizing mechanism of mass democracy. *New Media and Society*, 3(3):359–382.

53. Pew Research Center. (2008). The Internet gains in politics. Retrieved June 2, 2008 from, http://www.pewinternet.org/PPF/r/234/source/rss/report_display.asp. Accessed June 2, 2008.

Appendix 1

Methodology

The analyses in this book are based on a content analysis of network news coverage of the 1992, 1996, 2000, and 2004 elections. The sampling frame stretched from Labor Day to Election Day for each election year. This time period is routinely used in content analyses of presidential elections since it spans the traditional start of the general election campaign (Labor Day) to the day voters go to the polls. Moreover, the general election is the most closely watched phase of the campaign when the largest number of viewers are paying attention to the election (see Lichter, 2001; Moriarty and Popovich, 1991; Waldman and Devitt, 1998). Altogether, a total of 178 target newscasts were analyzed across a 12-year period.

Although the national news networks have been losing viewership to local, cable, and online news outlets (Iyengar and McGrady, 2007), our analyses focus on network news coverage for two reasons. First, it was the most widely used source of presidential campaign information over the course of the elections analyzed. Despite declines in network viewership, neither cable nor local television news has nearly the audience of network news. The audience size of the three networks combined is double that of cable news and Fox combined (Project for Excellence in Journalism, 2004). Second, network news has been stable in popularity among those who are likely voters (Pew Research Center, 2000).

During data collection we focused on the sound- and image bite content of all candidates who received coverage during the four election cycles analyzed. These election years featured an assortment of strong and weak incumbent office holders, third-party candidates who were well funded or well known to the media, and pressing public issues. The economy was weaker in some years (e.g., 1992) and stronger in others (e.g., 1996, 2000), and domestic issues that featured prominently in the first three elections were balanced by terrorism and national security concerns in 2004. Thus, these four races were representative of a variety of election conditions. The sample contained 42 newscasts each for 1992 and 2004, and 47 for 1996 and 2000. For each election year, composite weeks of evening newscasts were constructed, with a different, randomly selected network recorded each weekday (one from ABC, CBS, or NBC). For analysis purposes, we focused on Democrats and Republicans.

Three separate coding instruments, each representing a different unit of analysis, were designed. Coding sheet one used the individual-news broadcast as the unit of analysis, addressing matters related to the volume or overall amount of coverage. Coding sheet two employed the individual campaign story as the unit of analysis and featured categories related to journalists and story-specific dimensions. Coding sheet three entailed the most detailed categories, focusing on the individual candidate as the unit of analysis. Together, these different foci enabled comprehensive examinations of network news content across the different players in the election drama, both in the press and among political contenders.

Two primary coders, each with professional journalism experience, collected the data for this study while two secondary coders (the authors) served as reliability checks for the pretest. The testing of categories and training of coders extended over several weeks. During this time, refinements were made to the coding instrument. Overall, the pretest produced a reliable level of agreement (Krippendorff's alpha = .84) between all four coders. For the categories related to the individual news program as the unit of analysis, the reliability figure was .82, whereas for categories related to the individual campaign story the figure was .85. For categories related to the individual candidate as the unit of analysis, Krippendorff's alpha = .84. Although the pretest produced acceptable reliability figures, more training, specifically on how to accurately measure durations, ensued before the beginning of data collection. Details about specific categories and reliability estimates are reported for each chapter individually.

The following table (A1.1) summarizes the study sample as a whole, including the candidates featured, time periods analyzed, and number of individual stories by network for each year in the sample.

Table A1.1 Summary of the Study Sample

	Election Year			
	1992	1996	2000	2004
Candidates				
Democratic candidate	Bill Clinton	Bill Clinton	Al Gore	John Kerry
Republican candidate	George H. W. Bush	Bob Dole	George W. Bush	George W. Bush
Independent candidate	Ross Perot	Ross Perot	Ralph Nader	Ralph Nader
Network Campaign Stories				
ABC	$n = 54$ (35.8%)	$n = 30$ (31.9%)	$n = 38$ (39.2%)	$n = 36$ (38.7%)
CBS	$n = 51$ (33.8%)	$n = 40$ (42.6%)	$n = 31$ (32.0%)	$n = 29$ (31.2%)
NBC	$n = 46$ (30.5%)	$n = 24$ (25.5%)	$n = 28$ (28.9%)	$n = 28$ (30.1%)
Total	$N = 151$	$N = 94$	$N = 97$	$N = 93$
Campaign Stages				
Stage 1	Sept. 7–Oct. 9	Sept. 2–Oct. 4	Sept. 4–Oct. 3	Sept. 6–Sept. 30
Stage 2	Oct. 12–Oct. 21	Oct. 7–Oct. 18	Oct. 4–Oct. 19	Oct. 1–Oct. 15
Stage 3	Oct. 22–Nov. 3	Oct. 21–Nov. 5	Oct. 20–Nov. 7	Oct. 18–Nov. 2

Only those independent candidates who appeared on network news in our election sample are listed in the table. Results pertaining to Democrats and Republicans are reported in this book.

Appendix 2

Image Bite News

Coding Instrument

To assess the overall volume or amount of coverage, the individual newscast was employed as the first unit of analysis with campaign stories as a recording unit. A campaign story was defined as one in which presidential and vice presidential candidates were central to the narrative, including stories that focused on the candidates' wives. Brief appearances by candidates in stories about election-related issues such as voting machines, voter registration, or congressional debates about campaign finance reform were not coded as campaign stories. The number of campaign stories and their duration were recorded. The duration of each newscast and number of news stories overall were also noted.

Second, to investigate questions related to sound and image bites, individual candidates for president and vice president were used as the unit of analysis. Sixteen candidates representing five political parties—Republicans, Democrats, Independents, the Reform Party, and Libertarian Party—were identified as options within this category. The "other" option was included to make this item exhaustive.

Measuring sound bites. Four categories were developed to measure dimensions of sound bites. A sound bite is defined as an audiovisual segment in which a candidate is simultaneously shown and heard; in other words, where the audio in whole or part matches the accompanying video of a candidate talking. Sound bites can originate from a variety of settings, including speeches, sit-down interviews, or press conferences. An important defining characteristic of a sound bite is the representation of a candidate in official talking mode—comments are being made formally, whether to the press or a live audience, and the candidate is wired or miked for sound recording. Typically in sound bites the candidate wears a lapel microphone, holds a microphone in hand, or is facing free-standing microphones.

On account of video editing techniques, candidates do not necessarily appear visually uninterrupted for the full duration of the time they are speaking. These variations in visual and verbal appearances differ in representational weight. Seeing a candidate for the duration of a featured sound bite offers more opportunity for evaluation than hearing a candidate's voice while seeing something else. To parse out the visual and verbal nuances of sound bites, three categories were developed: bites in which candidates were *shown speaking,* bites in which they were *heard but not shown,* and bites in which they were *shown but not heard.*

To assess the average duration of instances where candidates were *shown speaking,* the number of times and durations (in seconds) in which candidates were portrayed in direct address with matching video were recorded. A *shown speaking* bite begins when the camera viewpoint features the candidate speaking as the primary sound. Such sound bites end when (1) the camera viewpoint cuts to something other than the candidate speaking (e.g., an audience member), or (2) the candidate is shown but what he says is not featured as primary sound.

The second sound bite scenario is the *heard but not shown* presentation mode. This production technique is known in the industry as a "soft cut": viewers hear but do not see the candidate. In a soft cut, the camera cuts away from the candidate to something else, such as a journalist listening, an audience member at a public speech, or video material related to what is being discussed. The duration (in seconds) in which candidates were *heard but not shown* on camera was recorded in seconds.

A third category was devised to capture the last sound bite possibility, the *shown but not heard* mode. Here, candidates are shown in conversation but with no sound. These instances are typical in interview situations where candidates are shown reacting nonverbally to a reporter's question. The duration of candidate *shown but not heard* appearances was recorded in seconds. Even though this category bears some semblance to sound bites, we contend that it should be classified as an instance of image bites and do not include it with our calculation of sound bites. An accurate account of sound bites in network news, therefore, can be determined by combining the *shown speaking* and *heard but not shown* categories. An image bite is markedly different from a sound bite in that it shows the candidate in full motion video but the footage is used to visually accompany the voice-over narration of a reporter or a reporter's question to a candidate; the candidate is therefore not heard.

To document the substance of candidate sound bites, seven content options were specified: speaking time devoted to policy positions, reactions to the news, attacks on opponents, defending one's role in a controversy (defensive rhetoric), predicting victory, rallying the troops, and an "other" option for cases that did not fit. The duration of sound bite substance was recorded in seconds, with each sound bite assigned to a single content option.

Measuring image bites. An image bite is defined as an audiovisual segment in which a candidate is shown but not necessarily heard. To document the different dimensions of image bites, three separate categories were specified. The most common image bite scenario is the *shown but not heard* presentation of candidates when they are not engaged in some form of public address. These are shots that portray candidates outside of speech settings. Candidates might be talking (perhaps while shaking the hand of a supporter) but the viewer does not hear what they say as primary sound. Instead, the reporter's narration dominates the audio track. The candidate might also be shown engaged in an activity such as walking his dog or exercising. Most important, these shots are accompanied by the voice-over narration of a reporter. The duration of these shots was recorded in seconds.

Another category was devised to capture a specific kind of *shown but not heard* appearance called "lip flap" among television news workers. Lip flap happens when the candidate is shown in formal speaking mode (during a speech, interview, or press conference) in a medium shot or close-up so that viewers clearly see the candidate's mouth moving but what he is saying is not heard as primary sound. In other words, the reporter's voice-over is aired while the candidate is shown speaking. Lip flap occurs, then, when a sound bite is used as an image bite. Generally, instances of lip flap are viewed as unflattering to candidates and are discouraged in industry circles as a means to generate video material for voice-over narration (video footage of related events is preferred instead). Lip flap appearances were recorded in seconds.

The last image bite scenario, referred to in the industry as a "sound-up," most closely resembles a sound bite. This technique can be described as a very short (2–3 second) sound bite of a candidate talking—but not in formal speech mode and not wired for audio recording. These short segments typically include comments that are recorded through directional microphones from long distance when candidates are on the campaign trail interacting with supporters or the press. Sound-ups might also entail a brief response, of only a word or two, from the candidate to journalists in different campaign settings. In a broadcast news report, sound-ups occur when the reporter's voice-over is briefly paused to make the candidate's informal response audible—that is, the *sound* brought *up*—after which time the reporter narration continues. The duration of sound-up comments from candidates was recorded in seconds.

News actors. To capture the prominence of news people (anchors, interviewers, and correspondents) in campaign stories, a third unit of analysis—the individual campaign story—was used and the individual reporter and anchor served as the recording unit. Categories were developed to document dimensions of anchor/reporter appearances and were compared with candidate categories. The presence of an anchor/reporter exchange and its duration was recorded in seconds, using the anchor's first mention of the reporter or first question as the starting point and the anchor's "thank you" at the conclusion of the exchange as the ending point. Using the same categories designed for candidates, coders measured the number of times and duration of anchor and reporter appearances in the following news-bite scenarios: *shown and heard, shown but not heard,* and *heard but not shown.*

Coders and Reliability

A posthoc reliability check was performed on 20% of the sample. Coders maintained a high overall level of agreement across sound and image bite variables (Krippendorff's alpha = .98), with a minimum score of .92 and a maximum of 1.00.

Analysis Strategy

Means comparisons between variables were subjected to homogeneity of variance analyses. When the Levene statistic indicated a violation of the equal variance assumption in one-way analysis of variance tests, the Welch robust test for equality of means was employed and posthoc paired comparisons were computed using the Dunnett C parameter (equal variance not assumed). If the Levene statistic indicated violations of the homogeneity of variance assumption in independent samples t-tests, robust mean test figures were reported.

Appendix 3

Visual Framing

CODING INSTRUMENT

Using the individual candidate as the unit of analysis, visual framing was assessed for each of the three character frames. The presence (value = 1) or absence (value = 0) of a visual category was coded for each candidate per news story and collapsed by news program to produce scores for each party per newscast. Several instances of a variable could be in play for a candidate within a single news story. Yet, only one instance of a given variable had to be present to be counted. Although this coding procedure does not assess the relative strength of a frame, it provides a conservative quantitative measure of the presence of frames within a story for each Democratic and Republican candidate. Coders were instructed to consider the foreground and backgrounds of televised scenes in which candidates appeared and to scrutinize shots adjacent to those of the candidate for associational juxtaposition.

The Ideal Candidate

The ideal candidate frame was measured as visual manifestations of statesmanship and compassion, using the following categories:

Statesmanship

1. *Elected officials and other influentials.* Candidate appearances with elected officials or other influentials—people with power, status, and money, whether on the national or local level

(e.g., former presidents, high-ranking members of Congress, industry, or the media, but excluding military dignitaries).

2. *Patriotic symbols.* Visual portrayals of the candidate that include patriotic symbols, such as monuments and memorials, the American flag, statues, military machinery and parades, paintings or photos of patriots as well as appearances with living heroes such as Colin Powell and Norman Schwarzkopf.

3. *Symbols of progress.* Linkage to symbols of economic or technological progress, including Wall Street, National Aeronautic and Space Administration (NASA), or high-technology manufacturing plants.

4. *Identifiable entourage.* Portrayal of an entourage, including security personnel, political aides, family, reporters, a motorcade, campaign caravan, or police vehicles.

5. *Campaign paraphernalia.* Clear visual representation of a candidate's name on campaign memorabilia, such as posters, banners, buttons, signs, clothing, or even campaign transportation.

6. *Political hoopla.* Candidate appearances amidst raining confetti, streamers, or balloons.

7. *Formal attire.* Shots of the candidate wearing a suit, defined in its full range from a tuxedo and black-tie evening wear to a conventional business suit.

Categories for the compassion subdimension included four visual association variables and three behavioral display measures, as follows:

Compassion

1. *Children.* Candidate appearances with children (interacting with, holding, or embracing).

2. *Family associations.* Visual connections to family members or historical family ties, affectionate displays with family members, or appearances with family.

3. *Admiring women.* Reaction shots or background footage of admiring women, expressing awe, wonder, excitement, or other signs of approval; also, enthusiastic female supporters shown smiling, cheering, or waving.

4. *Religious symbols.* Portrayals of candidates at places of worship, or among religious figures, or visual associations with religious symbols such as pulpits, crosses, candles, or religious scriptures.

The behavioral display measures used to represent compassion included the following:

5. *Affinity gestures.* Shots of candidates waving, fanning the crowd, giving the thumbs up or an informal salute, a "V" for

victory or peace sign, George W. Bush's three-finger "W" sign, both arms raised upward or a fist pump skyward to reflect the crowd's enthusiasm, a wink to someone in the audience or to the camera, tipping or waving one's hat.[1]

6. *Interaction with individuals.* Portrayals of candidates engaging with supporters and giving individual attention to well-wishers, without physical contact.

7. *Physical embraces.* Hugging, shaking hands with, embracing, or even kissing supporters.

The Populist Campaigner

The candidate's visual association with the plight of common people was coded in terms of mass appeal and ordinariness. In all, nine categories were used.

Mass Appeal

1. *Celebrities.* Shots of the candidate with celebrities, including movie stars, television personalities, musicians, rock stars, well-known athletes, and the like.

2. *Large audiences.* Shots of supporters tightly packed into a space or portrayals of the candidate appearing before a mass of supporters; also, aerial shots of mass attendance at rallies.

3. *Approving audiences.* Visual linkages to approving audiences shown applauding, waving, cheering, whistling, laughing, nodding in approval, wearing campaign paraphernalia, or toting campaign memorabilia.

4. *Interaction with crowds.* Shots of the candidate giving rapid, anonymous handshakes, grips, or touches to groups of supporters without individualized or fixed engagement with anyone in particular.

Ordinariness

1. *Informal attire.* Shots of the candidate wearing a tie without a jacket, shirtsleeves rolled up.

2. *Casual dress.* Shots of the candidate in khaki pants, slacks, or jeans with a long- or short-sleeve shirt or sport coat, bomber jacket, jean jacket, sweater, windbreaker, or other casual garment.

3. *Athletic clothing.* Shots of the candidate in short pants, jogging gear, or other athletic gear.

4. *Ordinary people.* Visual linkages to common folk, including visits to disadvantaged communities or manufacturing plants.

5. *Physical activity.* Depictions of the candidate participating in common athletic activities or performing physical work,

including chopping wood, clearing brush, serving meals at a homeless shelter, hunting, or other outdoor activities.[2]

The Sure Loser

The sure loser frame was operationalized in terms of unflattering visual depictions, typically connected to behavioral variables.

1. *Small crowds.* Shots of the candidate appearing with only a few supporters in attendance, shown scattered around, in sparsely filled spaces, often with empty chairs.
2. *Disapproving audiences.* Shots of citizens jeering, booing, signaling thumbs down, holding posters with disapproving comments, protesting, frowning, nodding off, or showing other signs of disinterest and disapproval.
3. *Displays of weakness.* Shots of the candidate tripping, falling, stumbling, or otherwise displaying clumsiness or lack of coordination; also, portrayals of the candidate with an illness.
4. *Defiant gestures.* Shots of the candidate punching the air, pounding the podium, or pumping a fist; also, finger pointing or wagging and hand-wringing to suggest mutilation of the opponent.
5. *Inappropriate nonverbal displays.* Visual portrayals of the candidate exhibiting facial expressions, gestures, moods, or an overall bearing that is incongruent with the news story context (e.g., the candidate shown in an upbeat mood following news of a terrorist strike, or displaying a sad and somber demeanor after winning a debate and opening a big lead in the polls).

CODERS AND RELIABILITY

Intercoder reliability was calculated using Krippendorff alpha; overall, reliability was high, Krippendorff's alpha = .92. Agreement across all 28 coding categories used in this analysis ranged from .81 to 1.00.

NOTES

1. Coders were instructed to record affinity displays only if they appeared without physical contact, which was coded separately.
2. Sports like yachting, golf, skiing, and windsurfing were excluded here because they suggest more elitist interests.

Appendix 4

Facing the Electorate

Individual candidates served as the unit of analysis for the results reported in Chapter 4. Within each campaign story, multiple sound and image bites were documented for each major party's nominees. Consistent with other analyses, a sound bite was defined as a piece of audiovisual material of a candidate in speaking mode, making comments to an individual reporter or larger audience. Image bites are individual shots of the candidate that visually cover the voice-over narration of the reporter. For the analysis, four kinds of variables were used. First and most central is a group that documented candidate displays of emotion in network news content. Second, daily tracking polls from Gallup and Rasmussen and postdebate polling data from CNN/USA Today were used to assess the front-runner or trailing status of each candidate. Third, in support of the critical events analysis, debate winners and losers were identified using poll data from surveys conducted for CNN/ USA Today by the Gallup Organization. A fourth class of variables categorized the different settings in which sound bites occurred, such as stump speeches or interviews. Fifth, a time variable necessary for making over-time comparisons was constructed, corresponding to three different stages of the campaign (early, debate period, and final stretch).

CODING INSTRUMENT

Agonic and Hedonic Displays

Central to this analysis is the assessment of nonverbal leader displays. For this aspect of the investigation candidate expressive behavior was scrutinized in sound and image bites. In sound bites, facial displays and the candidate's verbal tone were analyzed separately. In image bites, facial expressions as well as other nonverbal behaviors signaling emotion were examined. The coding categories are described below.

Sound bites. The candidates' facial expressions were scrutinized closely during all sound bites. To familiarize coders with the agonic and hedonic styles of candidate behavior, the codebook included several still images that exemplified these categories. A verbal tone category was included to capture the emotional quality of the candidate's voice during sound bites. Tone was primarily determined by the *manner* in which the candidate communicated, that is, by any vocal intonation, pitch, or modulation that conveyed an identifiable emotional state. Secondarily, tone was determined by the verbal content of what was said since voice inflections at times might remain relatively flat while the content is emotion laden.

Agonic expressive display variables included facial expressions of anger/threat and fear/evasion. First, the number of sound bites in which a candidate was shown displaying anger or threat was documented. These expressive displays were identified using the definitions of Masters et al.[1] and Sullivan et al.[2] The general sentiment expressed in an anger/threat display is negativity and hostility. Anger/threat was also assessed in terms of the verbal tone of sound bites. Often associated with challenges or boastful predictions, an angry or threatening tone was defined as menacing or hostile in intent. In other words, an angry or threatening tone signaled attack: the candidate might have sounded enraged, feisty, bold, aggressive, or eager and willing to do political battle. The number of sound bites in which the candidate sounded angry/threatening in verbal tone was coded.

The second agonic expressive display is fear/evasion. The number of sound bites in which a candidate perceptibly exhibited fear/evasion either facially or via verbal tone was logged. Displays of fear/evasion were coded employing the definitions of Masters et al.[1] and Sullivan et al.[2] A primary marker for a fear/evasion display is avoidance of direct confrontation, including expressions that feature furrowed brows and gaze aversion, a lowered head position, abrupt movement, or side-to-side head turning. In some cases the speaker's eyelids will be raised, as with the "deer caught in the headlights" look. Fearful/evasive verbal tone was defined as timid, unsure, or equivocal. A candidate's voice might tremble or he might stutter, misspeak, or be reluctant to answer a question. Sound bites evidencing fear/evasion revealed a tone of uncertainty, indecision, weakness, anxiety, uneasiness, apprehension, or agitation in response to a difficult situation.

Hedonic displays included depictions of happiness/reassurance. Coders documented the number of candidate sound bites in which happiness/reassurance was displayed facially and in verbal tone. Facial displays were identified using the following definitions. The general sentiment expressed in hedonic facial expressions is positive — they inspire confidence and signal affinity. Sound bites that were happy/reassuring in verbal tone were defined along the same lines: optimistic, cheery, full of hope, and channeling a positive feeling about what is likely to happen. In short, the tone of hedonic bites was described as inviting bonding with existing or potential supporters.

Image bites. The same facial display categories and definitions used for coding sound bites were used for examining facial displays in image bites. Three additional variables, one agonic and two hedonic, pertaining to nonverbal behavior other than facial displays were coded. On the agonic side of the ledger, coders logged the number of shots in which the candidate was shown exhibiting defiant hand or arm movements, suggesting aggression. These negative approach gestures included finger pointing or wagging, punching the air, raising a fist to issue a challenge or willingness to fight, and wringing one's hands to suggest mutilation of the opponent.

The two hedonic variables measured the frequency (number of individual shots) in which a candidate was shown exhibiting affinity hand gestures as well as making physical contact with supporters or staff. Affinity gestures consist of movements that imply bonding or a friendly relationship between the candidate and his audience. These positive approach gestures included waving, thumbs up, fanning the crowd, George W. Bush's three fingers ("W" sign), the "V" for victory (or peace) sign, an informal salute, both arms raised upward, a wink to someone in the audience or to the camera, and tipping or waving a hat. Hedonic contact was categorized as physical embraces of various kinds, including hugging; handholding; kissing; touching someone's cheek, shoulder or knee; or putting an arm around a supporter, well-wisher, or political ally as a type of bonding or reassurance display.

Sound Bite Setting

To investigate the candidates' expressive behavior in different campaign contexts, the setting of sound bites was analyzed. The first category consisted of stump or podium speeches, where the candidate was featured delivering an address rather than answering questions. Key to recognizing this setting is for the candidate to be depicted primarily speaking to supporters, not journalists or other politicians. The second category documented personal interviews, featuring the candidate in conversation with a journalist (or talk-show host) rather than in speech mode. Here, anchors or reporters are shown questioning the candidate one-on-one. Interviews can take place in a variety of settings, including television studios, outdoor locations, or on a campaign bus or plane. Other sound bite settings, including press conferences and debates, were coded but not used in statistical testing because they do not clearly represent the more formal speech or more personal interview modes that were of primary interest to hypothesis testing. A final category, "other," was included to document sound bites in settings not covered by the four above categories, for example, sound bite excerpts from political advertisements.

POLL DATA

To track candidate status throughout the general election, the analysis utilized daily tracking polls for each election year. A front-runner was defined as a candidate who led in the polls by one or more percentage points. Conversely, a trailer was defined as a candidate who was one or more percentage points behind the winner. If candidates were within 1 percentage point of each other in the polls, the race was treated as a dead heat and these cases were excluded from the analyses.

Although most tracking polls have a 3-point margin of error, we defined a front-runner as leading by one or more percentage points for two reasons, one practical and the other perceptual. Practically, eliminating those days where there was less than a 3-point difference between the candidates would have severely reduced the number of cases for analysis, compromising the reliability of statistical tests. Perceptually, we would argue that even a 1-point lead has potential value to close observers of the campaign since media coverage reports on the horse-race standings, however close. Even if the margin of error is reported to qualify a close race, it is usually mentioned as a caveat or footnote while the actual numbers are displayed in bold relief. To distinguish front-runners from trailing candidates, a categorical variable was constructed: a value of 1 was assigned to front-runners; a 2 was assigned to trailers; and a 3 was assigned if there was not at least a 1-point lead for one candidate. Analyses were performed using data for front-runners and trailers only.

For 1992, 1996, and 2000, tracking data from the Gallup Poll were used. Polling numbers for missing dates early in the 1992 general election (September 7–28) were filled in with tracking data from various polling organizations summarized in *Public Perspective* magazine, formerly published by the Roper Center.[3] In 2004, figures from Rasmussen Reports were used, since the Gallup Poll only tracked candidates at eight points in time during the general election that year. For Election Day of each year, percentages of the final presidential vote tally were used since polling ends before the election. Although criticized for using automated calling procedures,[4] Rasmussen Reports was widely recognized as one of the most accurate polling organizations during the 2004 campaign season.[5,6]

CRITICAL EVENTS ANALYSIS

For the purposes of this analysis, a critical event was defined as a presidential debate in which a clear victor emerged, becoming the object of favorable media coverage. Nationally televised presidential debates are significant in that they attract considerable media and public attention and have the capacity to solidify partisan support and move undecided voters; hence, a pivotal debate can have electoral significance. An examination of CNN/USA Today polling data revealed clear winners for at least one debate each election year. The poll question used to determine a debate winner was worded as follows: "Regardless of which candidate you happen to support, who do you think did the better job in the debate: [candidate A] or [candidate B]?"

In 1992, Bill Clinton was regarded as the winner of the second debate, a town hall meeting format, over George H. W. Bush and Ross Perot on October 15. Fifty-eight percent of voters thought Clinton did a better job, compared to just 16% and 15% for Bush and Perot, respectively. In 1996, Bill Clinton again prevailed in the second debate, also a town hall format, over Bob Dole on October 16. Fifty-nine percent of voters thought Clinton performed better in this debate, compared to 29% for Dole. In 2000, George W. Bush was deemed the winner of the second debate over Al Gore on October 11. Forty-nine percent of poll respondents favored Bush's performance, compared to 36% for Gore. In 2004 John Kerry was widely considered the winner of the first debate against President Bush on September 30: 53% of voters thought Kerry did the better job, compared to 37% for Bush. Polls were conducted for CNN/ USA Today by the Gallup Organization. For a summary, see http:// www.usatoday.com/news/politicselections/nation/polls/2004-09-30-debate-poll.htm.

Based on these polling numbers, candidates were assigned a 1 if they were a debate winner and 2 if they were the loser. Data from the post-debate period were used for analysis. Obviously, determining a debate winner from flash poll results does not reveal the quality of an individual debate performance or which candidate had stronger rhetorical arguments. We admit that declaring a debate winner or loser is somewhat reductionist; yet, our criteria for determining a debate winner was conservative—a clear consensus in subsequent press coverage *and* a clear separation (beyond the margin of error) of the candidates in post-debate opinion polls.

CAMPAIGN STAGES

To examine expressive displays across different stages of the campaign, a time factor was constructed using the date on which a candidate was featured on the news. The time variable had three levels, each representing a different stage of the general election campaign. The first stage ran from Labor Day to the day of the first debate of each election year. The second stage captured the spirit of the debate period, stretching from the day after the first debate to two days after the last debate for each election year. The third stage represented the final stretch of the campaign to Election Day. This approach is similar to the analysis strategy of Masters et al.,[7] who segmented the primary election into distinct phases for longitudinal analysis. The specific dates of each campaign stage are listed in Table 1.1 in Appendix 1.

CODERS AND RELIABILITY

Overall, the pretest produced a reliable level of agreement (Krippendorff's alpha = 0.84) between the four coders. For the categories related to expressive displays the overall figure was .81, whereas the identification of sound bite settings was conducted with a reliability alpha of .89. Although the pretest produced acceptable reliability figures, more training ensued before the beginning of data collection. A posthoc reliability check was performed on 20% of the sample. Coders maintained an acceptable level of agreement (Krippendorff's alpha = 0.83), with a minimum of agreement level of 0.80 and a maximum of 1.0 on individual variables.

ANALYSIS STRATEGY

Findings reported in this chapter are generally supported by data that do conform to the equal variance assumption. Indeed, some types of candidate behaviors are exhibited infrequently or not at all at certain points in the campaign but feature prominently at other times, such as after a strong debate performance or sudden dip in the polls. Not unexpectedly, standard deviations on some means suggest that certain variables do behave erratically. Thus, the Levene statistic was employed to assess equal variance within group means. In ANOVA tests where the homogeneity of variance assumption was violated, the Welch computation was used as a robust test of equality of means. Similarly, in t-tests the Levene statistic was employed to assess homogeneity of variance and robust test of means were reported for variables where violations occurred.

NOTES

1. Masters, Roger D., Dennis G. Sullivan, John T. Lanzetta, Gregory J. McHugo, and Basil G. Englis. 1986. Facial displays and political leadership. *Journal of Biological and Social Structures* 9:319–343.
2. Sullivan, Dennis G., and Roger D. Masters, with John T. Lanzetta, Gregory J. McHugo, Basil G. Englis, and Elise F. Plate. 1991. Facial displays and political leadership: Some experimental findings. In *Primate politics*, ed. Glendon Schubert and Roger D. Masters, pp. 188–206. Carbondale: Southern Illinois University Press.

3. Roper Center. 1992, November/December. The American Enterprise. Trial heats: Nationally ... *Public Perspective* 100–101.

4. Harris, John F. 2004, October 31. In such a tight race, pollster sees a profit; NJ-based business uses "robo calling." *The Washington Post*, p. A5.

5. Kenner, David, and William Saletan. 2004, December 9. Who nailed the election results? Automated pollsters. *Slate*. http://www.slate.com/tool-bar.aspx?action=print&andid=2110860. Accessed February 9, 2007.

6. Tarrance, V. Lance, Jr. 2005, February. The ABCs of the 2004 pre-election polls. *Public Perspective Online*. http://www.publicopinionpros.com/op_ed/2005/feb/tarrance.asp. Accessed February 9, 2007.

7. Masters, Roger D., Dennis G. Sullivan, Alice Feola, and Gregory J. McHugo. 1987. Television coverage of candidates' display behavior during the 1984 Democratic primaries in the United States. *International Political Science Review* 8(2):121–130.

Appendix 5

Visual Bias

CODING INSTRUMENT

To determine the amount of coverage, the campaign story was treated as the unit of analysis. The coding instrument differentiated between multiple-party campaign stories (featuring candidates from more than one political party) and single-party stories (featuring one political party's candidates). Brief mentioning of another party's candidate without visual material was coded as a single-party story. When a second party's candidate was shown and/or presented in a sound bite, the campaign story was coded as a multiple-party story.

In the case of a multiple-party story, coders determined which party's candidates dominated in the story, but with a "No one party dominates" option for this category. Dominance meant that a particular party's candidates were featured more often visually, they had more opportunity to speak, or they were described more thoroughly than the opposition. We employed these categories rather than attempting to measure durations for each candidate's appearance because in television news, multiple candidate stories are covered in an integrated way where it is often impossible to decide where one candidate's coverage starts or stops and another's begins and ends.

Visual weight of coverage was assessed using the individual campaign story as the unit of analysis. Six story types were identified: reader, voice-over (VO), voice-over/sound-on-tape (VO/SOT), interview, package, in-depth package, and other (to assure exhaustiveness). The position of campaign stories was coded as lead, before the first commercial break, and after the first commercial break.

Two editing and nine camera maneuver categories were utilized in the structural features analysis. For editing, the Goldilocks-effect was recorded in multiple-party stories. The options included Democrats, Republicans, and other candidates as well as "no sound bite featured." Lip flap was recorded in duration (seconds) using the individual candidate as the unit of analysis.

Camera maneuver categories included shot angle, length, and movement with the individual candidate as the unit of analysis. The codebook featured several photographic examples illustrating the threshold of counting a shot as angled and demonstrating shot lengths. The duration of shots in which candidates appeared in observable low and high angles was recorded in seconds. In addition, four different shot lengths were measured. The extreme close-up shot was defined as one in which the candidate's face appears to fill the entire screen without the shoulder or chest area visible. This might include a visual cut-off of the candidate's chin and forehead. The close-up shot shows the candidate's full head and shoulders and a small portion of the chest area (well above the waist and elbows). A medium shot depicts the candidate's full head, shoulders, and waist area but not the full body. The long shot reveals the full body, as well as contextualizing information including other objects and people. The durations of these shots featuring candidates were recorded in seconds.

The frequency and duration of zoom-in (movement from a longer to closer shot) and zoom-out (movement from a closer to longer shot) camera perspectives were measured. Finally, the duration of eyewitness camera shots of candidates was recorded in seconds. This viewpoint was defined as one in which the camera is placed on the operator's shoulder while subjectively pursuing the action. These shots are relatively easily distinguished from shots that are filmed by a stationary camera that is secured to a tripod.

CODERS AND RELIABILITY

A posthoc reliability check was performed on 20% of the sample. Coders maintained an acceptable level of agreement (Krippendorff's alpha = .83), with a minimum of 81% and maximum of 100% for the categories reported in Chapter 5.

Appendix 6

Visual Influence Analysis

CONTENT ANALYSIS DATA

The following key variables from each chapter's reported findings were selected for analysis:

1. Chapter 2: Sound and image bite volume, sound bite size, and sound bite content (issue statements, calls to rally the troops, attacks against opponents, and defensive rhetoric).
2. Chapter 3: Ideal candidate (statesmanship and compassion), populist campaigner (mass appeal and ordinariness), and loser frames.
3. Chapter 4: Hedonic and agonic verbal tone, facial displays, and gestures.
4. Chapter 5: Single-party story coverage, visual weight (story type and position in the newscast), beneficial packaging (last say opportunities, low angles, close-ups, zoom-ins, and eyewitness camera perspectives), and detrimental packaging (lip flap, high angles, extreme close-ups, long shots, and zoom-outs).

POLLING DATA

To investigate candidate support during the general election, bivariate and regression analyses utilize daily tracking polls for each election year. For 1992, 1996, and 2000, tracking data from the Gallup Poll were used. Polling numbers for missing dates early in the 1992 general election (September 7–28) were filled in with tracking data from various polling organizations summarized in *Public Perspective* magazine, formerly published by the Roper Center.[1] In 2004, figures from Rasmussen Reports were used, since the Gallup Poll tracked candidates at only eight points in time during the general election that year. For Election Day of each year, percentages of the final presidential vote tally were used since polling ends before the election. Although criticized for using automated calling procedures,[2] Rasmussen Reports was widely recognized as one of the most accurate polling organizations during the 2004 campaign season.[3,4]

METHOD

Content analysis data were aggregated by day, distinguishing between Democrats and Republicans and individual election years. The restructured dataset was then aligned with daily tracking poll data for each political party. Two statistical procedures were used to examine potential relationships:

1. Bivariate correlations between content analysis variables and poll data were performed.
2. Regression models were run using content analysis categories as independent variables in predicting candidate standings in the polls.

NOTES

1. Roper Center. 1992, November/December. The American Enterprise. Trial heats: Nationally . . . *Public Perspective*, pp. 100–101.
2. Harris, John F. 2004, October 31. In such a tight race, pollster sees a profit; NJ-based business uses "robo calling." *Washington Post*, p. A5.
3. Kenner, David, and William Saletan. 2004, December 9. Who nailed the election results? Automated pollsters. *Slate*. http://www.slate.com/toolbar.aspx?action=print&id=2110860. Accessed February 9, 2007.
4. Tarrance, V. Lance Jr. 2005, February. The ABCs of the 2004 pre-election polls. *Public Perspective Online*. http://www.publicopinionpros.com/op_ed/2005/feb/tarrance.asp. Accessed February 9, 2007.

Subject Index

Note: Footnotes are indicated by n. after the page number. Figures or tables are indicated by *f* or *t* after the page number, respectively.